A Republic of Righteousness

A REPUBLIC OF RIGHTEOUSNESS

The Public Christianity of the
Post-Revolutionary New England Clergy

JONATHAN D. SASSI

OXFORD
UNIVERSITY PRESS

2001

OXFORD
UNIVERSITY PRESS

Oxford   New York

Athens   Auckland   Bangkok   Bogotá   Buenos Aires   Cape Town
Chennai   Dar es Salaam   Delhi   Florence   Hong Kong   Istanbul   Karachi
Kolkata   Kuala Lumpur   Madrid   Melbourne   Mexico City   Mumbai   Nairobi
Paris   São Paulo   Shanghai   Singapore   Taipei   Tokyo   Toronto   Warsaw

and associated companies in
Berlin   Ibadan

Copyright © 2001 by Jonathan D. Sassi

Published by Oxford University Press, Inc.,
198 Madison Avenue, New York, New York 10016

Oxford is a registered trademark of Oxford University Press

Library of Congress Cataloging-in-Publication Data
Sassi, Jonathan D., 1967–
A republic of righteousness : the public Christianity of the post-revolutionary
New England clergy / Jonathan D. Sassi.
p.   cm. — (Religion in America series)
Includes bibliographical references and index.
ISBN 0-19-512989-X
1. Clergy—New England—Political activity—History.   2. Congregational churches—
New England—Clergy—Political activity—History.   3. Church and state—New England—History.
4. New England—Church history.   5. New England—Politics and government—1775–1865.
I. Title.   II. Religion in America series (Oxford University Press)
BR530 .S27 2001
277.4'081—dc21   00-053075

1   3   5   7   9   8   6   4   2
Printed in the United States of America
on acid-free paper

To Laura, for everything

Acknowledgments

Hope deferred maketh the heart sick: but when the desire cometh, it is a tree of life.

—Prov. 13:12

It is my great joy to recognize and thank the many people and institutions who have helped me in researching and writing this book. Its publication marks the fulfillment of a long-term hope.

My study of the early republic began when I was a graduate student at the University of California, Los Angeles. The history department there generously supported my education with a number of fellowships and teaching appointments. The UCLA Center for 17th- and 18th-Century Studies also hired me as a research assistant. Since I came to the College of Staten Island in 1998, an award of reassigned time in the spring of 2000 enabled me to devote myself to revising the manuscript, and my colleagues in the history department have provided a welcoming atmosphere. This work was also supported (in part) by a grant from the City University of New York PSC–CUNY Research Award Program for 1999. That same summer, my research into Worcester County materials was made possible by an American Antiquarian Society—American Society for Eighteenth-Century Studies fellowship.

My time in Worcester was so productive thanks to the outstanding staff at the AAS. The professionals there truly set the standard for other research libraries to emulate. Among the many people at the AAS to whom I am grateful, I especially thank Tom Knoles, the curator of manuscripts, for his sage advice. I also thank the AAS for permission to quote from its manuscript holdings. Other archives that have granted me permission to quote from their collections include the Congregational Library, Boston, Massachusetts, and the Worcester Historical Museum, Worcester, Massachusetts. At the Worcester Historical Museum, the executive director, William D. Wallace, went out of his way to provide me with a photograph of Joseph Goffe's portrait. In addition, I thank the publisher for permission to reprint excerpts from *New England Dissent: The Baptists and the Separation of Church and State* by William G. McLoughlin, Cambridge, Mass.: Harvard University Press, Copyright © 1971 by the President and Fellows of Harvard College. At Oxford University Press, Cynthia

Read, Ellen Guerci, and Theo Calderara have patiently and efficiently guided this first-time author through the publication process.

Many friends and colleagues have read all or part of the manuscript, and their suggestions have greatly improved the final product. Although the responsibility for the book's argument rests solely with me, I am delighted to acknowledge the advice and encouragement I received from Bob Abzug, Joyce Appleby, Phil Goff, Chris Grasso, Mark Hanley, Dan Howe, and Gary Nash. Ruth Bloch deserves special mention. As my dissertation advisor, she had an early faith in this project that never waned and that sustained me at numerous points along the way. Her rigorous and constructive criticism has improved this work immeasurably, and she deserves my deepest thanks.

The members of my family have always supported my work in ways that no academic institution ever could, and I am thankful for all of them. My wife, Laura, has enthusiastically lived with this project for years on end. Without her, it probably would never have been completed. This book is dedicated to her with love.

Cranford, New Jersey   J. D. S.
September 2000

Contents

A Republic of Righteousness

Introduction

Ye are the light of the world. A city that is set on an hill cannot be hid.

— Matt. 5:14

ON THE FOURTH OF JULY, 1825, sixty-four-year-old Samuel Austin addressed an assembly of Christians in Worcester, Massachusetts, "convened for the purpose of celebrating this event religiously." Austin had recently retired from the pulpit after a twenty-five-year ministry at Worcester's First Congregational Church and briefer stints as president of the University of Vermont and pastor in Newport, Rhode Island. In his interpretation, the anniversary of American independence was an occasion for rejoicing, primarily because God had used the Revolution as "a providential event" to advance "the Church." Austin made the usual observation that the Revolution staved off political tyranny, too, but for him the religious achievement was paramount. "What comparison can a mere civil institution, however well it may be organized, whatever temporal hopes it may suggest, or whatever secular advantages it may in fact yield, hold with that kingdom which is properly the kingdom of heaven, and which we are assured can never be moved? Let every man understand that but for the influence of our holy religion, and the purpose of God respecting his own Zion, never would the design have been formed to plant a settlement like that which the pilgrims sought and established on the barren shores of New-England."[1] Thus Samuel Austin fashioned a tapestry of historical understanding that wove together along one providential framework the colonization of New England, the outcome of the American Revolution, and the expansion of the kingdom of God.

Not only did Austin interpret the past, but he also issued instructions for the present with an eye to the future. He delighted in the fact that in the years since the Revolution, American Christianity had grown and seen "a glorious flowing together of repenting sinners to Zion." He foresaw a prominent role for American Christians in the preparation for the millennium, and closed with a call to collective action toward that end. "Let us put our religion, which is [the Lord's] most reasonable service, into its full influence over ourselves, over those committed to our care, and, as far as we can, over the favoured country we enjoy. O that it had its genuine dominion over all the population of these United States . . . and we should indeed be that happy peo-

3

Samuel Austin. Courtesy University of Vermont Archives.

ple whose God is the Lord."[2] According to Austin's prescription, the American churches would actively engage in the project of social sanctification.

How does one interpret Austin's blend of such patriotic, providential, and covenantal languages? Clearly he was mining a rich vein that extended back to the Puritan and Revolutionary eras. But Austin was not just a living anachronism, mouthing the rhetorical incantations of his youth. His speech did not simply repeat the sentiments of 1776 in a frozen formula; his ideas had evolved with the times. His closing call to reform, for instance, wedded a Puritan understanding of the sanctified community with contemporary initiatives to improve American society. Moreover, Austin was not alone in voicing such opinions but was joined by a younger generation of clerical spokesmen. To understand Samuel Austin's providential account of American identity and destiny circa 1825, one must realize that it reflected the developments of the past half century since the outbreak of the Revolution.

The adult life span of Samuel Austin (b. 1760, d. 1830), and his generation more generally, coincided with what is now known as the early republic. The early republic has emerged in the past quarter century of historical scholarship as a period of central consequence to the formation of subsequent American culture. The Revolutionary movement, it is now clear, had been a coalition of diverse elements united against a common threat. Once the British threat had been defeated, a vacuum of sorts resulted, in which social groups and their values jockeyed for supremacy and earlier cultural formulations had to be renegotiated. The post-Revolutionary period was one of the most hotly contested in American history. It lay at the nexus of elemental developments in the character of the new nation, including its politics, economy, and culture. Historians now view the early republic as an important period in its own right, not simply as a brief postscript to the Revolution or as a prelude to the antebellum era.[3] Religion, too, emerged as a fundamental part of this ferment, regardless of the Constitution's overall silence on the issue.[4] The early nineteenth century witnessed a tremendous spurt of evangelization and organization on the part of American Protestantism. By the Jacksonian era, Christianity played, if anything, a more salient public role than it had a half century before.[5]

Analyzing one aspect of this formative era, *A Republic of Righteousness* examines the evolving character of Christian social ideology in southern New England during the fifty years after the American Revolution. Within the context of enormous institutional and intellectual change, a corporate religious ethic endured within the region's social ideology well into the nineteenth century. This study seeks to understand the complex juxtaposition of Christianity and the American Revolution, of the kingdom of God and the United States, and of an identity as God's people and American nationalism—themes typified in Samuel Austin's July Fourth address of 1825. Clergymen never gave up the struggle to define the righteous community and comment on the relationship of Christians to the new nation, yet within the tumultuous environment of the early republic, their public Christianity had to adapt to new circumstances. In the latter part of the time period under consideration, they made a seminal contribution to American reform.

Statements like Samuel Austin's appear anomalous in the light of the secondary literature on religion in the early republic. The available interpretations cannot accurately account for his complicated synthesis of corporate concepts such as church, nation, and social reform. Certainly, the topic of the New England ministry did not suffer from scholarly inattention during the twentieth century. But historians studying the clergy have tended to "caricature" their subject in one of two ways.[6] For approximately the first two-thirds of the century, most of them overemphasized the clergy's political motives and public influence. Since then, the interpretative pendulum has swung to the opposite extreme, and leading scholars have largely consigned the Congregational clergy, at least, to the dustbin of social irrelevance. Although the last decade has seen a positive reappraisal of some of the Congregational clergy's initiatives, these ministers' political and social detachment is still overstated.

In the first part of the century, the Progressive historians depicted the Congregational ministry as locked in a rearguard political action. Typical of his muckraking generation, Richard J. Purcell found that the crux of the matter regarding religion, society, and politics in the post-Revolutionary era lay in class conflict. In his expla-

nation, Connecticut in the thirty years after the Revolution was undergoing a transformation "from an aristocratic, paternalistic into a modern democratic state . . .
[caused] by a natural movement of forces imperceptibly gradual in action."[7] The two
political parties embodied either end of this transition. On the one hand, Federalist
leaders conspired to buttress the aristocracy of traditional sources of mercantile and
financial wealth and the Congregational standing order. They were able to cling to
power despite the tides of change brought in by the Revolution because the lack
of a frontier in Connecticut retarded social development.[8] The Republicans, on
the other hand, represented small farmers, mechanics, and entrepreneurs in new
economic sectors like manufacturing, as well as non-Congregationalists. Purcell's
characterization of the Republicans as representing everything modern overdeter-
mined the story's outcome, as the Federalists receded into the background as futile
opponents of change. In this depiction, Congregational ministers, led by Timothy
Dwight, played the part of overt reactionaries. In the similar estimation of a fellow
Progressive, Vernon Louis Parrington, Dwight was "little more than a walking repository of the venerable Connecticut *status quo*."[9]

Although pointing to status rather than class as the primary factor driving change,
historians writing in the 1950s and early 1960s likewise cast the New England clergy
in the role of reactionaries. According to these scholars, ministers responded to their
supposed loss of status in the early nineteenth century with contrived efforts to bat-
ten down the hatches of orthodoxy and reestablish social control. For example, in
John R. Bodo's interpretation, the waning of their traditional "influence and pres-
tige" amid changing social relations inspired "the theocrats," his term for college-
educated clergy, to articulate a reform agenda for the United States with the goal of
reasserting their "ideological control over the nation." Clifford S. Griffin offered an
even more extreme statement of this perspective in *Their Brothers' Keepers*. In his
analysis, clergymen and their collaborators among the laity during the early republic
"feared new forces in American life, worried about political and social upheavals, deplored new moral standards, and lamented the decline of religion in an increasingly
secular age." Although they may have "claimed that they were being benevolent,"
their reform agencies were in reality "laboring to make men behave." As Griffin summarized, "Religion and morality, as dispensed by the benevolent societies throughout the seemingly chaotic nation, became a means of establishing secular order."
This type of approach, which emphasized the effects of status in the minds of historical actors, was quite popular in the literature on antebellum reform during the
1950s and the early 1960s and still crops up occasionally today. These various works
share an emphasis on the negative motivation of anxiety over declining social status
and an impending breakdown in social order as what really drove the ministry to
launch its multiform efforts to engage society.[10]

Over the next two decades, the accumulated pressure of new perspectives exploded the social control thesis. An influential 1973 article by Lois W. Banner
marked the beginning of the end for the conventional argument. She indicted Bodo
and other historians of his generation for portraying the antebellum reformers as
motivated by "the desire for 'social control' not social improvement." Rather than
dwelling on the purportedly negative and political motives of the clergy, Banner suggested that more benign impulses were at work. She pointed to ideologies such as re-

publicanism and millennialism as the driving forces behind the benevolent empire of missionary and reform organizations. Along the same lines, Richard D. Shiels's 1980 essay on "The Second Great Awakening in Connecticut" cast doubt on both the politicization of the ministry and the leadership of Yale President Timothy Dwight. Both arguments had been staples of the earlier historiography.[11] The essays by Banner and Shiels knocked the underpinnings out from the interpretative edifice that had been built up over the first two-thirds of the twentieth century regarding the New England clergy of the early republic. By and large, the two essays were more critical than constructive; that is, they helped to destabilize the older interpretation, but they sketched only some preliminary drawings for what a succeeding one should look like.

Rejecting the jaundiced view of the clergy in the then-prevailing social control thesis, Perry Miller was one scholar who had always given credence to the religious beliefs of historical actors. Like Banner would a decade later, he heaped scorn on his colleagues' "obtuse secularism," which, he argued, distorted the historical record and showed mainly that his peers had been "corrupted by the twentieth century."[12] Instead, Miller championed the centrality of covenant theology to Revolutionary America. In his depiction, the Revolution formed the high-water mark of the national covenant, as clergymen up and down the coast blended their jeremiads with the premises of the Lockean social contract. As Miller phrased the situation, "The jeremiad, which in origin had been an engine of Jehovah, thus became temporarily a service department of the Continental army." This was the clergy's most important contribution to the Revolutionary cause in Miller's estimation, because although a "pure rationalism such as [Jefferson's] might have declared the independence of these folk, . . . it could never have inspired them to fight for it."[13]

After the Revolution, however, Miller argued that the idea of a nation in covenant with God became untenable. The threats of the French Revolution and domestic partisan discord, together with the expanding frontier and the sheer scale of the United States, eroded clergymen's confidence in their ability to speak in terms of the corporate concept of a chosen nation. In place of the covenant, ministers promoted revivalism. "[American Protestants] did not need to renounce the Declaration, nor even to denounce the Constitution," Miller explained, "but only henceforth to take those principles for granted, yield government to the secular concept of the social compact, accept the First Amendment, and so to concentrate, in order to resist Deism and to save their souls, upon that other mechanism of cohesion developed out of their colonial experience, the Revival." In this analysis, revivalism differed from the covenant in two key respects. It was individualistic rather than corporate. "For these revivalists," wrote Miller, "it was no longer necessary to find space in their sermons for social theory." The revival was also geared toward the future, whereas the covenant had been "retrospective" and oriented toward preserving the historical legacy of the founders of New England.[14] Obviously, Samuel Austin's aforementioned 1825 speech, which was by no means idiosyncratic, contradicts Miller's scheme on both counts, but Miller's essay is nonetheless still significant historiographically. In addition to his cantankerous insistence on the importance for scholars of understanding religious belief, Miller also reformulated the idea that the early republic was a critical juncture in American religious history. At the same time, the period really constituted only an epilogue to his magisterial work on Puritanism. This tendency to treat the early republic's religion as a consequential, albeit little-studied aftereffect of the Revolution endured through most of the 1980s.

Important new scholarship during the 1970s and 1980s expanded on some of the themes that Miller had raised. Vigorous debates raged over the character of antebellum reform movements and over the link, if any, between religion and the American Revolution. These debates had indirect implications for our understanding of the post-Revolutionary clergy. Social historians' focus on nonelites continued to push the social control thesis further into obsolescence, because the old emphasis on a status-anxious and reactionary clergy became less necessary as historians examined the local figures behind various reform campaigns.[15] To put things another way, liberated from the responsibility for a supposedly reactionary reformism, the clergy was free to appear in a truer light. In addition, scholars following Miller and his student Alan Heimert, author of *Religion and the American Mind*, explored the connection between the First Great Awakening and the coming of the Revolution. They added to Miller's emphasis on covenant theology the importance of classical republicanism, millennialism, and Hopkinsian disinterested benevolence, among other ideologies.[16] While it is not clear that any of these ideologies exerted the predominating influence in Revolutionary America since claimed for them, all of them did contribute to the discursive inheritance of the early republic's clergy.

Despite this renewed attention being given to the role of religion in the Revolutionary era, these same scholars followed Miller's "From the Covenant to the Revival" in portraying the early republic as a time that saw the collapse of the Revolutionary synthesis of religious and political ideology. They also followed Miller in dispatching the early republic in brief epilogues to their more important work on earlier periods. As Harry S. Stout concluded in *The New England Soul*, regardless of the national covenant's persistence prior to the Revolution, this durable Old Testament symbolism could not withstand the tempestuous environment of the post-Revolutionary era. A new evangelicalism that was both individualistic and without the conventional New England orientation toward the past became the religious currency of the day.[17] Donald Weber also asserted that clergymen abandoned the public sphere: "They had once *acted* in history; by 1800 their secret desire was to get out of history, to a place where all 'remains the same.'"[18] In other words, scholars like Stout and Weber dismissed the Congregational clergy from the main current of American history after 1800. Therefore, by the end of the 1980s, historians had constructed a much more detailed, yet still incomplete rendering of the New England clergy of the early republic and its social ideology. They possessed a more sophisticated grasp of the clergy's multifaceted public Christianity and regarded their subjects in a less pejorative light. Yet, they still assumed that the early republic formed a point of radical disjuncture with the Revolutionary period immediately preceding it. The secondary literature could not explain the persistence of the clergy's social engagement or ministers' enduring ability to mingle past, present, and future in their public pronouncements that a closer examination of early-nineteenth-century sources would reveal.

The traditional discontinuity in the historical literature around 1800 reinforces the interpretation of a decisive break at the end of the eighteenth century. Most depictions of the period from the 1780s to the 1830s are fractured along chronological lines. There exist, as noted, outstanding literatures on the role of religion in both the American Revolution and the reform movements of the second quarter of the nineteenth century. However, fewer efforts have been made to draw connections between the two. Two examples, one sardonic and the other scholarly, point to the lacuna. Ralph Waldo Emerson once remarked that "from 1790 to 1820, there was not a book, a speech, a conversation, or a thought in the State [of Massachusetts]." Similarly, as Gordon S. Wood noted in an essay published in 1988, "the early republic tends to fall between two schools of the historical profession, and its significance and integrity are lost. One group of historians knows the period only as an epilogue; the other group knows it only as a prologue. Neither sees it whole."[19]

At the end of the 1980s, the early republic finally took center stage as perhaps the most important period in the overall history of American religion in two landmark books, Nathan O. Hatch's 1989 *The Democratization of American Christianity* and Jon Butler's *Awash in a Sea of Faith*, published the next year. Both marginalized the role of the New England clergy, a group that for most of the twentieth century had stood at the foreground of historians' analyses. According to Hatch, the really important aspect of the religious history of the early republic was how "religious outsiders" seized upon the democratic ethos of Revolutionary America to create popular religious movements that validated the visions and voices of ordinary men and women. In contrast to the conservative clerics who inhabited much of the earlier literature, Hatch found insurgent religious leaders among the Baptist, Methodist, Christian, Mormon, and African American churches who embraced the Revolutionary era's egalitarianism and liberalism. He dismissed Calvinist clergymen as hopelessly out of touch with the times and "bewildered" by their new antagonists. Butler's book was an even broader revisionist statement that sought to reorient the whole canon of early American religious history. Instead of emphasizing the New England clergy and its theological tradition, Butler's narrative placed all sorts of unorthodox beliefs and practices at the forefront. The early republic in this portrayal was the scene of "a dramatic American religious syncretism that wedded popular supernaturalism with Christianity."[20] Both books radically diminished the significance of the Congregationalists by casting them as a denomination far removed from the cutting edge of important new developments that shaped the era. The individualism and eclecticism stressed by Hatch and Butler, respectively, had little connection to the Congregational clergy and its corporate social vision.

This new portrayal of religion in the early republic dovetailed with wider syntheses of the period that told of a shift in the nation's cultural paradigm from a corporatist republicanism to an individualistic liberalism.[21] Gordon S. Wood's *The Radicalism of the American Revolution*, for instance, stressed the atomization of American society and the collapse of earlier authorities and traditions in areas ranging from politics and the economy to literature and the family. Religion was an important aspect of this overall change. "By concentrating on the saving of individual souls," Wood wrote of the early republic, "the competing denominations essentially abandoned their traditional institutional and churchly responsibilities to organize the world here and now along godly lines." Joyce Appleby also neatly summarized this interpretive stance. "Like Jeffersonian liberalism," she compared, "American Protestantism rejected the past, indifferent alike to the historic Church and its traditions. The individual, not the congregation, became the locus of religious power in America."[22] In short, we are told, religion became privatized, confined to the believer's heart, and divorced from its conventional concern with the larger society. Congregational ministers and their public Christianity appeared irrelevant to the really important developments in the religious history of the early republic. It is fair to say that this perspective exerts a powerful sway over the historical literature today.

By the middle of the 1990s, a few monographs had appeared that sought to rectify this dismissal of the Congregational clergy. For example, David W. Kling's study of the New Divinity revivals in northwestern Connecticut revealed Congregational ministers who were effective at making Calvinism relevant to a new generation. In Kling's story, the revivals they led were hopeful, rather than driven by anxiety, and had little to do with conservative political goals. Likewise, James R. Rohrer has persuasively shown that the missionaries sent from Connecticut to carry orthodox Congregationalism to the frontier were adaptable and successful, in contrast to the traditional view that they were aloof, hesitant, and ultimately scorned. He challenged historians like Hatch who "exaggerate . . . the 'competitive edge' enjoyed by Methodist and Baptist exhorters, and underestimate the ability of Congregational missionaries to build up large followings in the new settlements."[23] Both works, however, go too far in trying to distance the clergy from partisan politics. In reaction to the hoary image of standing order clergymen as virtual Federalist apparatchiks, both Kling and Rohrer strain a bit too much in emphasizing the spiritual priorities of their subjects and the ministers' concomitant lack of serious interest in politics and public events.[24]

A Republic of Righteousness joins Kling and Rohrer in seeking to rehabilitate the Congregational ministry from its displacement to the margins. What James M. Banner Jr. has recently written of the fate of Federalist politicians in contemporary scholarship could be applied almost word for word to the Congregational clergy.

> In the last twenty years the Federalists have been lost to view. Banished not because of their silence or the comparative weakness and size of their record but rather, on the contrary, because of their "conservative" politics, their race and gender, their symbolic place in our past history, their very articulateness . . . precisely because they lacked all exoticism and did not seem to need rediscovering, they have been excluded from the great reconsideration of American politics and society of our age. One can say without irony that it is the Federalists . . . who must now be rescued from the dustbin of historiography and the condescending regard of so many historians.[25]

This book goes beyond Kling and Rohrer in restoring politics and public life to a central place within the religious vision of these important ministers. It focuses squarely on the clergy's public Christianity, or the ways in which ministers tried to make religious beliefs and values speak to the problems of life in society. This book aims to find the balance that the secondary literature has been lacking with regard to our estimation of the New England clergy. It portrays these ministers as neither purely self-interested political operatives nor spiritually preoccupied and detached from their surroundings. It instead aims for a truer explication of the clergy's complicated, contested, and changing social ideology. Moreover, this book deals with an array of religious figures beyond the Congregationalists. Just as "American political culture was fashioned in a dialogue," so, too, the clergy's public Christianity is fully comprehensible only in terms of its pluralistic context.[26]

This study is deliberately centered in the early republic. It strives to interpret the developments between the Revolution and antebellum reform movements as a distinct period in its own right. It takes an in-depth view of a time period that should be, but often is not, conceived as a coherent entity.[27] It commences in 1783, at the end of the Revolutionary War and during a fleeting peak of high optimism regarding the new nation. It then carries through to 1833, the year that witnessed the final, formal disestablishment of Congregationalism in Massachusetts. It explores what Edwin Scott Gaustad in a pithy remark once called Congregationalism's shift during the late eighteenth and early nineteenth centuries "from that of a dominant, sometimes persecuting, majority to that of a sensitive, sometimes leavening, minority." This study traces not the breakdown of the clergy's social vision, as so many scholars from Perry Miller on have prematurely heralded, but the transformation of a distinctively New England variant of public Christianity. Chronologically and topically—if not always interpretatively—*A Republic of Righteousness* takes up a position between the colonial focus of Harry S. Stout's *The New England Soul* and the antebellum one of Mark Y. Hanley's *Beyond a Christian Commonwealth*.[28]

By finding that throughout the period from 1783 to 1833 there were Americans concerned with their collective destiny, this study belies the overall depiction of the post-Revolutionary period as the time of the individualization of American society. Specifically, important segments of the New England ministry retained a commitment to constructing a righteous community and assessing the cosmic meaning of the American experiment. New England's traditional religious leaders remained actively engaged in the search to maintain the connection between Christianity and the society at large; they stood against the liberal juggernaut and raised a prophetic voice.[29] This public Christianity had a number of significant ramifications for U.S. history. It both fostered and critiqued American identity, nationalism, and civil religion and contributed to the political ideology of the first and second party periods. The work of New England's clergymen also relates to the origins of reform in the early nineteenth century. From their pulpits and church-related voluntary societies, ministers continued to question their society's values and meaning. To the extent that the health of a democracy is dependent upon robust debate, the New England clergy furthered the vitality of early republican culture through the application of its social ideology to public issues. In this final sense, ministers acted in a progressive manner, not as knee-jerk or inconsequential conservatives.

The public Christianity of the early national period descended from the Puritans' national covenant. In his famous address to his shipmates aboard the *Arbella* in 1630, John Winthrop had set the tone by calling upon them to "be knitt together in this worke as one man." If they slacked off in their commitment to one another or God, Winthrop warned, "the Lord will surely break out in wrathe against vs be revenged of such a periured people and make vs knowe the price of the breache of such a Covenant." Winthrop further sought to inspire everyone to commitment, in an oft-quoted passage, by portraying their colonizing project in world-historical terms: "wee must Consider that wee shall be as a Citty vpon a Hill, the eies of all peo-

ple are vppon vs; soe that if wee shall deale falsely with our god in this worke wee
haue vndertaken and soe cause him to withdrawe his present help from vs, wee shall
be made a story and a by-word through the world."[30] This Puritan social vision had
been much contested, attenuated, revived, and reformulated in the ensuing century
and a half because of the impact of the Enlightenment, Great Awakening, and
American Revolution, among other factors.[31] Yet, ministers continued striving to link
heaven and earth. Like Winthrop, they proclaimed a vision of a godly society and
warned of the frowns of Providence. The southern New England clergy's public
Christianity in the post-Revolutionary era included elements of the national covenant, the jeremiad tradition, millennialism, republicanism, liberalism, and even the
great chain of being, but went beyond any of these discrete discourses. Clergymen
drew on all of these threads as they wove a Christian social ideology.

In their preaching, ministers related Christianity to social existence mainly in
two ways. In the first place, ministers—especially the Congregational ones, who regarded themselves as the watchmen over the public culture—kept a running account of the community's status before a providential God. They addressed questions
such as How had Providence guided New England's (and later, America's) history?
What role would the nation play in bringing about the millennium? Was this a nation with a special covenant with God? Or was divine chastening imminent? Samuel
Austin's 1825 address, discussed at the outset, touched on all of these issues. This interpretative tradition was premised on a belief in the direct rule of the living God.
The stream of ministerial commentary also connected to the issues of patriotism and
national identity. And as we shall see, ministers' reading of the community's standing
with Providence closely depended on current events. Second, ministers such as
Austin offered their prescriptions for how Christians and their churches should act in
society. They did so based on their belief that social stability required Christianity. H.
Richard Niebuhr has termed this ongoing debate over the relationship between
Christians and society the question of "Christ and culture."[32] Over the course of the
half century following 1783, ministers offered a variety of responses to this question.
They especially wrestled with the competing natures of Christianity's relationship to
society; that is, would it take a conservative or reformist approach? Their answers
tended to be intertwined with the state of partisan politics. Non-Congregationalists
made the debate over Christianity and society quite dynamic. The dissenters challenged the standing order's formulations, especially regarding the establishment.

This study is based on the premise that such religious language is an important
cultural category that must be studied on its own terms. Religious discourse cannot
be reduced to a derivative of its social or material contexts; it has a semiautonomous
integrity. In other words, this study seeks to avoid what Mark A. Noll has called "the
imperialism of social science" or the "aggressive determination to transpose religious
language and behavior into what was really going on." Similarly, I concur with Perry
Miller that "no interpretation of the [clergy's] religious utterances as being merely
sanctimonious window-dressing will do justice to the facts."[33] The older literature
tended toward such reductionism and has long been exposed as simplistic. Already
in her 1973 article, Lois W. Banner blasted the social control thesis for always insisting on sordid motives behind reform. Banner's essay belonged to a broader revolution taking place in the human studies during the 1960s, led by the anthropologist

Clifford Geertz. His criticisms of "interest" and "strain theory" likewise pinpoint the deficiencies in the earlier approaches to the New England ministry. In the place of a fixation on interest or social disorder, which posits that human beings only "pursue power" or "flee anxiety," Geertz argued for the centrality of meaning.[34] The language used by early-nineteenth-century clergymen, to use an example that Geertz did not, was not arbitrary or the mere reflection of something else in the social structure. Rather, it should be seen as part of an ordered, symbolic system that worked to carry meaning and in turn to order the perceptions and activities of actors.[35]

For evidence of the clergy's social ideology, the study draws on a large body of sermons, orations, and polemical treatises published throughout Massachusetts, Connecticut, and Rhode Island. Harry S. Stout has noted that most scholars use these more easily obtainable printed sermons and overlook manuscript ones. I accept the validity of his argument that "only from the vantage point of unpublished sermons, however, can the full range of colonial preaching be understood." The reliance on published sermons introduces a distortion into studies of Puritanism, Stout argues, because it does not portray accurately what ministers preached on a typical Sunday. A disproportionate number of published sermons were not *regular*, Sunday ones, but *occasional* sermons delivered for a special event, such as a fast or election day. Nevertheless, for the purposes of this study, published sources largely suffice. This is a study of the ministry's public Christianity, its utterances on the relationship of faith to life in society. It was in their occasional sermons—the kind that tended to wind up in print—that ministers discussed such matters. Stout writes that "each generation of New England ministers invented and institutionalized a growing range of occasional sermons that allowed for pulpit commentary on social and political themes without corrupting the enduring concern of regular preaching, which was the salvation of the soul."[36] Therefore, we can safely rely on the vast sample of printed sermons as a good source for the content of the clergy's public Christianity.

The book is also premised on the belief that ideas can be understood fully only within their historical background. While concentrating on the *content* of religious beliefs, the study also recognizes the importance of their *context*, without subordinating either one to the other.[37] It does not examine the religiosocial pronouncements of southern New England ministers in a vacuum but situates the ideology under study within the context of the political, intellectual, and religious culture and institutions. As the foregoing discussion makes obvious, many of the developments that influenced the clergy's public Christianity were national if not global in scope, ranging from the American Revolution to the French Revolution and from the struggles of the first party period to the rise of the missionary movement. Yet, other settings for our story are more appropriately smaller in scale, and thus the book also attends to both regional and local contexts.

The proper regional frame of reference for understanding the clergy's public Christianity is the tristate area of southern New England. Massachusetts, Connecticut, and Rhode Island were the historic homes of the Puritan tradition and its dissenting alternatives. The three states had individual histories, of course, but they also had a long cultural background with much in common. Jerald C. Brauer is correct to complain of the tendency to treat the national religious history as "Puritanism writ large," but on the other side of the coin, the regional history must not be enveloped in the mists of national generalizations either.[38] Although it is true that "everywhere in the new republic literate citizens were busy harmonizing the two faiths [of Christianity and republicanism]," their activities produced different syntheses in different regional contexts, which need to be recognized.[39] During the period under study, southern New England was set distinctively apart from some of the trends shaping the rest of the new nation. The area deviated from the norm in the early republic with its ethnic homogeneity and staunch attachment to Federalist politics.[40] Compared with the rest of colonial America, the Puritan colonies had always had a well-developed and relatively stable religious tradition, and all of the New England states save Rhode Island maintained the establishment of Congregationalism into the nineteenth century. "Congregationalism," writes one scholar, was deeply rooted "at the heart of New England culture."[41] This contrasts with the situation in the South during the early republic, where the Anglican church, which was not strong to begin with, had suffered a tremendous setback from the Revolution, and evangelicals essentially had to begin the process of Christianization over again.[42] As several historians have demonstrated, the frontier arc stretching across northern New England from Maine to Vermont really does not match this characterization of the religious culture of southern New England on account of the frontier's rapid growth, the newness and flatness of its social institutions, and its religious heterogeneity.[43] To say southern New England was unique—and even unrepresentative of national trends in the early nineteenth century—is not to deem it less representative than any other particular region. Specifically, many New England tendencies in the 1810s emerged on a national scale in the 1820s and 1830s as part of a new "northern" regional culture.

If the language of their public Christianity sounded across the region of southern New England, individual clergymen lived and acted mainly within more local horizons. "Indeed, above all else," writes Donald M. Scott, "the sacred office in eighteenth-century New England was a local office, derived from a special blend of congregationalist ecclesiastical theory and the social order of the New England town."[44] Despite the conspiratorial charges that were sometimes leveled by its enemies, the standing order of Congregational ministers was not much of a statewide monolith. Except for the annual conventions of ministers that were held in Boston and Hartford each spring at the time of the election day festivities, the standing order was mainly a local organism. Clergymen conducted many of their professional activities within networks of other ministers in their vicinity. They associated formally with nearby colleagues to hold discussions, examine and license candidates for the ministry, resolve disputes, and coordinate other activities. Informally, they exchanged pulpits and otherwise supported one another. Ministers joined together to lead revivals in nearby churches. Likewise, reform societies were usually begun locally, and even after the subsequent creation of statewide or national organizations, the local auxiliaries were still critical for grassroots mobilization. Conflicts with regional ramifications often played out locally as well. For instance, the Unitarian controversy was fought out at the level of the parish and church; William G. McLoughlin noted that "the fight for religious liberty was primarily a neighborhood affair."[45] Thus, many of the ministry's utterances about the interface of religion and society were cast in a local frame of reference. Even though the bulk of this study focuses on translocal

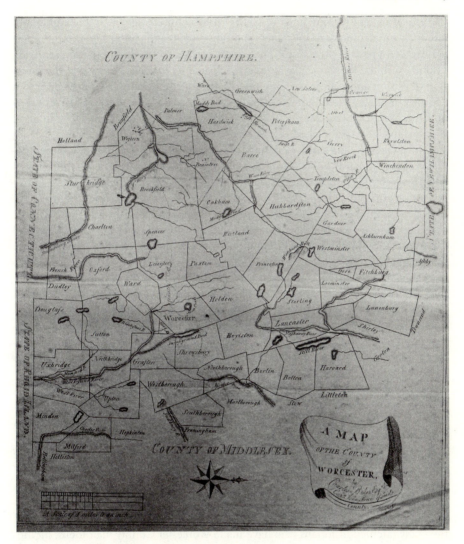

A map of the County of Worcester, 1793. Courtesy American Antiquarian Society.

themes such as the providential shaping of regional and national history or the pre-scribed structure of the righteous society, it is important to appreciate the local roots of a good deal of ministers' social ideology.

It would be beyond the scope of this study to investigate the local contours of every occasional sermon or to take a comprehensive look at the activities of each ministerial association. Selection is necessary. Fortunately, the confines of Worcester County, Massachusetts, brought together in microcosm most of the important reli-gious developments from across the region. The county was literally a crossroads, and people and trends from every corner of New England intersected there. As John L. Brooke writes in his study of the county's social and political history, "Worcester

County provides a comprehensive view of Massachusetts society in the eighteenth and early nineteenth centuries, incorporating themes and patterns that characterize very different parts of the state."[46] The county's religious development in the early republic exhibited the same "comprehensive" quality. From the east, from the direction of Boston and Cambridge, the county felt a strong Unitarian influence. From the west resonated the orthodox Congregationalism of the Connecticut River valley and the Nutmeg State itself. Up the Blackstone River valley from the southeast, Baptists and Quakers pushed into the county from the direction of Rhode Island. The northwestern and southwestern corners of the county were home to other sectarians, and itinerants passed through as well. In addition to its representative diversity, Worcester County was also the home to several long-serving and active ministers.[47] For instance, Samuel Austin, pastor of Worcester's First Church from 1790 to 1815, was also the editor of an eight-volume set of Jonathan Edwards's works and a principal figure behind the Massachusetts Missionary Society. At the Second Church, Aaron Bancroft served from 1786 to 1839. A luminary of the first magnitude among the religious liberals, he was president of the American Unitarian Association from 1825 to 1836. Joseph Goffe, minister of the North Parish of Sutton, later Millbury, between 1794 and 1830, also had his hand in a host of benevolent and clerical associations. These and other ministers made Worcester County the scene of a full array of ministerial, evangelistic, and reform organizations. Therefore, study of Worcester County sheds light on the history of the larger New England ministry and its public endeavors, and *A Republic of Righteousness* visits the county from time to time to contextualize the ministry's social ideology.

Of course, this local aspect of the book calls for a different body of source material than the sermons and orations that illuminate the ministry's public Christianity. Thanks to great archives, there are outstanding records with which to work.[48] A variety of organizational records are extant. For example, the records of the Brookfield Association of churches are intact for the years from 1757 to 1837, and there are similar records for missionary organizations, individual churches, reform societies, and the like. There also is an abundance of personal papers. Joseph Goffe's diaries and letters, to cite just one example, provide tremendous insight into ministerial networking and revivals. These manuscript sources are supplemented by the works of the many talented historians who have made Worcester County their focus, including both nineteenth-century ministerial authors and twentieth-century academics.

The story of how New Englanders sought to construct their public Christianity falls into three chronological periods. From the early 1780s until the turn of the century, the established ministry aligned church and government in a hierarchical social vision aimed at the creation of a righteous community. The standing order's predominant place in the region's socioreligious pecking order encouraged Congregational clergymen to posit a salient public role for themselves. Convinced of the providential direction and worldwide ramifications of the American Revolution, Congregational ministers worked to secure the republic through the cooperation of magistrate and minister. Congregational clergymen advocated a distinctive ideology that defies categorization as either liberal or republican.[49] However, to a greater degree than is sometimes recognized, they hesitated to endow the new republic with the seal of the national covenant. While some hailed the United States as a chosen nation, others denied it or carefully qualified the announcement.[50] Dissenters from the establishment challenged the Congregationalists' church-state alliance, but the political turmoil of the 1790s only drove established clergymen into a heightened defense of the status quo. The period from the 1780s to 1800 is the subject of chapters 1 and 2, which also lay the groundwork for later developments in the nineteenth century.

Rising opposition ignited a contentious second period, analyzed in chapter 3, that spanned the first two decades of the nineteenth century. Although dissenters were growing in number, it was not until the late 1790s with the rise of the Republican opposition that they made their presence decisively felt on the question of the religious basis of the social order. Competing political, theological, and ideological factions debated the proper place and extent of Christianity's role in the public sphere. The Democratic-Republicans presented dissenters with a powerful new stick with which to cudgel the standing order. Most tangibly, these years yielded the disestablishment of religion in Connecticut in 1818, but they also precipitated a crisis of ideology. The Congregational ministry had to reevaluate its earlier partnership with the state. As political groups critical of the ministers' social pronouncements and involvement came to power on both the national and state levels, the earlier reliance on the magistracy became problematic. Furthermore, the Congregational ministry interpreted the results of the first party competition by rejecting the U.S. government as a blessing of Providence and now portrayed it as one of God's judgments on a wicked land.

While disaffection with government grew in the years before 1815, the rising tide of evangelical awakening began to foster an alternative vision of the godly community. This is the subject of chapter 4. Successes in both faraway missionary endeavors and homegrown revivals were renewing the church, which suggested a new hope for corporate righteousness arising from the church acting on society. An important group of evangelical Congregational ministers began to articulate how this revived church would have a profound and salutary influence on the surrounding community. They organized a variety of new institutions to put their ideas into effect. The activities of clergymen in Worcester County epitomized all of these developments, as revealed particularly by the manuscript record left by Joseph Goffe.

By the late 1810s and 1820s, the period covered in chapter 5, the 150-year-old division between the standing order and the dissenters was finally giving way to a new alignment. The Connecticut establishment had fallen to the Republican coalition. In Massachusetts, the standing order broke up over an internal debate within Congregationalism, the so-called Unitarian controversy, that split the denomination into Unitarian and Trinitarian wings. The Unitarians, while theologically unconventional, remained conservative socially; they were the last defenders of the establishment. The Trinitarian (or orthodox) Congregationalists likewise retained elements of their traditional corporate ethic but were compelled to innovate without the establishment. The orthodox came to espouse new strategies of implementing their belief in the social necessity of religion. Orthodox ministers called for a conscientious electorate and a revitalized church to fulfill the roles formerly occupied by the establishment. They pioneered new organizational forms to carry this into practice. In their move away from the establishment, orthodox Congregationalists found common ground with the old dissenting groups, particularly the Baptists. A new, evangelical coalition emerged that would send powerful ripples through antebellum politics and reform nationwide. Both sides of the new evangelical-liberal divide voiced renewed patriotism around the nation's semicentennial in 1826, reaffirming hope in the providential destiny of the United States.

Yet the ministry's public Christianity, as shown in chapter 6, could also censure nationalism, along with other perceived defects in the national character, such as intemperance, intoxication with the emerging market economy, violations of the Sabbath, and chattel slavery. Both evangelicals and Unitarians critiqued national values from a standpoint apart from both the expanding market and the state. The reform initiatives of this period are better understood with this study's perspective on their roots in New England religious culture, rather than by simply invoking concepts such as status anxiety that make them appear as an ad hoc response to the immediate social environment.[51]

Overall, this study challenges the portrayal of the early republic as a period of secularization, individualization, or the withdrawal of religion from public life. Rather, ministers found new strategies for staying engaged with their society. Their public Christianity evolved over the period from 1783 to 1833 but continued both to endow social experience with providential meaning and to offer a program for the godly society. Evangelicalism ultimately proved it could carry with it a collective identity and was not synonymous with individual piety alone. Thus, the clergy's social ideology became an engine for reform and missions in the antebellum period. For the socially critical voice it inspired, New England's public Christianity deserves credit as an important element in the intellectual world of antebellum politics and reform. The Congregationalists' corporate ethic was a countervailing integrative force in an era better known for its social atomization; hyperindividualism was not the only ideology conducive to social ferment in the early republic. Ultimately, *A Republic of Righteousness* raises the (admittedly anachronistic) question of which Americans in the early republic were the most "modern." Nathan O. Hatch claims the title for his "insurgent religious leaders," others for secular liberals, but surely those who were the predecessors of Protestant liberalism, a progressive evangelicalism, and the Social Gospel could also stake a legitimate claim to the designation.[52] By articulating, often in opposition, an inclusive ideal that went beyond partisan political ideologies, the clerical figures under study stimulated a debate over social morality that was vital to the development of American culture.

ONE

The Standing Order's Corporate Vision
1783–1795

IN A 1783 PAMPHLET titled *Observations upon the Present State of the Clergy of New-England*, the Rev. Peter Thacher gloomily assessed the damages that the American Revolution had inflicted on the ministerial profession in New England. Thacher, the Congregational minister of Malden, Massachusetts, decried the depreciation of clerical income caused by wartime inflation. Not only had the real value of salaries eroded but also townsmen were often tardy in paying their ministers. Thacher cast this scenario as a classic case of declension, as a fall from the lofty "principles and spirit which distinguished the fathers of New-England," under whose paternal guidance "the clergy were tolerably supported and were highly respected." Even more threatening, Thacher suspected a newfound readiness on the part of churches to fire their ministers whenever the congregation pleased. "The people," he reasoned, "having emancipated themselves from the British government, and felt their competence to carry every point they chose, have, in some places at least, forgotten that they could never be emancipated from the bonds of justice. They have been too ready to suppose that their declaration and authority were sufficient to dissolve the most solemn engagements [like that between a church and its duly settled pastor], and that *the people could do no wrong*." The injustice of the situation was compounded by the New England clergy's patriotic support of the Revolution. "There is not the body of men among us of any description whatever," Thacher reminded his readers, "whose exertions had a greater tendency first to excite, and afterwards to keep up that indignation, at the usurped power of our enemies, that steady firmness in opposing it, or that chearful [*sic*] compliance with the measures necessary to our defence, which so greatly contributed to bringing about the glorious revolution, that hath distinguished the present period of existence in the annals of the world."[1] In Thacher's eyes, the established ministry stood ill prepared to exercise similar leadership in the early republic.

Historians have tended to agree with Peter Thacher's assessments. As far back as 1781, when the Tory writer Peter Oliver blamed the "black Regiment" of the New England clergy for fomenting rebellion, scholars have acknowledged the important role that the ministry played in the Revolutionary struggle.[2] Thacher's pamphlet gives two more impressions, both of which have left their mark on the secondary literature on religion in the early republic. Historians have used remarks like his to depict the Congregational clergy as in a steep decline in the post-Revolutionary years. Confronted with a surge in religious dissenters, we are told, the old standing order appeared ossified and irrelevant. Moreover, one could extrapolate from Thacher's pamphlet a general inference that by 1783 the established clergy's mood was downcast and its fund of social pronouncements depleted.

This chapter instead seeks to rectify these two misperceptions. Without denying the validity of Thacher's complaints, it first contends for the ongoing strength of Congregationalism in southern New England relative to other denominations during the 1780s and 1790s. Compared with the Episcopalians, Quakers, Methodists, or Baptists—if not to the halcyon days of "the fathers of New-England"—the Congregationalists ranked far ahead in terms of resources, influence, and organization. Patricia U. Bonomi has characterized the colonial-era "political and social preeminence" of the New England Congregationalists as a "hegemony," and the depiction remains valid for the first two decades after the War for Independence.[3]

After setting the context of the Congregationalists' hegemony, the chapter focuses on the content of the ministry's pronouncements. The chapter begins to unpack the established clergy's public Christianity, finding it vibrant and upbeat, Peter Thacher's forebodings notwithstanding. Reflecting their predominant place in New England culture and society during the critical period and Federalist era between 1783 and 1800, the Congregational establishments of Massachusetts and Connecticut sought to maintain the connection between religion and society through their public commentary. Clergymen drew this connection along two axes. In the first place, they interpreted the nation's role in the unfolding of the providential scheme of history in the wake of the American Revolution. By narrating a providential history of the Revolution, ministers situated the regional community in a transcendent framework and imparted sacred meaning to collective experience. The American Revolution did color their view, but not by casting a dark shadow; rather the Revolution's effect was more like the radiant glow of the setting sun, which cast a golden light on their retrospects. Second, and the subject of chapter 2, the Congregational clergy depicted the righteous community as one in which magistrate and minister closely cooperated.

This first chapter explores the providential worldview through which the ministry understood social experience. The Christianity of the southern New England standing order in the 1780s and 1790s was thoroughly and deliberately committed to society as a whole. This corporate ethic was a complex blend of several distinct yet interrelated elements. Contrary to the claims of some recent scholars, it consisted primarily of neither a national covenant nor republicanism. Rather, the standing order's corporate ethic drew on these and other discourses to explain the links between Christianity and the destiny of society as a whole. If there was one overarching theme to this creole of inclusive languages, it was the conviction that God's Providence oversaw and guided human affairs. Faith in the providential superintendence of nations had become especially relevant at the time of the American Revolution, because it made the momentous upheavals of the 1770s and 1780s explicable. For example, Isaac Morrill, the preacher at the fifth anniversary commemoration of the

Battle of Lexington, argued that "faith and trust in the government of divine providence, is the great support of God's people in the most perilous and distressing times." Amid the battle's carnage, recalled the pastor of Wilmington, Massachusetts, applying Ps. 27:13, "We had fainted, unless we had believed to see the goodness of the Lord in the land of the living."[4] Non-Congregationalists, too, joined in this kind of providential reading of events, although they generally lacked the standing order's broader concern for society. A belief in the providential guidance of American affairs also yielded insight into the future and contributed, in a diffuse way, to the development of nationalism in the last quarter of the eighteenth century.

In their providential interpretations, ministers perpetuated a New England tradition that stretched back to the region's seventeenth-century beginnings and adapted their reading of the region's ultimate meaning to incorporate the American Revolution. The ebullience precipitated by the Peace of Paris in 1783, however, obscured potential inconsistencies and unexamined implications within the clergy's public Christianity, which would become clearer over time. As a result, in the early nineteenth century many Congregational ministers would deny that the American republic was intended by God to elevate humankind. Nevertheless, by continuing to search for providential meaning in regional and national events, established clergymen nourished an important source of corporate identity. The very malleability of that corporate meaning was the source of both its ambiguities and its continuing relevance in the early republic.

The Congregational Establishment

> And thou shalt put [the vestments] upon Aaron thy brother, and his sons
> with him; and shalt anoint them, and consecrate them, and sanctify them,
> that they may minister unto me in the priest's office.
>
> — Exod. 28:41

Although dramatic developments were to transform the religious landscape between 1783 and 1833, by every measure the Congregational establishment occupied a predominant place in southern New England during the last two decades of the eighteenth century. Law and custom privileged the Congregational churches fiscally above their rivals, allowing them to collect taxes for ministerial support and building maintenance. Numerically speaking, the Congregationalists outpaced all others combined in terms of churches and clergymen. Although its cultural salience cannot be similarly quantified, the standing order also had influence not enjoyed by the Baptists, Episcopalians, Methodists, or Quakers. Established ministers buried their disputants in terms of the sheer volume of material they published. They associated closely and frequently with laymen at the center of political power in Massachusetts and Connecticut. The states' days of fasting, thanksgiving, and election disproportionately allowed the established ministry to reach the public audience with its prescriptions for the godly community. Finally, their local networks allowed standing order clergymen to advance their goals more effectively than some of their less organized competitors.

To say that the standing order retained power runs counter to a hoary tradition in the secondary literature that views its demise as a foregone conclusion in the wake of the American Revolution. The Revolution, we are told by an august list of scholars, seriously disrupted American Christianity, as preachers and the populace focused on the struggle for political independence. As Leonard Woolsey Bacon wrote, typifying this interpretation, "The closing years of the eighteenth century show the lowest low-water mark of the lowest ebb-tide of spiritual life in the history of the American church."[5] The source of this historiographical tradition, more so than Peter Thacher, is no less a towering figure than Lyman Beecher. His memories of deism running rampant during his undergraduate days at Yale, replete with students calling each other "Voltaire" and "Rousseau," have made a vivid impression on historians.[6] When religion revived in the Second Great Awakening, sectarian newcomers chiefly benefited. Sometimes this conventional chronology serves denominational purposes. At other times, historians simply find it convenient to invoke the Revolution itself as a cause of change.[7]

However, one must avoid the fallacy of overemphasizing the significance of future trends in their preceding time period. There is a rush to the explanatory thesis of "democratization" in the post-Revolutionary period. Contrary to studies that proleptically grant cutting-edge status to dissenters from the standing order, this study steadfastly insists on beginning the story at the beginning. Although not in a period of vigorous growth, the establishment was also not in a state of breakdown during the 1780s and 1790s. Elites mattered. The New England establishment enjoyed an Indian summer prior to the momentous and destructive changes of the nineteenth century.[8]

By "the establishment," I mean two things. Informally, I use the term to denote the dominant religious group, the ascendancy, in New England's denominational pecking order, as opposed to those groups on the social or cultural margins. Some religious groups were on the fringe of the debate over public Christianity because of a self-imposed exile, such as the Quakers or Shakers; others were relegated there on account of the hostility and disdain of the majority, as was the case with the Universalists. Formally, establishment signifies the churches that received legal and fiscal privileges from the state.[9] In either usage, the Congregationalists were New England's legal and traditional establishment. Although similar, the specific mechanics of the formal establishment differed in Massachusetts and Connecticut.

In Massachusetts, the formal establishment rested on the state constitution of 1780, in particular articles 2 and 3. These two articles of the "Declaration of Rights" embodied a seeming contradiction. Article 2 declared that "no Subject shall be hurt, molested, or restrained, in his Person, Liberty, or Estate, for worshipping GOD in the manner and season most agreeable to the Dictates of his own conscience, or for his religious Profession or sentiments," as long as such worship "did not Disturb the public peace, or obstruct others in their religious Worship." Yet in the next article, the constitution gave the legislature the power to restrain people's wealth in order to support religion. Specifically, article 3 stated that "the people of this Commonwealth have a right to invest their legislature with power to authorize and require . . . the several Towns, Parishes, precincts, and other bodies politic, or religious societies, to make suitable provision, at their own Expence [*sic*], for the institution of the Public worship of GOD, and for the support and maintenance of public protestant teachers of piety, religion and morality, in all cases where such provision shall not be made Voluntarily." Article 3 might be said to restrain people's bodies as well in giving the legislature power "to enjoin upon all the Subjects an attendance upon the instructions of the public teachers aforesaid, at stated times and seasons, if there be any on whose instructions they can Conscientiously and conveniently attend." The constitution tried to reconcile the conflicting demands of freedom of conscience and public support of religion by allowing dissenters from the established churches to earmark their taxes for "the support of the public teacher or teachers of his own religious sect or denomination, provided there be any on whose instructions he attends." Although the framers tried to make room for religious dissent, they were not about to countenance an anarchic individualism in which such an important matter as public morality was allowed to lapse into deregulation.[10]

The key to unlock the apparently contradictory tendencies of articles 2 and 3 lies in understanding that a Massachusetts citizen had both religious rights and duties. The beginning sentence of article 2 announced that "it is the right as well as the Duty of all men in society, publickly, and at stated seasons to worship the SUPREME BEING, the great Creator and preserver of the Universe." The state would tolerate those who pleaded a serious, conscientious objection to Congregationalism but not those who were just too stingy or too lazy to attend and to pay for worship. In addition to such ideological reasoning, these two articles represented a purely political compromise between those favoring religious liberty and those for the establishment, aimed at getting everyone on board to ratify the constitution of 1780.[11]

In practice, the constitution allowed the towns and parishes to tax residents for the support of the Congregational church, which was almost always the majority's church. However, the ambiguities and contradictions of the two articles regarding the dissenting sects created a rash of further legislation, litigation, contention, and confusion over the next three decades. There were at least five "reasonable" interpretations of the way article 3 was supposed to work. For example, did the third article mean that dissenters had to pay the religious tax like anyone else and then apply to have the money donated to their minister, or could they avoid paying the tax in the first place by turning in a certificate of membership in a church other than the established one, as they had done in the colonial era? Were they exempt outright? Could a town treasurer disperse publicly gathered tax money to any dissenting minister or only to those whose churches were incorporated by the state legislature (as none of the dissenting churches were before 1785) and thus had a legally recognized institutional existence? Only the 1811 Act of Religious Liberty, discussed in chapter 3, resolved these issues. Until then, a confusing and conflicting set of court decisions and local compromises led to no uniform, statewide application of article 3. Facing Baptist resistance, "many towns . . . ceased even to assess those Baptists who turned in certificates and thus placed the matter back where it had been before 1780." Nevertheless, throughout Massachusetts the Congregational churches were able to garner tax support from their adherents, those with no other preference, and those without the means or morale to fight the levy.[12]

In Connecticut, which was one of only two states not to adopt a new constitution in the Revolutionary era, the establishment relied on an older tradition.[13] However, the colonial procedures had been modified in a "general revision" of the state's laws in 1784. According to a 1784 law, dissenters of any Christian denomination, either full members or adherents, could receive a tax exemption from support of the standing order simply by handing in certificates signed by "dissenting deacons or church clerks as well as ministers." The Connecticut law, therefore, basically codified the same system that evolved informally in Massachusetts with local resistance to article 3. This 1784 legal housecleaning also led to the quiet deletion of the Saybrook Platform from the Connecticut books, which meant that "the state no longer gave its civil support to the actions of the various Congregational associations and consociations nor any civil endorsement to the Savoy Confession of Faith which was imbedded in the Platform." Thus, the Connecticut establishment of the 1780s and 1790s was like that of Massachusetts: loosely defined and with allowance for dissenters but one that still "gave certain privileges, *de facto* and by tradition, to the Congregational churches." An attempt in 1791 to make the certificate exemption harder to fulfill by requiring the signature of a justice of the peace, not just a dissenting church official, backfired and led to a new certificate law. This new law of 1791 did away with the requirement of any verifying signature and instead required only the individual's own. As time went by, the Congregational churches would feel the pinch financially, as more and more people opted out of the tax collector's grasp. The state legislature tried other means of funneling money to the standing order, such as lotteries, pew rents, and the sale of western lands.[14] Ultimately, the Connecticut establishment would come crashing down in 1818. But this is jumping ahead; during the last two decades of the eighteenth century, the Congregational establishment continued to be the dominant religious presence in Connecticut.

Rhode Island, as is well known, never had the religious establishment of its neighbors. This befitted a colony that was founded by and for outcasts, whose one thing in common was their inability to live under Puritan rule. Rhode Islanders also never instituted the tradition of an annual election sermon.[15] Instead of being a beacon to the world of the positive possibilities of religious liberty, however, Rhode Island had a pariah's existence. "During and after the colonial period, Rhode Island, 'the licentious Republic' and 'sinke hole of New England,' was an example to be shunned." Nevertheless, there are valid reasons to include Rhode Island sources in the present study. Primarily, I have cast my net beyond Connecticut and Massachusetts in order to take in a broader sample of evidence that includes Baptist publications. Rhode Island had always been a Baptist haven, and in the period under study it was the home to such leading figures in the denomination as James Manning, Jonathan Maxcy, and Francis Wayland, all of whom served as president of Rhode Island College (Brown University) in Providence. But the choice to take in Rhode Island also reflects the practical, lived realities of coexistence in southern New England. The borders between Rhode Island and Connecticut or Massachusetts were permeable, with a free flow of people and ideas across state lines. For example, James Manning often itinerated in eastern Connecticut during the summers. The Warren Association, the flagship grouping of Baptist churches, contained under its umbrella churches from throughout New England.[16] Therefore, although Rhode Island lacked a standing order of the type found in the other two states of southern New England, it was not outside the regional debate over religion and society.

A simple examination of some quantifiable indices graphically demonstrates that Congregationalism loomed large on the religious landscape of New England. Unfortunately, we lack uniform, readily comparable statistics for denominational size, number of adherents, or number of churches. The figures often must be taken from denominational histories that are of limited scope and possibly biased. Nevertheless, rough comparisons are possible. That Congregationalism formed the largest denomination in post-Revolutionary Massachusetts appears clearly in the tabulations of Joseph S. Clark, a nineteenth-century secretary of the Congregational Library Association. In fact, the Congregationalists claimed more than three times the number of churches in the state than all other denominations *combined* in 1790. Whereas there were 330 Congregational churches, the Baptists were a distant second with 68. All other denominations had less than a dozen: one for the Roman Catholics; three and six for the Universalists and Quakers, respectively; and eleven for the Episcopalians. The numbers for 1800 show the rapid expansion of dissenters but also the predominance of the Congregationalists, who still had more than a two-to-one advantage. There existed 344 Congregational churches in Massachusetts, and all others totaled 151, "namely: — Baptists, ninety-three; Methodists, twenty-nine; Episcopalians, fourteen; Quakers, eight; Universalists, four; Presbyterians (counting only those which continued such), two; Roman Catholic, one."[17] In Connecticut, meanwhile, the Congregationalists displayed a similar dominance. As of 1792, the Congregational churches made up roughly two-thirds of all churches in the state.[18]

While from a distance Congregationalism cut an imposing profile, a closer inspection reveals cracks just below the surface. These divisions, which would split the denomination and sap its strength in the first quarter of the nineteenth century, were now mostly latent, but festering. Since the 1730s at least, due to the influence of the Enlightenment, Arminianism had been seeping into New England thought and undermining its historical, Calvinist foundations. The contest between grace and works in New England theology exploded in the Great Awakening of the 1740s and pitted the Congregational clergy against one another in Old Light and New Light factions. In the Awakening's aftermath, the theological factions acquired further definition. The liberals continued down the road that would lead them to Unitarianism in the nineteenth century. As the Arminian movement's leading historian, Conrad Wright, has written, "Two generations of Arminians amassed the intellectual capital on which the liberals drew in the Unitarian Controversy." The liberals' opponents continued to develop as well in the mid-eighteenth century, as the students and intellectual heirs of Jonathan Edwards, the New Divinity men, renewed the vigor of New England Calvinism.[19]

However, in the eighteenth century, these theological disputes did not reach the point of schism for the standing order, as they would later on. The political crises of the 1760s through the 1790s tended to foster an artificial unanimity among New England Congregationalists, regardless of their intramural squabbling. They generally stood together in their public pronouncements, although theological segmentation did contribute to a breakdown in consensus regarding the national covenant. I concur with the assessment that "preoccupied with tracing every political distinction between evangelical and rational religion, [historians] have missed the most towering feature before them, the overwhelming political unity of the Congregational clergy."[20] It bears repeating that the theological balkanization of New England had profound ramifications for the debate over public Christianity in the nineteenth century. However, as for the last two decades of the eighteenth, one can still speak of a standing order of basically uniform social and political outlooks; this is the perspective of this chapter and the next.

Other denominations lagged behind the Congregationalists, and many were beset with serious handicaps. The Anglican church had suffered a devastating blow from the Revolution. During the colonial period, it had presented a rising challenge to Congregationalism with an aggressive missionary campaign in and beyond New England. This was especially so in Connecticut, where Anglicans had established more than forty churches by the eve of the Revolution.[21] The Revolution, however, threw into confusion a church that recognized the Crown's sovereignty in its governing structure and prayers: "When allegiance to the British king was no longer possible for a citizen of the United States, the Church of England in America was left without its accepted supreme governor." The break with England also severed the access of American Anglicans to their bishops, which meant that "the colonial clergy were deprived of their direct ecclesiastical superior and of their only source for the ordination of candidates to the ministry." Worst of all, the loyalism of the Anglican clergy forced a high percentage of ministers to flee and tainted many of those who remained with a smudge of suspicion.[22] In the immediate post-Revolutionary period, churchmen struggled to reorganize themselves as the Protestant Episcopal denomination and stanch the hemorrhaging of the war years. Intradenominational disputes over ecclesiastical restructuring largely preoccupied their energies. It was not until 1789 that Episcopalians hammered out a compromise among their regional and ideological factions. Once reorganized, the Episcopal church did not prosper. In his denominational history, Charles C. Tiffany dubbed the years from 1789 to 1811, "A Period of Suspended Animation and Feeble Growth."[23]

Like the Episcopalians, the Quakers, too, were stuck in a period of numerical stagnation, even decreasing in real numbers. In contrast to their seventeenth-century roots, Quakers in the new nation were not proselytizers. They turned inward, and the Society of Friends focused on "maintaining its special traditions, preserving itself basically as a hereditary organization, and improving its discipline." Although the Quaker reform movement may have tightened discipline and refined membership standards, it also caused less ardent adherents to the faith either to leave on their own accord or face expulsion. "As a result, with so many members being disowned and so few new members being added, the Society [of Friends in New England] started about 1780 to decline rapidly in numbers. This enforcement policy and its effects on the size of membership were not temporary, but continued well into the next century." Clearly, the Quakers would be unable to challenge Congregational hegemony.[24]

The Methodist denomination, which would attain such prominence in nineteenth-century America, only slowly penetrated New England. Methodists counted zero adherents in the region before 1789, when Jesse Lee entered Connecticut as a missionary. By June 1790, Lee had recruited a grand total of nine followers. The Methodists did not organize their first society in Boston until 1792 and laid the cornerstone of their first church there in 1795. Although the Methodists quickly set up circuits on the New England frontier, in more settled areas, with the notable exception of Lynn, Massachusetts, they encountered much more resistance and even overt hostility. Like the Anglican church, from which Methodism was an offshoot, the episcopal structure of Methodist governance had to withstand charges of ecclesiastical tyranny. Also like the Anglicans, the Revolution dealt a setback to the Methodists in the Middle Colonies. Every Methodist annual conference between 1776 and 1787 met in Maryland, Virginia, or North Carolina. Early Methodism was clearly a southern phenomenon, which reiterates the importance of regional specificity in early American religious history.[25] The Methodists' growth was rapid, but their numbers were small; by 1796, they had just under three thousand members in all of New England.[26] Again, one must be careful not to assert too large a role for Methodism in southern New England in the last two decades of the eighteenth century, regardless of future trends.

The most serious challenge to Congregational hegemony came from the Baptists. The Baptists' explosive growth dated back to the divisions of the First Great Awakening and showed no signs of abating in the early republic. For instance, in Connecticut between 1760 and 1790, Baptist churches multiplied from three to fifty-five.[27] Yet here again, the denomination's future strength should not color our perceptions of its real numbers in the last two decades of the eighteenth century. More important than its numerical strength, though, is the fact that the Baptists spearheaded resistance to the Congregational establishment through local protest, statewide organization, and an ongoing ideological confrontation in the newspapers and pamphlet literature. The Warren Association was one group that was capable of matching the standing order in terms of exerting local influence.[28]

Aside from a simple (and simplistic) enumeration of churches or adherents, less tangible factors add to the picture of the standing order's preponderance in the public realm. For instance, the standing order enjoyed access to public influence through its close interconnection with the region's ruling elites. The denominations did not operate on a level playing field either politically or culturally: some, like the Quakers, deliberately shunned public engagement; others were marginalized geographically and/or socially. The board of trustees of the Missionary Society of Connecticut illustrates perfectly the cooperation of magistrate and minister within the standing order. The board consisted of six laymen and six clergymen.[29] Their collective biographies reveal the tightly interwoven structure of authority at all levels of church and government that characterized Federalist Connecticut.[30] Of the five laymen I have identified, all held high governmental office in 1800, such as lieutenant governor, councillor, or congressman. Two of them united their government service with lengthy tenures as deacons of their local Congregational churches, and one, John Treadwell, also later helped found and served as president of the American Board of Commissioners for Foreign Missions. In addition to an orientation toward New Divinity theology and revivalism, the ministers all earned the status that came from a lengthy pastorate in one pulpit.[31] Aside from membership on the Missionary Society's board, other common traits drew these twelve men together. All of the ministers plus three laymen were Yale alumni, and at least two lay members and three clergymen knew each other from having served together on the Yale Corporation. Commitment to the patriot cause in the Revolution constituted another common link among those serving on the board.

This short review of the overlapping resumés of these twelve prominent figures illustrates the Congregationalists' sociopolitical hegemony in late-eighteenth-century Connecticut. The Congregational ministry shared the background and outlook of those in positions of social leadership. Ministers of the standing order associated on numerous occasions with members of the state's political leadership, which was significant because the governing class concentrated political power. "Offices sometimes came in a troop to the same beneficiary, as in the case of the pluralist who was clerk of his ecclesiastical society, clerk of the school district, clerk of the town, clerk of the probate court, clerk of the county court, and clerk of the Superior and Supreme Court of the State. He held all these clerkships at the same time, and of course he held them all till he died."[32] In an era of deference politics like the late eighteenth century, when the ruling class did not require or seek frequent public input on its decisions, Congregational clergymen held a privileged position.[33] They enjoyed a precious commodity generally denied other denominational leaders in New England: access to those whose hands were on the levers of power and who set the tone of regional high culture.

Congregational ministers sometimes tapped their friends in high places to try to stymie the dissenting sects. For example, Jesse Lee, his biographer reported, "scarcely entered a place without having to run the gauntlet with the minister of the parish, or a knot of selectmen, who, having custody of the townhouse, felt themselves the guardians of the morals and manners of the place." The experience of another Methodist itinerant, Freeborn Garrettson, bore this out. When he visited Worcester, Massachusetts, in 1790, he wrote in his journal, "I went from one end of the town to the other and could get no one to open the court house and gather the people."[34] Such treatment at the hands of Congregational clergymen and their friends in local government perhaps marginally slowed the spread of dissent, but it also bred a smoldering anger that would soon burst forth with destructive consequences for the establishment.

The establishment's ritual practice further raised its public stature. As Ronald P. Formisano has phrased matters, "ceremony, celebration, and sermon remained conspicuously alive" in Massachusetts until the 1830s. Not only did the ministers of the standing order frequently interact with New England's governing elite but also they put this association on display for all to see. This was especially the case on the general election day, during which "members of the senate and the house organized themselves in order to choose presiding officers in the morning, then in the afternoon went in procession with the executive to religious services and for the preaching of an Election Sermon."[35] David Tappan, minister of Newbury, Massachusetts, described the election day of 1792 as an occasion when the idealized unity of magistrate and minister became incarnate: "This joyful anniversary collects our civil and sacred leaders from various parts of the State, to one consecrated spot. It unites them, methinks, into one happy brotherhood. It brings them together to the altar of GOD, their common Founder, Master, and Judge. It makes them joint partakers in a kind of yearly festival, sacred to liberty and to religion — a festival, which seems to renew and to seal mutual friendship, and their harmonious ardent affection to the general interest." The annual election sermon, as well as days of fasting and thanksgiving, also placed an officially sanctioned religious presence into public life. These annual occasions acted as a stage from which the ministers of the standing order could publicly broadcast their ideology. What David D. Hall has written of public rituals in seventeenth-century Massachusetts still held true in the late eighteenth: "Ritual practice had much to do, as well, with these people's sense of corporate identity. Ritual reaffirmed the ideal nature of the body social and protected it from danger."[36] The sermons delivered on these occasions, many of which were subsequently published, record the ongoing clerical meditation over the question of Christianity's relationship to social life. They form the main primary-source basis for the following chapters.

Finally, the activities of local networks of clergymen furthered the Congregationalists' predominance, inasmuch as they strengthened the clerical profession and enabled ministers to work toward common objectives. The standing order had a loose, statewide coherence in both Massachusetts and Connecticut, as ministers met annually in convention, for instance. But the local associations formed the standing order's real sinews, because they grouped neighboring ministers into a grassroots professional network. Ministers had started organizing the several associations during the last decade of the seventeenth century and the first decades of the eighteenth. By the 1780s, ministerial associations existed across southern New England. For example, the Hartford North Association played a key role in igniting the revivals of the Second Great Awakening in northwestern Connecticut. At the other end of the region, six months after the Rev. Ephraim Abbot was ordained over the Congregational church in Greenland, New Hampshire, in 1813, he became involved in the meetings of the Piscataqua Association.[37] Thus, local associations were widespread across the region, and the records of the Brookfield Association of the western part of Worcester County are typical. The secondary literature has emphasized the negative aspects of this clerical associationalism, pointing out its tendencies to foster aloofness, complacency, and the suspicions of laypeople.[38] Without denying that these negative outcomes did sometimes occur, there was also a positive side to ministers' networking that needs to be appreciated. In addition to promoting professional regularity, the standing order also provided support for coordinated action. Eventually, these eighteenth-century networks would provide one of the key foundations for nineteenth-century missionary, benevolent, and reform societies and revivalism.

Ever since the last decade of the seventeenth century, Massachusetts clergymen had been holding an annual convention. They scheduled it for the day after the general election because many of them would be in Boston then, and it provided another occasion to rub elbows with the political leadership. Ministers trekked to the capital from throughout the state. For instance, the terse 1787 diary of Ephraim Ward, the Congregational minister of West Brookfield, records that he made the trip to Boston on May 28 and 29 and returned home again on June 1 and 2; that would place him in town for the election on May 30 and the convention the following day. Ministers such as Ward, although he was active locally in the Brookfield Association, were not confined to a parochial orbit or outlook. He set out again in October on a nearly three-week tour of eastern Massachusetts, during which he visited and dined with friends, preached in the pulpit of the Rev. John Prince at Salem's First Church, and took in a couple of lectures in Boston. The annual convention of ministers allowed men like Ward to renew old acquaintances and stay abreast of events. Most important, the convention enabled the ministry "to concert measures for the propagation of religion." It served as a hub for exchanging information among the assembled ministers and their several associations. It also provided an occasion for the ministry to utter its unified "testimony against prevailing errors in doctrine, discipline, or manners . . . and to recommend whatever may be of general use to ministers and churches, or to the commonwealth and country." The Connecticut clergy held a similar annual convention, although "it was not a gathering of all of the ministers of the province who wished to attend; instead it consisted of two or three representatives from each association." Given the new nation's paucity of other strong institutions, the New England clergy was probably one of the best organized and most influential bodies in society. Thus, the conspiratorial fears of critics of the standing order, analyzed in subsequent chapters, were grounded in reality. Still, the statewide convention, useful as it could be, took place just once a year. The real locus of clerical activity was to be found at the more frequent gatherings of the local associations.[39]

The eighteenth-century records of the Brookfield Association show how ministers worked together to enforce the clergy's professional standards and advance common goals. At the association's first meeting back on June 22, 1757, the five founding ministers had pledged "to comfort, strengthen, & quicken one another in the great Work we are jointly engaged in." Their overall aim was to "endeavor that our Ministry may hereby be rendered more successful," so that "the Interest of Religion" would be advanced. By and large, the association's ensuing records paint a picture of ministers trying to realize these founding goals.[40]

The associations were responsible for regulating entry into the standing order through the process of examining and licensing ministerial candidates. The experience of Joseph Goffe demonstrated the standard procedure. After his 1791 graduation from Dartmouth College, Goffe spent six months in New Haven studying with Jonathan Edwards Jr. At the end of that time, he was examined and licensed "by the Association of the Western Division of the County of New Haven" on October 30, 1792. Once licensed, a candidate could preach and receive a call. Ordination marked a minister's official installation over his church and into "a professional ministerial community." Here again, the local clergy played a key role in offering prayers and delivering the sermon, charge, and "right hand of fellowship." Goffe noted in his diary when he first took part in an ordination other than his own, which indicates that the ministers involved considered the ceremony a major event. In addition to licensing new preachers, the association could also vouch for an experienced colleague whose pastorate had come to an unsuccessful end. In October 1773, the Brookfield Association gave a letter of recommendation to "Revd. Mr. Strickland, . . . [who] tho' dismissed from Oakham," was "still in good standing with this Association" and came recommended "as a Christian & Minister wherever Providence shall open a Door for his Usefulness." In short, the associations upheld the standing order by maintaining the standards for entry into the ministry.[41]

Although the case of Rev. Strickland ended with his dismissal, the associations did try to intervene before difficulties between ministers and people became irreconcilable. When the Brookfield Association met at New Braintree on October 3,

1781, some members of the church there complained about the doctrinal errors of their minister, Rev. Foster. "After due Deliberation," the six ministers present "drew up their pacific Advice." Likewise, at the meeting of May 2, 1792, "Rev. Mr. [Ebenezer] Chaplin of Sutton laid before the Association the situation of affairs between him & his people. Advice was given him."[42] The founders of the Brookfield Association had pledged to "comfort" one another, and one can see here evidence that the ministers attempted to assist in times of trouble.

Even if it lacked much direct authority beyond licensing candidates, the association could try to compel obedience through less formal channels. Although these men were Congregationalists with a tradition of jealously guarded local autonomy, they nevertheless acted together in ways that could sometimes still prove to be effective for marshaling consensus. The experiences of two young ministers, Joseph Goffe and Aaron Bancroft, both of whom ran afoul of their local colleagues, demonstrate the ways in which ministers could just as easily withdraw comfort as offer it. Goffe settled in the North Parish of Sutton in September 1794 after the aforementioned "advice" of the Brookfield Association had proven fruitless and the church had dismissed Ebenezer Chaplin. As a way of showing their displeasure with Chaplin's ouster, the area ministers shunned Goffe. He had no one with whom to exchange pulpits, and his neighbor in Sutton's South Parish, the Rev. Edmund Mills, even refused to perform Goffe's marriage ceremony in December 1796, saying, as Goffe recorded in his diary, "that the ch[urc]h & people here are in error, & that he will not acknowledge me in the character of a minister." Instead, Goffe was married by Aaron Bancroft of Worcester's Second Church, a man who, too, had been shunned by his clerical brethren. Bancroft had come to Worcester amid a division in the First Church, where a majority of the members had opposed his settlement on theological grounds. (The majority eventually settled on Samuel Austin, a consistent Calvinist.) Nevertheless, the minority withdrew and formed the Second Church in 1786. Bancroft was ordained by a group of five ministers, three of whom were theological liberals imported from eastern Massachusetts for the occasion. Some of the local ministers tried giving Bancroft the cold shoulder, as only the two local clergymen present at his ordination, Zabdiel Adams of Lunenburg and Timothy Harrington of Lancaster, would exchange pulpits with him. Nonetheless, Bancroft withstood the pressure. His presence divided the local association in a harbinger of the Unitarian controversy of the early nineteenth century. For Goffe, it was only after he had pastored his church for half a dozen years and proven his mettle by both surviving the snubs of the clergy and leading a revival in 1800 that he was accepted into the clerical fraternity. Both men would recount these experiences decades later, which shows that these episodes left lifelong scars.[43] Probably some aspiring ministers would be reluctant to cross their colleagues' wishes and endure the kind of treatment meted out to Bancroft and Goffe. It was by means of such unofficial coercion that the local associations could enforce their will.

Besides trying to control membership in the standing order through either the formal mechanism of licensing or the informal power of shunning, the ministers of the Brookfield Association had also pledged to "quicken one another" with the goal of being "more successful" in ministry. The association's members accordingly en-

Aaron Bancroft. Courtesy American Antiquarian Society.

gaged in a variety of mutual support and professional development activities. One of the most important favors that ministers did for one another was to exchange pulpits. The refusal of Bancroft's and Goffe's neighbors to exchange with them as punishment for their stepping out of line indicates the practice's significance. Pulpit exchanges relieved a minister of the burden of having to prepare a new sermon every week. Ephraim Ward arranged two exchanges during July 1787, the month when he and his neighbors were preoccupied with gathering in their hay. At their meetings, the members of the Brookfield Association also sought to sharpen each other's theological awareness and pulpit presence. In September 1782, they discussed the controversial pamphlet *Salvation for All Men*, perhaps with an eye toward issuing a rebuttal. On August 13, 1794, the association made this practice of conversing upon theological topics a regular part of its activities; a doctrinal question was to be posed at each meeting for discussion at the next. Moving from content to delivery, in January 1799 the members "voted that in a brotherly and candid manner we should hereafter remark on the [meeting's] preacher as to matter and manner." In these various ways, the ministers of the Brookfield Association sought to build up each other.[44]

The activities discussed to this point all centered on the internal tasks of sanctioning and strengthening the association's clerical membership. However, the association's primary goal was to forward "the Interest of Religion," and to do so clergymen had to reach out to their people and colleagues elsewhere. For example, as patriot troops besieged Boston in early 1776, the association "drew up an Agreement concerning supplying Col. Larned's Regiment at Roxbury, as Chaplains." At the same meeting, in light of "the present gloomy State of Affairs in N. England, both civil & moral," the ministers decided "to appoint a Lecture, or Season for special Worship in each of our Parishes; & to assist one another in carrying on the Work." Likewise, six years later the association planned "to have frequent Lectures for the Revival & Promotion of Religion, & to assist one another in carrying them on." The Brookfield Association could also combine its efforts with those of other associations, as when it received a letter from the Boston Association in May 1799 "requesting our concurrence with them in devising some method to check the progress of Licenciousness [sic] & Infidelity and promoting virtue & piety."[45] Through the coordinated work of different associations and the annual convention, Congregational clergymen could leverage their activities for maximum impact.

In sum, the organization of its members into local associations provided the Congregational ministry with some useful tools. The associations maintained the entrance standards for the ministry, mediated disputes, provided a forum for discussion, and served as a launching pad for endeavors of mutual interest. In the first quarter of the nineteenth century, clerical innovators would draw on their preexisting network of colleagues in the associations to carry out the work of revivals, benevolence, and reform.

Anyone looking to understand religion and society in post-Revolutionary New England must begin with the Congregationalists. Not only were the Congregational churches the oldest in the region, the most numerous, the best supplied with clergymen, and supported with public funds but also they were home to the civil and social leadership. This predominance gave established ministers both the elevated angle of vision to view their society inclusively and the confidence to assert an important place for themselves in maintaining social stability. Corresponding to its numerical, cultural, and institutional strength, the southern New England standing order articulated a distinctive, corporate ideology that joined Christianity and social thought. A detailed examination of that ideology as it appeared during the last two decades of the eighteenth century is the subject of the remainder of this chapter and chapter 2, which explore how older, Puritan languages of Providence, the covenant, and the godly society entered the era of the early republic.

Providence and Other Bases of the Clergy's Corporate Ethic

> At what instant I shall speak concerning a nation, and concerning a king-
> dom, to pluck up, and to pull down, and to destroy it; If that nation,
> against whom I have pronounced, turn from their evil, I will repent of the
> evil that I thought to do unto them.
>
> —Jer. 18:7–8

New England's established ministers, and many dissenters as well, hailed the American Revolution as a providential event of major world-historical significance. Since the seventeenth century, clergymen who styled themselves God's "ambassadors" had assumed the prerogative of interpreting New England's divine status.[46] Their providential worldview made elucidating the nation's significance imperative, and in the wake of the American Revolution they extended this long, regional tradition to the United States. Although some repudiated assertions of a national covenant, the sounds of covenantal language continued to echo within a more capacious providentialism. Not only did established ministers explain the Revolution within a providential frame of reference but also they used that framework to speculate regarding the new nation's implications for the future and to warn of judgments in the jeremiad tradition. From outside the established clergy's theological constructs, other streams of eighteenth-century thought fed into its corporate outlook. On account of this preoccupation with corporate life, the Congregational ministry made a leading, albeit ambiguous, contribution to the growth of nationalist identity. Overall, post-Revolutionary New England Congregationalists evidenced a commitment to social life, not just a concern for the inward state of the individual soul. Their public Christian ethic formed a rich religious social ideology, yet its very richness contained within it points of latent contradiction.

The New England ministry's most fundamental article of faith was its providential perspective on history and global affairs: God utterly controlled the universe.[47] To take one example, Eliphalet Porter of Roxbury, Massachusetts, observed that "divine Providence is the necessary result and consequence of those glorious attributes, which are essential to Deity. . . . And even the most minute and inconsiderable events and occurrences, are under his divine inspection and controul." True to Calvinist principles, Joseph Huntington of Coventry, Connecticut, depicted this providential control as predestined in his 1784 Connecticut election sermon.[48] At this basic level of belief in a providential God, there was unanimity among New England ministers both across the Congregationalists' theological spectrum and between different varieties of dissenters.[49] This providentialism clearly distinguished them from deists, whom they regarded as serious rivals in the late eighteenth century, because for deists God had absented himself from the scene.[50] Ministers lamented, however, that a seemingly self-evident proposition such as Providence escaped people's notice at times. In the words of Nathan Williams of Tolland, Connecticut, shortsighted men tended "not to be led thro second causes to the great first cause and disposer of events."[51] Beneath all events moved the invisible hand of God, guiding history to its appointed telos.

Ministers made the interpretation of God's providences a part of their privileged role. Citing Ezek. 3:17, ministers claimed the authority of "watchman unto the house of Israel" with a sacred duty to comment on public affairs. "Publick teachers" were needed, according to Joseph Lathrop of West Springfield, Massachusetts, in order "to open the important truths, and inculcate the sacred duties of religion," even if, added Worcester's Samuel Austin, they offered "truths which are grating to [the congregations'] natural feelings." Both reason and revelation assisted in the understanding of God's plan on earth, explained Joseph Willard in 1783. As Josiah Whitney pointed out, providential interpretation functioned best in retrospect: "Often when particular events take place, we cannot at first tell, whether they are the effects of the favour, or displeasure of the world's great Ruler: Time, the great expositer [sic] of events can only satisfy us." Ultimately, said David Osgood, Congregational pastor of Medford, Massachusetts, at the end of time, events "which are now esteemed dark and mysterious" would be clarified, so as to "induce enraptured saints, with astonishment, to exclaim, [Rom. 11:33] O *the depth of the wisdom and knowledge of God!*" Millennialism can be viewed as providentialism projected into the future on the basis of the biblical prophecies.[52]

God's providential control extended over everything, of course, but the clergy specified that it applied with particular force to both national life and the Christian church. "All nations of the earth are at the absolute disposal of the Most High, to be divided and separated at his pleasure," summarized Joseph Huntington.[53] A favorite biblical passage along these lines was this section's epigraph, Jer. 18:7-8. Certainly if God noticed the sparrow's fall or numbered the hairs on one's head, then something as momentous as war or revolution was also under his control.[54] This national conception of providentialism formed the underlying rationale for the annual fast and thanksgiving days. For example, Governor John Hancock declared a thanksgiving day in 1784 because, he wrote, it was "our indispensable Duty as a People, in a public and religious Manner, to acknowledge the preserving and governing Providence of Almighty GOD, and more especially to celebrate the Divine Goodness in the various Blessings confer'd upon us in the Course of the Year past."[55] At the same time, ministers described how Providence worked especially for Christians and the church. "We might sweetly employ our meditations upon . . . God's love, care, and watchful providence over his church: how he hath frowned on kings for her sake," observed Rozel Cook of New London, Connecticut. "How all the great revolutions that have taken place in the world, have been made subservient to prepare the way for, and assist in carrying on the work of redemption." The Warren Association of Baptists joined in linking the Revolution to the providential direction of the church.[56] Similarly, it was divine Providence alone that initiated conversions and revivals; in accordance with Calvinist doctrine, these works of God came from the Holy Spirit.[57]

In describing the providential care of nation and church, ministers established a latent tension: which institution would take precedence if a conflict should arise? Clearly, they would answer that in all things God worked for the church, but initially some failed to anticipate the potential contradictions of their position. After 1800, when the national government came under the control of the Jeffersonians, the standing order sought to separate the church from any identification with the Union.

However, for the last quarter of the eighteenth century, ministers readily, if recklessly, asserted the providential sanctification of both American and Christian history.

One reason for the clergy's myopia regarding this potential conflict was the blinding effect of post-Revolutionary optimism. No event loomed larger in the scheme of Providence for this generation than the American Revolution. A review of that event left the established ministry and dissenters alike with no doubts that it showed the hand of God at work. "It was the will of heaven, and agreeable to his general plan, that the *principal part* of *America* should become *separate* and *independent* of *Britain*," summarized Zabdiel Adams, minister at Lunenburg, Massachusetts, and cousin of the second president. Concluded Rozel Cook, "It is abundantly evident, that the Lord hath been on our side, hath fought our battles, and delivered us from the hands of our enemies. Can the wonders done for our land be ascribed to fortuitous hits and accidents? no, my friends, they are the effects and productions of the wise and steady counsels of heaven."[58]

The clergy attributed several factors in the American victory to Providence. Ministers often mentioned the improbable intercolonial unity that had coalesced. "In the first years of the contest, and indeed throughout the whole, we must have been blind, and utterly inattentive to the government of divine providence, not to have been convinced that heaven was supporting our important interests," commented John Lathrop, pastor of Boston's Second Church. "One common soul seemed to animate the great political body."[59] Ministers invoked Providence as the only way to explain upset military victories; as John Marsh phrased it, at Trenton, Princeton, and Saratoga, "the interposition of divine providence on behalf of these states, was too conspicuous not to be discerned and owned by the most unobserving and unbelieving mind."[60] The success of American diplomats, who were able to secure valuable allies, was cited by Rozel Cook as another example of providential intervention. A similar instance of providential control concerned the way in which the patriots were able to seize British supplies; sometimes war matériel seemed to fall into the Americans' laps.[61] Ministers furthermore mentioned the Americans' preservation from the likes of Benedict Arnold.[62] They delighted to show how God could foil human intentions. Henry Cumings noted how British actions sometimes had seemingly unintended consequences, but which were actually intended by Providence. "Their arts of intimidation," he pointed out, "far from answering their purpose, rather served to strengthen the zeal and resolution of the friends of liberty, and to add desperation to their courage, by giving a most alarming view of the awful consequences, to be expected from the success of their arms."[63] Rozel Cook thanked "God's great goodness, and watchful providence" for "turning the counsels of our enemies into foolishness."[64] For the generation that lived through the conflict, the Revolution was anything but expected, predictable, or mundane. Rather, to make sense of it all, ministers delved deep into sacred meanings. They connected the Revolution to their most elemental foundation of understanding, their providential faith.

Many clergymen singled out George Washington as a particularly shining example of providential assistance. In John Marsh's interpretation, God directed Washington's early career to fit him for the task at hand and placed him in a position where (1 Kings 1:20) "the eyes of all Israel [were fixed] on him as the man most suitable, in every respect, to sustain the high, arduous and most important office of

Captain-General and Commander in Chief of the Patriot Army."[65] Providence usually manifested its hand through human instruments; God only rarely acted in an extraordinary manner, as in the burning bush or a thunderclap.[66] After this fashion, explained Ezra Stiles, the president of Yale, George Washington had advanced God's plan: "Posterity, I apprehend, and the world itself, inconsiderate and incredulous as they may be of the dominion of Heaven, will yet do so much justice to the divine moral government as to acknowledge that this American Joshua was raised up by God, and divinely formed, by a peculiar influence of the Sovereign of the universe, for the great work of leading the armies of this American Joseph (now separated from his brethren), and conducting this people through the severe, the arduous conflict, to liberty and independence."[67]

Finally, of course, Providence also deserved thanks for peace. *"Glory be to God in the highest,"* trumpeted Henry Cumings, "who has been pleased to dispose the belligerent powers to sheath the devouring sword, and put a stop to the effusion of human blood." Samuel Langdon concisely summarized the providential view of the Revolution during the 1788 New Hampshire election sermon. He was then minister at Hampton Falls and had served as president of Harvard from 1774 to 1780. Langdon admitted that "the God of heaven hath not indeed visibly displayed the glory of his majesty and power before our eyes, as he came down in the sight of Israel on the burning mount." Nevertheless, "the signal interpositions of divine providence, in saving us from the vengeance of a powerful irritated nation, . . . in giving us a Washington . . . in carrying us through the various distressing scenes of war and desolation . . . and finally giving us peace, with a large territory, and acknowledged independence; all these laid together fall little short of real miracles, and an heavenly charter of liberty for these United-States."[68] In hindsight, ministers could clearly discern the hand of God in the American Revolution, and they fitted that event seamlessly into their providential reading of the past.

As the language of the preceding paragraphs indicates, the deliverance of the Israelites from Egypt served as a common metaphor for the American experience. There was, said Boston's Samuel Cooper during a sermon preached at the inauguration of the Massachusetts constitution in 1780, "a striking resemblance between our own circumstances and those of the antient Israelites." Both revolutionary America and biblical Israel had been "chosen by God [as] a theatre for the display of some of the most astonishing dispensations of his Providence."[69] These examples illustrate the residual pungency of the national covenant. Earlier in New England history, in the seventeenth century, Puritan ministers had grounded the religious basis of society in the theology of the national covenant. The national covenant stipulated that God entered into relationships with chosen nations, whereby he promised special protection in return for obedience. In the Old Testament, of course, the people of Israel had been selected by God for a redemptive mission, rescued from Egypt, and shielded from hostile neighbors until it apostatized and forfeited its privileges. So, too, Puritan divines maintained, New England could be a chosen nation if it abided by the terms of God's covenant.[70]

By 1783, however, Congregational clergymen spoke with more than one voice on the question of whether the United States was a nation under a covenant with God.[71] At one extreme, some clergymen strongly asserted a traditional covenant for the new nation. At the opposite end, there were ministers who categorically denied a covenantal relationship between the United States and God, as did dissenters. In between, most Congregational ministers were less precise in their use of covenantal language. Some of these clergymen described the United States with covenantal terminology without going so far as to explicitly affirm a national covenant. Others bestowed the covenant mantle upon the church, in which case the nation became important in its role as home to the church. The national covenant no longer was the defining ideology that some scholars have made it out to have been.[72] For most ministers, it provided only a kind of illustrative analogy to their providential reading of events.

While some ministers expressed without reservation their belief in the identification between the United States and ancient Israel as covenant nations, others flatly rejected the idea. John Murray, the Presbyterian pastor of Newburyport, Massachusetts, was astounded by the parallels between the story of the Israelites under Gideon and the Americans under Washington. Both of these covenant nations had been attacked and threatened with slavery, only to be saved by Providence acting through a great leader. Murray concluded his extended analogy with these rhetorical questions: "Pause, my hearers, review the several parts of this sacred story; and say, does it not seem to be written for an history of the American war—only allowing for the change of name—places—and times? Are not we the children of Israel too—a professing covenant-people, in a land peculiarly privileged with gospel-light?"[73] Samuel Austin also presented an analysis of the United States as God's chosen "American Israel." Because Washington was soon to leave office, Austin used the occasion of the 1796 thanksgiving as an opportunity to reflect back on God's hand in the Revolution. Austin reviewed the covenantal status of the Israelites under Abraham's line and then applied the same to the United States: "The interposition of God, in behalf of his American Israel, has been as signal, and ought to be as devoutly honored. . . . The God of our fathers . . . heard our prayer, in heaven his holy dwelling place, and [Judg. 3:9] *raised up a deliverer, to us, the children of* his American *Israel, even* GEORGE WASHINGTON." In contrast, another group of Congregational ministers explicitly denied any pretensions to national chosenness, election, or mission. Samuel Wales's 1785 Connecticut election sermon made this point most clearly. "The ancient Israelites," explained the Yale divinity professor, "were under a dispensation of grace different from ours, and, for a long time under the peculiar kind of civil government which has been called *a Theocracy*. National blessings are not promised, and national judgements are not threatened under the gospel in like manner as they were under the law." Wales based this position on a moral law interpretation of scripture, arguing that Deut. 8:11-14 did not bind Americans because they were a special nation like Israel but because there was a tendency in human nature for anyone to become self-assured when flush with success. Thomas Brockway advanced an interpretation similar to that of Wales. Noted Brockway, "the war which the Canaanites waged with Israel, differed from that which England has been levying against us. England came not against the covenant people of the Lord. We had no such national covenant to plead, as had the Jews: for it is but a scattered few, in this vast continent, that can claim even the visibility of a covenant relation to God."[74] The idea of the United States as a new, covenanted Israel, strictly defined, provoked sharp disagreement among Congregational clergymen.

The utterances of most Congregational ministers tended to fall somewhere between the poles of outright covenant proclamation and denial. Some ministers implied only loosely a traditional definition of Americans as a chosen people, their language remaining merely suggestive rather than explicit. John Marsh's thanksgiving sermon of December 11, 1783, took for its chosen text Ps. 147:12-14, which reads, "Praise the LORD, O Jerusalem; praise thy God, O Zion. For he hath strengthened the bars of thy gates; he hath blessed thy children within thee. He maketh peace in thy borders, and filleth thee with the finest of the wheat." Later in the same sermon, after reviewing all of the instances of providential assistance in the American Revolution, Marsh stated, "Praise the LORD, O America: Praise thy GOD, O United States: For he hath strengthened the bars of thy gates: He hath blessed thy children within thee. He maketh peace in thy borders." Marsh's insertion of America into the biblical text suggests an identification between the United States and the chosen people. Yet it remains unclear exactly how far Marsh would have carried the analogy. Did he mean to imply that the United States was a nation in covenant with the Lord or, more broadly, that the American Revolution bore signs of providential direction? Henry Ware, then a minister of Hingham, Massachusetts, prior to his election to Harvard's divinity chair, used the same text as Marsh for his thanksgiving sermon of February 19, 1795. He, too, aligned the United States with Israel: "[The chosen text] may be applied, perhaps, with as striking propriety to the present circumstances of the inhabitants of this country, as it ever could be to those of any people, since its original application, by the sacred penman, to the situation of the children of Israel, at a time of great prosperity." Without digging into an analysis of America's elect status, Ware, as a leading liberal divine, probably did not mean to assert a national covenant. Yet his language clearly drew on older precedents of covenantalism and remained elusively open-ended.[75] As these examples show, even if no longer rooted in a clear theological premise, the language of the national covenant could continue to provide some rhetorical contribution to collective identity. If no longer an immediate, central reality for ministers like Marsh or Ware, the Old Testament vocabulary of the national covenant still had strong metaphorical power for them.

Still other ministers used covenantal terminology with reference to the church. This interpretation of the church's central role introduced an important distinction between civil society and the kingdom of God; the United States was only a chosen nation inasmuch as it preserved the true Christian church. This last group of ministers anticipated, albeit unknowingly, a position that would become prominent in the nineteenth century. At that future time, most of New England's Congregational clergymen would separate God's dealings with the nation from his church. In the late eighteenth century, while one can detect the seeds of a future development, this church-covenant position, too, remained largely indistinct. According to Joseph Huntington, all of history revolved around the church: "God, from eternity, in his most glorious plan, his infinitely kind decree; set the bounds of all nations, with a most tender regard to his own covenant people, in every age, wherever they might dwell, or whatever their number might be; and in his almighty Providence carries the whole into effect." The American Revolution took on significance in this reasoning, because it provided an environment that was hospitable to the church. Huntington further described how the kingdom of France had unwittingly assisted the kingdom of God. It did so not through its Roman Catholicism but through its support of the American Revolution, which helped save "the glorious cause of liberty and religion among the nations." New Haven's Jonathan Edwards Jr. considered the question of when a people have the Lord for their God in his 1794 Connecticut election sermon. He based the question on his chosen text, Ps. 144:15, "Yea, happy is that people, whose God is the LORD." He answered not by asserting a covenant for Americans, but by stating that they would be a people of God if they accepted Christianity. "The answer is, when they believe, worship and obey the Lord or Jehovah, as the only true God, and that according to his revealed will. The Lord was the God of the Israelites, when they complied with the dispensation, under which they lived; and he is our God, when we cordially believe and comply with the gospel."[76] The position of these clergymen might be called the contingent definition of American chosenness, because only to the extent that Americans embraced Christianity or expanded the church did they become God's people.

For all the apparent prescience of these ministers, however, they, too, muddied the clarity of their analysis. Although they point the way toward a future trend, in the 1780s it was still inchoate. David Osgood, for example, argued on the one hand that the church lay at the center of God's plans on earth, saying that it "shall be as certainly under the divine care and guardianship, as were God's people of old, . . . and shall as fully experience the happy effects of his Almighty protection." Further along, on the other hand, he elevated his region in particular over the Christian church in general, lauding "the churches of New-England" as "the freest of any in the world; and in their mode of worship and method of discipline approach[ing] the nearest to the simplicity of the gospel and the forms in use with the primitive christians."[77] The lines separating church and nation blurred for Osgood as of 1788, as the language of the national covenant had become similarly indistinct to most ministers.

Ezra Stiles's well-known Connecticut election sermon of 1783, *The United States elevated to Glory and Honor*, epitomizes the difficulty in pinpointing the clergy's interpretation of the significance of the United States in terms of a national covenant. In his introduction, Stiles flirted with an American covenant. He noted that the populations of biblical Israel and the United States in 1783 were roughly the same and that both nations were under the Mosaic law. He closed this section with the remark, "I have assumed the text only as introductory to a discourse upon the political welfare of God's American Israel, and as allusively prophetic of the future prosperity and splendor of the United States." Clearly, the reference to "God's American Israel" carried the specter of the national covenant of New England's founders. In the body of the sermon, however, Stiles did not return to the concept of a national covenant; it was as if this "omnivorous" intellect could not be bound by one theological framework alone.[78] Instead, he depicted the real importance of the United States in terms of its example and location as center in the distribution of the republican Christian Enlightenment: "Knowledge will be brought home and treasured up in America, and, being here digested and carried to the highest perfection, may reblaze back from America to Europe, Asia, and Africa, and illumine the world with truth and liberty." Most important, the United States would be home to the religion that would evangelize the world. In this sense, Stiles joined with those who saw the deepest significance of the nation in its hosting of the true church.[79]

The national covenant obviously no longer compelled the kind of broad-based allegiance that it had in seventeenth-century New England. The explanation for this lies in the doctrine's history in the eighteenth century, which provides a classic example of the failure of the center to hold. From both the left and the right of the theological spectrum, the national covenant had come under assault. On the left, those most influenced by Enlightenment ideas moved away from what seemed to them the national covenant's bigoted God, who capriciously chose one nation over another.[80] At the other end of New England Protestantism, the Separates spawned by the First Great Awakening also rejected the national covenant, but for different reasons. They wanted to withdraw from established churches, which they viewed as impure and "spiritually dead." Therefore, they repudiated the corporate grasp of the national covenant, while still affirming providential sovereignty. In response to the Separates, the standing order had not employed the national covenant; rather, it denied the Separates validity by pointing to the state's regulatory prerogatives and the contractual obligations of the churches. As Christopher Grasso concludes, "The authoritarian 'we' of covenant rhetoric was a fiction that could no longer be used to cover the fractious midcentury debates."[81] Between these two poles of liberalism and Separatism, the New Divinity theologians also abandoned the national covenant for the most part. They tried to rescue Calvinism from the liberals' aspersions and the radicals' abuse. To answer the liberals' criticism of the covenant's arbitrariness, they downplayed the covenant in favor of moral law, because "the terminology of law, in contrast, implied that divine justice was not partial toward any one nation." Their New Light lineage also encouraged a renewed emphasis on the church as the redemptive instrument as opposed to the nation.[82]

The national covenant could no longer be the cord by which ministers bound religion and society because it had become too frayed in the religious tug-of-war of the mid-eighteenth century. Those defending a strictly and conventionally defined understanding of New England's chosen status occupied a smaller piece of ground by the century's end. Nevertheless, if no longer a unifying theology, the national covenant still evoked a collective identity, if perhaps only in an illustrative or equivocal manner.[83] The discourse of a national covenant bequeathed to late-eighteenth-century New England a tradition of searching for the meaning of corporate life. Although Congregational divines could not agree whether there was a special covenant between the nation and Jehovah, they unanimously shared in a more general providentialism, which clearly saw God's guidance of American history.

Such interpretations of the hand of Providence in American history did not cease with the Revolution. Clergymen extended the practice as the years rolled by in the early republic. Samuel Langdon credited God with the framing of the Constitution. "Wisdom is the gift of God, and social happiness depends on his providencial [*sic*] government; therefore," he reasoned, "if these states have framed their constitutions with superior wisdom, and secured their natural rights, and all the advantages of society, with greater precaution than other nations, we may with good reason affirm that God hath given us our government."[84] In contrast to his attitude in the early nineteenth century, Newburyport's Samuel Spring also gave thanks in 1793 for the federal government. "God has not only granted us the best constitution of government in the world," Spring boasted, "but he has filled the offices of government with men of influence and reputation." Jonathan French, minister of the South Church in Andover, Massachusetts, outdid the others. His thanksgiving sermon of 1798 traced the blessings of God to New Englanders from the 1620s all the way to the 1790s. The Plymouth landing was part of "the great designs of heaven in spreading the glorious gospel, and extending the Redeemer's kingdom." The same had been true throughout the eighteenth-century wars with France and in the Revolution. "What cannot a people do," French asked rhetorically, "when the LORD is on their side?" And regarding the 1790s, he gave thanks that the United States had been preserved from "dangerous secret societies."[85] Nearly all the ministers of the standing order freighted the new nation with real importance. Although they disagreed over the specific reasons, they found common ground in reading a salient place for the United States into the story of God's providential oversight of history.

Looking forward, clergymen anticipated global ramifications for the American Revolution. They presented various scenarios as to how these would come to pass. Ministers emphasized the transforming effects of either American politics, civilization, or spiritual life, although the three themes frequently melded. Some foresaw millennial consequences resulting from the ways in which American political institutions would emancipate mankind. For example, Henry Cumings predicted that "should the principles, upon which we have erected ourselves into an independent nation, in consequence of our success, be adopted by other countries, tyranny would fall before them; the kingdom of satan and of antichrist would receive a terrible shock." While not exactly foretelling an American millennium, David Osgood did borrow the prophetic language of Isa. 35:1 to describe the significance of the new nation: "Wise and just political institutions, a free and happy government will encourage that industry which turns *the wilderness into a fruitful field*, and causes *the desert to blossom as a rose*."[86] Like Cumings, he highlighted the potentially millennial impact of the liberal government established in the United States.

Several ministers painted a lush landscape of American progress across a broader canvas of human endeavors. American civilization in all its diverse components would reshape the world. Samuel Cooper presented this common, eclectic view: "We seem called by heaven to make a large portion of this globe a seat of knowledge and liberty, of agriculture, commerce, and arts, and what is more important than all, of christian piety and virtue."[87] Enos Hitchcock of Providence, Rhode Island, mingled liberty, the American economy, and the Holy Spirit in his vision of the Revolution's millennial effects: "What glorious prospects open to view when we contemplate the scope given to the human mind for exertion,—the extension of commerce—the progress of science, agriculture, manufactures, and all the pleasing and useful arts of refined society, which naturally flow from independence, and a government as just in its principles and firm in its texture, as it is free in its formation? . . . The wilderness shall blossom as a rose—the desert become vocal with the praises of God."[88] Obviously, it is an understatement to say that the ministry invested the new nation with major significance. A new society was being born in America, where the combination of freedom and Christianity would yield unprecedented felicity.

In addition to politics and civilization, ministers stressed the importance of American religion to the rest of mankind. In the 1784 Connecticut election sermon,

Joseph Huntington linked the outcome of the Revolution to the dawn of the millennium in the Western hemisphere: "May we not reasonably hope God has done all these things to prepare the way for the most glorious effusion of his holy spirit in this western world: and to bow the hearts of millions to himself? That the latter day glory may soon break out here in its meridian lustre and diffuse over all the world, soon darting its blessed beams to the farthest borders of the east." Ammi Robbins of Norfolk, Connecticut, offered another detailed blueprint of the way in which the expansion of the United States would forward the kingdom of Christ. He anticipated that by spreading out across the Appalachians, Americans would convert a huge swath of territory from heathenism to Christianity. Because, he argued, "the special *agency of Heaven* was so visibly manifest, in the late American Revolution, as forced the acknowledgment of it, even from the inattentive as well as the attentive mind—from the profane and impious, as well as the virtuous and sober," Providence must have still more significant things in store for the new nation. Robbins did not contend that the United States was synonymous with the kingdom or that all Americans were the people of God, but he did attach potentially millennial import to the new nation's expansion. His interpretation was similar to those ministers, previously discussed, who depicted a covenant with the church and an important role for the early republic as its home. In short, although many ministers had reservations about anointing the United States a chosen people with a special, covenantal relationship to the Almighty, they nevertheless clearly envisioned a large role for the new republic in global history. For instance, Thomas Brockway, although frankly rejecting a national covenant, could still, like Robbins or Stiles, foresee how the American Revolution could be "a leading step" toward the millennium.[89] Providence would use the nation to advance the kingdom of God and shorten the time until the millennium.

These ebullient interpretations of the new republic must have joined wider channels of early American nationalism. For instance, nonministerial, patriotic orators, such as the New Haven lawyer Simeon Baldwin, sometimes adopted the providential language surrounding the Revolution. In a July Fourth oration in 1788, he declared that "the clear manifestation of providential beneficence in this event, calls for gratitude and joy."[90] Several historians have drawn a link between clerical pronouncements of providential guidance and the coalescence of American "civil religion" and nationalism. Nathan O. Hatch, for one, writes that "Yankee ministers who watched the dawn of the new century did not stumble unawares upon the road of civil religion; they actively sought a way of assigning to the American republic a major role in the scheme of providential history."[91] However, the extent to which the ministry *consciously and deliberately* contributed to nationalist sentiment is unclear. On the one hand, ministers did see some patriotism as useful, inasmuch as it built up public-spirited virtue.[92] As far as many could foresee circa the 1780s and early 1790s, God was going to use these United States for important purposes in the advancement of his plans. On the other hand, the ministry was divided over the extent of America's chosenness. Those ministers who explicitly separated the United States from any ideas of national election cannot receive full credit or blame for stoking the flames of nationalist fervor. At least partly, then, ministers' interpretation of the hand of Providence in the Revolution only unintentionally led to a general cultural pattern of celebratory nationalism. In the 1780s, they apparently anticipated little conflict between the new nation and the kingdom of God and may have plunged ahead with drawing the two spheres together without considering all the ramifications. To the degree that ministers joined in the proclamation of hopeful American nationalism, this would make their later disillusionment with the country all the more poignant.

The established ministry further avoided a complete fusion of nationalism and providentialism by issuing warnings in the tradition of the jeremiad.[93] The belief in the providential correction of backsliding nations put a brake on the rush to nationalistic exultation. The ministry's providential worldview did not only explicate past events and shed light on the future but also contained cautionary lessons about current events. It elevated concern for the behavior of others into a pressing obligation, because the standing order's conception of sin was eminently social. Ministers often cited Prov. 14:34, "Righteousness exalteth a nation: but sin is a reproach to any people."[94] This corporate conception of sin ministers conveyed chiefly by means of two metaphors, disease and pollution. Sin was said to spread like an infectious disease through society. Zabdiel Adams employed this idea when he described the British example during the colonial period as "extremely contagious; and if we had been *connected* with and *dependent* on them, should have been very prone to have aped them in their vices as well as in their virtues; and such vices as those above-mentioned, would have been highly detrimental to an infant country."[95] John Murray gave a typical example of pollution imagery when he urged his listeners, "let us be humbled before the Lord for all our sins, and the sins of this guilty land." It was as if the very earth beneath one's feet recoiled from the violations of sin.[96] Since Providence made the oversight of nations a special priority, God punished these corporate sins with "tremendous judgments," "chastisement," "high displeasure," or "frowns."[97] "It is the nature of vice to provoke the displeasure of God, and draw down his judgments, to complete the ruin of a people," Nathanael Emmons of Franklin, Massachusetts, stated matter-of-factly. Leonard Woods, then a young minister of Newbury, Massachusetts, concluded his 1799 fast sermon on profanity with a similar warning: "Can we expect uninterrupted public prosperity, while this is our national character? Will his patience last forever? *Will not God visit for these things? Will not his soul be avenged on such a nation as this?* Yes, my brethren; goodness, long neglected and abused, becomes indignation and wrath."[98] Early New England antislavery drew upon this jeremiad tradition, on the grounds that "[the slaves'] cries will sooner or later reach the ears of him to whom vengeance belongeth."[99]

Finally, besides a faith in the providential oversight of nations, other concepts added to the ministry's social vision and further impelled the established ministry to extend its watchful eye over the community. Some of these corporate ideas were rooted in the theology of the established ministry. Others were the common currency of eighteenth-century social thought, in which concern for the public good "reflected the received Western wisdom of their age." As illustrations of the latter, several points of clerical social ideology overlapped with that of the nascent Federalist party. Ministers of the standing order shared with Federalist politicians the "basic motifs" of "harmony, unity, order, [and] solidarity." For example, the ministry depicted the role of government as, in the words of Levi Hart of Preston, Connecticut, "the good of society." Rulers, according to Portland's Samuel Deane, "must enact no laws but such as have the publick welfare for their object: For God invests them with no authority, but to do good."[100] Similarly, the ministry subscribed to widely held views of social unity. "A community is but one great family; in which, every member ought to consider his own interest, as involved in that of the whole; and this whole ought to swallow up every private or detached interest," advised Isaac Lewis of Greenwich, Connecticut. Timothy Stone based unity also in the theory of the social contract, because "covenanting with each other, to observe such regulations, and perform such duties as may tend to mutual advantage," the people "become one great whole, cemented together by voluntary engagements."[101] For reasons beyond its interpretation of Providence, the established ministry adhered to a corporate ethic, or a belief that the community as a whole possessed a moral dimension.

With this frame of reference, the ministry could not imagine legitimate dissent or diversity. In the analysis of Elizur Goodrich, lifelong pastor of Durham, Connecticut, society's survival and success depended on unity. When a political opposition did form, the standing order delegitimated it by casting it as a motley and pernicious faction, as will be discussed further in the next two chapters. "The disappointed, and restless, persons of broken fortunes, and characters, will at times excite, and foment disturbances," noted Josiah Whitney, in 1788. "*These*, when formed into little political clubs, and allowed to lead others, as uneasy, and mischievously inclined as themselves, are always troublers of a State, and should be treated as *pests* in society." The standing order did not want to rock the boat.[102]

Some of their particularly theological convictions, in addition to a faith in Providence, also impelled ministers to adopt a corporate outlook. Although there were affinities between the ministers' and the politicians' ideologies, the two were not identical; clergymen brought other doctrines of their own to bear on issues of social morality. Disinterested benevolence was one. Jonathan Edwards had written that the renovated Christian heart would be motivated by pure love toward others, and his followers in the New Divinity movement made disinterested benevolence into one of their signature doctrines.[103] For instance, in a sermon of 1790, Samuel Austin chose for his text Phil. 2:4, which reads, "Look not every man on his own things, but every man also on the things of others." "The great duty which it teaches us," he explained, "is, to regard with a benevolent affection, and to endeavour to promote with correspondent engagedness, the temporal, social, and spiritual interests of our fellow men." In other words, this doctrine made a paternalistic attitude a moral necessity. The virtuous person, in this definition, would be entirely other-directed.[104] This kind of benevolent outlook also militated against slavery in the early republic. As Jonathan Edwards Jr. asked simply, "Should we be willing, that the Africans or any other nation should purchase us, our wives and children, transport us into Africa and there sell us into perpetual and absolute slavery? . . . Yet why is it not as right for them to treat us in this manner, as it is for us to treat them in the same manner."[105]

Established ministers also taught that man was created as a social being. As Josiah Whitney remarked, "Man is evidently formed for society. When GOD made the first man, he saw [Gen. 2:18] it was not *good for him to be alone*; therefore *made an help-meet for him*. He formed him for society, and disposed him to enter into it."[106] By teaching that man was inherently sociable, established clergymen rooted their corporate views squarely in a biblical basis. Moreover, the established ministry harked back to older, medieval notions of social organicism and the great chain of being. They used the doctrine of God's superintending Providence to argue that everyone in society should have a role assigned to them. At the top of the hierarchy stood God, who then authorized the government and rulers.[107] As Cyprian Strong of Chatham, Connecticut, described matters, "The kingdom which is the Lord's does, in a sense, embrace the *universe*; consisting of all ranks and grades of creatures, throughout all worlds. . . . The various orders of existences, from the archangel to the most inconsiderable insect, constitute the links of a perfect chain, and are like wheels which are necessary to complete a perfect machine." Within the society, men and women fit neatly into "orders" and were expected to fulfill their social role faithfully and obediently. "Every man is a member in the political body; and every member hath a place in which it may be useful," Nathan Strong pointed out. "If any are not useful, it is their fault; for divine wisdom hath so organized the body, there is a place, a business and a duty for all." In Moses Hemmenway's similar depiction, "The order and interest of a civil society require that there should be different ranks of men, with different civil rights and privileges annexed to them; and subject to different restrictions. Nor is the true liberty of any rank infringed by this subordination, but rather secured, improved and enjoyed by all to better advantage."[108] The established clergy drew on a range of religious ideas to construct its corporate ethic, which went beyond the bounds of what Federalist statesmen stood for.

Although they had retreated from covenant theology by the latter part of the eighteenth century, Congregational ministers of southern New England remained committed to connecting religion and society on the ideological level. Primarily they did so through the language of Providence, which posited divine control over life on earth. Established ministers used a providential vocabulary to explain major historical events such as the American Revolution, to discern the future, and to warn of the consequences of national sins. Additionally, other elements of eighteenth-century social discourse reinforced the ministry's commitment to societal engagement. As a consequence, the standing order identified rather uncritically with the new nation. After 1800, when disappointment with national policies set in, the ministry would develop dimensions of its social discourse to register its dissent. Because it had not totally endorsed a national covenant and still argued that God punished national iniquity, it could find a voice with which to challenge what it perceived to be a wayward nation. But this development lay in the future; in the warm afterglow of the Revolution, the standing order celebrated the birth of a nation.

Christian Liberty

> For, brethren, ye have been called unto liberty; only use not liberty for an occasion to the flesh, but by love serve one another.
>
> —Gal. 5:13

Classical republican ideology also contributed to the clergy's public Christianity in at least three ways. The two overlapped in the high degree to which each valued liberty, and both privileged the commonwealth above individualistic concerns.[109] Most important, ministers borrowed from republican writers a vocabulary for talking about politics in terms of the threat to liberty from tyranny and corruption.[110] However, the extent to which the ministry imbibed republican ideology has been overstated. While ministers praised political liberty and thought it worth fighting for, it did not become the singularly defining element of their worldview.

On the surface, ministers did appear to be apostles of republicanism, inasmuch as they spoke highly and frequently of liberty. The salvation of personal and political liberty emerged as a salient theme in their interpretations of the Revolution's significance. They commonly argued that the American Revolution had preserved from being snuffed out the earth's last flicker of freedom. As David Osgood summarized, "Liberty, banished from the other quarters of the globe, has withdrawn to the American shores. In these States she has found an asylum, and seems to be fixing her residence." Many justified the Revolution with the remark that the Americans had no choice but to resist or to submit to British slavery.[111] By acting, Americans had achieved "the maintenance of our rights and liberties [and] the ultimate acknowledgment of our freedom, sovereignty, and independence." Having saved liberty, Revolutionary Americans, as noted previously, would then set a pattern to follow for other subjugated peoples around the world. Enos Hitchcock hoped, for instance, that "the spark of liberty, which has been kindled on the American altar, [would] be blown into one pure universal flame, and irradiate the whole world of intelligent beings."[112] In addition, the heightened awareness of liberty's value led some concerned ministers to appreciate anew the injustice of African American slavery. As Jonathan Edwards Jr. noted, "We all dread political slavery. Yet such a state is inconceivably preferable to the slavery of the Negroes. Suppose that in the late war we had been subdued by Great-Britain; we should have been taxed without our consent. But these taxes would have amounted to but a small part of our property. Whereas the Negroes are deprived of all their property."[113] The New England clergy joined other American patriots in articulating the ideas of liberty's preciousness and its need for nurture and protection.

Furthermore, some clerical spokesmen draped the term *liberty* in the garb of the sacred. Hitchcock described the Fourth of July in the terms of sacred ritual and architecture: "To sacrifice, at the shrine of liberty, 'the fat of fed beasts,' and pour out the generous libation, if conducted with prudence, may not be unsuitable expressions of the pleasure we this day experience. But a nobler employment now awaits us—we ascend from gratulations and amusements to contemplate, in the temple of liberty, the various beauties of the edifice,—to recount the multifarious blessings she proffers our favoured land." As some Congregationalists did, Thomas Baldwin, pastor of the Second Baptist Church of Boston, recounted the familiar assertion that Providence had chosen America "as the favoured spot, on which Liberty (which had long been imprisoned in other parts of the globe) should erect her spacious temple."[114] William Emerson, then serving as pastor in Harvard, Massachusetts, employed a favorite biblical text in the sacralization of liberty in his 1794 July Fourth oration. It was the latter half of Gal. 5:1, "be not entangled again with the yoke of bondage." Verses like this one lent a powerful aura of authority to the concept of liberty.[115] Some ministers also reinterpreted their collective memory around the theme of liberty. They stressed the centrality of liberty in the history of New England's founding and in their reading of the Old Testament.[116]

From this ubiquity of the word *liberty* in the clerical language of the period, some scholars have argued that republicanism became the predominant ideology of eighteenth-century ministers. Certainly, it is correct to draw our attention to the ways in which clergymen appropriated the republican vocabulary of liberty and virtue.[117] However, it must be pointed out that when they discussed "liberty," they did not solely refer to secular or classical republican freedom. Rather, liberty was a "multivalent" term that could carry republican, liberal, or Christian meanings.[118] Although there certainly was a synergy between republicanism and clerical social ideology, it is a mistake to believe "that, despite the renewed use of providential vocabularies, the real center of New England's intellectual universe had become the ideals of liberty defined by the eighteenth-century Real Whig tradition."[119] In the first place, the "providential" elements in ministers' statements were far from moribund or vestigial, as previously shown. In addition, eighteenth-century Americans loaded *liberty* with at least eight different meanings.[120] Although ministers of the standing order extolled liberty, they used the term in particularly qualified ways. Far from dwelling in the "Real Whig tradition" alone, they endowed liberty with a distinctly Protestant definition and warned of liberty's potential excesses if not bounded by Christian restraint. They also advocated the cooperation of magistrate and minister as the strategy, detailed in the next chapter, to achieve their twin goal of a godly community with liberty.

Moses Hemmenway and John Mellen—two ministers who provided unusually thorough and illuminating discussions of the standing order's understanding of liberty—each began his analysis of liberty by grounding the concept not in classical literary references but in biblical Christianity. According to Hemmenway, liberty sprang from Christianity. "We are more beholden to the oracles of GOD than to the schools of philosophy, for just and generous notions of the rights of mankind," he declared. In his reading, the Bible abounded with evidence in favor of the right to liberty.[121]

Among the different types of liberty, ministers regularly gave highest priority to the kind enjoyed by Christians. Hemmenway drew a common tripartite distinction when he defined liberty as consisting of "those liberties which belong to us either *as men*; or *as citizens*, or *as christians*."[122] The liberty of men, was, as in the Declaration of Independence, rooted in "the law and light of nature," whereas the liberty of citizenship was specific to a given polity. Christian liberty meant two things: freedom from "the power of sin" and freedom of conscience "in matters of faith and worship." It was the highest form of freedom, especially the freedom from sin through God's grace, which had ultimate consequences for eternal life. "It is the true Christian alone who is the LORD'S FREE MAN, and a denizen [*sic*] of the new Jerusalem."[123] Like Hemmenway, Ezra Stiles warned that "the most essential interests of rational beings are neglected when their secular welfare only is consulted," because "although [Christianity] subserves the civil welfare infinitely beyond the morals of deism and idolatry, yet it also provides for the interest of eternity, which no other religion does." Isaac Morrill also put Christian liberty above civil liberty when he praised the veterans of Lexington for having fought against political tyranny, yet reminded them to fight "the great christian warfare." "Ever hold in mind the opposition you must make to the enemies of your souls, and take heed your spiritual adversaries do not prove victorious."[124]

John Lathrop rejoiced in the second type of American religious freedom, liberty of conscience. "In religion, our conscience is not hurt by *oaths* and *subscriptions*. We are allowed to *enquire* for ourselves, and to speak what we think. No man shall be injured, in his person or property, for worshiping God in the way he chooses. This right is fully secured, in the constitutions of the several states. — On this ground alone, may we expect a *pure* and *rational* kind of religion, will flourish."[125] (How the standing order embraced freedom of conscience and the establishment without, its defenders insisted, any contradiction, is discussed further in the next chapter.) During the 1760s and 1770s, one pronounced threat to religious liberty, in clerical eyes, came from the possibility of an American colonial bishop for the Church of England.[126] In brief, one reason the ministry was so receptive to the language of "liberty" was because it was rich with religious significance.

Moreover, some ministers argued that the other types of freedom were dependent on Christianity; liberty and Christianity were said to be indivisible. Henry Cumings called for "that *glorious* internal *liberty of the sons of God*" as the only thing capable of enabling Americans to subdue "every vicious habit." "Without it we shall be slaves, in the worst sense, how much soever we may hate the name, and whatever outward liberty we may be in possession of." Christianity fostered civil liberty on the macro level too, like yeast leavening a loaf, to use the imagery of Matt. 13:33. This was David Osgood's chosen text in a 1798 sermon in which he said, "The throne of violence is alike supported by irreligion, ignorance, and superstition. Remove these props, and its fall will be inevitable. Extend the knowledge of the Lord throughout the earth, and you will give liberty to the world — you will communicate the blessings of a free and just government to all nations." Similarly, David Tappan thought that a Christian belief in the ultimate sovereignty of God would naturally work to "prevent a cowardly, degrading submission to the claims and measures of imperious despots, or a fawning, idolatrous, prostration at the feet of a dignified fellow-worm." In reverse, liberty could not endure in the absence of Christianity. "Just in proportion, as the restraints of religion are taken off, the cords of civil government must be strengthened: And in proportion as men become immoral, they must be impelled to duty, and restrained from mischief, by the force of arms," cautioned John Lathrop. Nathan Strong concluded, "we find that wherever a just understanding of christianity hath obtained, and its duties been practised, they have had a benign influence on the liberty of nations: And where a contrary effect hath been aided by what men called religion, as was the case in the Papal Hierarchy, it was owing to a subversion of the true principles of christianity."[127] Protestant Christianity, ministers said, produced personal and collective freedom. On the one hand, it gave men the self-discipline they needed to control destructive passions. On the other, it fostered, in the spirit of the Reformation, critical thought and a sense of self-worth, which were believed to be incompatible with either religious or political authoritarianism.

The concept of civil liberty championed by the standing order was also not an unbridled individualism; on this point, ministers agreed with more secular republican writers in attacking libertarian ideas of freedom.[128] To cite one example from among many, Josiah Whitney made absolute freedom look most unattractive: "Should a nunber [sic] live together without government, and every one *do what is right in his own eyes*, what must the consequence be in such a lapsed, disordered world as this? Why, they would soon prey upon, and devour each other. Neither life nor property could be secure. *The earth would be filled with violence*."[129] Yet ministers went beyond republican writers on this point as well. The reason they gave for qualifying freedom was not merely the good of the commonwealth or personal virtue, but individuals' subordination to God. As John Mellen succinctly argued, "no natural liberty gives men a right to be *libertines*, or renders them *lawless*, for all are under law to God and nature. . . . The true notion of liberty consists rather in the privilege or license to do *right*, or what we conscientiously think to be so; and in pursuing our true happiness, in this way of well doing, without any hindrance or controul from others." These ministers furthermore thought that total freedom was impossible on account of human sinfulness.[130] These ideas of corporate and limited liberty reached far back into New England's Puritan past; they long antedated ministers' adoption of republican terminology, which sometimes carried the same overtones.[131]

Moses Hemmenway warned most clearly of the antinomian dangers of liberty in his explication of Gal. 5:13, which became a favorite verse during the Revolutionary era. For Hemmenway, liberty and Christian responsibility, or "right" and "duty," if correctly understood, presented no inherent contradiction, that is, if liberty were bordered by a sound Christian understanding.

> We should take heed that *Liberty of thinking* for ourselves, or the right of private judgment become not an occasion of infidelity, or scepticism, or of our being carried away with unsound doctrines, and our minds corrupted from the simplicity that is in Christ. *Liberty of speaking* out thoughts must not be abused to the dishonor of God, and religion and virtue; to the encouragement of vice, or hurtful errors; to the detriment of the commonwealth; or to the injury, grievance, or scandal of any one. *Liberty of conscience* must not be abused into a pretence for neglecting religious worship, prophaning [sic] God's sabbaths and ordinances, or refusing to do our part for the support of government and the means of religious instruction. In a word, — as we would avoid the abuse of liberty, let us all take heed that we use it not *irreligiously*, by transgressing God's commands, or by neglecting or prophaning [sic] his worship and ordinances; *nor undutifully*, by refusing due Honor and subjection to rightful authority, in families, churches or commonwealth: *nor injuriously, unkindly, and uncharitably*, to the wrong, the damage, the grief and offence of our brethren: *nor inordinately*, exceeding the bounds of moderation, sobriety and expediency, even in things that are in themselves lawful.[132]

As Hemmenway and the rest of the standing order discussed liberty, they situated it within their broader corporate ethic, within a matrix with God and society. Liberty, according to Hemmenway, "consists in a person's being allowed to hold, use and enjoy all his faculties, advantages, and rights, according to his own judgment and pleasure, in such ways as are consistent with the rights of others, and the duty we owe to our maker and our fellow creatures."[133] The established ministry had not become the prophets of republicanism above all else, but it did appropriate a republican vocabulary in important and undeniable ways within its corporate, Christian framework.

In a complex fashion, therefore, the established ministry of southern New England built an ideological structure that housed Christianity and society as a whole under one roof. Situated at the hegemonic center of their society, established clergymen asserted it as their prerogative to enunciate such a Christian, corporate vision. The central pillar of the clergy's public Christianity, to continue the construction metaphor, was a faith in divine Providence's control over earthly affairs. Other elements buttressed this corporate ethic. For some, a national covenant provided the plumb line for their comprehension of God's dealings with the nation, but for many more the covenant's vocabulary and imagery added only ornamental trim. Republican themes reinforced the clergy's corporate outlook but did not serve as the foundation. Other ideas, such as disinterested benevolence, unity, and the great chain of being, also were attached to the structure. None, however, had the centrality of Providence. This providential framework gave meaning or a cognitive order to past, present, and future. Clergymen described how the Revolution had especially manifested the providential care of the nation and church, and they presented eclectic scenarios of American-led progress. As Benjamin Trumbull expressed the dual significance of the American Revolution, "Every thing which could be dear to us, either as men or christians, was at stake."[134] By dwelling on the importance of the new nation, ministers furthered American nationalism, but in their post-Revolutionary enthusiasm, they lacked a full realization of the potential pitfalls of this position.

The southern New England standing order had recounted the many "favourable interpositions of Providence in our behalf" with thanksgiving. Yet interpreting God's handiwork, while essential in its own right, did not complete the ministry's task. Clergymen also had to work to consolidate the Revolution's gains for liberty and the kingdom of God because they, like other "men of extensive political information, and sagacious forecast," "frequently trembled for our national existence." Their diagnosis of the threats facing the early republic and their prescriptions for organizing the godly community are the subject of the next chapter. In its own unique way, the established ministry sought to resolve the "democratic dilemma" of joining freedom with order that faced all Americans in the post-Revolutionary era.[135]

T W O

—⚬—

The Two Kingdoms in Concert
1783–1799

IN THE LAST QUARTER of the eighteenth century, the southern New England ministry sought to comprehend social experience through a specifically Christian framework. It posited the providential direction of nations and elevated communal values over individualistic ones. However, to say that clergymen were committed to relating Christianity to society as a whole does not explain what they prescribed for a righteous social order. Ministers not only gazed upward, so to speak, to discern the divine meaning of corporate events but also looked down from the pulpit to dictate about the organization of human society. Just as the Revolution had compelled ministers to interpret events providentially, so the prospect of launching a new nation made it essential for them to outline Christian principles for social order.

More than fifty years ago, H. Richard Niebuhr recognized this issue of "Christianity and civilization" to be an "enduring problem" in Western history.[1] The post-Revolutionary New England standing order propounded one particular solution of its own: it emphasized the mutual submission of church and state. While fulfilling distinct roles, church and state were to pursue a common end. The kingdoms of God and this world, so often posed antithetically in Christian history, were to work in concert. Ministers of the establishment saw themselves as co-leaders in an era when elites presumed to rule.[2] They cast themselves in the role of society's moral stewards. Their social hegemony facilitated this outlook. Because the Congregationalists were numerically superior to any other denomination and their clergy enjoyed singular influence with the ruling class, ministers could comfortably imagine for themselves a leading role in establishing the well-being of New England society. This clerical ideology, neither entirely republican nor liberal, set forth a vision of a godly society that would be shielded from the threats of social sin and a decay of virtue.

This prescription for church-state cooperation roughly exhibits the characteristics of Niebuhr's "Christ above culture" "type." As he and Mark A. Noll point out, this "Christ above culture" position is usually identified with medieval Roman Catholicism, but the late eighteenth-century standing order exhibited many of the same features. The standing order was, in Niebuhr's phrases, a "church of the center" that

52

sought a "synthesis" of Christianity and New England culture. It was committed to the world, yet distinguished religion from it. Also, Noll's descriptions of the Catholic stance as one in which "the institutions of religion and of government were integrated . . . [and] church and state were different, but were joined under a common divine sovereignty" aptly characterize the position of the standing order. By the late eighteenth century, the descendants of the Puritans had lost the reforming fire of the Reformed tradition; they were no longer outsiders burning to transform their culture, but the keepers of their culture who wanted to integrate Christianity and society harmoniously.[3]

Religious minorities, however, vigorously dissented from the standing order's construction of church-state interdependence. They objected that this close association of church and state both threatened religious freedom and represented a misreading of biblical principles. The Baptists in particular felt oppressed by the system of tax levies for the Congregational churches. This early dissent foreshadowed the severe turbulence that the standing order would encounter in the early nineteenth century as it presumed to chart society's moral course.

During the late 1790s finally, the Congregational ministry's public Christianity contributed to its negative reactions to both the French Revolution and the first rumblings of party politics. These developments seemed to challenge both Christianity and ordered liberty, to which established clergymen had attached such social significance. Therefore, Congregational ministers called on the people to renew their support of religion and government. At the same time, the political and foreign policy crises of the 1790s pushed the ministry's stance in a more conservative direction and clarified its ideas regarding Providence and the United States.

The Threat of Sinfulness, The Hope of Piety

> Beware that thou forget not the LORD thy God, in not keeping his commandments, and his judgments, and his statutes, which I command thee this day.
>
> —Deut. 8:11

By 1783, the Revolution had been won but remained to be stabilized. With words that would echo down through the Gettysburg Address, David Osgood of Medford, Massachusetts, said, "*With us* it lies to give an example, whether mankind are capable of freedom? Whether the justice, good faith, peace and happiness of the Community are safer and best promoted, when the power is ultimately lodged in the hands of the people, or when it resides in a Master over them?"[4] The Constitution's framers and supporters grappled with essentially the same challenge Osgood identified. As Joel Barlow, lawyer, poet, and proponent of a stronger federal government noted in a Hartford speech as the Philadelphia convention was meeting in July 1787, "the blessings, claimed by the sword of victory and promised in the voice of peace, remain to be confirmed by our future exertions."[5] Clergymen did not reject constitutionalism—in fact, they welcomed the new federal structure—but thought that it did not and could not go far enough. They feared that the republic would fall victim to a variety of social sins. A decline of virtue appeared especially threatening.[6] Within the ministry's providential outlook, the possibility of divine displeasure and rebuke on account of sin never moved far offstage. The diffusion of vital Christianity throughout the populace appeared as the only viable solution with which to avoid the new nation's pitfalls.

The expansive, at times millennial, optimism of 1783 proved to be a mile wide and an inch deep. In 1788, Charles Backus of Somers, Connecticut, rebuked his audience on the annual fast day for having "had too high expectations from the world." He recalled that when peace was declared, "the imagination of the Poet knew no bounds, in describing what America *would* be. The Philosopher became a Rhapsodist, in contemplating the importance of the American Revolution." However, Backus warned that such laudatory sermonizing had been overdone. "We raised our expectations of happiness from the world, beyond what it can afford," he regretted. "In the most eligible and promising state of human society, man is still born to trouble." He advised instead that Americans needed to be more realistic, reassess their priorities, and regain their self-possession. "If the United States are not wanting to themselves, they may hope [1 Kings 4:25] to sit as quietly under their vines and fig-trees, as at the present state of man will permit. If none of us overrate sublunary enjoyments, we shall pass our few days upon the earth with contentment. Without this, we should be miserable [Exod. 3:8] in a land flowing with milk and honey."[7]

A nagging worry that the country's morals were crumbling settled over the ministry like a blanket of fog rolling in off the ocean. Ministers seldom found themselves at a loss to locate and name the sins undermining American society. Their long enumerations of public sins divided into four basic categories. To begin, clergymen decried a rash of personal vices. Profanity, "the intemperate use of strong drinks," sexual impurity, indolence, and "extravagant modes of living" all evidenced a pervasive moral breakdown.[8]

Ministers next pointed to interpersonal sins like injustice, perjury, litigiousness, faction, and disrespect for authorities, all of which were rooted in pride. "So long as we love our sins, we must expect trouble," said Isaac Morrill of Wilmington, Massachusetts. "Our covetousness, injustice, oppression and hard heartedness, must be put away, as we desire to see prosperous days." Such interpersonal sins violated the principles of unity and benevolence within the standing order's public Christianity. Joseph Huntington, the 1784 election-day preacher from Coventry, Connecticut, protested about "that unreasonable, raging spirit of jealousy pointed against all in power." "The people will inspect [our rulers] *with a jealous mind*, and the certain consequence is, they judge very falsely and abusively of them."[9] These sins of injustice were not confined to relationships within New England society but could also characterize relations between regions, nations, or races. For instance, Newburyport's Samuel Spring interpreted warfare with the Indians on the western frontier in 1793 as "a righteous scourge of Providence," because Americans, "a wicked people," had intruded on the Indians' territory and had "not, in many instances, treated them according to the common principles of justice and humanity." Similarly, slavery constituted a variety of interpersonal sins of the deepest turpitude. "Who can attend to the Slave-Trade, in the manner in which it has been prosecuted, with the extent and consequences of it," asked Samuel Hopkins of Newport, Rhode Island, "and not be convinced that the hand and power of satan has been in an extraordinary degree exerted and manifested in it, stirring men up to a kind and degree of wickedness and mischief, which was not known before?"[10] Americans, a people so blessed, were throwing everything away in a fit of backstabbing and oppression.

Ministers also upbraided their people for religious omissions such as neglect of the Sabbath and inattention to religion in the home. "Great pains should be taken by all parents, and head of families," advised Charles Backus, "to instruct those under their government, in the first principles of religion; to restrain them from vice, and to enforce all their counsels by a holy example." Without home instruction, there was trouble for society down the road. "Ungoverned children are commonly vicious in their lives, and become turbulent members of society. . . . How often have felons confessed from the gibbet, that they were undone, by the indulgence and bad examples of their parents or masters."[11] The most glaring of these failures in religious duty was ingratitude to God. Ingratitude seemed to be a particularly obnoxious trespass for Americans in the 1780s and 1790s in light of all the providential blessings they had so recently received. Like the ancient Israelites, Americans, according to Backus, had forgotten their God in the aftermath of their rescue. This invited trouble. "When we have experienced publick deliverances, we have refused [Ps. 150:2] to praise GOD *for his mighty acts, and according to his excellent greatness. . . .* But, alas! *America, saved by the LORD, while one of the most potent nations, on the face of the whole earth, lifted up the sword against her, has forgotten* [Ps. 77:10] *the years of the right hand of the Most High."*[12] Samuel Hopkins linked the theme of ingratitude to the slave trade. He anticipated the wrath of God in light of the fact that the Continental Congress in 1774 had forsworn the slave trade and then gone back on its promise. The implication was ominous. "When all this is taken into view by the truly pious, who fear God, and believe his word, is it to be wondered at, that their flesh trembleth for fear of the righteous judgments of God? Are they to be condemned as superstitious enthusiasts? Have we not all reason to fear that the vengeance of heaven will fall upon us, as a people, in ways perhaps which are not now thought of, unless we repent and reform?"[13] As the priesthood of New England society, established ministers were quick to call attention to lapses in religious observance and to warn the community of the perils of neglect.

Along the same lines, ministers complained of "infidelity," a pervasive decline in religiosity, and/or a rise in error. "Is it not a sad truth," asked Samuel Wales, Yale divinity professor, in 1785, "that since the commencement of the late war, and especially since the restoration of peace, the holy religion of Jesus, that brightest ornament of our world, is, by many less regarded than it was before?" In 1789, Joseph Lathrop of West Springfield, Massachusetts, warned that "this is a time when errour and wickedness much abound; when new and strange doctrines are taught; and when teachers, of one sort and another, are starting up with pretensions to guide souls in the way to heaven." "We must value the gospel, if we would have it continued to us," summarized Isaac Morrill for the people gathered to mark the fifth anniversary of the Battle of Lexington.[14] Infidelity formed a blanket indictment that summarized and explained all of the other sins. Ammi R. Robbins, the 1789 Connecticut election preacher from Norfolk, mapped the outbreak in vice resulting from the germ of religious infidelity.

> *O Connecticut*, how art thou fallen! Once famous for benevolence, righteousness
> and the fear of GOD—for the belief and practice of religion—even the religion of
> JESUS, which alone bring sinners to heaven. Now abounding with impenitence, in-
> fidelity and all manner of impieties.—The precious word of GOD disregarded.—
> The holy sabbath treated with growing neglect.—The sacred institutions of the
> LORD JESUS, by many dispised [*sic*].—Family-prayer awfully out of fashion. And
> of consequence, all manner of violations of the duties we owe to one another. In-
> justice, fraud, violence, profaness [*sic*], debauchery, intemperance, deceit, falshood
> [*sic*], and covetousness—these and many more evils which are the genuine offspring
> of these; too much mark our towns and communities. Meanwhile the God of our
> Fathers in anger withdrawn, and the necessary influences of the blessed spirit with-
> held!—Is it not time to stop in our career, and enquire—where are we—and what
> must we expect?[15]

As discussed in the last section of this chapter, the fear of infidelity became especially
pronounced after the appearance of French Revolutionary radicalism in the 1790s.[16]

Although these sins may have been individual or religious in origin, they also
carried grave public consequences. For one, God held nations as a whole accountable for their sins. Americans seemed to be antagonizing the Almighty, whether deliberately or unconsciously, and such behavior invited retribution. As Robbins
warned, "the God of our Fathers [had] in anger withdrawn." Moreover, the ministry
shared with Federalists in general the conviction that a principal threat to the society came from a decline of civic virtue. Nathanael Emmons was repeating a plati-
tude when he remarked that a republic "is built upon the pillars of virtue." Republicanism provided a vocabulary and model for the way in which the political world
worked.[17] Ministers and laymen believed in common that the new nation "must sink
into contempt and ruin" if it should "become depraved in principle and dissolute in
manners, till the pulse of republican virtue shall cease to beat." As Henry Cumings
of Billerica, Massachusetts, asked in light of the United States' natural endowments
and liberty, "what appears to hinder us from becoming a great and happy people, if
it be not our own fault? Religion and virtue will raise and exalt us; vice only can sink
and depress us."[18] Ministers easily incorporated republican themes within their larger
corporate ethic. The republican concepts of virtue and vice easily became—and, in
fact, originally derived from—the Christian concepts of morality and transgression.[19]
Timothy Dwight, for instance, defined *virtue* "in that enlarged and Evangelical
sense, which embraces Piety to God, Good-will to mankind, and the effectual Government of ourselves." John Murray, a Newburyport Presbyterian, to take one more
example, argued, "Righteousness is the only thing that really exalteth a nation. In the
honest cultivation of virtue, and the zealous promotion of vital religion—we must
seek our establishment."[20]

Because virtue was subject to corruption by sin, reliance on it was fraught with
perils. The flimsiness of virtue became a salient theme during the critical period. Puritan ministers had always warned of the dangers of public sins, but in the post-
Revolutionary era these warnings took on renewed urgency as Americans were attempting to launch the republic. David Osgood concluded that in the new nation,
"if [the people] are ignorant and vicious, abandoned to idleness, pride and extravagance; if they are selfish and fraudulent, disorderly and factious, impious towards

God and unjust and injurious towards one another—all must be anarchy and confusion, riot and licentiousness, where such a people hold the powers of government."[21] Virtue was an important matter because it had an irresistible tendency to act on society. Samuel Wales drew this connection in his Connecticut election sermon of 1785. "By the constitution of nature which God has established," he explained, "vice tends to the misery, and virtue to the happiness not only of individuals, but of public Communities."[22] Spokesmen for the standing order also denounced slavery on the grounds of its ruinous impact on the virtue and morality of both blacks and whites, in addition to their aforementioned criticisms based upon providential wrath, benevolence, and liberty. On this point, at least, they agreed with Thomas Jefferson.[23] The new nation was teetering on the edge of a canyon, so to speak, and the ground of virtue holding it up did not look entirely steady.

In light of these dangers, the clergy contended that only Christianity provided the means to prevent sinfulness, promote social virtue, and hold society together. As Elizur Goodrich of Durham, Connecticut, concisely stated, "Religion and virtue, are the strongest bond of human society, and lay the best foundation of peace and happiness in the civil state." Ministers and lay politicians relentlessly drove home the point that Americans had to attend carefully to their public duty. But clergymen argued that Christianity alone produced the right public spirit; neither power, self-interest, nor classical virtue would go far enough to foster unity. Instead, only Christianity would internalize virtue as a function of a renovated conscience and render it efficacious to the state. Perhaps the most important way in which religion influenced social life was through its influence on public virtue. When ministers discussed virtue, they put a Protestant slant on an often secular and republican term. As with their usage of liberty, ministers' attachment to virtue shows how they adopted republican discourse without enthroning republicanism in the central place in their social ideology.[24]

Ministers seeking a social adhesive scrutinized the available alternatives to Christianity and found them all wanting. In contrast to adherents of a secular republicanism, clergymen flatly stated that classical virtue was insufficient. "How much soever we may admire the morals of Plato or Epictetus," cautioned Ezra Stiles, president of Yale, "they are not to be compared with those taught by Moses and the divine Jesus." New Haven's Jonathan Edwards Jr. also dismissed antique models of virtue, in that the worship of the ancients involved "the practice of every lewdness and debauchery." Modern deism, in Edwards's opinion, was no better: "It is a maxim of infidelity to follow *nature*. Now to follow her, is to follow all the appetites and passions of which we are naturally the subjects; and this will lead to all kinds of vice. But it is a maxim of christianity, to follow the divine law, the precepts of the gospel and the example of Christ: and whether these lead to vice or virtue, I need not inform you."[25] In addition, Hartford's Nathan Strong attacked public policy that was either upheld by the iron fist of dictatorial power or based on "the selfish passions." "Justice, truth, righteousness and mercy are the solid basis of empire," he concluded instead, "and these are but branches of religion or christian love."[26] The limited reach of law enforcement provided the ministry with another often-cited reason for the necessity of Christian virtue. If virtue were not internalized, society could never be upheld with the police power alone. Only "a full belief of a final judgment," in the words of the younger Edwards, would keep people honest. He sketched a dismal picture of a world without Christian morality, in which the amoral person would be a scourge to society, a public nuisance who would bring others down with him amid "animosities, law-suits and contentions in every form."[27] Christianity surpassed rival moral systems, ministers said, in its ability to foster social peace.

The ministry argued that only Christianity provided the motivation to make one seek the public good. Levi Hart of Preston, Connecticut, and Ammi Robbins explained why most clearly, although other examples abound. According to Hart, "No other [religion], teaches its votaries to place their felicity in the public good, and to think and act on the extended scale of the most perfect general happiness. But christianity not only *teaches*, but *inspires* its subjects with this truly noble liberality of sentiment and affection. It expands the heart of each individual to embrace the good of all, and to rest ultimately, in the perfection of the divine glory, and of the felicity of God's kingdom. And, surely, a heart thus dilated with public affection, can not fail to exert itself for the good of society." Robbins made the same point in his 1789 Connecticut election sermon. Christians, "being born from above," were uniquely capable of "virtuous conduct, and holy practice, both towards GOD, themselves, and mankind." This made them the best of citizens. "They are disposed not to be factious, turbulent and boisterous; but rather to feel the influence and obligation of true patriotism—to seek the real prosperity and good of their country."[28]

Ministers especially highlighted the importance of Christianity to a ruler's virtue. The leadership's piety and moral fiber were important safeguards to society. "It cannot be expected that things will go well, when persons of vicious principles, and loose morals are in authority," observed Josiah Whitney of Brooklyn, Connecticut, in the 1788 election sermon. "If they are unfaithful to GOD, and their own souls, will they probably be faithful to the public? Every friend of virtue says no. They want something sufficient to controul their lusts. Without the aids of religion, and virtue their best motives will be feeble, and inconstant." Whitney based his sermon on one of the establishment's favorite verses on the subject of civil leadership, Exod. 18:21, "thou shalt provide out of all the people able men, such as fear God, men of truth, hating covetousness; and place such over them."[29] Preaching the Massachusetts election sermon that same year, Amherst's David Parsons chose for his text another favorite of the standing order, Prov. 29:2, which reads, "When the righteous are in authority, the people rejoice: but when the wicked beareth rule, the people mourn." The principle applied in the 1780s.[30] Timothy Dwight's 1791 Connecticut election sermon, *Virtuous Rulers a National Blessing*, made a similar point. "The [ruler's] natural conscience, then, carefully cultivated by education into habit, enlivened by a fixed sense of accountableness to God, and strengthened by the belief of future eternal retribution, as revealed in the scriptures of truth, forms another, and it must be confessed, a much more solid foundation [than honor or self-interest], on which to rest the welfare of a community."[31] Chandler Robbins, the 1791 Massachusetts election preacher from Plymouth, added a further distinction to this debate. He pointed out that he was not advocating the seventeenth-century Puritan idea of rule by the visible saints only, what he called "the absurd heresy of '*dominion founded in grace*.'" Nevertheless, godliness was still an important prerequisite for "public rulers." "This will regulate their passions—dignify and enlarge their minds, and form them for noble and benevolent actions. This will inspire them, with undaunted firmness, to pursue the path of duty."[32]

In the post-Revolutionary years, the established ministry had cause for unease. It feared that although the United States had been providentially blessed and was pregnant with future significance, the nation now had to confront a thicket of sins, and God would be watching. The canons of republicanism compounded the problem, because they taught that the decline of virtue was especially threatening. As the antidote to the poison of vice, the ministry prescribed Christian piety. Joseph Huntington captured the mood of the times, when he concluded in 1784, "There is but one way to [secure and improve our blessed inheritance], and that is to keep the commandments of our God. This will secure to us every blessing, and make us [Deut. 26:19] 'high above all nations,' — 'great in name, in praise and in honor;' but if we rebel against God we shall be miserable. We must, above all things, attend to true religion, and practise every moral virtue, even that righteousness that exalteth a nation, and fly from every vice and abhor the ways of immorality."[33] Having shown the providential direction of the new nation and the necessity of Christianity to corporate existence, Congregational ministers then turned to address specific strategies for the propagation and perpetuation of godliness.

The Standing Order Secures the State

> Thou leddest thy people like a flock by the hand of Moses and Aaron.
> —Ps. 77:20

To meet the formidable challenges posed by sin and vice, the standing order put forth an institutional strategy. Cooperating institutions such as the school, family, church, and magistracy would develop the needed public virtue and Christian piety. Only the combined action of the civil and ministerial leadership, so Congregational ministers argued, could yield the oversight and godliness requisite to maintain order, suppress vice, and disseminate social virtue. "Moses and Aaron," although each operating within separately defined spheres, were to pursue the same goals, namely, the common good and the service of God. They would prop up each other and, in so doing, safeguard the republican experiment and build a righteous society. The established ministry assigned itself a central role in the project because it assumed a position of moral oversight. As Donald M. Scott has written, "The ministry in seventeenth- and eighteenth-century New England was a form of public office . . . [which] had particular responsibility for the preservation of social order." Deference for society's leaders and public support for the churches were two other crucial underpinnings of the southern New England establishments.[34]

Both education and the family, ministers said, were cornerstones of the righteous community. According to Enos Hitchcock, a Providence, Rhode Island, Congregationalist, history showed that when empires ignored education they soon collapsed. Samuel Langdon, minister at Hampton Falls, New Hampshire, and president of Harvard from 1774 to 1780, contended that both religion and government required an educated public. "An ignorant people will easily receive idolatry for their religion, and must bow their necks to the tyrant's yoke, because they are incapable of using rational liberty."[35] Likewise, the family formed a second key institution in the formation of virtue and the preservation of society. In a 1790 discussion of the United States' moral shortcomings, Nathanael Emmons named a decline of family religion as a likely cause of social disintegration. "These prayerless and irreligious families are the hives of vice. And from these, we may expect, will issue swarms of prayerless children, prayerless parents, ungovernable subjects, and prodigies of wickedness, to disturb the peace of society, and to propagate irreligion and immorality from generation to generation." Congregational clergymen, the descendants of the Puritans, kept up their ancestors' belief in the central social importance of school and home.[36]

Of utmost importance to public well-being was the cooperation at the top of the social order of magistrate and minister. Here ministers departed from a general republican or Federalist framework to articulate a peculiarly clerical perspective on public life. Amid the general cultural and theological milieux emphasizing the values of the common good, unity, and order, the Congregational ministry posited its particular strategy for attaining these goals. By teaming up with society's civil leadership, the ministry hoped to inculcate Christian virtue and suppress vice. Because vice and irreligion were so intertwined, an approach was needed to both problems. Church and state would work toward the same end, the righteous community. Good government would carve out a space within which the church, the institution of ultimate importance in providential history, could operate. In turn, the church would reinforce the state. However, cooperation did not equal Erastianism. Ministers labored to clearly distinguish cooperation from unjustifiable melding of church and state. David Tappan's 1792 Massachusetts election sermon justified Congregationalism's tax-supported status, but he first of all denied that he was improperly confusing the two kingdoms. "We mean not to advocate such a union or cooperation of the two orders, as involves a heterogeneous mixture of civil and spiritual objects; as places the Magistrate upon CHRIST's throne, in the Church, and invests the christian Minister with the honors and the powers of the State: Such motley alliances are the offspring of political and priestly ambition, aided by equal cunning; are the main pillar both of civil and religious tyranny; and the source of infinite mischiefs to the intellectual and moral character as well as the temporal condition of mankind."[37]

Two biblical texts frequently recurred in the ministry's discussion of this joint strategy. The first was Isa. 49:23, which begins, "And kings shall be thy nursing fathers, and their queens thy nursing mothers." In his election sermon of 1784, Joseph Huntington called on the legislators "to be nursing fathers to the church of God, and [to] promote the interest of that kingdom which shall finally triumph over all."[38] The other favorite verse in this regard, Ps. 77:20, formed the theme of David Tappan's 1792 Massachusetts election sermon. Tappan used this text as the basis for his argument that magistrate and minister should use "their reciprocal influence, and their conjunct operation" to advance "the common good."[39] In the words of John Marsh of Wethersfield, Connecticut,

> Though not sharers in the administration, [clergymen] have an important influence on the object of government. In laboring to promote the spiritual and eternal interest of mankind, which is the immediate object of the institution of the evangelical ministry, they co-operate with the civil Magistrate in promoting their temporal in-

terest. The wise and benevolent Governor of the world, in the appointment of magistracy and the priesthood, has expressed a tender regard to the happiness of men, and is pleased to make use of both conjointly, for accomplishing the purposes of his good pleasure. He led his ancient people like a flock, by the hand of MOSES and AARON.[40]

Although there were dissenters who challenged the standing order on scriptural grounds, the established ministry possessed its own quiver of biblical references.

These calls for cooperation were also based on the ministry's conception of the purpose of government, which was the good of the whole. However, this must be placed in its religious context. Beneath the ministry's providential cosmology, the common good could be realized only through public Christianity. Although separate, both church and state were to pursue a unified goal, the service of God, and were to assist each other in attaining it. Elizur Goodrich voiced the relationship perhaps most clearly: "The immediate ends of the magistracy and ministry are different, but not opposite: They mutually assist each other, and ultimately center in the same point," he argued in his 1787 election sermon. "The one has for its object the promotion of religion and the cause of CHRIST; the other immediately aims at the peace and order of mankind in this world: Without which, there could be no fixed means of religion; nor the church have a continuance on earth, but through the interposition of a miraculous providence, constantly displayed for its preservation." Andrew Lee, the 1795 election preacher from Lisbon, Connecticut, reminded rulers that they "should always consider themselves as subordinate rulers, who are exercising only delegated powers, and exalted to rule, not for themselves, but for him whose they are, and whose majesty in which they shine."[41] The 1799 Connecticut electionday preacher, Cyprian Strong of Chatham, also argued that civil government had to be subordinate to the church in the advancement of the kingdom of God. "I beg leave to inquire," he asked, "Whether the prosperity and advancement of a kingdom of holiness and righteousness among men, be not the great object of civil government?"[42] In other words, church and state would combine to yield the happiness of society and the advance of God's will. Ministers could place themselves on the same plane as the new republic's elected leaders, because they held that both adhered to the same corporate and religious goals for society.

Although magistrate and minister were pursuing the same goal, they had, like husband and wife, different prescribed roles toward attaining that end. The Congregational ministry expected civil rulers to do three things on its behalf: maintain the establishment, exemplify godliness, and prosecute sinfulness. Cyprian Strong summarized these three tasks, although in a different order, when he said, "It is in the power of civil rulers, in many respects, to prepare the way, for an advantageous tender of salvation to mankind. They may set up their banners against vice—encourage men of religion and virtue, and support the institutions of Christianity." The ministry relied on civil rulers to uphold the standing order's legal establishment. "The good ruler," as defined by John Marsh, "will cheerfully give his assent to laws calculated to promote the education of youth in virtue and knowledge, and the training them up for public usefulness in the Church and State; and *which will most effectually provide for the support of public worship and instruction,* and are friendly to the general diffusion of knowledge and true religion."[43]

The established ministry also sought a good example from society's leaders. Like Federalist politicians, Congregational ministers placed great weight on the influence of elites over the common people. "We know, that so long as all the governors, senators, and representatives of this Commonwealth, were public professors and zealous promoters of religion, the sabbaths were sanctified; the houses of God were filled; divine institutions were attended; family religion and parental authority were maintained; cards, and balls, and theatres were unknown, and all open vice and infidelity were treated with general and just contempt," claimed Nathanael Emmons. "It was never known, that the house of Israel reformed one of their loose, irreligious kings; but it was often known, that one pious, exemplary king reformed the whole nation." Those holding conspicuous places in the public eye would model godliness for others. As David Tappan remarked, "The efficacy of example, when arrayed in all the splendour of high office, is not to be described."[44] The Congregational ministry had a trickle-down theory of public influence.

On a more active note, whenever they had the chance, ministers implored the magistracy to work toward "the suppression of all vice and immorality." David Parsons argued that "the magistrate bears the sword in vain, who pays no attention to a matter [public morality] which so much concerns the peace of society." Parsons was referring to another defining text of the standing order's public Christianity, Rom. 13:4.[45] According to Timothy Dwight, the magistracy would be involved along several fronts, "by steadfastly opposing immorality, by employing and honouring the just, by contemning the vicious, by enlarging the motives to righteousness, by removing the temptations to sin, and, in a word, by that general train of virtuous measures, which, like a magical charm, unobservedly spreads its influence over moral things, and, in a gloomy waste of vice and impiety, calls up a new creation of beauty, virtue, and happiness." In the crisis atmosphere of 1798, the Connecticut General Assembly issued a special proclamation that called "upon all officers, judicial and ministerial, to whom the execution of the laws is intrusted [sic], to exert themselves by their united councils, and in their several stations, and by wise and prudent measures to give energy to the laws against Sabbath-breaking, and profaneness, and to those which relate to unlicensed houses, and to houses of public entertainment."[46] Dire consequences would follow if rulers neglected this duty. "When known breaches of law pass with impunity, and open transgressors go unpunished," warned Timothy Stone, "when executive officers grow remiss in their duty, especially, when they connive at disobedience: all distinctions betwixt virtue and vice will vanish, authority will sink into disrepute, and government will be trampled in the dust." The magistracy also had to combat vice because it was not confined to the individual, but rather could characterize a whole society.[47]

The established ministry, too, made the war on vice an integral part of its public role, but whereas Moses bore the sword, Aaron relied on lung power. The pulpit still thundered with jeremiad preaching, as clergymen alternately threatened and pleaded with their congregations to repent and turn from their sins. This was the first way in which the ministry assisted society's civil rulers with governing. Charles Backus called for "unfeigned repentance" in the light of the dangers of public sinfulness. "When GOD's hand is lifted up in wrath," he reminded his auditors in 1788, "we are solemnly warned, to search and try our ways, and turn unto him. If we forget the mighty works of our great REDEEMER, we provoke him to cast us out of his holy protection. Nothing will make real good times but reformation."[48] Likewise, Thomas Barnard cried, "Hear ye me, all ye people, this day! We have no reason to expect continued mercies, unless we repent and reform. Let us therefore seriously consider our ways, and return unto the Lord our God whom we have forsaken. . . . But, if we continue growing in corruption, we have no reason but to think the judgments of God, which are many, will be upon us." Typical of the standing order, Barnard called for a cooperative campaign of magistrates, ministers, and Christian heads of households.[49] The vigilant God of the clergy's providential worldview required upright conduct and humiliation for sins. Mindful of this signal doctrine, ministers constantly deplored vice through their preaching.

The ministry could assist the state in at least two other ways, namely, by teaching obedience and by sowing piety. Josiah Whitney detailed how he and his clerical brethren would make the civil magistrate's job easier if they were to "recommend obedience to lawful authority—the observance of the wholesome, and necessary laws of the State—reprove vice and immorality—shew the ruinous tendency of discontent and faction—and the salutary effects [1 Tim. 2:2] of *leading quiet and peaceable lives in all godliness, and honesty.*" "If at propertimes [*sic*] we judiciously treat these subjects, and influence others, to pay a practical regard to them," he thought, then ministers "shall be essentially useful to the commonwealth."[50] Isaac Lewis pointed out that the ministry's top priority was "to prepare men for the kingdom of heaven." However, this work could have important side effects for the state. "If [ministers] can become the happy instruments of leading those among whom they labor, to forsake sin, to embrace the gospel, to love God and practise every branch of true piety; they will no doubt obey magistrates, and submit themselves to every ordinance of man, for the Lord's sake. The more we promote the interest of religion, the more shall we advance that of civil society." To Timothy Dwight at least, Connecticut presented a perfect picture of the standing order's success, because public education and the established church had succeeded in diffusing "knowledge" and "virtue." "Every parent in the State has a school placed in his neighbourhood; and every child is furnished with the means of the most necessary instruction. To aid, and to complete, these peculiar advantages, a church in every district of a moderate size, opens its doors to the surrounding inhabitants, and invites every family to receive the knowledge, communicated by the Word of God."[51] Thus the clergy's ordinary duties of teaching and preaching bore important social responsibilities.

The occasions of the Sabbath and the annual election day enabled the ministry to fulfill these functions of exhortation and Christian education. "It concerns us to do all in our power, and use every suitable mean, for diffusing the knowledge and establishing the principles of religion and virtue among us," noted the Cambridge, Massachusetts, ministerial association in conventional fashion. "These purposes cannot be more effectually promoted than by a *due sanctification of the Sabbath.* The weekly return of this day of rest gives the whole community an opportunity for intellectual and moral improvement."[52] If the Sabbath were designed to reach "the whole community," the annual election was geared toward those chosen to hold the levers of power. Ministers used the election sermon to offer "pertinent religious discourses, concerning the duties incumbent on rulers" or, in other words, to remind the assembled legislators of their godly role from the perspective of the clergy's public Christianity. David Parsons most clearly depicted a key purpose of the annual election as a day in which Aaron spoke to Moses from a biblical perspective concerning the latter's duty: "The preacher considers it to be the special design of our present meeting in this place (according to common usage, and the laudable example of our pious Ancestors) to seek the divine influence and direction in the important concerns of the day—to express our grateful and devout praises for the inestimable blessings of government—to implore the divine blessing upon our civil magistrates in the discharge of the duties of their several departments—and to meditate on such suggestions from the oracles of truth, as may be pertinent to such an occasion."[53] Established ministers thought that their preaching fulfilled important social functions. They therefore instituted regular occasions at which to deliver their message to the public.

The established ministry's top-down theory of social influence, typified in the election sermon, derived from its hierarchical view of society. Hierarchy formed a central element in Congregational clergymen's social ideology. To some extent, it grew out of their fundamental belief in a world ordered by Providence. Jonathan Edwards Jr.'s discussion of Matt. 7:12 allows a revealing window into the ministry's hierarchical principles. The text—"Therefore all things whatsoever ye would that men should do to you, do ye even so to them: for this is the law and the prophets"—must be one of the Bible's most egalitarian. Obviously enough, Edwards used it as the basis for an antislavery sermon. However, he qualified it so as not to run counter to the ministry's conventional social assumptions.

> This precept of our divine Lord hath always been admired as most excellent; and doubtless with the greatest reason. Yet it needs some explanation. It is not surely to be understood in the most unlimited sense, implying that because a prince expects and wishes for obedience from his subjects, he is obliged to obey them: that because parents wish their children to submit to their government, therefore they are to submit to the government of their children: or that because some men wish that others would concur and assist them to the gratification of their unlawful desires, therefore they also are to gratify the unlawful desires of others. But whatever we are conscious, that we should, in an exchange of circumstances, wish, and are persuaded that we might reasonably wish, that others would do to us; that we are bound to do to them. This is the general rule given us in the text; and a very extensive rule it is, reaching to the whole of our conduct: and is particularly useful to direct our conduct towards inferiours, and those whom we have in our power.[54]

The egalitarian thrusts of the American Revolution only partially penetrated the standing order, which remained a bastion of hierarchy and order.

In its public pronouncements, the established ministry tended to speak in terms of a society divided between rulers and the ruled. Moses Hemmenway, the 1784 Massachusetts election preacher from Wells in the District of Maine, most clearly stated this idea. "The order and interest of a civil society," he argued, "require that there should be different ranks of men, with different civil rights and privileges annexed to them; and subject to different restrictions. . . . But though the several ranks in a political system may rise one above another in a long scale of subordination, yet we may conveniently distribute them all into two general classes, viz. RULERS and

SUBJECTS." David Parsons was just as summary in his dismissal of the democratic aspirations of ordinary people to participate in government. "It would be happy," he remarked curtly, "if inferiors would not employ themselves too much in disputing the policy and prudence of their rulers, and the propriety of their laws."[55] The closing ritual for a typical New England election sermon reflected this view of society as composed of orders. The preacher addressed the different ranks represented in the audience in turn. Starting at the top, he spoke to the governor and then the lieutenant governor. Next the minister applied some of his earlier remarks to the legislators, perhaps adding some specific policy recommendations. In a manifestation of the establishment's belief in the cooperation of magistrate and minister, the preacher then directed his remarks to his fellow clergymen in attendance. Finally, he addressed himself to the people at large. This formula, which concluded most of the election sermons in this time period, encapsulated in an institutional setting the standing order's hierarchical and ordered view of society.

Hemmenway hastened to add that by discussing hierarchy he was not preaching unlimited submission and that rulers had to respect the boundaries set by "the laws of morality." Josiah Whitney also distanced himself from the doctrine of unlimited submission: "Government cannot exist, nor its advantages be felt, without proper submission, *proper submission* I say, *not absolute, unlimited subjection,* for this is fit for brutes only, not for men." Nevertheless, it is easy to see how this talk of differential rights and subordination began to grate on the nerves of men fired with the sentiments of democracy and equality.[56] When the Democratic-Republican party formed in the years around 1800, it made the assault on hierarchy a central issue, and the established clergy made a fat target for Republicans' ridicule.

The established ministry's hierarchicalism also derived from its belief in the difficulty of leadership. These ministers saw ruling as something that was both demanding and critical to social well-being. "Civil government is extremely complicated and extensive, both in theory and in practice," observed Nathanael Emmons. "It embraces all the objects in this world, and all the interests and concerns of men, in this life. No species of human knowledge is foreign to the business of a statesman, who needs to be universally acquainted with men and things." Their position was a far cry from laissez-faire. According to David Tappan, the qualified ruler was "like the central orb of the planetary world, [that] enlightens and animates, cements and beautifies the whole political system. With a skilful [*sic*], steady, yet gentle hand, he moulds a confused mass of discordant materials into one regular and harmonious compound, and holds it together with a silken, yet invincible chain." Again, the ministry's fear of society's naturally anarchic tendency asserted itself. Only someone of uncommon skill could manage society. Josiah Whitney presented a demanding list of prerequisites for office in his 1788 Connecticut election sermon. Rulers "should be men of such health and strength as to be capable of bearing the burdens and fatigues of their office. —They should be men of so much interest or wealth, as shall raise them above the temptation of *transgressing for a piece of bread.* —*Men of parts,* of such natural and acquired accomplishments, as to understand well the constitution and laws of their country; as well as the duties of the place to which they are raised."[57] According to Nathan Strong, public leadership exposed a man to great "temptations." "When the respectable citizen rises from private into public life, he must expect to exchange quietness for trouble; honor, though alluring, has its bitterness and its dangers; enemies before unknown, will rise up; the jealous will sift all his actions. . . . To support the mind under these evils, and lead it into the exercise of prudence and patience, religion is necessary."[58] Established ministers elevated governing to a herculean task that required knowledge, wisdom, and Christian virtue.

In sum, the standing order advocated a symbiotic relationship between magistrate and minister, emphasizing the importance of elite action upon society. Magistrates had significant services that they could perform for the church, such as prosecution of vice, maintenance of a godly public image, and provision of financial support. The reverse was true as well; ministers made governing much smoother through cultivation of public virtue and condemnation of dangerous and antisocial behavior. Although the civil and clerical spheres would take care to maintain separate bounds, this did not mean that they could not engage in close action for a common end.

Two further consequences followed from the standing order's emphasis on the cooperation of Moses and Aaron. In the first place, there was not a clear sense of detachment from the state in the ministry's thinking in the late eighteenth century. The ministry's hierarchicalism and focus on a common good led it to assign responsibility for society's orderly righteousness to those at the top of the social order. By aligning themselves with the civil leadership, ministers were also predisposed to side with the magistracy when it came under attack. As the nation divided into opposing camps, established ministers were inclined toward the Federalists.

Second, the promotion of the idea that magistrate and minister were pursuing essentially the same goal enabled standing order clergymen to rationalize the establishment of Congregationalism. The ministry defended the establishment as another dimension of the cooperation of magistrate and minister in pursuit of the righteous community. It did not justify the establishment as a theological necessity—say, as part of the national covenant. While ministers' high regard for religious liberty led them to insist that "in matters of faith every one hath an unalienable right to judge for himself," they united liberty of conscience with the religious establishment.[59]

William Symmes, who delivered the 1785 election sermon in Massachusetts, justified the establishment by means of this syllogism: the state needed morality for stability; morality came from religion; therefore, the state should support religion in some form. Levi Hart employed the same reasoning as Symmes. It was, argued Hart, "the proper object of civil government" to see to it that the "heart[s] [of men are] animated by the spirit of true religion," inasmuch as such "evangelical obedience" was "essential to the well being of society." This appears to have been the standard logic behind the establishments in both Massachusetts and Connecticut during the last two decades of the eighteenth century. It was also the justification found in and for article 3 of the Massachusetts constitution of 1780. Although they unanimously denied the state any prerogative to interfere in doctrinal matters, Congregational ministers nevertheless recommended state support of religion on utilitarian grounds. Jonathan Edwards Jr. added his assent to these principles in the 1794 Connecticut election sermon. "Since christianity appears to be necessary to the public good of the state," he asserted, "[magistrates] are bound to encourage, promote and inculcate that, by their example and profession, . . . by supporting christian ordinances and worship, and by promoting to places of trust and profit those who profess it and live agreeably, and who are otherwise properly qualified. Magistrates are called to do all this on the ground of the soundest policy."[60] According to ministers of the standing order, the state's financial support of the Congregational churches had nothing to do with denominational partiality. Rather, they argued that it was simply in the state's best interest to ensure the diffusion of morals, and nothing fostered morality like Christianity. The establishment rested on "the soundest policy," not just sound doctrine.

For ministers of the standing order, the public support of religion was analogous to today's system of public education, in that it was seen as a public good for which everyone should bear some of the burden.[61] Samuel Langdon denied any authority on the part of the state to legislate on matters of "faith or modes of worship," yet he still thought the state had an interest in seeing that the populace had access to the services of the clergy. He called upon state legislators "to make provision that all the towns may be furnished with good teachers, that they may be impowered to make valid contracts, and that the fulfilment of such contracts should be secured against the fickle humours of men, who are always ready to shift from sect to sect, or make divisions in parishes that they may get free from all legal obligations to their ministers." "Fulfilment" of ministerial contracts was a euphemism for state enforcement of tax support for the standing order. Another example of such coded terminology came from Samuel Deane's 1794 Massachusetts election sermon. Deane, pastor of the First Church in Portland (now in Maine), called on magistrates to "enable Christian societies to raise contributions among themselves, to serve religious purposes." The establishment simply did not trust the populace to support its churches automatically. "Only fanatics had the unmitigated self-assurance (so similar to vulgar pride or arrogance)," thought ministers of the standing order, "to assume they could maintain religion merely by the zeal of their preachers and the truth of their persuasion."[62] Such "fanatics" as the Baptists had no concern for the larger society and probably did not realize the cost of maintaining a preacher and meetinghouse in every parish.

The need for a religious establishment derived, in part, from the standing order's presumption that the people needed instruction at regular intervals. David Tappan thought that society needed "public religious instructors" or "the friendly voice of STATED MONITORS, to recal [sic] our forgetful, wandering feet; and to enlighten and warm our hearts afresh with the divine principles and motives of religion! . . . Without this, how shall [the inferior members of the community] obtain a competent knowledge, or an abiding practical impression of their various relations and duties to GOD, to man, to civil society?" The public was too prone to "wander" without the reminders of its ministers. Samuel Deane was even more condescending when he argued that "if, with political views, [magistrates] may enforce the support of schools for the instruction of youth, why not that of meetings for the instruction of grown up children in religion and morality, so far as they shall judge it needful to promote the welfare of society?" Seeing most members of society as "grown up children" surely alienated many who had come to believe that all men were created equal.[63]

Ministers of the standing order often dismissed calls for more religious liberty as either insincere or a smokescreen for some sinister purpose. They frequently charged that objections to the establishment were nothing more than tax evasion. In the 1788 Massachusetts election sermon, David Parsons asserted that "the pleas of conscience are frequently made to cover a design, and with intent only to form an excuse from contributing to the support of religion, or upholding any form of social worship. In this case the constitutional power of government ought to be employed to disappoint the dissembler, and enforce the *rights* of religion."[64] Certainly, the dissenters must have taken this brush-off as a slap in the face; here was a minister of the standing order suggesting that their complaints arose from stinginess, not conviction. Also noteworthy is Parsons's use of the term "*rights* of religion." Whereas dissenters argued for a right to be free *from* religious establishments, Parsons made the argument that the majority had a right *to use* the government to set up their ministry. If the Baptists and others who dissented from the standing order were not just cheap, perhaps they were unstable. Noah Worcester charged that the Baptists attracted "ignorant" people, who were "more charmed with sound than sense" in their preaching. Samuel West, Congregational minister of Dartmouth, Massachusetts, proved yet more insulting when he likened them to "the troubled sea, whose waters cannot rest, but being driven by furious winds are constantly casting up mire and dirt." Furthermore, he smeared the standing order's critics as an unholy combination of "disguised tories, British emissaries, profane and licentious deists, avaricious worldlings, disaffected sectaries, and furious, blind bigots."[65] Standing order ministers obviously did not engage in a meaningful dialogue with their critics. Thus, dissenters had to find other means to challenge their overlords. The first party competition would prove to be a powerful lever with which to budge the standing order.

When not engaged in such ad hominem attacks, established ministers corrected their opponents' mistaken ideas about religious liberty. Liberty, they maintained, had to be protected from degenerating into licentiousness. The corporate concern for the stability of society overrode individualism. "We cannot set too great a value on our civil and religious liberties," granted William Symmes. "But," he warned, "we can place ourselves in no point of view, in which we can have the least colour of right to any kind of liberty that disturbs the peace of society, or discharges us from the service of God."[66] Ministers of the standing order especially had to set itinerant preachers straight about the limits of religious liberty, lest the irregular ministers produce "endless confusion." The itinerants did not understand the principle [from 1 Cor. 14:40], that "all things are to be done decently and in order." These interlopers threatened to trample the carefully measured bounds of the parish system and sow seeds of dissatisfaction. "Ministers," said Joseph Lathrop, employing a Newtonian simile, "are not to cross each other's lines, and interfere in their motions; but, like the heavenly system, to run, each in his proper circuit, around the common centre. They are to contribute, each in his sphere, to the general order and harmony."[67] The Cambridge, Massachusetts, ministerial association used the same logic of limited liberty to argue for the enforcement of the Sabbath, basing itself also in article 3's provision "that the citizens at large shall worship God in some form or other." "The liberty not to worship him at all, for which some seem disposed to contend," the association decreed, "would hold forth to the citizens a license to degrade themselves from the dignity of rational beings to a level with the brute animals, among whom no other law or order prevails than that which the stronger impose upon the weaker. Such a kind of liberty would, in all probability, soon terminate in the dissolution of all order and government."[68] Again, the standing order's definition of liberty fit within its larger corporate framework.

The standing order asserted that its arrangements did not infringe on anyone's rights of conscience, properly understood. According to William Symmes, a minimal level of state involvement in religious affairs should have offended no one (although, of course, it did): "And when all the members of a community enjoy the free use of their reason in matters of religion; when they are left to pursue the dictates of their own consciences, which are subject to God only, and no particular mode of worship is established by law; where is the grievance if public worship is required in some mode or other, to preserve order, and prevent the infection of bad examples?"[69] In other words, liberty rightly understood had boundaries, because the standing order understood liberty not solely from an individual basis but from the perspective of the society as a whole. Like the other ministers of the standing order, David Tappan did not think that some kind of tax support for religion, with appropriate loopholes, could offend a reasonable person. Such support, he contended, did not "make the least approach to a political establishment of any particular religious profession, nor consequently invole [sic] any invasion of the prerogative of CHRIST, or the sacred rights of conscience." Symmes and Tappan, as representatives of the establishment, apparently thought that the constitution of 1780 had struck a judicious balance between liberty of conscience and society's need to support public religious instruction.[70]

During the last two decades of the eighteenth century, the established ministry articulated a distinct and detailed formulation of the correct constitution of New England society. The established church and the civil government were to pursue the shared goals of the common good and service to God. The cooperation of magistrate and minister would also shield society from its greatest dangers. In the social ideology of Congregational ministers, Christianity was absolutely essential, because it yielded Christian civic virtue and ameliorated other social sins. The state would repay the church for this service with legal privileges and aggressive moral policing. This hierarchical church-state connection was the ministry's first post-Revolutionary answer to the question of how to organize the righteous community.

Dissent

> Jesus answered, My kingdom is not of this world. . . .
>
> —John 18:36

Those outside the standing order challenged its linkage of church and state as unnecessary to the righteous community. The Baptists led this dissent, but other denominations and even some idiosyncratic individuals joined them. Before exploring the dissenters' complaints with the Congregational establishment, however, it should be noted that there were points of overlap between the dissenters and Congregationalists on the issue of public Christianity. Their disagreements should not be overemphasized because in their points of consensus lay the seeds of future cooperation.

The Baptists had a concern for social morality similar to the Congregational-ists'.[71] For instance, the 1785 circular letter of the Warren Association discussed "the importance of family religion and government." This was an important matter be-cause, among other reasons, it had implications for social order; people who did not learn order at home could be counted on to be troublemakers in society. "Gaming, swearing, drinking, nocturnal revelling, uncleanliness, profanation of the Lord's-day, &c. which have arrived to such an awful height, if checked at all, must be checked by the united influence of those whose relation to their families, whose age, and whose examples, give them importance." These are the same kinds of sins that alarmed the standing order. Likewise, Samuel Stillman, the prominent pastor of Boston's First Baptist Church, called for virtue to support the republic, just as the Congregationalists did, and Thomas Baldwin of Boston's Second Baptist sounded like a member of the establishment in his discussion of the public's moral account-ability before God.[72] Isaac Backus of Middleboro, Massachusetts, the champion of Baptist resistance to the standing order, "had no quarrel with the general New Eng-land assumption concerning the necessity for the general diffusion of the Protestant religion in order to preserve the safety and happiness of the state."[73] The Baptists also spoke with essentially the same voice as the Congregationalists in attributing the out-come of the Revolution to providential influence. Religious denomination was not the sole determinant of political allegiance either. During the political crisis of the late 1790s, some leading Baptists came out strongly in favor of the Federalists. Both Jonathan Maxcy, president of Rhode Island College, and Samuel Stillman delivered highly partisan addresses in 1799. Sounding like Edmund Burke, Maxcy cautioned, "A good government . . . ought to be considered as an inheritance to be transmitted from one generation to another; and not as the capricious offspring of a moment, per-petually exposed to destruction, from the varying whim of popular phrenzy, or the daring strides of licentious ambition."[74] Finally, one can foresee the Baptists' later rapprochement with evangelical Congregationalists in their call from Jude 3 to "stand fast in this evil day, and contend earnestly for the faith once delivered to the Saints."[75] Doctrinally speaking, the two groups had so many points in common that they would eventually realize the advantages of cooperating against the threats of re-ligious liberalism and moral decline.

Other religious minorities in New England also had certain similarities to the Congregationalists. The social views of Samuel Seabury, Episcopal Bishop of Con-necticut, were every bit as statically hierarchical and providential as any member of the standing order. "[Religion teaches]," Seabury intoned, "that the various states and conditions of life are the result of that constitution, and the designations of that prov-idence, by which the world is sustained and governed—that, therefore, the several stations which men fill, and the different relations in which they stand to each other, are necessary for their mutual support and comfort, and productive of the greatest general happiness." Also, as descendants of the Church of England, Episcopalians "had no objection to an established church system or to religious taxes." Although Samuel Parker was the Episcopal rector of Trinity Church, Boston, he was chosen as Massachusetts election preacher in 1793. His sermon shared many of the establish-ment's axioms, including its chosen text, Prov. 14:34. As numerous Congregational-ists had argued, Parker said that "religion and virtue are the surest means of promoting national happiness and prosperity." Likewise, John Tyler fully concurred with Washington's national thanksgiving proclamation of 1795 (see later). His sermon comported with orthodox Congregational doctrine on the providential oversight of nations and the need for religion to foster public virtue: "Every Enjoyment we have, is the Effect of God's Bounty: and every Suffering we endure, either directly or indirectly, of his inflicting. The Connexions of all things, were by him originally appointed: and the whole Series of Causes and Effects, are continually under his Superintendence." John Murray—the Boston Universalist, not the aforementioned minister of Newburyport—expressed some rather conventional beliefs in the providential direction of the Revolution and constitution, regardless of his theological innovations. His "federal bosom" also "swelled with conscious pleasure," just like any member of the standing order, when Washington crushed the Whiskey Rebellion.[76]

However, religious minority groups rejected the justifications of the Congregational establishment from a variety of ideological perspectives, including liberalism, sectarianism, and antiauthoritarianism. Millennialism, too, sometimes fired their dissent. At bottom, the Baptists were outraged at having their property seized and being thrown in jail for failing to pay their taxes in support of their local Congregational church. Growing out of this practical grievance, the Baptists constructed their ideological defenses. For one, "the Baptists . . . explicitly invoked John Locke's ideal of voluntary association among rational individuals" as early as 1769 to critique the standing order's corporate ethic and tax support. To Locke, they soon added the libertarian legacy of the Revolution to argue that any kind of coerced funding of religion was, in the words of the Warren Association, "not only a violation of the law of God, but also directly against the fundamental principles of the late revolution in *America.*" In 1773, Isaac Backus also compared British tyranny in government to standing order tyranny in religion. Speaking to the citizens of Massachusetts on behalf of the Warren Association, he asked, "You do not deny the right of the British Parliament to impose taxes within her own realm; only complain that she extends her taxing power beyond her proper limits. And have we not as good right to say you do the *same thing?*" In contrast, the Baptists gave thanks that Rhode Island, at least, provided them with a haven from state coercion in New England. "What right has the arm of the magistrate to intrude itself into the field of religious opinion?" demanded an exasperated Jonathan Maxcy. "To the everlasting honour of Rhode-Island be it said, that her legislature has never assumed the authority of regulating ecclesiastical concerns. Religion here stands, as it ought to, on its own basis, disconnected with all political considerations."[77] The Baptists advocated a less constricted definition of liberty than the Congregationalists, and the rhetoric of the Revolution reinforced their logic.

No one made the argument for an inalienable right to conscience more powerfully than the iconoclastic Baptist, John Leland. He assailed the establishment as a procrustean bed that produced only either hypocrites or martyrs. Leland wrapped himself in a pure form of the doctrine of the free market of ideas: "It is error, and error alone, that needs human support; and whenever men fly to the law or sword to protect their system of religion, and force it upon others, it is evident that they have something in their system that will not bear the light, and stand upon the basis of truth." He brushed aside the standing order's description of the interdependence of

Painted by A.B.Moore   Eng.ᵈ by T.Doney. N.Y

John Leland. Courtesy American Antiquarian Society.

church and state, asking, "Did not the Christian religion prevail during the first three centuries, in a more glorious manner than ever it has since, not only without the aid of law, but in opposition to all the laws of haughty monarchs?" The established ministry, in his regard, was nothing more than a bunch of incompetent, money-grubbing loafers.[78]

Elias Lee, another Baptist minister, made comments similar to Leland's but with more attention to the millennium. This independent thinker from Ridgfield, Connecticut, came to the opposite conclusion from the standing order regarding the connection between Christianity and society. He started by reading up on politics and the Bible.[79] Lee's autodidactic research convinced him that a connection of church and state was erroneous, because it retarded the spread of Christianity. In Lee's analysis, Christ was the only one suited to be a monarch; fallible men should govern on a more equal basis. Religious establishments he decried as tyrannical. "When ever civil authority lends its aid, to the support and establishment of any particular mode of worship, or religious constitution, in distinction from others; that so far there is presumption and tyranny in the one and weakness and debility in the other." In contrast, he bragged that the Baptists were the only ones truly in sync with the age; their "Baptist republican church constitution" made them "friends, to both civil and religious liberty." On top of his republican analysis, Lee poured millennial speculation. Through its involvement during the American Revolution, France had caught the spirit of liberty. Lee linked this to prophecy: "The horn of Antichrist is broken amongst them, civil and religious monarchy expires; and true liberty and freedom, wafted on the wings of Providence, in defiance of millions of enemies, hail a general revolution."[80]

When a Baptist did address the question of religion and politics, he had to justify himself. Samuel Stillman's sermon on the national fast of 1799 revealed his discomfort. Perhaps because he did not have the standing order's tradition of public Christianity behind him, Stillman defended his remarks at length. He denied the argument that there should be a total separation between religion and politics. Ministers had the same rights as anyone else. "They are *citizens*, members of *civil* society; have civil rights as well as other men. . . . Because they are Christians and ministers of religion, shall they see ruin coming on themselves, their families, and their country, and say nothing?" Stillman also used the clergy's role in the Revolution as a defense, noting that ministers had been applauded then. "Now, as then, they espouse the cause of their own country, and with its peace and prosperity, as well as happiness to the whole family of man. But the objection does not lie so much against their '*preaching* politics,' as against the '*politics* they preach.' Should they take the opposite side of the question, those who now censure would applaud their conduct."[81]

In addition to arguments rooted in religious liberalism, the Baptists objected to the standing order's societywide view of an established church on the grounds of sectarian theology. Indeed, for them the sectarian objections were more fundamental; the aforementioned libertarian arguments were brought forth only to defend their dissent from the establishment.[82] The standing order's corporate outlook had originally been modeled, in part, after the Old Testament covenant between God and the whole people of Israel. That covenant had been sealed and signified by circumcision, which had been replaced by infant baptism in the New.[83] Instead, the Baptists viewed the church as pure, as consisting only of the confessing and baptized regenerate. Isaac Backus argued that "the twice born" were "the only *priesthood*, and *holy nation*, that God hath under heaven." Their church was localist, certainly not something with which the state legislature had to be concerned. The circular letter of the Warren Association from 1786 gave this definition: "What we mean by the Christian church is, Christ's church, which consists of many distinct bodies of believers; each is called a particular church; which is, a number of professed disciples of Jesus Christ, formed into a distinct body, by mutual compact; solemnly engaging to each other, to walk agreeably to the laws, precepts and examples of Christ, made known to us in the scriptures of truth; acknowledging Christ to be the only head of the same." Backus also attacked the standing order's broad-based idea of the church, saying that with Christ there came into the world a new covenant with a break from the past. If the Baptists had a broader concept of religious liberty than their standing order opponents, their understanding of the church was narrower.[84]

Whereas the standing order sought to bring the two kingdoms into alignment, the Baptists rejected this strategy. As the Warren Association wrote in its 1791 minutes, "we cannot consent to blend the kingdom of Christ with the kingdoms of this world; nor to support it by the power of the civil magistrates." Isaac Backus most clearly delineated this "true difference and exact limits between ecclesiastical and civil government," arguing "that the church is armed with *light and truth* to pull down the strongholds of iniquity and to gain souls to Christ and into his Church to be governed by his rules therein, . . . while the state is armed with the *sword* to guard the peace and the civil rights of all persons and societies." Furthermore, he warned, "where these two kinds of government . . . have been confounded together no tongue nor pen can fully describe the mischiefs that have ensued." If the standing order was a "church of the center" of the "Christ above culture" type of H. Richard Niebuhr, then the Baptists substantially adhered to the model of "Christ against culture" in their concern to insulate the church from the world's corruption. Of course, the Baptists were not separatists from the world in any extreme form, as seen in their aforementioned concerns for social morality. Yet, in their highly developed sensitivity to the church's purity and rejection of the established churches' corporate pretensions, they had pronounced sectarian leanings.[85]

Like the Baptists, the Episcopalians disagreed with Congregational ecclesiology, too, but for different reasons. The Episcopal apologist Jeremiah Leaming, rector of Christ's Church, Stratford, Connecticut, and recently a Tory during the Revolution, championed his church's apostolic succession, claiming that Congregational ordination was invalid. He attacked the standing order for linking church and state: "It is much to be lamented, that christianity is scarcely allowed by some, to be a divine institution. Its ordinances are viewed by many, as only *political*: and the ministers of Christ, as *officers appointed* and *empowered* by the people. Men who have no pretensions to a divine commission, think they may, and actually do undertake, *to regulate the faith of the gospel; and fashion and frame the church of Christ as they please*." New England Episcopalians like Leaming had more of a "Lutheran" view of the relationship between church and state, inasmuch as they wanted to divide the spheres of church and state carefully.[86]

The alienated, self-proclaimed prophet from western Massachusetts, Simon Hough, illustrates a third, antiauthoritarian basis of dissent from the establishment. In his criticisms, one can hear the echoes of the First Great Awakening's radical New Light wing, especially in his emphasis on the authority of spiritual experience over learning and institutional accreditation. Whereas the standing order openly stated its trust in the prevailing social and political hierarchies, dissenters scorned them.

Hough lashed out at the establishment in 1792; not that he confined his barbs to the Congregationalists, but he had nothing but hostility for the established ministers, whom he ridiculed as money-servers and Pharisees. "Well if you have no religon [*sic*] but what is upheld by money and civil authority, you may as well have none, for it will not carry you to Heaven!" He also noted that God did not choose the learned for his instruments. "He especially welcomed the thought that at the coming apocalypse the churches 'built on the sandy foundations of worldly wisdom, traditions of men, money, and liberal education will fall, and great will be the fall.'" Instead, the Bible could be comprehended only by those (like Hough) aided by the spirit. John Leland also rejected the standing order's hermeneutical elitism. "Is not a simple man, who makes nature and reason his study," Leland asked rhetorically, "a competent judge of things? is the Bible written (like Caligula's laws) so intricate and high, that none but the letter learned (according to common phrase) can read it?"[87]

The standing order's view of the church and state walking closely together while remaining distinct preponderated in the first two decades after the Revolution. That is not to say that the establishment went unchallenged. Religious minorities, small but growing in numbers and influence, challenged the social, political, and theological assumptions underlying the establishment. At the very end of the eighteenth century, this challenge took on new vigor as national political divisions electrified New England politics. This theme is examined in the next chapter.

The Conservative Reaction of the 1790s

> And I heard another voice from heaven, saying, Come out of her, my people, that ye be not partakers of her sins, and that ye receive not of her plagues.
>
> — Rev. 18:4

In the latter half of the 1790s, the standing order's public Christianity passed through the fire of domestic and foreign crises. It emerged from this crucible largely intact but subtly altered as well. The standing order responded to the French Revolution and the concomitant domestic political crises of the 1790s in light of its public Christianity. These events troubled the establishment because they threatened both religion and government.[88] Therefore, the clergy parried the Gallic and democratic thrusts with a combined action of its own, calling for a renewed attachment to piety and the republic. This strategy drew the ministry even closer to Federalist political leaders and accentuated its already conservative tendencies. The atmosphere of crisis also helped to clarify the ministry's stance toward the providential significance of the United States. Amid fears of impending anarchy, the ministry moved toward a greater faith in the church as the enduring institution. Although ministers preached obedience to authorities, they hedged their bets by emphasizing the providential protection of the church, not the state. This opening crack between church and state in the late 1790s foreshadowed the much more momentous break that would occur in the next two decades. In short, the standing order's public Christianity conditioned its response to events in the late 1790s at the same time as those events altered the ministry's social ideology. The process had the look of the double helix of DNA, as stimulus and response wrapped around each other in an upward spiral. The latter half of the 1790s served as a prelude to the more intense struggles over the issue of religion and society that occurred after 1800.

Two influential pamphlets of 1794 marked the standing order's growing anxiety over the French Revolution's implications for the United States.[89] *The Revolution in France*, by Noah Webster, a Connecticut lawyer and publisher then living in New York City, criticized the French Revolution for its assault on liberal government and rational religion. Webster detailed how the Jacobins had assumed a tyrannical hold on power through a *"principle of combination"* and then concentrated his fire on the revolutionary government's "inveterate war with christianity." Of course, the new regime had dealt a blow to Roman Catholicism, but it had now gone too far toward complete *"atheism* and *materialism,"* resulting, predictably, in "mental licentiousness." French affairs did not interest Webster so much for their own sake as for their impact on the United States, or in order "to ascertain the point . . . beyond which an introduction of their principles and practice into this country, will prove dangerous to government, religion and morals." French factionalism and atheism raised red flags for someone steeped in the public Christianity of the standing order. Webster argued that the lesson to take from the French experience was that Americans needed no "private societies to watch over the government," and he closed with a call to preserve the status quo against the threat of the Democratic-Republican societies. "Americans! be not deluded. In seeking *liberty*, France has gone beyond her. You, my countrymen, if you love liberty, adhere to your constitution of government. The moment you quit that sheet-anchor, you are afloat among the surges of passion and the rocks of error; threatened every moment with ship-wreck."[90]

David Osgood followed up on Webster's pamphlet in his thanksgiving sermon of November 1794, covering much the same ground and quoting *The Revolution in France* at length. This was a significant publication because "Osgood's sermon was the first step in the Congregational clergy's involvement in the political controversies of the 1790s."[91] Osgood blasted Citizen Genet, "a foreign incendiary," as the advance agent of a French plot to undermine the United States. He gave absolutely no credence to domestic dissent, instead labeling opponents of the Washington administration as merely jealous, "constitutionally turbulent and uneasy," or self-serving and prone to dangerous factionalism. Like Webster, he, too, urged support of the established authorities.[92] Osgood's sermon demonstrates how the established ministry moved into Federalist ranks during the initial period of party coalescence in the 1790s.

James Sullivan, Massachusetts's attorney general and member of Boston's own "self-created society," responded to Osgood's publication in an anonymous, mock sermon, *The Altar of Baal Thrown Down*. In it, Sullivan accused Osgood of issuing "slanders and calumnies" regarding France in order to advance a monarchist agenda. In a sense, Sullivan's work amounted to a backhanded compliment to the power and influence of the standing order, in that opponents of the establishment could not let conservative ministers have the mantle of godliness to themselves. Sullivan closed with a shot fired across Osgood's bow: "I shall now leave you sir, with only advising you never again to step out of your line to gratify a party; that whenever you ascend the sacred desk, you shall have your mind deeply impressed with a sense of your solemn obligation to truth and candour, and that laying aside a spirit of malice and envy, you shall feel the same tenderness for the reputation of others, which you wish them to possess towards yours."[93] *The Altar of Baal* pointed to the kind of resistance the standing order was to meet increasingly after 1800 as the Democratic-Republican opposition organized. The established ministry did not heed Sullivan's warning, and it would become further embroiled in disputes with Republican politicians like him.

Regardless of Sullivan's warning, the New England ministry grew more and more hostile toward revolutionary France in the latter half of the 1790s, and its criticisms followed in the tracks laid by Webster and Osgood. Like those two, most New England ministers vilified the French for a revolution gone haywire in factionalism and infidelity. Also like Webster and Osgood, most clergymen freely mixed criticisms of the French with warnings regarding home-grown anarchists and atheists. The established ministry, joined by some leading dissenters as well, moved en masse into the ranks of the emerging Federalist party. Politicians and divines both utterly ignored the claims of political dissenters and instead called on their audiences to rally to the government. The standing order reiterated that the nation's best hope lay in the partnership of Moses and Aaron. Azel Backus of Bethlehem, Connecticut, captured the sentiments of his ministerial colleagues when he said in 1798, "In times of seditious machinations, let us cleave to our religion, and our constitution, as the refuge of our hopes, as the haven and anchorage of freedom."[94]

Political and religious events both at home and abroad alarmed the established ministry. "The evils of faction and party spirit," embodied by both the French Jacobins and the American democratic societies, contradicted the standing order's principle of unity and the republican idea that everyone should be directed toward a singular common good. The French Revolution had obviously degenerated into a hideous scene of despotism, and now the French were bent on exporting "the *demoralizing Principles* of the *old* Continent" to the United States. "Yes, my brethren," bellowed Jedidiah Morse of Charlestown, Massachusetts, "it is a sacred truth, that our most precious religious and political interests are at this moment imminently endangered, by *the hostile designs, the insidious arts and demoralizing principles of a* FOREIGN NATION; and I plainly declare to you that I mean the FRENCH NATION."[95] The French were so "insidious" because rather than risk a frontal assault on the United States, they were trying to worm their way to influence by manipulating their American minions. The ministry deemed the gathering domestic opposition to the Adams administration illegitimate and instead characterized political dissenters as either dupes of the French or opportunists. In 1799, Nathanael Emmons could not acknowledge any valid complaint with the government and concluded that "there must be, therefore, some men behind the curtain, who are pushing on the populace to open sedition and rebellion. It is highly probable, that the late insurgents in Pennsylvania were corrupted and deluded, by some artful and influential characters, who have chosen to lie concealed from the public eye." Likewise, Azel Backus's 1798 Connecticut election sermon, *Absalom's Conspiracy*, catechized legislators on the problem of faction. He described how "ambitious and designing men commonly address men's passions and flatter their prejudices."[96] Indeed, the established ministry responded to its political opponents much as it did to its sectarian rivals: it painted both as at best misguided, if not downright sinister.

Equally as troubling as the problem of faction, if not more so, was the rising challenge of infidelity, which the ministry detected in both France and America. Infidelity appeared to be a social sin of epic proportions and abraded the establishment's belief in the social necessity of religion. Despite their many significant differences of opinion on other matters, both established and dissenting ministers could agree that the 1790s were a time of "open war with error and infidelity."[97] Once again, the French had innovated with "the revolutionizing maxims . . . that *religion* of all descriptions is a *cheat*—that there is no *Revelation*—no *Redeemer*—and no *God*" and then tried "to diffuse the poison of their irreligious and disorganizing sentiments among the people of America."[98] Moreover, there was no reason to praise France for having destroyed popery, according to Jonathan French, because "if the Pope be displaced, and the devil incarnate hath himself taken the chair; if instead of peace and tranquility though guided by bigotry and blind superstition; if instead of these, atheism, bloodshed, rapine, and tyranny have succeeded, with a train of tenfold greater evils than the popish hierarchy itself, bad as it was, does this look like the downfall of the man of sin?"[99] Not only were the French stirrers of faction, which was bad enough, but also, to make matters worse, they appeared to be flagrantly at war with Christianity.

Although analytically distinguishable, the threats of faction and infidelity were usually jumbled together by established ministers. These were men, after all, who had been trying to maintain the connection between government and religion since before the American Revolution. During the 1760s and 1770s, they had seen the British government as a threat to both political and religious liberty, and in the 1790s they regarded France as the source of a similar dual threat.[100] Opposition to government, in the minds of established ministers, went hand in hand with atheism. As John Prince of Salem, Massachusetts, asked, "who are the open and avowed opposers of christianity? Are they not those men who are endeavouring to put down all rule and all authority in every nation, that *their* will and power alone may govern the world?"[101] Jedidiah Morse depicted the two-pronged French assault in his sermon on the national fast in 1799. His chosen text was Ps. 11:3, which he paraphrased for the current situation as, "If RELIGION and GOVERNMENT, the foundations here meant, be subverted and overthrown, what could the best of men, however righteous their cause, hope to do to any good effect in such a state of things?" It was a critical time because, as the ministry had argued all along, without religion the republic could not endure. "Our dangers are of two kinds," according to Morse's analysis, "those which affect our religion, and those which affect our government. They are, however, so closely allied that they cannot, with propriety, be separated. The foundations which support the interests of Christianity, are also necessary to support a free and equal government like our own."[102] Samuel Austin rolled foreign and domestic faction and infidelity into one as he sought to separate the American and French Revolutions: "We deny, that we gave example, or furnished patronage, to that endless ringing of changes, which is heard on the other side of the Atlantic. . . . And are the factious among ourselves, the demagogues of a party, or the retailers of their infidelity, and calumny; are these the legitimate children of our country, as an independent, and consolidated Republic? No. They are a spurious offspring. Like mushrooms, they have a recent, and unsolid existence."[103]

In this context, the ministry's warnings reached a nearly hysterical and apocalyptic crescendo in 1798 and 1799.[104] At that time, the rumor of a conspiracy on the part of the Bavarian Illuminati gained repute among the standing order.[105] A transatlantic fraternity, the Illuminati purportedly aimed "to overturn all existing governments and religion." The Illuminati scare embodied all of the ministry's fears of foreign and domestic subversion and apostasy taken to their wildest extreme. It explained how both religion and government were under attack simultaneously.[106] Jedidiah Morse claimed to have a list of American "Illuminees" and blamed them for everything from domestic political animosity to "the industrious circulation of baneful and corrupting books, and the consequent wonderful spread of infidelity, impiety and immorality."[107] The social sins the ministry detected now were not the result of the usual backsliding or indifference but the poisonous fruit of a sinister conspiracy deliberately sown.

Moreover, the Illuminati scare was not confined to just a few paranoid cranks within the top echelons of the standing order, as the diary of Joseph Goffe attests. In the late 1790s, Goffe was an obscure minister laboring in the rural North Parish of Sutton, Massachusetts. Nonetheless, his reading connected him to the broader intellectual and political currents of the southern New England clergy. In November 1798, Goffe noted in his diary that he read both "Illuminati. — a discovery of dark & diabolical dangers against G[od] & men" and "Robison on Freemasonry." On August 9 of the following year, he "read the whole of the first Vol. of the Abbe Barruel, on the antixian [antichristian] conspiracy." In other words, Goffe was conversant with the key texts of the Illuminati episode.[108] Although we cannot know exactly how Goffe responded to these books, it is safe to assume, based on other diary entries, that he took from his readings the typical understandings of Congregational Federalism. For instance, on the federal fast days called by President Adams for May 9, 1798, and April 25, 1799, Goffe preached from two classic texts of the standing order's public Christianity, Jer. 18:7-10 and Prov. 14:34, respectively. Furthermore, he spent the evening of January 15, 1797, in conversation with several men, during which he "highly censured Tom Paine & all deists." Goffe's example shows how the Illuminati scare both informed the ministry's outlook on the world in the late 1790s and motivated clergymen to greater exertions in defense of government and religion.[109]

In the hour of crisis, many established ministers joined Goffe in summoning their congregations to stay the course. They circled the wagons, so to speak, around the Federalist party and New England Congregationalism. First, in response to the dangers of faction, they urged allegiance to the constitution and the Adams administration. Nathan Strong made a typical remark when he said, "The present state of Europe teaches us to reverence our own civil constitutions." Joseph Eckley of Boston's Old South Church proclaimed "supporting the National Government" to be a duty. He added, "Thanks be to *Heaven!* for giving us an ADAMS, with a WASHINGTON."[110] Such conservative pleading became the chief response of the standing order to the increasingly polarized atmosphere of the 1790s. For example, when President Washington issued a proclamation on January 1, 1795, for a day of thanksgiving to be held on February 19, the established ministry heartily complied.[111] In unsettled times, ministers built sermons around the themes of obedience and submission, using texts such as Titus 3:1, "Put them in mind to be subject to principalities and powers, to obey magistrates, to be ready to every good work," or 1 Tim. 2:1-3, "I exhort therefore, that, first of all, supplications, prayers, intercessions, and giving of thanks, be made for all men; For kings, and for all that are in authority; that we may lead a quiet and peaceable life in all godliness and honesty. For this is good and acceptable in the sight of God our Saviour." "It is extremely criminal to disobey civil rulers, and oppose the regular administration of government," Nathanael Emmons flatly declared.[112] Along these same lines, ministers stressed the virtues of patriotism. Boston's John Lathrop justified his pro-administration commentary by arguing that patriotism was eminently Christian. He even went so far as to claim, based upon Luke 19:41-42, that Jesus "was also a true patriot" because when "he foresaw, and predicted the miseries which were coming on Jerusalem, he wept over it." In short, the ministry held to its previously declared principles but tilted to the right in accenting the duty of supporting the authorities, in particular the administration of John Adams. "Congregational ministers," one scholar has concluded, "began sounding warnings based on old deferential politics, revealing an outlook very congenial with that of the Federalist party, an outlook which was, in fact, drawing them within its circle."[113]

Second, the clergy responded by calling for repentance and a renewal of godliness. The ministry had preached this before, of course, but now it became more urgent. Indeed, the call to obey and support the government hinged upon such piety, on account of "the folly of endeavouring to support good government and a system of rational and equal liberty without the aid of religion." John Prince also based this call to fidelity upon the wrath of Providence. He asked his listeners to reflect on their sins and compare them with all that God had done for them. He then said, "May a sense of the dangers which hang over us lead us to repentance, and fervent prayer, that God may turn from us these tokens of his anger, and cause us more highly to esteem and improve, in future, his spiritual and temporal blessings."[114] In a 1798 sermon, Timothy Dwight detailed the necessary kind of godliness. He chose as his text Rev. 16:15, "Behold I come as a thief. Blessed is he that watcheth, and keepeth his garments, lest he walk naked, and they see his shame." From this he explained, "To watch and keep the garments is, of course, so to observe the heart and the life, so carefully to resist temptation and abstain from sin, and so faithfully to cultivate holiness and perform duty, that the heart and life shall be adorned with the white robes of evangelical virtue, the unspotted attire of spiritual beauty." He hoped to stabilize the state through religion, knowing that "where religion prevails, Illuminatism cannot make disciples, a French directory cannot govern, a nation cannot be made slaves, nor villains, nor atheists, nor beasts. To destroy us, therefore, in this dreadful sense, our enemies must first destroy our Sabbath, and seduce us from the house of God."[115]

As Dwight's remarks indicate, part of repentance, or turning back toward God, meant turning away from France. Dwight and several of his colleagues cited this section's epigraph, Rev. 18:4, and interpreted it to mean that revolutionary France was to be avoided like the plague.[116] Like the Israelites at the Passover, Nathan Strong urged Americans to avoid the pollution of their enemies and take shelter until God's deliverance. "If there be any people so situated that they may possibly escape the weight of calamity (as it is hoped the people of this nation are) it becomes them to stand at a distance from the scene of plagues, and not come into a state of intimacy, lest they be necessitated to drink the dregs of a very bitter cup." Strong's advice forms an interesting contrast to the buoyant internationalism of the 1780s. At that time, clergymen expressed confidence that the United States would be a model for the world; now some washed their hands of events across the Atlantic, retreating to fortress America. "None but a person bereft of reason would chain himself to a burning pile," Strong concluded. Elijah Parish advised the same course of action, saying, "Be warned, oh my country, to fly the fatal abyss. To put the least confidence in French promises; to hazard any thing dear on the sincerity of their treaties, would be, like sailing to the torrid zone in a ship of ice."[117]

These calls to seek the old paths and walk therein, in the imagery of Jer. 6:16, were based in part on the standing order's self-concept as steadfast conservators of tradition. Establishment ministers had argued all along that law should be nearly immutable to protect the society from instability.[118] In the late 1790s, they joined Federalist spokesmen in portraying themselves as champions of tried-and-true common sense, as opposed to the speculative and untrustworthy plans of "philosophers" and social theoreticians. David Daggett, for example, a Yale alumnus, New Haven lawyer, and state legislator, satirized philosophical speculation and social novelty in his 1799 July Fourth oration, *Sun-Beams may be extracted from Cucumbers, but the process is tedious*. The title derived from a fictional land where scientists tried wrong-headed experiments that tried to create "a pin-cushion out of a piece of marble," a sheep without wool, a society without language, and a process by which sunshine could be recaptured from cucumbers in order to warm a garden in inclement weather. Daggett also sneered at Enlightenment projects ranging from balloon travel and scientific agriculture to new methods of child-rearing, which he contrasted with the old paths of wisdom and the Bible. The French, of course, were living examples of the plunge into experimental excess. The solution was support of the Adams administration and an allegiance to the fathers of New England, who had always followed "common sense." "They delivered [good government and good morals] to us as a sacred deposit, and if we suffer them to be destroyed by the tinselled refinements of this age, we shall deserve the reproaches, with which, impartial justice will cover such a pusillanimous race."[119] The standing order embodied the established center of New England society, and it prepared to defend that ground against newfangled challengers.

At the same time that the ministry redoubled its efforts to cement an attachment to patriotism and piety, it also began to revise its interpretation of the providential place of the United States. Toward the century's end, ministers of the standing order remained ambiguous regarding the providential purpose in American history. There were some, like Timothy Dwight, who continued to express confidence that the blessings of Providence would shelter the United States. "Look through the history of our country," he said. "You will find scarcely less glorious and wonderful proofs of divine protection and deliverance, uniformly administered through every period of our existence as a people, than shone to the people of Israel in Egypt, in the wilderness, and in Canaan. Can it be believed, can it be, that Christianity has been so planted here, the Church of God so established, so happy a Government constituted, and so desirable a state of Society begun, merely to shew them to the world, and then destroy them?"[120] Yet, a stronger consensus was beginning to crystallize around the idea that in tumultuous times, the church, and not necessarily the nation state, was the one institution God would uphold no matter what.

Most ministers of the standing order argued that regardless of developments in the political world, God would protect the church. They expressed faith that the church would be a shelter amid the storm. Nathan Strong, for instance, took the position that "the church wishes the favor of the state and thanks those pious rulers who say to her *God speed thee*; but she can stand without them; because she hath an Almighty King who rules in the midst of the nations, and in the midst of his enemies and has promised his protection." The following year, also on the anniversary thanksgiving, he sounded the same theme.

> The whole divine government of men is with reference to his church—to the interests of his kingdom, and the accomplishment of the purposes of his grace. The cabinet of earthly princes is subservient to the king of Zion; and the armies and the heroes of hostile nations, although they mean not to be thus considered and know not by whom they are girded, he calls his armies and his servants to execute the purposes of his counsel, and avenge him on his enemies who know not his name, or have departed from the faith which he gave them to keep.[121]

Ministers intended such upbeat forecasts to dispel anxiety. Jedidiah Morse projected a confident front when he argued, "The Wise and Mighty GOD is accomplishing his grand designs; and the winding up of the awful and tremendous scene now acting in our world, will doubtless be glorious to himself." Cyprian Strong, too, found "a stable and unfailing source of comfort, in the most dark and gloomy times, and amidst the changes and revolutions which take place, in the rotation of events, respecting the present world" in the fact that "God is both able and fully determined, to establish his kingdom."[122]

In conclusion, New England clergymen in the late 1790s responded to the French Revolution and domestic political contention with such antipathy because these events appeared to fundamentally negate their corporate outlook. The establishment's public Christianity extended along two lines in the period from 1783 to 1799. First, established ministers interpreted the place of the United States in the providential scheme of history. The American Revolution had challenged them to seek an understanding of its significance, which they found in the Revolution's protection of liberty and the church. Their discussion of the Revolution's likely providential ramifications contributed, although ambivalently, to the formation of embryonic American nationalism. Second, Congregational ministers prescribed the pattern of the righteous community, which they said would consist of an established church and closely cooperating state, both of which pursued a common goal of service to God. Magistrate and minister existed in a symbiotic relationship designed to foster social order and Christian virtue. The French Revolution and the concurrent domestic polarization not only appeared to deny claims of the global impact of the American Revolution and the necessity of church-state unity but also elicited an alteration in the standing order's social pronouncements. In the late 1790s, the established ministry raised the volume of its conventional calls for piety and order. The French Revolution and the initial rise of political party conflict also caused a slight separation to appear in the seam between church and state, which would develop into a more open rift in the years ahead. The ministry developed early doubts about the wisdom of placing so much reliance on the state, and many clergymen stressed instead the endurance of the church.

For their part, dissenters from the standing order rejected the establishment's formulation of the righteous community. Most obviously they did so on account of their objection to taxation in support of the established churches, but they also predicated their dissent on ideological issues of individual rights and their definitions of church and community, which were at variance with the standing order's. In the years after 1800, the challenges of the dissenters and domestic political rivals proved to be much more significant threats to the standing order than the French Revolution ever could be. These nineteenth-century events proved the wisdom of Joseph Eckley's observation, "*Convulsions* in the State, must always be productive of *Convulsions* in the Church."[123]

THREE

—⋖⋗—

Jeffersonian Disillusions and Dreams
1799–1818

D URING THE LAST TWO DECADES of the eighteenth century, the standing orders of
southern New England had built and defended a two-pronged link between religion and society. The establishments' public Christianity rested on the premises
that God's Providence superintended all human affairs, especially with regard to nations and the church, and that Christian piety played the critical role in fostering social harmony. In light of these convictions, Congregational ministers interpreted the
providential significance of the American republic and recommended strategies for
diffusing Christian virtue. Specifically, they discerned profound purposes for the new
nation and its system of government—even if they divided over the existence of a national covenant—and called for the close cooperation of magistrate and minister, or
Moses and Aaron, to promote societal godliness.

Social and political developments during the two decades from 1799 to 1818 presented the establishments in Connecticut and Massachusetts with colossal challenges to both aspects of this religiosocial ideology. Ministers at first reacted by reit-
erating many of their old prescriptions for the godly society. In the first years of the
nineteenth century, established clergymen preached repentance and a return to the
tried-and-true paths of the righteous founders of New England. They also adjured
magistrates to uphold their end of the partnership of Moses and Aaron. However,
growing frustrations with these defensive solutions, especially in their relationship
with the magistracy, left established ministers groping toward a new conception of
the godly society. Moreover, they could no longer envision any kind of a positive role
for the United States. As clergymen sought to stay abreast of the changing cultural
landscape, they could not escape an engagement with the partisan warfare that was
polarizing the country. Jeffersonian successes rekindled old, apocalyptic fears of a
conspiracy against religion and government. The first party competition between
Federalists and Democratic-Republicans forced the established ministry to reassess
both its understanding of the United States as an instrument of Providence and its association with the civil leadership.

The nineteenth century had seemingly begun well enough for the standing

84

order, as it welcomed the new century exuding a deep sense of confidence. Ministers expressed that assurance through a special sermon, the "century sermon." Several used the occasion of January 1, 1801, or January 4, the first Sunday of the new century, to preach a message dedicated to a review of past events, a restatement of the role of the United States in the plans of Providence, and a call to improve the passage of time by seeking faith in Christ. Deuteronomy 32:7, "Remember the days of old, consider the years of many generations," was the text chosen by Abiel Holmes, minister of Cambridge, Massachusetts, for his sermon, and it captured the tone for the day. Such a day of retrospection, clergymen argued, reaffirmed the belief in Providence's control of history. They traced the hand of Providence in American history from the founding of New England through the winning of the Revolution and beyond, to the drafting of the constitution and the preservation of the new nation from the recent European war. "If, my christian friends," concluded Timothy Alden of Portsmouth, New Hampshire, "we cannot see a special overruling providence, in these various mercies, and thousands of others, which have been poured upon us, like the manna upon antient Israel, from the first landing of our fathers, to the present day, neither should we see it, we may be bold to assert, though transported to the joys of the heaven of heavens." The eighteenth century had witnessed momentous events, and these merited a time of thanksgiving and praise on the part of grateful Americans. The future, too, looked bright to many clergymen, such as Joseph Lathrop of West Springfield, Massachusetts, who celebrated U.S. gains "in population, wealth, navigation and learning," in addition to a government that "rendered the nation prosperous and happy."[1]

Before the close of the nineteenth century's first decade, however, several prominent ministers of the establishment would denounce the federal government that they had so recently and lavishly hailed as a blessing of Providence. In contrast to the hopeful pronouncements with which so many greeted the nineteenth century, a host of leading clergymen braced for some sort of apocalyptic climax to events just a dozen years later. Dissenters from the establishment, however, found reason to exult in the course of American history in the first years of the century. They celebrated the Republicans' ascent and laced their denunciations of the establishment with the potent rhetoric of Jeffersonianism. The following two paragraphs sketch the changes that buffeted and altered the standing order's attempts to connect religion and society. They also reveal the shrill rhetorical pitch that the debate over Christianity's place in public life had reached by 1808 and 1809.

On April 7, 1808, the annual fast day in Massachusetts, Elijah Parish delivered a sermon before his church in Byfield. This Essex County Congregationalist warned that the United States was hurtling toward destruction on account of association with the French Antichrist. He accused the Jeffersonians on the state and national levels of being "friendly, and *partial* to the interests of Anti-Christ." It was incumbent on the clergy, Parish argued, "to instruct their people concerning the real state of the church and the world . . . [in order to] resist this gangrene of moral death." The United States had to enact a change of policy, shake off the ensnaring overtures of France, and keep from becoming collaborators in that unholy nation's plot to destroy Christianity. Parish directed his "piercing eye" to the congregation and concluded, "If you value your own peace and safety here; if you would not pull down the judg-

Elijah Parish. Courtesy American Antiquarian Society.

ments of God on your families, your neighbors, and your country; if you would not with all the friends of Anti-Christ sink into that lake, which burneth forever and ever; then fly from this unholy enemy."[2]

The political situation that so disturbed Parish elated Elias Smith. A little more than a year after Parish's fast-day sermon, Smith delivered a July Fourth oration at Taunton, Massachusetts. An independent editor and itinerant, he had formerly pastored the Baptist church in Woburn, Massachusetts, before rejecting all denominational traditions in 1800 and labeling himself simply as a "Christian." For Smith, the Democratic-Republicans had preserved the Revolution's heritage of liberty from a Federalist hijacking. He praised their commitment to religious freedom, as opposed to the practice of the standing order, which he lumped with other Federalist tyrannies. Whereas Parish viewed present events with apocalyptic dread, Smith was upbeat: "As it respects things of religion, the situation we are in as a nation, is truly

Elias Smith. Courtesy American Antiquarian Society.

pleasing and encouraging to all the friends of truth, notwithstanding many tell us it is a melancholy day as it respects the state of religion. . . . Thousands have of late been turned to the Lord; and while the sound of the trumpet and the alarm of war is heard in the different parts of the old lands, here the gospel trumpet is sounded . . . [and] thousands rejoice in the light of life, and in hope of glory, honor, immortality, and eternal life." Smith explicitly tied the rise of Jeffersonian politics and its defeat of Federalism to the birth of a Christianity unfettered by the tyranny of the established churches. He closed with a fusion of his Jeffersonian liberalism and his populist evangelicalism. "My brethren," he entreated, "while thus enjoying these privileges under a republican government, let us be *republicans* indeed. Many are *republicans* as to *government*, and yet are but half *republicans*, being in matters of religion still bound to a *Catechism, creed, covenant*, or a superstitious priest. Venture to be as independent in things of religion, as in those which respect the government in which you live."[3]

These excerpts are emblematic of the larger shifts taking place during the early 1800s in the debate over the connection between religion and society in southern New England. Both, for instance, point to the dramatic impact of the first party competition, which catalyzed an ideological reevaluation for the ministerial thinkers involved. For figures of the establishment like Elijah Parish, the rise of the Democratic-Republican party was symptomatic of a serious malady in the body politic. They criticized Republican men and policies, none more so than the War of 1812. Reasserting their role as prophetic interpreters of Providence, they reevaluated the meaning of the American experiment. As opposed to the optimistic conclusions they drew at the end of the Revolution or even the beginning of the nineteenth century, established ministers now feared God's judgment and national destruction, even going so far as to repudiate the constitution. Their earlier reliance on the role of the magistracy likewise became problematic.

Dissenters like Smith, however, took a far different lesson from the Revolution of 1800. They rebuked the established ministry for political meddling, while the rise of the Democratic-Republicans equipped them with new critical arguments and political allies. This change in political culture, which was interwoven with equally dramatic changes in the religious landscape, shifted the contexts in which the standing order had operated. The standing order had rested on a number of factors, including legal advantages, numerical dominance, and a supportive association with the region's ruling class. Beginning at the tail end of the eighteenth century and progressing with astonishing swiftness, changes of seismic proportions in New England politics, culture, and society undercut these old foundations of the standing order and toppled it.

The Standing Order's Disillusionment

> When the righteous are in authority, the people rejoice: but when the wicked beareth rule, the people mourn.
>
> —Prov. 29:2

Although always claiming to be nonpartisan, the Congregational clergy entered the political controversies of the first party period with a vengeance. Overwhelmingly Federalist, these ministers offered a detailed and sustained critique of Thomas Jefferson personally and the Democratic-Republican party he inspired, using the language of their public Christianity. Historians at least since Henry Adams in the 1880s have marked the New England clergy's utter loathing of the third president.[4] The ensuing section begins by analyzing the standing order's detestation of Jefferson in order to show how it grew out of the ministry's public Christianity and was not merely a partisan ploy. Ministers painted the Republicans with the same alleged qualities of infidelity and anarchy with which they had tarred the French revolutionaries in the previous decade. They then summoned their listeners to adhere to the wisdom of the New England past and to put their confidence in the leadership of Federalist magistrates and standing order ministers. However, over time the ministry's continuing disgust with the Jeffersonians altered its public Christianity. In the dozen years between 1800 and 1812, the standing order lost all of its earlier optimism regarding the providentially appointed role of the United States. The inability of New England to affect the course of national politics led established ministers to question the way in which they had endowed recent American history with such significance. The continuing control of the federal government by the Virginia dynasty and the policies enacted by the Democratic-Republicans soured the New England clergy on the union. From the perspective of established ministers, events of the early nineteenth century drained the reservoir of expectancy that they had built up behind the Revolution, constitution, and Federalist period. Meanwhile, the established clergy's natural allies among New England's Federalist political leadership had likewise proven to be a disappointment. By the outbreak of war in the summer of 1812, the standing order had lost faith in the magistracy, renounced the national government, and was predicting disaster.

The election of Thomas Jefferson as third president of the United States deeply troubled the overwhelming majority of New England's Congregational ministers. They had made it an axiom of their social prescriptions that a ruler needed to be godly above all else. As Ludovicus Weld of Hampton, Connecticut, remarked, "When men of corrupt principles and licentious lives, secure general confidence, we have just occasion for alarm. They will lead multitudes into their false principles, and extensively diffuse the poison of their vicious habits." Whatever his personal religiosity may have been in actuality, Washington had at least appeared to embody these traits of piety and had endorsed the connection between religion and society in his public pronouncements.[5] Jefferson, however, openly affronted the standing order's characterization of the godly ruler, and Congregational clergymen were not hesitant to raise their objections to his qualifications or to elaborate on the probable ill consequences of his holding office.

Ministers could register their dissent from the turn in national politics obliquely. For instance, William Emerson, minister of Boston's First Church, concluded his 1802 Independence Day oration on a conservative note by calling on his hearers to "preserve unchanged the same correct feelings of liberty, the same purity of manners, the same principles of wisdom and piety, of experience and prescription, the same seminaries of learning, temples of worship, and castles of defence, which immortalize the memory of your ancestors." In this way, they would "witness a reign of such enlightened policy, firmness of administration, and unvaried justice, as shall recal [sic] and prolong to your enraptured eyes THE AGE OF WASHINGTON AND OF ADAMS." He left it conspicuously unspoken that the age of Jefferson was not worthy of preservation.[6]

Other ministers refused to bow to the dignity of the presidential office and brazenly listed Jefferson's shortcomings. The most ingenious assault on Jefferson's character came from Nathanael Emmons of Franklin, Massachusetts. Emmons's 1801 fast sermon set a pattern in attacking Jefferson as an enemy of righteousness. Using his talents of biblical exegesis, he drew an extended analogy between Thomas Jefferson, the successor of Washington and Adams, and Jeroboam, the successor of David and Solomon, who was the wicked king who "drave [sic] Israel from following the Lord." Jeroboam had duped "the unthinking multitude" into believing that their taxes were onerously high, had "totally apostatized from the religion of his country" while living abroad, and "made himself king, by disaffecting the people to the administration of his predecessor; and he caused this disaffection, by basely misrepresenting the wise measures of that wise and excellent ruler." For anyone with the slightest awareness of current events, the parallel between Jeroboam and Jefferson was clear, and Americans had to beware lest they suffer as the Israelites had under Jeroboam. As Emmons concluded, "Let us all learn this lesson, and especially those, who have complained of the late wise and gentle administration of government. It is more than possible, that our nation may find themselves in the hand of a Jeroboam, who will drive them from following the Lord; and whenever they do, they will rue the day, and detest the folly, delusion, and intrigue, which raised him to the head of the United States."[7]

Jefferson's writings also opened him to criticism. Basing himself on Prov. 29:2, Elijah Parish asked, "If the people mourn when the wicked beareth rule, then have not the people of the United States reason to mourn?" The evidence for the wickedness of the nation's ruler was to be found in Jefferson's book, *Notes on the State of Virginia.* Parish contrasted Jefferson and his published skepticism regarding the biblical account of the flood, which he termed "frank, open and bold denials of revelation," with the "righteous" governor of Massachusetts, Caleb Strong. And to Jefferson's opinion that "'it does me *no injury* for my neighbour to say there are twenty gods or no God,'" Parish scoffed incredulously, "Is it no injury in a society of Christians to have men avow themselves pagans and atheists? Does it not tend to unhinge and destroy all social order? Would any Christian parent wish his children educated where men make a god of every thing but God; or where in their hearts and words they banish God from the universe? Do not such 'neighbours' grieve, and distress, and 'injure,' good men? do they not harden and render bad men worse?" Jefferson's unorthodox sentiments had to be exposed and countered, Parish reasoned, because "the depravity of a ruler as spontaneously descends to the people, as the rivulet runs down the hill."[8] Other clergymen assailed Jefferson as a toadying Francophile and an adulterous atheist. Along these lines, Festus Foster of Petersham, Massachusetts, accused Jefferson of having breached his own embargo to import a special shipment of the writings of Tom Paine, "the most obscene and scurrilous infidel of the age."[9] Thomas Jefferson appeared to contradict all the established ministry's prior instructions regarding the importance of Christian virtue to a ruler's character.

The Congregational ministry's criticisms extended beyond Jefferson personally to the movement he represented. Established clergymen portrayed the Democratic-Republican party as having contracted the anarchic and atheistic diseases of the French Revolution. In fact, the accusations of "infidelity" directed against the French Revolution in the 1790s were transferred to the ministry's domestic political enemies. For instance, Worcester's Samuel Austin drew a connection between the French Revolution, Jeffersonian democracy, and the destruction of religion and government when he asked,

> Have any of you gone to the school of French atheism and revolution, the hot-bed of faction and massacre, faction and massacre inevitably terminating in anarchy or despotism? . . . Have you conjured up, by the aid of political magicians, new-fangled notions of liberty and the rights of man, with which your forefathers had no ac-

quaintance? And have you entered upon the philosophic *projet* of extirpating Christianity; prostrating the most useful religious institutions, which it has been the glory of New England to have so carefully cherished; levelling all distinctions in civil society; equalizing property, and opening the flood-gates of lawless licentiousness?[10]

He asserted that there were "incontestible [*sic*] evidences" of a conspiracy to destroy Christianity orchestrated by the Democratic-Republicans in Washington, D.C., in concert with their French allies, who advocated "that system of European revolution, which is founded in Atheism, which has terminated in one of the most absolute and oppressive despotisms that the world ever felt, a despotism founded in infidelity, *founded in infidelity I say.*" Henry Cumings of Billerica, Massachusetts, also fretted over the threat of infidelity. In 1801, he warned that "the moral complexion of the times has become unusually alarming, on account of the uncommon prevalence of infidelity and diffusion of corrupt principles, tending to deprave the minds and manners of people." This moral decay had come from overseas, from "a great European nation, [that] hath given encouragement to infidelity in this happy country, and inspired our libertines and sceptics with unusual boldness, in their endeavors to rob us of our faith, and banish the light of the glorious gospel from the land!" This conspiracy against Christianity threatened to undermine American society, and Cumings knew who was at fault. The people behind this plot were "our leading disorganizers" because they saw Christianity "as the grand obstacle to the execution of their political schemes of licencious [*sic*] democracy." Clearly, Cumings meant to bring the Democratic-Republicans to mind when he pointed his finger at those advocating "licencious democracy." It is within this context that Elijah Parish made the previously mentioned remark about the Jeffersonians being "friendly, and *partial* to the interests of Anti-Christ." And not only were Republicans at the federal level infidels. Festus Foster, referring to the Religious Freedom Act of 1811 (discussed later), blasted the governor of Massachusetts and the state legislature for working to undermine the Congregational establishment.[11] In the eyes of standing order ministers, religious infidelity became a political party with the Jeffersonian Republicans.

In its fear of a Democratic-Republican conspiracy, the clergy joined other Federalists.[12] Ludovicus Weld warned that the Jeffersonians were up to no good. Although they were "those very persons who styled themselves '*The Friends of the People,*'" such professions were bogus and a cover for their actual, nefarious goal of a grab for power. Like Weld, Asahel Hooker of Goshen, Connecticut, alerted his listeners to beware of "a profusion of smooth words, and fair professions of regard to 'the rights and liberties of the people.'" The Republicans' incessant clamoring for the people's rights was really just a clever ploy, "the lullaby of liberty and equality," that they used to gain office. Once in power, the clergy cautioned, they would reveal their real motive of subverting religion and government.[13]

Within the foregoing context, one can better decipher the multiple messages contained within the well-known political cartoon, "The Providential Detection." There is some scholarly debate surrounding when this image was published. Stephanie A. Munsing contends for 1797, reasoning that the picture was produced in "celebration of the narrow defeat of Thomas Jefferson . . . in the election of 1796." The May 1797 American publication of Jefferson's letter to Philip Mazzei, featured prominently in the picture, supports Munsing's chronology. Earlier students of

THE PROVIDENTIAL DETECTION

The Providential Detection. Courtesy American Antiquarian Society.

American graphic arts had speculated that the print was brought out to influence the election of 1800, and certainly the conspiratorial themes it raises were more fevered in 1799 or 1800 than in 1797. Whatever the exact publication date, "The Providential Detection" is a magnificent Federalist fantasy of deliverance that encapsulates the Congregational clergy's estimation of Jefferson and his party. The cartoon depicts the sage of Monticello kneeling before the "Altar to Gallic Despotism," which certainly comports with the argument for his Francophilia. Jefferson carries with him his letter to Mazzei, in which he accused Federalists of being "an Anglican, monarchial and aristocratical party." He is just about to burn the "Constitution & Independence" of the United States in a fire fed by the writings of such notorious freethinkers as

Godwin, Paine, and Voltaire and leading Democratic-Republican newspapers. Obviously, here are references to the alleged Democratic-Republican and French revolutionary conspiracies against government and religion. To drive that point home, Satan or another of his demonic minions crouches below the altar. Just in the nick of time the national eagle—like the intervening angel of the Lord at Abraham's intended sacrifice of Isaac—swoops in, seizes the constitution, and is about to smite Jefferson's face with its other outstretched talon. Presiding over this scene of deliverance is a large eye, gazing down from the clouds. Munsing refers to this as "the eye of Liberty," but she should call it the eye of God in light of the suffusive providentialism of eighteenth-century rhetoric. "The Providential Detection" bears graphic testimony to the power of the Federalist clergy's hyperbolic portrayal of the Jeffersonians' Gallic infidelity and self-serving anarchy.[14]

The continuing appeal of the Democratic-Republican party, regardless of its obvious infidel tendencies, perplexed the Congregational clergy. Support for such candidates could indicate only that something was seriously amiss with the electorate, that Americans had become a "degenerate people." Ministers brought forth a string of diagnostic terms to account for Republican successes. The public, they said, had been seized with "delusion," "folly," "phrenzy," "infatuation," or "madness." "What astonishing delusions have prevailed, and are still prevailing in France, and in many of the states and kingdoms of Europe? . . . And who can tell when or where these delusions will end?" queried Nathanael Emmons. He answered somberly, "Human nature is the same in America, as in all other parts of the world. We are no less exposed to be carried down the current of delusion, than others were, who have been overwhelmed and destroyed." David Osgood, Congregational clergyman of Medford, Massachusetts, was likewise dumbfounded to ask whether it was "conceivable, that the nation of Gideon or the nation of Washington, after having for years rejoiced in the rich blessings derived from such rulers, . . . after having received from them their last solemn paternal advice, should, in direct contradiction to such advice, be capable of giving their suffrages for rulers known to be of a different and opposite character? Of all the follies to which human beings are liable, is there any more unaccountable, more astonishing than this?" The situation was one of the blind leading the blind because, according to Samuel Austin, not only the voters but also the rulers were gripped by "unaccountable infatuation, approaching even to phrenzy and madness."[15]

Ministers of the establishment who criticized the Jeffersonians did not limit their attacks to identifying such general tendencies as "infidelity" or "phrenzy." Rather, they also took aim at specific policies, which grew out of the Republicans' defective character. The Congregational clergy joined with other New Englanders in denouncing the embargo, an obvious product of "folly." David Osgood was bullish on trade as "preeminently useful and indeed necessary for promoting national wealth and prosperity, spreading general information, advancing arts and knowledge, increasing civilization, refining and polishing the manners of a people, and giving them those improvements which adorn society and constitute its highest felicity." Therefore, he attacked the embargo as sheer idiocy, contrasting the Republicans' incompetence and corruption with the godly paradigm of leadership found in Exod. 18:21, of "able men, such as fear God, men of truth, hating covetousness." Likewise,

Samuel Spring, from maritime Newburyport on the Essex County coast of Massachusetts, lamented the decline of trade, its consequent cost to the national treasury in decreased excise revenue, and the unemployment that resulted from it. He particularly blasted Jefferson's embargo for its pernicious moral tendency: "Idleness was the consequence. Vices of various complexions succeeded of course to the great disadvantage of individuals, families and the community. For idleness is the fruitful mother of wicked customs and habits, which are so destructive to the best interest of men." "*Who, where* is he who has done this mighty mischief?" demanded Elijah Parish. "Every child can answer. The heralds of the general government have passed through our towns; like the messengers of Job, each had a tale more affecting than his fellow. They have passed along; before them was the garden of Eden, a virtuous people, obedient to the laws. Behind them is the desert of Sodom, violations of law, perjury, and distress. Terrific architects of ruin, can they exult in their tremendous power of annihilation?" There is no more powerful statement of the way in which Democratic-Republican policies such as the embargo had alienated the standing order from the U.S. government.[16]

In short, the vast majority of Congregational clergymen explicitly interpreted the Jeffersonian movement and its policies as national sins. Yet almost to a man, they paradoxically insisted that their pronouncements were not part and parcel of partisan politics. Since the established ministry had advanced a key role for itself in the denunciation of social sins, clergymen argued that their behavior toward the Democratic-Republicans was just an extension of that outlook. Ministers defended their ability to draw a distinction between the bias of "a political partizan, anxious that one system of policy should succeed to the defeat of its opposite," and the disinterested candor of "a messenger of God, standing for the defence of his honour, and the interests of pure and undefiled Christianity."[17]

Joseph Lathrop discussed this difference most clearly. He agreed that clergymen should not embroil themselves in plans "to frame constitutions, settle forms of government, review the doings of legislatures, decide on the comparative merits of candidates for office, the wisdom of national treaties, and other high acts of government." These were the legitimate concerns of the electorate, not the clergy. However, Lathrop countered as erroneous the statement "that a minister ought not to *preach* on matters of government" because that argument "will import, that he may not teach morality, or may not shew its usefulness to society—may not state the principles of government, the social obligations, the relative duties, those which rulers owe to the people, and the people to their rulers and to one another—may not give warning of impending dangers and of divine judgments—may not bear testimony against the sins which cause, or mention the signs which forebode national calamities." Likewise, Samuel Austin admitted that his fast sermon of July 1812 contained "many observations in it, that have respect to the administration of our national government, and the state of our country." Yet, he insisted that "they are produced in evidence to a point of religious instruction. Moral and religious instruction is the drift of every thing that is said."[18] The established ministry boldly upheld its ability to distinguish base partisanship, in which it said it would never engage, from its exalted duty to bring the Word to bear on governmental affairs.

Although the distinction may have been straightforward to Lathrop and like-minded colleagues, the events of the early nineteenth century blurred the lines between the mundane tasks of citizenship and government and the sacred issues of morality and judgment. Furthermore, as analyzed in the next section, an increasing number of New Englanders no longer accepted the legitimacy of this differentiation between partisanship and disinterestedness; to them, the standing order was obviously and offensively Federalist. One senses a certain tone of frustration on this point in Austin's voice when he asked, "Can we not distinguish here? Or, are we determined to be blind to all distinctions which do not favour our prejudices?" The unpopularity of the ministry's pronouncements led Jedidiah Morse—himself no stranger to controversy since the Illuminati crisis in the late-1790s—to try a novel strategy to ward off criticism. Before launching into his denunciation of the War of 1812, Morse devoted the first half of his sermon to restating the case for the obedience due to rulers. This minister of Charlestown, Massachusetts, hoped to show thereby that he was no mere antigovernment ranter. The standing order recognized that some in its audience were chafing under its commentary. Abiel Holmes observed that "the more obviously just and necessary the admonitions which [a minister] utters, the greater reason has he to expect, that some persons, from ignorance and misapprehension; some, from passion and prejudice; some, from devotedness to party; and some, from absolute hatred of all truth, will refuse the counsels, which are offered, and be displeased with the messenger, who delivers them."[19]

Nevertheless, ministers of the standing order claimed to be unconcerned with popularity because they had a higher calling. A deep sense of the "duty" of their office impelled ministers "to bear public testimony against all attempts of those in authority, to destroy the religion and morals of the people," regardless of the consequences. As Holmes had said, they were "messengers" from God, and "wo [*sic*] be to that minister, who dares not apply to the times, in which he lives, those truths of the sacred volume, which are most applicable to them." Many Congregational ministers struck the pose of an Old Testament prophet. For example, Ludovicus Weld devoted most of his sermon on the annual fast of 1804 to explaining the difference between the true prophets who proclaimed God's righteous message and the false ones who pandered to what the sinful wanted to hear. "God's messages to a sinful people are always grating," he noted, "but they must be faithfully delivered by the ambassador, that he merit not the appellation of *false prophet*, and receive not his *fearful doom*." Many applied to themselves Ezekiel's words regarding the duty of the "watchman unto the house of Israel" to warn of approaching disaster.[20]

In addition to issuing their warnings and criticisms of Jefferson and his party, standing order ministers also articulated a conservative message aimed at inoculating the region from the political contagion. In order to wipe out the plague of Jeffersonianism, the standing order initially sought to reiterate its social ideology. Over against the double-headed political and religious disease of the Democratic-Republicans, established ministers urged repentance. After turning away from their folly and sin, New Englanders were advised to turn toward the God-fearing ways of their fathers. Established clergymen advocated education as one important means to foster an adherence to correct principles. Ministers may have claimed that they were advocating traditional, nonpartisan nostrums regarding education and New England traditionalism, and indeed their conventional wisdom antedated the first party struggle. Nevertheless, the implied partisan import of the Federalist clergy's pronouncements cannot be denied. In addition, some clergymen even partook in more or less open support of Federalist politicians. In turn, ministers also renewed their call for the cooperation of Moses and Aaron; troublesome times called for vigilant magistrates and ministers. The standing order's first response to the tumultuous developments of the early nineteenth century was a conservative one.

Standing order ministers in the first dozen years of the nineteenth century repeatedly urged repentance and reformation. The people needed to throw themselves on God's mercy because they were already beginning to feel the sting of his judgments. Samuel Spring's remarks were entirely typical of a host of others: "Nothing less than our deep humiliation[,] genuine sorrow and repentance of sin, will correspond with the obligation of the day [the annual fast of 1809]. . . . The sorrow we ought to feel in the view of the sins we have committed is enough to make hearts of stone melt and bleed." With the uncompromising theological rigor of the New Divinity, he concluded that "your sins and your danger, the mercy of God if you repent, and the vengeance of God if you will not repent, are now before you. Take which you please, God will be glorified. For his justice is as dear to him as his mercy." Such repentance, said Nathan Perkins of Hartford, Connecticut, showed "true patriotism" because it would "bring down a blessing on our land."[21]

After repentance, ministers of the standing order counseled a renewed consecration to "the principles and habits of their ancestors." According to Joseph Strong of Norwich, Connecticut, "the joint demand of gratitude and interest, [dictated] that we carefully select its virtues [the age of the fathers'] and copy them into our own practice." "Innovation," like infidelity, appeared as a dangerous and subversive force to be shunned. Chauncey Lee of Colebrook, Connecticut, for example, railed against "upstart pretenders, visionary theorists and projectors, strutting upon the stilts of *philosophy*, and swelling with the wisdom of Solon, while ignorant of the alphabet of legislation and government." Such warnings carried with them an implicit condemnation of Jeffersonianism.[22] This innovation appeared to be such a threat because it could wipe out the achievements of generations in an instant; it was like a hurricane that could level a forest that had grown over the course of decades, leaving ruin in its wake.[23] The texts from which spokesmen for the establishment chose to preach in the early 1800s well illustrate their conservative mood. For instance, the 1801 Connecticut election preacher, Benjamin Trumbull of North Haven, selected 1 Kings 2:2-3, in which David exhorted Solomon to "keep the charge of the LORD thy God, to walk in his ways, to keep his statutes, and his commandments, and his judgments, and his testimonies." The next year, Joseph Strong preached from a similar text, Jer. 6:16, "Thus saith the LORD, Stand ye in the ways, and see, and ask for the old paths, where is the good way and walk therein, and ye shall find rest for your souls." The incredulous query of Worcester's Aaron Bancroft epitomized the feelings of the rest of the standing order: "Shall we part with the maxims of our venerable ancestors, which time has proved to be wise, for a spirit of innovation, which nothing sacred or profane can restrain?"[24]

Consistent with this emphasis on the conservation of society's ancestral values, ministers of the establishment repeatedly beat their drums on behalf of education. Education, they recognized, could serve as a powerful weapon in the contest "to secure the rising generation from that spirit of innovation, and rage for change, which endanger the primary principles of good order."[25] A focus on knowledge and education appealed especially to the nascent Unitarian wing of the Massachusetts standing order. For instance, as hostilities with Britain were approaching in 1810, Boston's William Ellery Channing called on men in positions of social influence "to fix the understandings of the people on the calamities, that are approaching them; to enlighten the public mind; to improve our moral feelings; to breathe around you an elevated spirit; to fortify as many hearts as possible with the generous purpose to do all, which men can do, for the preservation of their country." In so doing, these shapers of public opinion were not to resort to the vulgar methods of common newspaper editors or demagogic politicians, which were so abhorrent to a refined mind like Channing's.[26] While education may have had a particular resonance with the proto-Unitarians, evangelical Congregationalists took very similar positions. Benjamin Trumbull, pillar of Calvinist orthodoxy and trustee of the Missionary Society of Connecticut, had an equally high view of the importance of education.[27]

Of utmost importance was the education of youth. By attending to the formation of the next generation, ministers could attempt to stamp out the brushfires of innovation before a general conflagration erupted. Or, to change the metaphor, they realized that "it must be a great force indeed, which bends the full grown tree into a new direction. Bent aright at first, very little after labor is required to mould it to that particular situation in the great political machine, where it is most needed."[28] In this regard, women played an essential role. Jesse Appleton's 1814 Massachusetts election sermon best encapsulated the establishment's appeal to education. Appropriately enough, Appleton, as second president of Bowdoin College, preached from Isa. 33:6, "And wisdom and knowledge shall be the stability of thy times, and strength of salvation: the fear of the LORD is his treasure." His one sentence summarized the standing order's thoughts on education in the early nineteenth century: "Those intellectual and moral qualities, so essential to the permanent prosperity of a state, can be promoted extensively in no other way, than by education, early begun and judiciously prosecuted."[29]

Besides uttering such platitudes about preserving the legacy of their ancestors, some ministers engaged in active politicking. If there was a problem with the political system, after all, then perhaps a little ministerial tinkering could set things right? The Rev. Joseph Goffe of the North Parish of Sutton, Massachusetts, for example, dabbled in Federalist politics during the pivotal year of 1800. On January 15, he, along with five thousand other people, attended an elaborate ceremony in nearby Oxford, Massachusetts, in commemoration of Washington's death. The event featured a long procession of soldiers and Freemasons, who marched to the meeting-house, where Goffe's colleague and friend, Samuel Austin, opened the meeting with prayer. Goffe presumably walked with the other clergymen in attendance, located in the line of march between the fifers and drummers in front and the mock funeral bier to their rear. By taking part in the day's festivities, Goffe lent his clerical authority to the Federalist cause. Back in Sutton on February 22, Goffe celebrated Washington's birthday at the South Parish by preaching from 2 Sam. 1:27, "How are the mighty fallen, and the weapons of war perished!" Such events commemorating Washington were important sites for Federalist politics in the late eighteenth and early nineteenth centuries. Again on March 31, Goffe got involved in politicking, this time from behind the scenes. He "prepared an electioneering piece to put in the papers."[30] In these small ways, Goffe employed his talents as a writer and speaker, as well as his status as an ordained clergymen, on behalf of Federalist conservatism. In so doing, he belied his ministerial brethren's professions of complete nonpartisanship and provided ammunition to Democratic-Republican critics.

A full study of such clerical involvement in political activity has yet to be undertaken, but the available evidence suggests that ministers did not rely on it as their primary tool for engaging society. As a more immediate strategy to turn back the Jeffersonian tide, established clergymen looked to their partners among the civil leadership. Just as many established ministers denounced Jefferson on account of their expectation of a ruler's godliness, they responded initially to the political changes of the early nineteenth century by beseeching local and state-level officials to manifest their depiction of the righteous magistrate. One could pile up ad infinitum their insistent claims that "civil rulers . . . must be truly and eminently religious."[31] A favorite biblical text in this regard was Exod. 18:21. In that verse, Moses' father-in-law, Jethro, had advised him to "provide out of all the people able men, such as fear God, men of truth, hating covetousness; and place such over them, to be rulers."[32] Such God-fearing public officials, standing conspicuously before the community, would project a sound example and set the moral tone of society. As Elijah Parish so redolently phrased this belief, "if magistrates be good men, their virtues, like the blossoms of spring, will perfume the country."[33] Therefore, Christian freemen should cast their votes only for such candidates.[34]

Clergymen exhorted such godly magistrates to stand up and do their duty. "The ruler should stand like a rock in the sea, which keeps its place though the storms arise, the billows roll and dash themselves upon it with the greatest violence," said Benjamin Trumbull. "Especially, is this necessary in popular governments; that rulers may act impartially, do justice and judgment, faithfully pursue their own opinions and the public good, though popular prejudices and the popular breath should sometimes be against them." Regardless of the cost, it was the magistrates' duty to track down and extirpate vice. Intoned Amos Bassett of Hebron, Connecticut, "A temperate, yet faithful execution of the laws enacted for the suppression of vice and the preservation of order, is of great importance as a guard to the morals of a people." The magistrates really had no choice; according to Zebulon Ely of Lebanon, Connecticut, "Unrighteous laws and an unfaithful administration of justice tend to unhinge all good order and throw every thing into confusion."[35] As ministers vowed not to flinch in the face of criticism, because they were messengers from God, so they charged magistrates with a similarly sacred calling.

Congregational ministers also commended the safekeeping of the establishment to those in positions of political power. Zebulon Ely waxed joyous over "the idea which makes civil government an handmaid to religion." "A sweet and harmonious union of church and state to promote the general good, must meet the full approbation of heaven," he reasoned (although it clearly met the disapprobation of the Baptists). The ministers of the established churches viewed disestablishment as a misguided crusade pregnant with social disorder. In response, no doubt, to the attacks of dissenters, Joseph Lathrop parried, "If from government you banish religion, the latter will live; but it will take with it all that is amiable and excellent; and government will be like that putrid carcass. . . . Religion is connected with government by the principles of morality, as the soul is connected with the body by the principles of animation; and in both cases, a separation, though it will not extinguish the former, yet will be death to the latter."[36] To support the churches was in the civil leadership's best interest anyway, on account of Christianity's promotion of the virtues necessary to society. Asserted Aaron Bancroft, "it clearly falls within the province of a christian legislature, to support institutions, which facilitate the instruction of people in the truths and duties of religion, which are the means to give efficacy to the precepts of the gospel, and are calculated to instill the spirit of morality and order into the minds of the community." "Thus co-operating like Moses and Aaron," Ely concluded in his 1804 address to the executive and legislators of Connecticut, "may we not confidently hope that our American Israel will present a brazen front to her enemies, supported by the mighty God of Jacob."[37] As part of their overall pattern of taking up defensive positions in the early nineteenth century, established clergymen urged political leaders to stand firm on behalf of the standing order's privileges.

In sum, the established ministry's first response to the political and cultural transformations of the early nineteenth century was to restate the main points of its prior social vision. Congregational ministers called their people to repent, eschew dangerous "innovations," and rely on the trusted team of magistrate and minister to keep the community on an even keel. The standing order had pursued a similar, conservative strategy of admonishment in the 1790s and had beaten back, in New England at least, the perceived threat of French revolutionary infidelity. In the last two decades of the eighteenth century, there had been a mutually recognized convergence of interest between the established ministry and the political leadership of southern New England. The clergy had subserved the governing class through its moral instruction and denunciation of public sinfulness, while the government had set a good example, suppressed vice, and given certain privileges to the church. One hand washed the other, so to speak. The two groups actualized, to a significant degree it appears, the ideal of the cooperation of "Moses and Aaron."

However, by the second half of the nineteenth century's first decade, the standing order was starting to feel frustrated with its conservative battle plan. This feeling settled in most obviously because "innovation" abounded as Virginians kept a lock on Washington, D.C., the number of dissenters surged, and even Massachusetts elected a Democratic-Republican governor in four of the six contests from 1807 to 1812.[38] Less visibly yet ultimately more significantly, even within the Federalist party Moses and Aaron found themselves increasingly at odds during the period of rapid politicization in the first decade of the nineteenth century. The Federalist political leadership, in the interpretation of James M. Banner Jr., instead of concentrating on the clergy's prescribed dicta of godliness, now became preoccupied with getting a leg up on the Democratic-Republicans. Federalist politicians built a party machine aimed at mobilizing voters and winning elections. At the same time that they became "more professional," they also became more adept at the types of electoral "chicanery" that characterized the nineteenth-century urban machines. Banner sees a growing estrangement between the "party figures," who worked in the interests of the organization above all else, and the "occasional politician," chief among whom was the Congregational minister, who remained committed to older, antiparty ideals. Friction generated between the two groups' divergent agendas. Party leaders grumbled that the clergy meddled with the workings of the party machinery and, like a rogue elephant, threatened to trample "the political leaders' [carefully coordinated] control of the people" through undisciplined extremism. For their part, clergymen decried the changes in the party. They continued to voice what was right or wrong with society as they saw matters, regardless of the popularity or expediency of their pronouncements.[39] Not only the results but also the organizational processes of the first party competition disturbed standing order clergymen.

After 1805, established ministers began to openly express their dissatisfactions with the magistracy. They groused that magistrates were failing to do their job. Amos Bassett obliquely indicated their irritation in 1807 when he asked, "What, then, shall be thought of the fidelity of civil officers, in places where sabbath-breaking and riotous collections are publicly known, and yet meet with no legal censure? What of their fidelity, who by improper forbearance, give countenance to places employed as retreats for intemperance and various species of disorder?" He answered, "To pass by such places and not censure them is to sanction them." By 1814, Dan Huntington of Middletown, Connecticut, was blunter. Amid other signs of declension, Huntington complained of "silent laws" and "inefficient magistrates." The vigilant and pious ruler, he noted in contrast, would not be "unwilling to stand forward, and own himself the friend of that Emmanuel."[40]

An asymmetry developed in the relationship between magistrate and minister, which embittered the clergy even more. At the same time that the standing order "appeared to be almost entirely dependent upon Federalist political supremacy for the protection of its privileged position," the clergy became more expendable to the Federalists as politicians reduced the level of the church in their order of priorities in order to appeal to a broader base.[41] Moreover, orthodox Congregationalists felt further alienated from the innermost circles of the Federalist party in Massachusetts, which were dominated by Unitarians from Boston and Essex County. Jedidiah Morse expressed this feeling in 1805 when he wrote, "It is unfortunate that a number of the ablest federalists are engaged (with truly Jacobinic arts) in revolutionizing [Harvard] college, in which I am bound to oppose them."[42] The demands of electoral competition were driving a wedge between Moses and Aaron.

The more perspicacious among the established ministry realized that there was a problem not just with unfaithful magistrates; rather, the root of the problem reached into American democracy itself. Stephen W. Stebbins, pastor of the First Church of Stratford, Connecticut, recognized the pressure public officials were under in the new, highly competitive political environment of the early 1800s. In 1811, he told Connecticut legislators to do "what is fit and right in itself . . . [or] what will stand the awful trial of the Supreme Governor of the universe, and meet his final approbation" and not to ask themselves "what measure will most contribute to my [the legislator's] popularity, to secure my present station, or advance *me* to an higher office; nor what will be most for my personal interest, or the advantage of those with whom I am particularly connected." Chauncey Lee also realized that in a democracy training godly rulers did not go far enough because "the character of rulers will ever be formed by that of their constituents." Because citizens elected the government, they, too, needed reformation.[43]

Indicative of their growing frustrations with conventional solutions, a few established ministers went beyond crying repentance and obedience and pushed for more assertive measures by the time of the War of 1812. Jedidiah Morse maintained that it was the "duty" of conscientious citizens "to refuse their aid" in support of an unjust war, "as they would avoid partaking in the guilt of shedding innocent blood." He further declared that the best course of action was to vote the war hawks out of office and replace them with the standing order's model of the godly officeholder. Consistent with his other sentiments, Elijah Parish staked out even more extreme ground. "Have you concluded, for yourselves, your children and children's children," he baited his audience, "to subject to greater commercial restrictions, voluntarily to submit yourselves to the miseries, now endured by a hundred million slaves in Europe? then, it is suitable and fit, that you should be slaves." Of course, his listeners did not want to accept slavery, and Parish shouted, "if you have some of your father's blood, yet in your veins, then protest against this war. Protest did I say, protest? *Forbid this war to proceed in New-England.*"[44] Ministers like Parish obviously contributed to New England's foot-dragging during the War of 1812.

The radical resistance advocated by Morse or Parish, however, was challenged even within the standing order itself. More representative, perhaps, was the advice of William Ellery Channing. He agreed that "it is your duty to hold fast and to assert with firmness those truths and principles on which the welfare of your country seems to depend," but he advised a different plan of action. He cautioned people against the excesses of partisanship. "Remember, that in proportion as a people become enslaved to their passions, they fall into the hands of the aspiring and unprincipled; and that a corrupt government, which has an interest in deceiving the people, can desire nothing more favourable to their purposes, than a frenzied state of the publick mind. My friends, in this day of discord, let us cherish and breathe around us the benevolent spirit of Christianity." Likewise, Yale President Timothy Dwight asked, "My friends and brethren, will party-politics carry you to heaven?"[45] In response to their problems with the civil leadership, most Congregational ministers did not call for a redoubling of political activism. They also rejected as too risky any extreme plans for resistance to government or rebellion.

Instead, most ministers fell back on their traditional role as "watchmen" and detailed the nation's sins through their preaching. In addition to the Democratic-Republicans' "infidelity" and the public's "phrenzy," ministers enumerated other complaints that were familiar from the 1780s and 1790s. Samuel Austin gave a typical list when he railed against "vice," which he defined as "irregularity of behaviour, counter to wholesome civil laws, and those precepts of the Bible which have respect especially to our moral conduct. Intemperance, luxury, prodigality, lewdness, gambling, night-frolicks, lying, profaneness, perjury and fraud, belong to the catalogue of vices, and are the principal of them." As a result, he verbally scowled, Americans had "become assimilated in our moral character, as a people, to the notoriously wicked inhabitants of Sodom."[46] Never shy about lambasting social sins, the established ministry intensified its denunciations as the nation's political situation grew worse.

Disregard of the Sabbath and a decline in religion generally were also frequently listed as reasons "by which we are constantly provoking the Holy One of Israel unto anger."[47] Sometimes this complaint about religious slackening seemed to refer only to the standing order's problems with rising dissent. John Smith of Salem, New Hampshire, just across the border from Massachusetts, cited "religious delusions, which abound." When he described these more specifically, however, they sounded like the appearance of Universalists or Shakers, perhaps. "Deceivers have entered into many of our towns, who deny the fundamental doctrines of the gospel, and the power of godliness; and, in order to gain the favor of their hearers, flatter them in their sins, and aim to reconcile the practice of iniquity with the hope of salvation; teachers, who falsely pretend to be inspired."[48] The fact that all of these sins flew in the face of Americans' manifold blessings only compounded the problem. A wayward people had seemingly forgotten the providential deliverances of the founding of New England and the Revolution.[49] To put the ministry's assessment succinctly and bluntly, as Ludovicus Weld did in 1804, "Stupidity predominates. . . . What vice can be mentioned, which here is not fashionable?" The United States had become "a nation of sinners with but few exceptions."[50]

At about the same time that this disgust with national sinfulness and frustration with the magistracy were setting in, the state of the nation was going from bad to worse with the approach of the War of 1812. No policy of the Democratic-Republicans came in for a more withering fusillade from the standing order than "Mr. Madison's War."[51] The War of 1812 also formed the last in a line of public crises that had pushed together the rationalist and evangelical wings of the standing order. The imperial wars of the 1750s and 1760s, the War for Independence, the French Revolution, and now the War of 1812 all rallied Congregationalists around their common concern for social order and an external threat.[52] Timothy Dwight and William Ellery Channing, for example, both joined in condemning the war. With the return of peace, their other antagonisms would come to the fore and divide their corporate outlooks, but for now the standing order united once more to face a threat.

Established ministers opposed the War of 1812 on a number of grounds. First, they argued that the United States had instigated an offensive, not a defensive, conflict. "This opposition [to the war] is defensible," argued Samuel Austin, "upon the ground that the war is most plainly repugnant to the entire spirit, and the express precepts of our holy religion. This is not a defensive war."[53] Second, like the embargo or slavery, the war would surely undermine public morality because "war directly leads to profaneness, to customary swearing in common conversation, to the neglect of the holy sabbath, and of public worship, to fraud and dishonesty, to infidelity, and a stupid inattention to divine things."[54] Third, the war was further misguided in that it pitted the United States against a nation that should have been an ally. Jedidiah Morse echoed the words of Governor Caleb Strong in calling Britain "the bulwark" of Christianity, a country "which has done for years past, and is still doing, under Providence, more than all other nations beside for its defence, and its propagation through the world."[55]

Fourth, and perhaps worst of all, going to war with Britain meant an implicit alliance with Napoleonic France, which was then Britain's wartime opponent. For about fifteen years, the Congregational ministry had been warning of the Republicans' servile commitment to France and French principles. Now the War of 1812 not only confirmed this analysis of national infidelity but also deepened the turpitude of the nation's sins. "The obsequiousness of this country to the despot of Europe needs no proof or illustration from me," remarked Elijah Parish. "If we engage in this war, then we take side with the despot; we enlist under his fatal banner; we make a common cause with him, and must share in his approaching destruction." Alliance with France yoked the United States to the Antichrist. Both Nathan Strong of Hartford, Connecticut, and Samuel Worcester of Salem, Massachusetts, cited with reference to France the admonition of Rev. 18:4, "And I heard another voice from heaven, saying, Come out of her, my people, that ye be not partakers of her sins, and that ye receive not of her plagues." As the ever-quotable Parish cried in exasperation in 1810, "The atheists of France, and the Puritans of New-England; was ever an alliance so monstrous!" Or, as Timothy Dwight phrased matters, "To ally America to France, is to chain living health and beauty, to a corpse dissolving with the plague."[56]

Given all their accumulated disappointments by the 1810s, ministers added a novel trespass to the catalog of national sins: they now proclaimed the U.S. Constitution to be one of the nation's affronts to God. Ministers of the standing order decried the fact that the Constitution did not contain a statement, in the preamble perhaps, that it was based on Christianity. The Constitution's "one capital defect," in Samuel Austin's opinion, was that "it is entirely disconnected from Christianity. . . . Its object is not, more or less, to subserve it." This he compared unfavorably to the British government, which "does not barely tolerate Christianity as a harmless thing. It has embosomed it, in the strict and orthodox sense. It has wrought it into its very constitution." Chauncey Lee pointed out that the Constitution "has not the impress of *religion* upon it," and asked, "whether, *if God be not in the camp, we have not reason to tremble for the ark?*" Similarly, as Timothy Dwight noted, the delegates at the Philadelphia convention had ignored Christianity. "We formed our Constitution without any acknowledgment of God; without any recognition of his mercies to us, as a people, of his government, or even of his existence. The Convention, by which it was formed, never asked, even once, his direction, or his blessing upon their labours." The implication was that the Constitution was fatally flawed—conceived, as it were, in original sin. In addition, and in reference to their attacks on the infidelity of Jefferson and Madison, these clergymen regretted that the Constitution contained no religious test for office. This loophole, thought Jedidiah Morse, was the Constitution's "essential defect," which meant "that even an Atheist may be constitutionally placed at the head of our nation." Finally, Nathan Perkins anticipated the radical abolitionists' indictment of the Constitution by some two decades: "ALL THE UNION it must be expected will have to suffer [for the sin of slave-holding], in the righteous retributions of Providence. And the punishment," he warned, "will not be light."[57] The ministry's disgust with the Constitution on religious grounds coincided with the more secular critique of New England Federalists that led to the Hartford Convention.[58] Ministers such as these had done an about-face from the optimistic days of 1783, when the Constitution had appeared as one instrument in the providential program to redeem the world. The ascendancy of the Democratic-Republicans since 1801 had opened their eyes to the defects inherent in the framework of government, defects they had been unable to see while basking in the glow of the first two Federalist presidents.[59]

A crushing load of sin, therefore, threatened to sink the nation. God, though merciful and patient, would not suffer a people to rebel indefinitely; no, his justice would not allow it. Explained Nathan Perkins, "The honour of divine Providence requires that great national sins and errors should be punished by national calamities and public judgments." If one paused "to consider how we stand in relation to the great Sovereign of the world, to contemplate our concerns as under his administration, to view things in the light of his law and truth," there was reason for unease. "The nation is manifestly in circumstances of adversity," thought Samuel Spring, "and we are sure that the Lord is the author of it because we have sinned against him as a nation."[60] To ministers of the standing order, God's punishment already appeared to be breaking out, as demonstrated by bad harvests, the collapse of trade, the explosion of partisan contention, and, of course, the War of 1812.[61] In this analysis, the war had a dual meaning: it was not only a sin committed *by* the United States but also a "scourge" sent *upon* the country for all its other offenses. "No person, seriously conversant with the divine oracles," Samuel Worcester pointed out, "can disbelieve that war, whether defensive or offensive, just or unjust, expedient or inexpedient, is a token of the Divine displeasure. It is one of God's expressly appointed judgments, for the punishment of guilty nations."[62] Just three decades after the end of the War for Independence, the United States appeared to be sinking fast amid the clergy's worst-case scenario of national sins and providential judgment.

The ministry's assessment of the nation's prospects had reached ebb tide. The texts on which ministers chose to base their sermons captured the mood of the times. Worcester, for example, chose Ps. 60:1-4, which begins, "O God, thou hast cast us off, thou hast scattered us, thou hast been displeased; O turn thyself to us again. Thou hast made the earth to tremble; thou hast broken it: heal the breaches thereof; for it shaketh. Thou hast shewed thy people hard things; thou hast made us to drink the wine of astonishment." As Festus Foster wrapped things up, "the dark cloud which hangs over our land and threatens to burst upon us" had turned the annual thanksgiving into a day of humiliation. "The glory of the Lord is departed from us," he concluded and could only plead, "*God save the Commonwealth of Massachusetts!*"[63]

Indeed, some ministers' disillusionment became so deep that it led to a recrudescence of the kind of apocalyptic millennialism not seen since the 1790s. As they searched the prophetic writings, these clergymen came back to report that things looked bleak. Certain passages foretold a period of tumult and destruction, "a time of remarkable indignation upon the world," before the millennium would begin.[64] Events around 1812 again appeared to bear a disconcerting resemblance to these end times. Asked John Smith, "can we turn our attention to the state of Europe, at this time of God's indignation, without seeing some similarity between the judgments threatened in the word of God, and those now experienced by the nations? by the nations, who have been enlightened with the beams of gospel mercy, and have shut their eyes against the light; persecuted the religion of CHRIST, and shed the blood of martyrs?" "At no time, since the deluge," opined Timothy Dwight, "has the situation of the human race been so extraordinary; the world so shaken; or its changes so numerous, sudden, extensive, and ominous." In Elijah Parish's reading, Napoleonic France was belching forth "the disgorgings of the infernal world, the pandemonium of every species of licentiousness and abomination." He concluded that "after more than half a century of war and devastation among the nations, the last enterprize of this terrible power [the French Antichrist] is called by way of distinction the battle, the battle of the great day of God Almighty, preparations are making for this closing scene, the final catastrophe."[65] To many ministers of the standing order, the dark night of the apocalypse was at hand.

This is the context in which Parish, as quoted in the chapter's introduction, had advised his parishioners to flee from the pollution of Antichrist and the eternal conflagration. For many ministers of the standing order, the state of the nation appeared dismal by 1812. They painted in the darkest hues a vision of coming destruction on account of a bevy of national sins, not the least of which were the infidel Republican leadership and a godless Constitution. Even New England's own magistrates seemed feckless. In the twelve short years between Jefferson's election and the War of 1812, the established ministry had rejected the U.S. government as a blessing of Providence and now portrayed it as one of God's judgments on a wicked land. The standing order's public Christianity remained intact to the extent that ministers still sought to interpret the nation's status before God and identify national sins. However, due largely to the rise to power of the Democratic-Republican party, the New England ministry's disillusionment with its earlier understanding of the significance of American history was now complete. "To conclude the subject," sighed Parish, "we discover the malignant nature of American democracy. . . . In other quarters of the globe, tyrants entrench themselves, behind the shields of their standing armies. But *here* the people *themselves* produce their own calamities, defend their own tyrants."[66]

Dissenters and Democratic-Republicans

> The LORD hath done great things for us; whereof we are glad.
>
> —Ps. 126:3

Unlike Parish, there were those who reveled in the concept and very words of "American democracy." In the 1809 Fourth of July oration referred to in the introduction, Elias Smith replied pointedly to the kind of despair and disgust voiced by Parish. "The government adopted here is a DEMOCRACY," he instructed his auditors. "It is well for us to understand this word, so much ridiculed by the internal enemies of our beloved country." Smith meant to defend democracy as both a general principle and a partisan label. He exclaimed, "My Friends, let us never be ashamed of *Democracy*! Never think it a reproach to be called a DEMOCRAT!" Moreover, Smith wrought his defiant political language into his religious faith. He challenged his audience to become "*republicans* indeed" by repudiating not only the conventional authorities in politics but also the religious tyrannies of "a *Catechism, creed, covenant,* or a superstitious priest."[67]

Smith's remarks point to the fact that many people rejected the established ministry's reading of events at the beginning of the nineteenth century. The rise of the Democratic-Republican party, to which the standing order reacted so adversely, occasioned rejoicing and a sense of opportunity from a diverse coalition of New Englanders. As standing order ministers and Federalist magistrates grew apart, religious dissenters and Republican politicians found common ground in attacking the standing order and its partisan utterances. The Democratic-Republican party provided an umbrella under which an array of "outsiders" could gather and share their dissatisfactions with a range of issues, including the religious establishment.[68] Roughly half the electorate in southern New England wore the label of "Democrat" with pride. In addition to facilitating the formation of an antiestablishment coalition, the Democratic-Republican party also gave dissenters powerful new language that was more in the mainstream with which to criticize the standing order. Dissenters fused earlier grievances over the establishment with a new, Jeffersonian critique. As the standing order's optimism and attachment to the United States waned, the dissenters' waxed. The Democratic-Republican party, combined with the rising number of religious dissenters and the Congregationalists' own internal divisions, eventually undermined the standing order as it had been known in the late eighteenth century.

Southern New England politics polarized rapidly and dramatically in the dozen years between 1798 and 1810.[69] Along with the rest of the nation, the region divided into two antagonistic camps with different perceptions and programs. On the one side, Federalists defended the policies of the incumbent governments of Washington and Adams. On the other, the Democratic-Republican opposition organized in reaction to what it perceived as a monarchical tendency within those administrations. The Republicans advanced two main arguments against the Federalists, each of which became entangled in the debate over the proper relation between Christianity and society. These issues are well known to historians of the early republic and can be summarized briefly. Both of them appeared in the 1799 July Fourth oration of Ezekiel Bacon, a twenty-two-year-old lawyer from Williamstown, Massachusetts, and ardent defender of the Democratic-Republican cause. Primarily, Republicans like Bacon championed "liberty and equality." This was the foundational ideological cleavage separating the two parties; as Ronald P. Formisano has written, "if the Federalists were the party of 'law,' then the Republicans were the party of 'liberty.'" The Republicans were out to halt what they perceived as a Federalist threat to liberty. As Federalists attacked them as anarchists, Republicans replied that their adversaries were bent on establishing tyranny. Bacon, for example, quoting from the Declaration of Independence, drew parallels between George III and John Adams. Turning the tables on the Federalists' usual charges, Bacon argued that it was they who were under "popular delusion and political infatuation." In addition, Republicans tried to blunt the Federalists' attacks on Jefferson, whom Bacon described as among those patriots "whose philanthropy, disinterestedness, moderation, and virtue, should ever endear them to a grateful people."[70] These domestic issues were intertwined with the two parties' divergent responses to the French Revolution and the ensuing European wars; Federalists favored Britain, while Republicans were sympathetic toward France.[71] The activities of partisan organizers furthered the process of polarization. In an unprecedented mobilization, party committees blanketed the states' counties, towns, and wards. Events at three levels then—state, national, and international—led both sides to gather into parties.

The bifurcation of politics permeated deeply into public life. Party organization quickly succeeded in heightening electoral participation. Through the 1780s, politics had been factional, fluid, and characterized by low voter turnout. However, "if the year 1800 be taken as a starting point, the contest between rival political machines almost doubled the proportion of voters who turned out at the polls [by 1810]," from roughly 32 to more than 60 percent. Newspapers, now blatantly partisan, aided the task of organization and fanned the passions of the average voter. Thousands of people on both sides, obscure and heretofore nonparticipants in the political process, underwent an awakening through newspaper reading. During the early nineteenth century in Massachusetts, the parties fought a close contest in which "the margin of one party's victory over the other rarely exceeded 3 per cent of the total vote," until the War of 1812 tilted the electorate substantially in favor of its Federalist opponents. Connecticut, meanwhile, remained securely in the Federalist camp until after 1815, but even there the Republicans organized an opposition not to be ignored.[72] In short, the first party competition profoundly changed the political culture of southern New England, forcing voters to choose sides on contentious issues.

The relationship of Christianity to public life became one of the questions swept into the partisan maelstrom. Although the vast majority of Congregational ministers reacted with hostility toward the upstart Democratic-Republicans, the standing order's critique did not exist in isolation. Rather, the first party contest produced a broad spectrum of ideological responses. There were several other positions in addition to the establishment's on the issue of public Christianity. In the first place, a few Congregational ministers broke from the main body of the standing order and called for a more irenic spirit with respect to political engagement. A second small group of Congregational clergymen went further and joined the Republican party, but their otherwise traditional outlook tempered their dissent from the establishment's Federalism. Jeffersonian Republicanism also produced two white-hot reactions against the standing order. Republican politicians attacked the Federalist clergy with no holds barred. Religious dissenters joined them, fusing earlier grievances over the Congregational establishment with a new, Jeffersonian critique. These four groups challenged the standing order's interpretations and advanced their own counterclaims at every point. They defended Jefferson, his policies, and the Constitution, inverted the established ministry's portrayal of who threatened the nation, and put forward a hopeful and celebratory providential outlook. Indicative of the heightened contention concerning religion and politics, a parishioner of Henry Channing, the theologically liberal but politically conservative pastor of New London, Connecticut, griped, "we agreed with you to preach Jesus Christ, not John Adams, in that most Holy Place, I mean the pulpit."[73]

A few Congregational Federalists left the fold of the standing order for fear of engaging in a destructive rage of partisanship. Not every member of the standing order greeted the rise of the Democratic-Republicans with the unmitigated loathing of the majority. There were a small number of clergymen whose commitment to the ideal of respect for civil rulers overrode whatever distaste they may have felt for the Democratic-Republicans. On the same day that Nathanael Emmons delivered his sermon comparing Jefferson to Jeroboam, the annual fast of 1801, Joseph McKeen preached *A Discourse against Speaking Evil of Rulers*. McKeen was the pastor of the First Church in Beverly, Massachusetts, located in Federalist Essex County, and his own politics inclined toward that party. Yet despite these facts, and although an enthusiast of the sport of wrestling, the political wrangling of the recent presidential election had gone too far in his opinion. Basing himself on the standing order's high regard for the magistracy, McKeen reminded his partisan listeners that "civil government is a divine institution, though its particular forms are human. And the Scriptures frequently enjoin obedience to the lawful commands of the magistrate, and they forbid, on severe penalties, disobedience, and speaking evil of dignities." He thought that the bitter vituperation of men like Emmons undermined proper social order and threatened that dreadful situation of Judg. 21:25, in which "every one [felt] at liberty to do what was right in his own eyes." He concluded in the conservative and deferential mode of the standing order, "We ought not to determine beforehand that we will be displeased with the measures of our new rulers. . . . No one, who is really a friend to good order and government, thinks it of so much importance *who* does the business of the state, as *how* it is done. . . . And I freely confess that in my opinion we have less to fear from the men who do or may administer the government, than from the prevalence of a licentious spirit among the people, which makes them impatient of the most wholesome and necessary restraints."[74] The Jeffersonians' ascent forced the recognition of a jarring contradiction between the establishment's belief in deferential hierarchy and its exposé of the leadership's sinfulness.

Also on that fast day in 1801, Stephen West of Stockbridge, in western Massachusetts, cautioned against excessive partisanship. His sermon focused on "the evils comprehended in this awful threatening of *being forsaken of God.*" Unlike some other ministers of the period, West did not point to Jefferson as proof of God's departure. Rather, he decried the people's political intoxication, which led them astray from their true Christian responsibilities. Like McKeen, he recalled for his congregants biblical passages that implored Christians to respect and pray for their rulers. Furthermore, West contended that politics was of little ultimate importance: "Of how little avail to the peace and interest of those, who are strangers and enemies to Christ, whether this political party, or the other prevail!" Drawing on the standing order's ideal of a unified, nonpartisan society, he concluded, "Cultivate a spirit of harmony, of union, of love. Without this, let our outward circumstances be as they may—let political matters go as they will, we must, we shall be an unhappy people."[75]

With their sermons, McKeen and West set a pattern for other Congregationalists who disagreed with the ardent Federalism of their colleagues: they turned the principles of the anti-Jeffersonian majority against itself. They exposed a contradiction in the logic of the established clergy, in that they showed that it was not always possible both to warn of the danger of an ungodly politician and at the same time to inculcate obedience, deference, and hierarchy. During the Revolution, of course, this tension had been ripped open, as patriot and loyalist ministers emphasized either the necessity of resistance or submission. The standing order had tried to patch the wound in the post-Revolutionary period, but the jostling and scraping of the first party tussle tore off the bandage and exposed it again.

The handful of Congregational ministers who openly identified themselves with the Democratic-Republican party—probably not many more than a dozen in Connecticut and Massachusetts—extended the line of criticism blazed by the likes of McKeen and West.[76] Like those two moderates, the Republican Congregationalists harpooned the Federalist clergy with its own logic but pushed their thrust deeper. Not only did they call for respect for elected (Republican) rulers but also they chastised Federalist ministers more harshly and defended the policies of the Jefferson and Madison administrations. Republican Congregational ministers rebuked the Federalist standing order by using their party's language but with the distinct accent of the establishment. They were a small but revealing group of clergymen who staked out a slice of ground between the bulk of the standing order and the more radical dissenters.

Republican Congregational ministers can be said to have taken a middling stance; although they were obviously aberrant in their partisan allegiance, they also affirmed many of the standing order's corporate axioms. Like other Congregationalists, they believed in the primacy of "the public welfare," accepted the argument that society needed religion, and never favored disestablishment.[77] In keeping with this traditional style of public Christianity, Republican Congregationalists voiced their grievances through the form of the jeremiad. They identified corporate sins and declensions from ancestral standards and urged people to repent. Newburyport's John Giles called on his listeners on the national fast of August 1812 to "humble ourselves under the mighty hand of God, and by faith in the Redeemer, and genuine repentance, disarm a frowning God of that vengeance which we have demerited at his hand." Joseph Richardson of Hingham, Massachusetts, could have agreed with any Congregational Federalist when he called the fast day tradition part of "the good old paths of our ancestors" and urged people to repent of the "prevailing looseness of morals."[78]

These Congregational clergymen departed from their Federalist brethren, however, in their interpretation of the sins that called for repentance. They employed the same basic theological foundation as the rest of the established ministry but inverted its conventional application. Joseph Richardson, for example, interpreted outbreaks of sin, sickness, and "scarcity of bread" in Massachusetts in 1813 not as judgments for the War of 1812 but for the state's nonparticipation. "As a State, no one in the Union has more cautiously avoided all participation in the war, yet this State lies under a heavy judgment, more severe than has been, by an immediate providence, inflicted on any other. . . . Has this taken place on account of prosecuting the war, or for our strange love of what is called peace?"[79] The Republican Congregational ministers form an intriguing little band of Jeffersonians because they resembled the Federalist clergy in so many ways except political allegiance.

Republican Congregationalists also argued that the Federalist clergy had sinned by violating the boundaries separating religion and politics. They rejected Federalist ministers' protestations of nonpartisanship and accused their adversaries of being enemies of government. This was the most important service rendered by the Republican Congregationalists: they denied Federalist clergymen their prophetic pretensions and thereby diluted the standing order's pronouncements. Federalist ministers were false prophets, warned Joseph Richardson. Regarding those established ministers who had plunged into supporting Federalism, Thomas Allen of Pittsfield, Massachusetts, said that "if men of a party spirit have opposed their rulers without charity, and without regard to the public good, and under the cloak of religion have violated the principles of religion, we may be assured they have not been actuated by the gentle, humble, holy spirit of the gospel." John Giles blasted ministers "who dragoon religion into their service, and make it the trumpet of sedition and rebellion." Worse yet, such men had injured the status of the clergy as a whole; "when the sacred desk, is converted into a vehicle of scandal, and calumny, and charges predicated on misrepresentation and the most glaring falsehood; this is a prostitution, not only of place, but office, and sinking the ministerial character into that of a public informer. Such conduct . . . flies in the face of divine authority, and subserves the cause of infidelity; for no truth is more explicitly revealed, than due subordination to government."[80] Solomon Aiken, Congregational minister of Dracut, Massachusetts, criticized Samuel Spring for this reason. Aiken said that the partisanship of his Merrimack Valley neighbor had brought the ministry and religion into disrepute.[81] The Republican Congregationalists unfrocked their Federalist brethren as a merely political priesthood. Moreover, they could not be written off as just another group of fanatical partisans because they shared so much of the background and outlook of other established ministers. The Republican Congregationalists created a dissonance that shattered the standing order's pretensions to speak with a unified voice. Their disaffection shows one way in which the acerbic quality of the first party competition corroded the standing order's ideological synthesis.

These Republican Congregationalists went beyond lambasting the sinfulness of the Federalist clergy and positively defended Republican politicians and policies. William Bentley of Salem, Massachusetts, offered a mild but firm corrective to all of the abuse heaped on the third president when he said, "Gratitude bids us to remember our national benefactors. Washington employed our arms with glory, and Jefferson has instructed us in the arts of peace." Although the Federalist clergy repeatedly expressed alarm over the prospect of an infidel at the head of the nation, Solomon Aiken rebutted the charge: "Whether Mr. Jefferson be a man of real piety or an infidel, I know not. I am informed that he is a constant attendant on public worship, when in his opinion it is performed with decency; and that he liberally contributes to the support of the public worship of God. I have no evidence of his infidelity in any of his writings, nor from any other quarter which should satisfy a candid mind."[82] Stanley Griswold, Congregational minister of New Milford, Connecticut, mounted an implicit defense of candidate Jefferson in 1800 when he denounced "all that private slander which many think themselves at liberty to utter against others on account of religious sentiments, and which of late with unblushing impudence has crept into public Gazettes, Magazines and Pamphlets and swollen their impure pages, branding the worthiest men with infamy."[83] These Republican ministers further showed that they were a rare breed of New England Congregationalists by defending the embargo and the War of 1812, both of which were highly unpopular. They justified both on account of attacks against American shipping. Thomas Allen tried to show that, despite the embargo, things were not so bad as Federalists liked to say, and America certainly was "not the abode of wretchedness." In the War of 1812, said Joseph Richardson, "God is on the side of our country."[84] These positions carried the Republican Congregational ministers further than moderates like McKeen and West.

The fact that Republicans like Bentley and Allen gave the Massachusetts election sermons in 1807 and 1808, respectively, reveals that in the early nineteenth century, the choice of election preacher had become a partisan issue. At one time, the election sermon ritual had aspired to be an expression of consensus, but any harmonious pretensions were swept away in the flood of the first party competition. Republicans made sure that when they came to power, they would call only a sympathetic cleric to deliver the election sermon. When Federalists retook control of the state in 1809, they responded with their own artillery, appointing David Osgood in 1809 and Elijah Parish in 1810. Indeed, Parish's sermon was deemed so partisan by the Republican legislature that that body broke with tradition and refused to publish it. Federalists, of course, rushed it to the press privately.[85] The transformation of politics in New England and the nation in the early nineteenth century meant that old issues like the relationship of Christianity and society took on partisan overtones.

Republican politicians did not seek out a debate over Christianity's place in public life. The issue was not their top priority, but they were drawn into the fray in self-defense. The standing order had reacted to the rise of the Democratic-Republicans by portraying that party as a hotbed of infidelity, as "a set of unprincipled and abandoned Democrats, Deists, Atheists, Adulterers and profligate men," in Noah Webster's scattershot defamation. Republican politicians could not let such accusations go unanswered. Indeed, by engaging in political controversy, established ministers created a self-fulfilling prophecy: they hardened the Republicans into enemies of the standing order. In addition to rebutting the accusation that they were atheists bent on toppling Christianity and government, Republican spokesmen went further and turned on the established clergy. They attacked Federalist ministers as hypocrites who were naive at best and cynically self-serving at worst. Republican politicians had to undertake these counterattacks, because they believed "that clerical influence played a crucial role in helping the Federalists maintain their political dominance."[86] Republican critics of the role of the clergy in politics such as Abraham Bishop and William Plumer shared many of the same issues with Republican Congregational ministers. However, the politicians generally lacked the ministers' concerns for the common good and the status of the ministry. They ratcheted up the level of hostility toward the standing order and trashed the clergy's aspirations to public guardianship.

Republican spokesmen began by trying to deny the aspersions cast on their party's character. Both Abraham Bishop's *Connecticut Republicanism* and William Plumer's *Address to the Clergy of New-England, on their Opposition to the Rulers of the United States* well illustrate Republican complaints with clerical interference in politics. These two works, published in 1800 and 1814, respectively, also roughly bracket the time period of this chapter. Bishop, a New Haven Jeffersonian, replied to Federalist allegations of an infidel conspiracy by emphatically declaring, *"there is not an atheist in the State nor a single modern philosopher among the republican party."* During the War of 1812, Plumer was still fighting the same set of charges. Plumer served as governor of New Hampshire in 1812 and 1813 and stood alone among New England chief executives in supporting the war. On account of this support and his failure "to appoint a state fast in the summer of 1812," Plumer became embroiled in controversy with Federalist clergymen. Like Bishop, he prefaced his *Address to the Clergy,* a collection of reprinted newspaper essays, by insisting that he bore no "hostility against Christianity itself." Such denials were probably important to the Republicans for internal party cohesion. No party of infidels and freethinkers could win in the United States. Pious dissenters and Congregationalists were the foundation of the Republican coalition, and they had to be reassured that the party held no actual animosity toward religion.[87]

After denying the verisimilitude of the standing order's portrayal of the Democratic-Republican party, spokesmen like Bishop and Plumer took a step further and denied the established clergy's knowledge and authority. They portrayed ministers as in over their heads. In a direct hit to established ministers' pretensions as community watchmen, Plumer depicted the ministry as generally provincial and learned only in abstruse theology and dead languages. He likewise dismissed ministers' claims to be messengers from God: "The Israelitish *prophets* were divinely *inspired by* GOD, and expressly commanded by HIM, at certain times and on particular occasions to denounce the wickedness and tyranny of particular rulers. But you are not *prophets*—you are not endowed with divine *inspiration*." Republicans also argued that the ministry had stepped out of its place in advancing political opinions. "How much, think you, has religion been benefited by sermons," asked Bishop, "intended to show that Satan and Cain were jacobins? How much by sermons in which every deistical argument has been presented with its greatest force as being a part of the republican creed?" Plumer warned that "the moment [clergymen] attempt to fight the battles of *party* with the weapons of religion," they were fair game. "If he will wallow in the mire of *factious opposition*, he cannot expect his cassock and band will protect him from the filth and slander which he delights in handling."[88] Like the Republican Congregational ministers, men like Plumer and Bishop did not accept the standing order's repeated insistence upon its own nonpartisanship.

More seriously, Republicans charged that the clergy's pronouncements were cynical and deliberately hyperbolic. At election time, according to Bishop, "*the clergy*, preachers of the word of life[,] deign some days to waive their sacerdotal functions, to descend from their high seats made venerable by the respect of the people for religion and . . . shout from every quarter, THE CHURCH IS IN DANGER!" Ministers then went on to cast "all holy men of every age as federalists." Plumer highlighted an apparent contradiction in the establishment's sermonizing by juxtaposing remarks by Elijah Parish and David Osgood from the 1790s with some of theirs from the 1810s. He portrayed these leading exemplars of the standing order as insincere partisans, who in the earlier period had preached obedience to government and resistance in the latter. The ministry would stoop to such levels, Republicans mocked, because its own pecuniary self-interest was at stake. They alleged that ministers were in cahoots with Federalist politicians in a desperate bid to retain or win back power. At this point, the Republicans' critique of the established clergy merged with their wider conspiracy theories. As Federalists suspected a conspiracy against all religion and government, so, too, the Republicans harbored their own theories of a plot aimed at subverting liberty. Both Bishop's *Connecticut Republicanism* and Plumer's *Address to the Clergy* were grounded in a vision of sinister and far-reaching machinations. Bishop, for example, detailed how Federalist bankers, merchants, military officers, and professionals planned to establish themselves as an American aristocracy. The clergy was a key cog in the antilibertarian cabal.[89]

The Democratic-Republican party's appeal to religious dissenters should be readily apparent, given the antagonism of the party's leaders toward the established ministry. Dissenters were delighted to find new allies in their battle with the standing order. They joined forces with Republican spokesmen like Bishop and Plumer but launched their attack on the establishment from a different vantage point. Their basic grievances with the Congregational establishment continued to be founded on practical and doctrinal matters that were neither originally nor inherently partisan. The process of political polarization, however, with the standing order overwhelmingly taking one side, gave dissenters a home in the opposition. To their older issues, which reached back to the First Great Awakening, dissenters added Republican themes like individual liberty and small government. Like the Republican Congregationalists, their position was a blend of old and new. As New England's Republican politicians "mediated" between local interests and nationwide party issues, so dissenters, too, were engaged in translating sectarian concerns into a broader, partisan idiom. The rise of the Democratic-Republican party and the articulation of its ideology empowered the dissenters' critique of the standing order.[90]

To emphasize the impact of Jeffersonianism is not to say that dissenters had forgotten the fundamentally sectarian grounds of their disgruntlement. Rather, they were still preoccupied with two issues that antedated the first party system: what they regarded as the standing order's erroneous, even heretical doctrines, and their perceived persecution under the laws of the establishment. The Congregationalists' interposition of state authority into religious affairs was the major sticking point. The dissenters' shibboleth remained John 18:36, "My kingdom is not of this world." "In no part, of countries at this time under the administration of the clergy of the church of Rome, is the kingdom of Christ perverted so much to a kingdom of this world, as in Connecticut," charged the fierce Episcopal critic of that state's standing order, John Cosens Ogden. Likewise, the Baptist Nehemiah Dodge held "that God has allowed no connection between the spiritual kingdom of Christ and the carnal policy of the world."[91] Dodge based his position on an interpretation of the Bible different from the Congregationalists'. He contended that they made an anachronistic application of Old Testament principles to their public Christianity when those principles had been supplanted by the New. In other words, dissenters like Dodge dismissed the relevance of the standing order's frequent appeals to the example of Moses and Aaron.[92] Dodge went even further and accused the standing order of partaking of the character of Antichrist for this violation of the church and kingdom. The Congregational churches would not be blessed by God, he predicted, being "worldly churches, who have nothing better to lean upon, than human wisdom, wealth and power, parts and learning, legislative skill and civil establishments."[93] The Baptists continued in the early nineteenth century to posit a stark separation between church and world. Their doctrine of the church depicted it as a realm set apart. "By a Christocracy," said John Leland, "I mean nothing more than a government of which Christ is law-giver, king, and judge, and yet so arranged, that each congregational church is a complete republic of itself, not to be controlled by civil government or hierarchy. Let this government be called by what name soever, it is not of the world, and therefore the rulers of this world have nothing to do with it, in their official capacity." God protected his church with a wide gulf that kept out the corruptions of a fallen world: "Though kingdoms and states be in confusion, embroiled in wars, tossed with tumults, and their governments in continual revolution; tho' their powers combine against the church and people of God, aim at no less than their ruin, and go very near towards gaining their point; yet will not we fear, knowing that all these troubles will end well for the church."[94] Dissenters remained fearful that the church would be polluted by contact with the state or world.

In addition to the question of the kingdom of God, dissenters fired other sectarian criticisms at the establishment. John Leland, a Baptist from Cheshire, Massachusetts, charged that levying taxes to support religion—what he dubbed "turnpiking the way to heaven by human law, in order to establish ministerial gates to collect toll"—had no scriptural warrant. "The people of Massachusetts boast of their religious knowledge; to them I appeal. Pray tell me where Jesus, or the apostles, ever called upon rulers of state to make any laws to oblige people to part with their money to hire preachers or build meeting-houses." Some added a shot of eighteenth-century New Light reasoning, ridiculing established ministers as feckless, unconverted, and greedy. Elias Smith relished resurrecting these old taunts. "Wherever the people have been brought up under what is called a settled minister, they are generally the most *ignorant* of the scriptures of any people I meet with," he observed. "This is easily accounted for, their ministers never say but little about the scriptures; their written discourses are generally from ten to forty minutes long, and commonly the matter is of a worldly nature." He also reprised the dangers of an unconverted ministry, saying that "a man without regeneration can no more preach the gospel of the grace of God, than a blind man can judge of colours, or a deaf man teach music."[95] The controversy over infant baptism remained central to the Baptists' and Christians' repudiation of Congregationalism as well. Nehemiah Dodge reviled the Congregationalists for "introducing the mark of the beast in the forehead, called infant sprinkling, which they have held up as regeneration; teaching ignorant hearers, that they were thereby born again, and introduced into the holy city or church of God."[96] Although the establishment, too, stood upon biblical grounds, dissenters rejected the standing order's arguments as either uninformed or deliberately deceptive.

Related to these doctrinal matters were the dissenters' continuing, practical difficulties with the laws governing the establishment. They complained of harassment. "Men have been dragged to prison, and their property sold at public auction, to maintain systems of faith and discipline, which they neither believe nor follow," objected John Cosens Ogden. Elias Smith stated simply that "those who, contrary to the constitution of the United States tax other denominations, carry them to prison, &c. would be very much disturbed, were they treated in the same manner they treat others."[97] In short, the issues that had rankled the dissenters since the 1740s and before continued to be sources of alienation in the first decades of the nineteenth century.

One could conceivably imagine that, given the salience of these old, sectarian concerns, there would be little to attract dissenters to the party of Thomas Jefferson. However, the Democratic-Republicans' attack on the Congregational clergy's Federalism created a mutual interest for pietist and politico.[98] Dissenters happily seconded the call for the ministry to get out of politics, although their reasoning may have been based more on the doctrine of the kingdom of God than on partisan calculations. They found especially repugnant the way in which established ministers supposedly prostituted the pulpit for Federalist ends. Nehemiah Dodge thought that "ministerial influence in political affairs has done much more hurt than good in the world for a long time." Both Dodge and John Cosens Ogden alleged that established clergymen pulled strings behind the scenes—using "interference with elections, recommendations of Candidates for civil office, denunciations of those who have resisted their discipline, and usurpations"—in order to manipulate politics to their advantage. In the same way that standing order clergymen were not just mouthpieces for political Federalism, dissenters were not lockstep Republicans either but had an idiosyncratic synthesis of their own.[99]

In a fascinating process of cross-fertilization, dissenters quickly appropriated the language of the Democratic-Republicans for their own ends. They cudgeled the standing order with arguments picked up from Jeffersonian liberalism. For example, as Republicans lashed Federalist extravagance and made economy in government their watchword, dissenters employed this criticism against the established churches. "No christian State of equal numbers, has submitted to heavier burdens in support of its clergy than Connecticut," claimed John Cosens Ogden. "Large sums are constantly paid as settlements, which become the property of the ministers, and enable them to extend their purchases to the enriching of themselves and their families. The clergy pay no taxes. . . . They have annual salaries and perquisites, which give not only a competency, but independence and affluence. All of which is collected from the sweat of the people and their labors." John Leland called for minimal government, which one would never hear from ministers of the standing order, who believed in the difficulty and monumentality of governing. Likewise, developing the Jeffersonian theme of the equality of men, dissenters cultivated a certain strain of anti-intellectual populism against the standing order. Elias Smith mockingly contrasted Rom. 10:15, "*And how shall they preach except they be sent?*" with what he claimed was the standing order's rendition, "*And how can they preach except they are sent to college?*"[100] To suit their needs, dissenters easily transferred from the political realm to the religious the Jeffersonian assaults upon taxation and privilege.

Most important, dissenters embraced Republican paeans to liberty. Feeling that their "natural inalienable rights" were being trampled by the establishment, they used Jeffersonian language to hammer away at the standing order, "an aristocratical hierarchy in religion."[101] J. C. Ogden's *An Appeal to the Candid upon the Present State of Religion and Politics in Connecticut*, for example, was an extended assault on Yale as a Calvinist-Federalist monopoly. "President Dwight is making great strides, after universal controul in Connecticut, New-England, and the United States, over religious opinions and politics," Ogden asserted, invoking Republican images of a Federalist conspiracy. "He is inspiring his pupils with political prejudices against some of our best fellow citizens, in warm and unbecoming language. He is seeking to establish the Edward[s]ean system of doctrines and discipline, from pride for his grandfather's (Predent [*sic*] Edwards) talents and fame. . . . With a large salary paid from public bounty, he is maintained in his place, and excites and perpetuates party designs." The school ignored the interests of "every man" in favor of a privileged clique, he said, striking the chord of equality. Like Abraham Bishop, Ogden assailed the tyranny of the established clergy. "President Dwight, elected by ecclesiastics who maintain their own succession, and pay obedience to no authority on earth, who controul the votes of eight of our first civil magistrates, in an institution where the general opinion and sentiment are formed upon all subjects, is a more formidable character than the Pope of Rome." He also alleged that the school ran roughshod over the religious rights of non-Congregational students, compelling them to attend the college chapel under the president's watchful eye.[102]

The ultimate fusion of Jeffersonian and dissenting languages came from Elias Smith. He exhorted his listeners on the Fourth of July 1809, "Many are *republicans* as to *government*, and yet are but half *republicans*, being in matters of religion still bound to a *Catechism, creed, covenant*, or a superstitious priest. Venture to be as independent in things of religion, as in those which respect the government in which you live." In other words, Smith sought a consistent libertarianism that rejected the standing order in religion as it repudiated Federalism in government. "The republican class," in John Leland's similar analysis, "contains those who fought, not only to be independent of Britain, but also from that policy which governs her—those who contend for the civil and religious rights of all men."[103] Religious dissenters harmonized their voices with the Jeffersonian-Republican chorus's incessant chanting for liberty and equality.

Based on their identification with Jeffersonian liberalism, New England dissenters idolized the third president, "the defender of the rights of man and the rights of conscience."[104] They ripped the standing order for its hostility toward him. "A man needs not a great share of knowledge to see, that as a body of men, [established clergymen] are professed enemies to our Republican government, and open enemies to the President," observed Elias Smith. Added Nehemiah Dodge, "if Jefferson, or any other honest man, has too much good sense to favor their scheme, do they not degrade him to the lowest hell as near as they can, and deal forth the thunders of heaven in full detail, against all who will not curse him?" Dissenters also went on the offensive and praised Jefferson as a providential blessing. "A wonderful mercy of the great God indeed!" exclaimed Dodge, "that he hath so caused the wheels of providence to roll in these United States; that we have a Jefferson at the helm of government, who is fully convinced that the church of God needs none of his unasked-for aid." In 1804, Elias Smith even went so far as to identify Jefferson as "the sixth angel of the apocalypse" from Rev. 16:12.[105]

Hence, as the standing order's attachment to the nation plummeted on account of the Republican ascendancy, the dissenters' patriotism rose proportionally. "When taking a retrospective view of our nation and country," opined Asahel Morse, "modern history affords no manifestations of the divine favor to any people, comparable with the history of our own." Dissenters based their sermons upon joyful texts, which stood in contrast to the establishment's mood of gathering gloom. Morse, for example, chose this section's epigraph, Ps. 126:3, "The LORD hath done great things for us."[106] The celebratory defense of Jefferson was an item common to the agendas of dissenters, Republican Congregationalists, and Republican politicians.

The dissenters' allegiance to the Democratic-Republican camp became politically significant on account of their growth. Of course, not every dissenter sided with the Republicans, nor did the Congregationalists vote Federalist en masse. Nevertheless, every student of New England politics in the early republic has concluded that religion formed one of the surest indicators of party identification.[107] During the early nineteenth century, dissenters from the Congregational establishment continued to make rapid numerical gains, which derived in part from the divided state of the standing order. In Connecticut, the combined number of dissenting churches passed the number of Congregational ones in 1806, and in 1818 non-Congregational churches outnumbered Congregational ones by roughly 225 to 204.[108] In Massachusetts, the Congregationalists managed to retain more numerical strength, with dissenters in 1810 accounting for "less than 5 per cent of the population."[109] At least from the Episcopal church, the establishment appeared to face little challenge, because "Massachusetts had a bishop for only six of the twenty-two years between 1789 and 1811, and even as late as the latter date there were only fifteen clergy in all New England outside of Connecticut." Yet even here, under the leadership of Bishop Alexander Viets Griswold of the Eastern Diocese, which embraced all the New England states except Connecticut, greater organization yielded a doubling in the number of Episcopal communicants between 1810 and 1818.[110] And in a period of sharp party competition, these dissenting numbers eventually translated into Republican votes. The Democratic-Republicans' rise both energized religious dissenters' ideology and gave them a practical political context from which to operate.

Many factors such as aggressive evangelism, appealing theology, a populist style, and their tax-exempt status contributed to the advances made by Baptists, Methodists, and others. Additionally, the Congregationalists in Massachusetts could not compete effectively because of their own internal furor over theological diversity. Coincident with the establishment of party divisions, the Congregationalists in Massachusetts fell out among themselves over "the Unitarian controversy." The Unitarian controversy came into the open in 1804 and 1805, when the Harvard Corporation chose Henry Ware to succeed the deceased David Tappan as Hollis Professor of Divinity. Led by Jedidiah Morse, theologically conservative members of the Harvard Board of Overseers criticized Ware's liberalism, arguing that it deviated from both Harvard tradition and the intent of the Hollis chair's patrons.[111] The bases of the controversy had been building since the 1730s, as religious liberals had come to reject core beliefs of Calvinism, such as original sin, justification by faith alone, and the Trinity. However, major public issues such as the Independence movement and the French Revolution had engrossed people's attention and forestalled a full airing of the disputes.[112] The argument between the Unitarians and the orthodox, as the Trinitarian Calvinists called themselves, did not arise simply from generational differences between old conservatives and youthful liberals. Rather, it represented a sea change in New England thought, as the Unitarians rejected Calvinism in favor of the Scottish philosophy of Common Sense.[113] By the end of the first decade of the nineteenth century, it was clear that Massachusetts Congregationalists had divided into two separate camps. From then on, it would be impossible to speak of Congregationalism singularly.

The Unitarian controversy issued in a number of baneful consequences for the standing order in Massachusetts. For one, theological dissension set congregations against themselves. The orthodox began to withdraw from Unitarian-controlled parishes and formed churches of their own, and vice versa; divided houses could not stand.[114] The controversy also wrecked the harmony of the established ministry and belied its pretensions to represent the commonwealth as a whole. Two parallel and competing sets of institutions emerged from the dispute, and Congregational ministers hived off into separate connections. On the local and personal level, pulpit exchanges, ordinations, and ecclesiastical councils also ceased to include anyone from outside one's own theological party.[115] This internal skirmishing retarded the Congregationalists' denominational growth. Their preoccupation with parish controversies both abdicated the mission field to the dissenters and led some congregants to wash their hands and leave such scenes of acrimony. The Unitarian controversy goes far toward explaining the establishment's loss of earlier dominance. It weakened the Massachusetts establishment's supports, including the Congregationalists' numerical superiority and their ministers' alliance with the ruling class.[116]

All of these developments—the escalation in political contention, the increasing proportion of the population that identified with churches other than Congregational, and the divisiveness of the Unitarian controversy—combined to precipitate a movement for disestablishment. The movements to disestablish the Congregational church followed separate paths in Massachusetts and Connecticut but reached similar ends toward the end of the second decade of the nineteenth century.[117]

The Massachusetts establishment, as codified in article 3, remained on the books until officially deleted by constitutional amendment in 1833. However, it died a gradual death over the two preceding decades, succumbing to internal breakdown resulting from the aftershocks of the Unitarian controversy. In contrast to the situation in Connecticut, where a political coalition of dissenters and Republicans brought down the standing order, the Massachusetts establishment collapsed more on account of its own self-destruction. The extended process of the establishment's decline played out as substantially in the courts as in the legislature or on election day. During the Republicans' first period of control of the state house in 1807–1808, they did not advance the dissenters' cause one inch.[118] The first major alteration in the establishment followed the Massachusetts Supreme Judicial Court's 1810 decision in *Barnes v. Falmouth*. This decision was meant to clarify once and for all the ambiguities surrounding article 3. It ruled that "only incorporated dissenting societies could recover religious taxes paid to the established parishes; all other congregations were not recognized by law." This was "the most conservative, if not reactionary, interpretation possible to Article Three of the Declaration of Rights."[119] The *Barnes* decision outraged dissenters because many of their churches remained unincorporated. They threw their weight behind the Republicans' successful election campaign of 1811, and in response the Republican legislature passed the Religious Freedom Act of 1811. This put into law a mechanism similar to Connecticut's 1791 statute, in that certificates were still required but standardized. It also reversed *Barnes*, opening up the policy of tax distribution to unincorporated societies, too.[120] After the 1811 legislation, the establishment reached another state of legal equilibrium until disturbed by the 1820 state constitutional convention. Initially, the separation of Maine as an independent state caused the convention, but once begun it raised other issues for review, including article 3. The convention provided the establishment's opponents with a forum in which to advocate disestablishment. However, the convention deadlocked on the issue: Unitarians supported the establishment just as strongly as the Baptists denounced it, while most orthodox Congregationalists and Republican politicians were divided. Therefore, the standing order remained intact as of 1820 because the stalemate meant that nothing could be changed.[121]

In Connecticut, enemies of the standing order finally achieved their goal of disestablishment in 1818. The Baptists, in the dissenting vanguard once again, began the push in the early 1800s with a nonpartisan petition drive. They submitted petitions to the state legislature in 1802, 1803, 1804, and 1806, calling for an end to the state's establishment and certificate system. However, they soon learned that a nonpartisan tack was a nonstarter. Lack of results from the petition drive led the Baptists to enter the Republican camp by 1804. Only slowly did Republican politicians wake up to this potential pool of voters, according to McLoughlin, who stressed the tensions between Baptists and Republicans. But the politicization discussed at the beginning of this chapter gave dissenters a new platform. Party competition meant that those shut out from the standing order's access to the state leadership and ritual events now had an avenue along which to carry their grievances. For instance, Republican Fourth of July celebrations became an important site for orations that did the ideological work of unifying the Jeffersonian-Baptist coalition. Furthermore, the coalescence of a political opposition facilitated coalition building. "The history of disestablishment in Connecticut after 1800 is the story of how each of these four groups of dissentients [anticlerical radicals, liberal Congregationalists, Episcopalians, and adherents of smaller sects] felt gradually more alienated from the narrow, partisan conservatism of the Federalists and the Beecherite clergy; how each in its own time and for its own reasons sided with the voluntaristic pietists to end the Standing Order which bent but which would not break its ties to the past." Of greatest importance in this process was the Episcopalians' decision in 1816 to join the Republicans. Although they had been mostly Federalists up to this point, accumulated grievances, especially regarding perceived slights at Yale, left them cold. In a fusion of religion and party politics, the Republicans renamed themselves the "Toleration Party" for the 1816 election, stressed the issues of the dissenters' grievances, and made major gains. Finally, in 1818 the Toleration Party seized both houses of the legislature, called a state constitutional convention, and guided the ratification of a new constitution of 1818 that disestablished Congregationalism in Connecticut.[122]

The Connecticut election sermon of 1818 encapsulated many of the themes of the foregoing section. Copying a page from their Massachusetts partisans, Connecticut Republicans appointed a sympathetic clergyman to deliver the annual election sermon once they took control of the state government. Instead of choosing a Republican Congregationalist, as had been done in Massachusetts, Connecticut Republicans named an Episcopal priest, Harry Croswell, rector of Trinity Church, New Haven, to the honor of election preacher. This choice acknowledged the Episcopalians' position as the keystone of the party's coalition. Predictably, Croswell's sermon was, in essence, a rebuttal of the political preaching of the Congregational ministry. His chosen text reflected the dissenters' central belief in the need to separate church and state. It was Luke 20:25, "Render therefore unto Cæsar the things which be Cæsar's, and unto God the things which be God's." He lectured the magistracy on the Republicans' soon-to-be-enacted platform of disestablishment. "Aware, that it is the prerogative of God, solely and exclusively to judge the heart; and aware also, that all men are accountable to Him alone, for the motives which govern them in their intercourse with heaven, the civil government will abstain from every measure, which may seem to usurp the rights of conscience, or which may obtrude on ground forbidden to any earthly power." To the ministry, he directed his thesis that "it is both improper and hazardous for those who minister in holy things, to intermeddle with the party-politics of the times in which they live."[123] Thus, Croswell's sermon typified two important changes. It symbolized the arrival of the Episcopalians and other dissenters at the political mainstream as part of a majority, Democratic-Republican electoral coalition. It also showed the dissenters' opportunistic ability to mingle their sectarian concerns over the worldly corruptions of Christ's kingdom with their Jeffersonian defense of mankind's inalienable rights.

The advent of the first party competition dramatically changed the terms and temperature of the debate over the relationship of Christianity to society. To the standing order, it signaled a need to warn of the perils posed by the Republicans and to reinterpret the providential meaning of the American nation. For their trouble, established ministers received a torrent of abuse. Even within the standing order, a few moderates and Republicans bolted from the leading camp. Dissenters meanwhile embraced the change wholeheartedly. Jeffersonianism fueled the standing order's opponents with a new language with which to communicate their grievances. The dissenters' critique of the establishment became more mainstream, as they utilized popular Jeffersonian rhetoric. Furthermore, the Democratic-Republican party provided a vehicle under whose aegis a coalition of political and religious dissenters could gather. While the rise of the Democratic-Republicans filled the establishment with woe, it ignited a burst of optimistic activity from a host of others. The coalition partners—Republican Congregationalists, religious dissenters, and party spokesmen—all repudiated the pronouncements of the established ministry, ordered the standing order to quit its political meddling, and, when that failed, led the charge for a revision of the laws governing the establishment, if not complete disestablishment.

A stalwart of the establishment, Nathan Perkins, also attended the Connecticut election-day festivities in 1818. He was in a surprisingly good mood, given that Croswell's sermon represented the close of the standing order's reign. "At the annual celebration dinner," Perkins spoke with Croswell, "and joked that when he had catechised children in Hartford years before, he had never dreamed that one of them would grow up to be an Episcopal clergyman and give the election sermon."[124] How ministers of the old standing order like Nathan Perkins regained the gift of laughter, overcame their sense of despair, and maintained their corporate ethic is the subject of the next chapter.

FOUR

❧

Grassroots Changes and Regional Ideology
1800–1815

T HE DEVELOPMENTS of the early nineteenth century dealt the standing order in
both Connecticut and Massachusetts a startling combination of blows. The
deep dissension of the first party period made the established clergy's relationship
with the Federalist magistracy problematic, and the Jeffersonian ascendancy disillu-
sioned most Congregational ministers with their post-Revolutionary proclamation of
America's providential significance. In turn, the newly forged alliance between the
Democratic-Republicans and the surging numbers of dissenters rebuked the established clergy with increasing effect. Movements for the disestablishment of Congregationalism started to gain momentum. Moreover, the outbreak of the Unitarian
schism retarded the Congregationalists' ability to respond to these disorienting
changes. As a result, by 1812 many standing order ministers preached apocalyptic
messages of national sinfulness and divine wrath.

The Worcester County ministry found itself in the thick of this regional controversy. In the wake of Jefferson's inauguration in 1801, the Massachusetts establishment tapped Aaron Bancroft of Worcester's Second (Unitarian) Church to come to
Boston and deliver the election sermon. Although the Jeffersonian victory meant radical changes in public policy at the national level, for the Bay State Bancroft urged
continuity with the past. His election sermon epitomized the standing order's conservative response to the revolution of 1800. Bancroft designed his sermon "to review
the principles and habits, under the influence of which this Commonwealth has attained to its present state of population and strength, wealth and dignity; and to enforce the necessity of their preservation." According to him, the founders' principles
featured "the love of civil and religious liberty" circumscribed by "the wholesome restraints of government." The colonists' habits had also been pious, moral, industrious, and committed to education, all of which resulted in "a state of social order and
happiness as near perfection, as the world has known." Because obviously no one
would want to tamper with a state of "near perfection," Bancroft warned his listeners to beware of the introduction of "a national administration in politicks and morality, upon abstract principles." Instead, he concluded this prudential address by asking

rhetorically, "Shall we part with the maxims of our venerable ancestors, which time has proved to be wise, for a spirit of innovation, which nothing sacred or profane can restrain?" A decade later, Samuel Austin of Worcester's First Church was launching similarly partisan attacks but in much less temperate language than the circumspect Bancroft. On the annual fast day of April 11, 1811, Austin denounced "our moral character, as a people," which this orthodox Congregationalist compared "to that of the notoriously wicked inhabitants of Sodom." As proof of his charge, in addition to mentioning the usual sorts of vice and irreligion, Austin decried the U.S. Constitution as "entirely disconnected from Christianity." He warned that "we must be nearly ripe for some terrible convulsion, and perhaps for a final overthrow." The next summer, at the commencement of the War of 1812, Austin continued his tirade. "This war is a providential event," he argued. "It has been sent upon us by God, and is evidently an awful scourge of his hand, expressive of his wrath." He singled out for blame "the unaccountable infatuation, approaching even to phrenzy [sic] and madness, which has possessed, and continues to possess the minds of those who have the management of our government."[1] Austin's philippic was similar to a host of others that rang across southern New England that summer as the Congregational clergy plunged into apocalyptic cries of despair. In short, the Worcester clergy was deeply implicated in the acrimony of the region's first party competition. Moreover, this engagement with regionwide controversies seeped down to the grassroots level, watering the rank weeds of local contention.

Several members of the First Church objected to Samuel Austin's partisan preaching, and they demanded a meeting to consider his dismissal. When the parish meeting voted not even to discuss the complaints against Austin and adjourned forthwith, the disgruntled laypeople left the church. They were then instrumental in organizing Worcester's First Baptist Church. As a result, Elder William Bentley of Tiverton, Rhode Island, was installed on December 9, 1812, as the new pastor of the Baptist church in Worcester. Present were representatives from Baptist churches in Charlton, Grafton, Leicester, Sturbridge, and Sutton, Massachusetts—all Worcester County towns—as well as from Boston's Second Baptist Church and the Baptist churches in Pawtucket, Providence, and Warren, Rhode Island. When Austin not surprisingly refused the Baptists the use of the First Church's meetinghouse for the occasion, Aaron Bancroft allowed them the use of his, whether out of genuine hospitality or in order to spite his orthodox neighbors is unclear. The new church became part of the Warren Association before the end of the year.[2] This episode reveals Worcester's connection to two larger trends. It demonstrates the intertwining of religion and politics during the first party competition, particularly the correlation between Republicanism and dissent, and the detrimental consequences this had for the standing order. It also shows the Baptists' expanding presence, which in Worcester County especially came from the direction of Rhode Island.

The Unitarian controversy likewise produced its own Worcester County manifestation in the dispute over the selection of a new minister for the Congregational church in Princeton. Samuel Clarke, a theological liberal, was the choice of the Princeton parish, but not the church, which was more orthodox. An ecclesiastical council called to resolve the dispute in 1817 sided with the parish on a 5–4 vote. Joseph Goffe of the North Parish of Sutton, a member of the council minority, lambasted the decision as "a prostitution of ecclesiastical power!!!" He charged that the council had tossed the traditional prerogatives of the New England churches to the wind in favor of "the horrid maxim of Illuminism, that the end sanctifies the means." Clearly, Goffe's reference to the bogeyman of "Illuminism" reveals the depths of the dispute. In response, Aaron Bancroft wrote for the majority. He refuted Goffe's case, arguing that the parish paid the bills and ought to have the final say in choosing a minister. He also chided Goffe for his "intemperate zeal." The council's division and the subsequent pamphlet war over the selection of a new minister in Princeton show how the Unitarian controversy divided the standing order from within in Worcester County as elsewhere. Goffe and Bancroft, after all, had formerly been neighbors and friends. In December 1796, Bancroft had performed Goffe's wedding ceremony when other local ministers were shunning him, and the following spring the two were exchanging pulpits. Both men also shared an active involvement with Federalism, but the Unitarian controversy made bitter antagonists of them.[3]

Thus, Worcester County experienced all the turbulence that buffeted the standing order anywhere in southern New England. Yet, despite all these problems, despair or resignation surprisingly did not take hold. That is because the Spirit of revival was moving in Worcester County during and after 1800. Joseph Goffe could curse the rise of Unitarianism and sourly note in his diary after the Democratic-Republican victory in the state elections in 1807 that "Massachusetts turns Jacobin this day." Nevertheless, he could also find reason to praise God—"Gloria Deo," he wrote in his diary—over what was happening in his parish during the fateful year of 1800. "Many people among us remain deeply impressed in religion," Goffe summarized at the end of April. "Several souls, I think have lately been new born."[4] Eventually, orthodox ministers like Goffe would use the energy and optimism of the revivals to reformulate their public Christianity.

The sermon of Timothy Dwight, the president of Yale, at the opening of the new Andover Theological Seminary in September 1808 was one that pointed toward the new formulation. Whereas anxious Federalists, such as Samuel Austin in the previously quoted remarks, depicted God coming in wrath to judge the world, Dwight accented the triumphal elements of the Second Coming. He found reason for hope because of the renewal he saw taking place in the Christian church throughout the world. "In this terrible day, as in every other, the church of GOD is the safeguard of mankind; the *salt*, which keeps this putrid world from absolute corruption." News of revivals and the missionary movement and new institutions like Andover gave this spokesman for the establishment cause for optimism, despite his common apprehension that "the aspect of the political horizon" was "gloomy and dreadful."[5]

Grassroots changes like those Goffe experienced in the North Parish of Sutton during 1800 ultimately drove this broader ideological transition. This is not to say that regional ideology followed in Worcester County's wake, but that the county had a representative experience for southern New England. There was a reciprocal connection between national, regional, and local changes. If the story of the last chapter was how national developments eroded regional ideology and precipitated the local conflicts previously mentioned, then this chapter is one of influence acting in the reverse direction. Local changes as epitomized in Worcester County, such as grassroots revivals, ministerial networking, and novel forms of organizing, nourished a new regional conception of public Christianity. In time, this regional ideology would yield national ramifications.

The Awakening of Worcester County

> Wilt thou not revive us again: that thy people may rejoice in thee?
>
> —Ps. 85:6

The diary of Joseph Goffe for 1800 affords an intimate look at the Second Great Awakening in one Worcester County town. Back in the 1740s, the First Great Awakening had had a powerful impact on the area. For example, the English evangelist George Whitefield passed through in 1740, touching off a revival in Brookfield. In Sutton, the Rev. David Hall, a friend and ally of Jonathan Edwards, also led revivals in 1741–1743, 1757, and 1768–1769. In other towns, Sturbridge being a prime example, the awakening led to church separations and gains for the Baptists, who also experienced a revival in 1778–1782. Thus, what occurred in 1800 was not unprecedented. Still, it had been decades since the fires of revivalism had burned through the county, and the Second Awakening had not appeared there yet, although it was already underway in Connecticut. As Goffe recollected, the 1800 revival "was a new thing in this part of the country, and a new era in this church and vicinity." The Second Great Awakening has generated a voluminous secondary literature.[6] The purpose here is to view the movement from the clergy's perspective, that is, how ministers tried to direct spiritual energy and how they themselves were transformed in the process. For Goffe, the revival resulted from both his own tireless exertions and his collaboration with neighboring colleagues. It brought a host of new members into his church. More broadly, news of this revival and others like it influenced how ministers across southern New England understood the connection between religion and social life.

The revival in Sutton's North Parish can be attributed first and foremost to Joseph Goffe's method of preaching. As he described it, he employed "a plain and simple exhibition of divine truth, declaring to the utmost of my ability the whole counsel of God, and keeping back nothing that is profitable, through fear of offending my hearers." Like other New Divinity men—Goffe had studied for six months under Jonathan Edwards Jr. in New Haven, Connecticut, after graduating from Dartmouth in 1791—his preaching was "chiefly of a *doctrinal* character," aimed at "the understanding, judgment and conscience of my auditory." Many of the texts he chose from which to preach in 1800 sought to arouse his listeners from their indifference and stir a revival. For example, Matt. 25:10, "And while they went to buy, the bridegroom came; and they that were ready went in with him to the marriage: and the door was shut," drove home the urgency of conversion, lest one miss this time of the Spirit's outpouring. Likewise, both Isa. 60:1, "Arise, shine; for thy light is come, and the glory of the LORD is risen upon thee," and Isa. 55:6, "Seek ye the LORD while he may be found, call ye upon him while he is near," formed the bases for arresting calls to self-examination.[7] In combination with his other pastoral activities and in collaboration with his ministerial brethren, Goffe's energizing preaching brought about a revival.

Joseph Goffe. Courtesy Worcester, Mass. Historical Museum.

Goffe followed up his formal, Sabbath-day presentations with more informal opportunities to interact with his people. On at least ten occasions in 1800, he recorded
in his diary meeting with parishioners for "religious conversa[tion]." For example, on
January 22 he noted, "The minds of my people appear to be stirred up a little[.] Two
came to me to day, enquiring after salva[tion]." On August 7, Goffe "talked about 3
hours with Mr. Phelps upon religion." As part of his pastoral duties, Goffe took time
to counsel his flock, speaking with inquiring men and women. With even greater fre-
quency, Goffe attended regularly held conference meetings. Conference meetings

were weekday gatherings that might include a sermon but also featured conversation, prayer, singing, and testimonies by laymen. For instance, in the evening of January 23, Goffe went to a "very full" conference, where "Mr. Phelps & Col. Holman spake considerable." That night's meeting was held "at Mr. Jos. Waters'," which was typical of these meetings. Although they were sometimes held at the meetinghouse, more normally they took place at one of the schoolhouses or in one of half a dozen private homes. Thirty-one times during 1800, Goffe recorded his attendance at conference meetings, including seven of them in January alone, when the revival was just gathering steam. As a result, at the end of that month Goffe concluded, "There appears to be a considerable attention among my people. I think I have seen more success of the gospel this month than in the whole 7 years I have preached here besides— Blessed G[od], go on [Rev. 6:2] from conquering to conquer." Indeed, the revival continued throughout that year. In the fall, Goffe observed, "Blessed be G[od] he yet continues pouring out his Spt. upon us.—Many of the young people are under serious impressions, & many hopefully converted."[8] Joseph Goffe was an effective revivalist, in part because he descended from the pulpit to meet face-to-face with men and women throughout his parish.

Goffe would not have been able to sustain this level of activity had he not been able to draw on the support of his neighboring clergymen. Throughout 1800, he often collaborated with a group of five other ministers. Goffe worked most frequently with Edmund Mills, his neighbor in Sutton's South or Old Parish, and Worcester's Samuel Austin; the three others were Isaac Bailey of Ward, John Crane of Northbridge, and Grafton's John Miles. All of these men were located within about a twelve-mile radius of Goffe's parish in the southeast quadrant of Worcester County along the Blackstone River. With this group plus Nathan Holman, a ministerial candidate who was ordained later that year at Attleboro, Goffe exchanged pulpits on four occasions in 1800. Swapping pulpits relieved a minister of the responsibility of always having to prepare a new sermon, gave the congregation the opportunity to hear a different voice on Sunday, and ever since the First Great Awakening had been used to fan the glowing coals of a revival. On five other occasions that year, Goffe also invited his colleagues to come to the North Parish of Sutton to lecture for him. Lectures were special messages, like sermons, that were usually delivered during the week, sometimes at the conference meetings. As the revival gathered momentum in Goffe's parish during 1800, he deftly pushed things along by inviting outside speakers to sustain the movement.[9]

The revival clearly benefited from Joseph Goffe's employment of his neighboring clergymen. At the same time, the success of the revival redounded to his credit among them, raising his stature and legitimacy in the eyes of his colleagues. Remember that when Goffe was ordained over Sutton's North Parish in 1794, he had been an object of scorn among the area clergy. Edmund Mills of the South Parish had refused to perform Goffe's marriage in 1796, saying, as Goffe wrote in his diary, "that the ch[urc]h & people here are in error, & that he will not acknowledge me in the character of a minister." The 1800 revival erased this ill will. As Goffe recalled, "The ministers in the neighborhood looked on, and, convinced that it could be no other than the finger of God, they dropped their opposition to the church and to me, and became cordial and helpful in carrying on the work." Indeed, Goffe pointedly recorded on January 26, that when he and Mills preached at one another's churches, "this is the 1st time of our exchanging."[10]

Sometime shortly thereafter in the early 1800s, Goffe and his ministerial brethren cemented their new friendship by forming the Worcester South Association. On June 3 and 4, 1806, Goffe noted that he was in Worcester "to help form an associa." He even entertained a half-dozen ministers at his house for an association meeting on October 6, 1807. However, the beginning of their formal collaboration dates to before 1806; in 1802 and 1803, Goffe regularly recorded in his diary his attendance at "the ministers['] meeting." As the founding ministers of the adjacent Brookfield Association had pledged to "comfort, strengthen, & quicken one another" with the goal of being "more successful" in ministry, so Goffe and his friends worked together to promote revival.[11]

To keep the revival going and moving in the right direction, Goffe had to overcome a number of obstacles. Foremost among them were the challenges from sectarian rivals. At the end of February 1800, Goffe was pleased to note the "considerable" "religious attention" in the parish. But he was also concerned that "great exertions are made by the devil's agents—the universalists—the methodists, & a runabout baptist; to divide, distract, & lead off many. May G[od] confound their wicked devices & keep the devil from injuring or impeding his work." As a consistent Calvinist, Goffe especially loathed the Universalists, who had been active in Worcester County since the 1770s under the leadership of Caleb Rich. When Hosea Ballou itinerated through the area in 1800 and preached at the North Sutton schoolhouse, Goffe remarked that "Satan is exerting himself for our destruction." Moreover, one of Goffe's handful of published sermons, *Spirits in Prison*, was a theological blast against the doctrine of universal salvation. Goffe also had to deal with Baptist efforts to reap the fruits of the Sutton revival. He spent the evening of November 4 "in endeavoring to counteract Baptist influence." Perhaps the "runabout baptist" who so annoyed him was John Leland, who preached in town on September 19. However, it should be pointed out that Goffe had generally cordial relations with those Baptists who were not of the "runabout" variety. When Goffe traveled to either Providence or Boston, he called upon Dr. Jonathan Maxcy and Dr. Samuel Stillman, president of Rhode Island College and the prominent pastor of Boston's First Baptist Church, respectively. Goffe even preached in the vestry of Stillman's church during "a time of special attention among the Baptists in Boston" and lectured in the meetinghouse proper before "a large assembly." Furthermore, when Goffe "heard Mr. Andrews a Baptist preach . . . at the brick school house" on Prov. 10:29, "The way of the LORD is strength to the upright: but destruction shall be to the workers of iniquity," he deemed it "an excellent sermon." Apparently the Baptists' Calvinism, moralism, and growing respectability all made them palatable to Goffe. If he detested the "runabout" types like Leland, Goffe could collaborate with more settled Baptist leaders. This Congregationalist's working relationship with Baptists foreshadows the later unity between evangelicals of both denominations.[12]

Regardless of Goffe's exasperation with sectarians, he admitted a raft of new members to the church. Between January 30, 1800, and April 12, 1801, he recorded in his diary the admission of forty-five men and women. Perhaps taking a somewhat longer time frame or counting other people not listed in the diary, Goffe later claimed that the total "fruit of this revival" amounted to "about seventy new members." Especially memorable was November 16, 1800, when twenty-one people joined the church. Goffe described it as "a scene superior to what ever took place in Sutton, even in its most religious days. — The work appears to be of G[od], & to him be ascribed all the glory." Here was tangible proof to match Goffe's impressionistic sense of the revival's currents.[13]

By early 1801, just as quickly as it had developed, the revival in Sutton's North Parish dissipated. On January 31, Goffe observed that "the extraordinary work of the Spt. of G[od] among us appears to be abating. — But few new subjects of grace appear. — I fear G[od] is departing from us. — O that he might leave a rich blessing behind him." By May 31, he was even gloomier: "My people appear to be falling into a state of Sptl. deadness & stupidity — The Spt. of G[od] is withdrawn, O when will he return again? I fear never." Goffe tried reviving conference meetings in the fall, but little spiritual excitement generated.[14]

Notwithstanding this ebb tide in the North Parish of Sutton in 1801, revivals would continue to surge during the ensuing years in scores of other towns throughout southern New England and the nation. To cite just one example, the South Parish experienced its own revival in 1810–1811 under Edmund Mills's supervision. That revival followed the familiar pattern of "pungent" preaching, "solemn" and heavily attended meetings, "assistance" from neighboring clergy, and a large increase in membership. And as a matter of fact, despite Joseph Goffe's understandable disappointment in the aftermath of his first revival in 1801, he would lead several more over the course of his career. In thirty-six years as the pastor in Sutton's North Parish (known as the town of Millbury after 1813), Goffe oversaw seven revivals that brought in close to four hundred members to his church. During the first third of the nineteenth century, revivals became a repeated and regular fixture on the religious landscape of southern New England.[15]

These revivals became news events that left a lasting imprint on the clergy's social ideology. Even when his own church was languishing in the spiritual doldrums, Goffe would take note when revivals were occurring elsewhere. For instance, in the fall of 1803, when it was "rather a dry time" in his own community "as to Sptl. influences," he learned "by report" that "G[od] is still refreshing some of his Chhs [churches] in our land." Goffe was a consumer of the new periodical literature that carried updates of revivals in New England and worldwide. His personal library, for example, contained volumes one through five of the *Connecticut Evangelical Magazine*, five volumes of the *Massachusetts Missionary Magazine*, and three volumes of the *Panoplist*. Goffe and ministers like him were also the producers of this reportorial fare; he noted in his diary when he was drafting his own submissions. Ministers shared accounts of their own experiences as leaders of local revivals.[16] Perhaps other ministers would read them and hope to replicate an awakening of their own. Over time, revivals and the news thereof became ingrained into the texture of the public Christianity of the orthodox wing of the established clergy. Revivals were seen as a countervailing positive development amid the other wrenching changes of the early nineteenth century.

An Alternative Vision Germinates among the Orthodox

> God is our refuge and strength, a very present help in trouble. Therefore
> will not we fear, though the earth be removed, and though the mountains
> be carried into the midst of the sea.
>
> —Ps. 46:1-2

The first dozen or so years of the nineteenth century were pivotal ones for the public Christianity of the Congregational clergy. Both the first party competition's robust
contentiousness and its electoral outcomes dissolved with caustic persistence the established clergy's post-Revolutionary ideological synthesis. Ministers lost confidence
in magistrates' assistance and repudiated their earlier reading of the new nation's
providential destiny. Yet, their corporate ethic endured in its essence, as established
ministers continued to preach God's oversight of nations and the need for religion in
society. Moreover, the news of successes in missionary endeavor and local revivals
suggested by around 1810 a new hope for societal righteousness. Orthodox Congregationalists began to emphasize the importance of the church acting on society.
While the nation's political culture seemed headed for disaster, these ministers rallied to the revived local churches as the hope for social sanctification and the millennial promise. From this creative vision, new institutions and ideas began to ger-
minate, which would sprout and yield much fruit in the 1820s. Thus, instead of
cowering in the face of impending destruction, bumbling when confronted with opposition, or withdrawing from a corrupted environment, standing order clergymen
stepped up to meet the problems posed by political and religious rivals.[17] They transformed their commitment to the collective welfare of society through a new model
of public Christianity that was rooted in the kind of grassroots developments found
in Worcester County.

There can be no question that Congregational ministers continued to preach
that it was a providential God who directed the plight of nations. The annual fast day,
reminded Boston's William Ellery Channing in 1810, was designed to get people "to
ask ourselves whether we have not provoked divine judgments, and whether divine
judgments are not hanging over us; and to implore with humble importunity the for-
giveness and blessing of Him, whose word fixes the destinies of nations; whose good
providence has been our refuge in the past, whose favour is our only hope for the future." Likewise, in the definition of Dan Huntington of Middletown, Connecticut,
real "prosperity" had both individual and communal elements. "That people may be
said to prosper," he said regarding communities, "who, elevated as to their national
character, and happily exempted from national judgments, are, under the divine
smiles, making improvement in their laudable pursuits."[18] The sermons from the
time of the War of 1812 had shown this corporate concern with their diagnoses of national sins and punishments. These pronouncements of communal guilt and danger
were not merely a partisan rhetorical trope but reflected a fundamental of the standing order's outlook. It was a staple of the establishment's social ideology that "public bodies and communities only exist in this world, and of course, can only be rewarded and punished in this world by Divine Providence."[19]

Providence normally acted through the channels of moral law. For instance,

Asahel Hooker of Goshen, Connecticut, pointed out that "mankind are subjects of a divine moral government" with laws "sanctioned by divine authority, and enforced by adequate promises and threatenings;—promises of due reward to the obedient, and threatenings of just punishment to such as disobey."[20] The history of the Israelites as recorded in the Old Testament provided a case study of the ways in which infidelity led to national reverses. "One grand object indeed in chusing [the Israelites] to be [God's] people," argued Hartford's Nathan Perkins, "was to shew all mankind, that he rules in the world; disposes of nations; and loves righteousness, and hates iniquity; that national virtue will be rewarded; and national wickedness punished. He, in general, deals with nations, in a similar manner, to what he did with the Jews, as their history fully evinces. The Lord ruleth among all nations."[21] As a general proposition, therefore, Congregational ministers clearly continued to affirm that nations lived under Providence, the rule of law, and the prospect of judgment.

Established ministers further continued to contend that government and the very possibility of social existence itself depended on the influence of religion in society. Reason or government unaided by religion would never suffice to preserve society from a vicious state of war, or so claimed Matthias Burnet of Norwalk, Connecticut, in an 1803 reiteration of conventional wisdom. "Banish a sense of religion and the terrors of the world to come from society," he solemnly warned, "and you at once dissolve the sacred obligations of conscience and leave every man to do that which is right in his own eyes; you let mankind loose like so many beasts of prey, to roam at large, to deceive, destroy and devour all whom fraud or force may put in their power." "In a word," summarized Reuben Puffer, the 1803 election-day preacher from Berlin, Massachusetts, "religion is the palladium of social order and happiness." Nathan Perkins used this logic to rebut the arguments of dissenters and Republicans, who were always clamoring for a more scrupulous segregation of church and state. Alluding obviously to the Jeffersonians, he noted that there were "philosophers and statesmen" who "conceive that religion is only an AFFAIR BETWEEN GOD AND THE SOUL." Such men admit religion to "be necessary to a preparation for future happiness" but think "that it is of little or no consequence to the state, whether the christian religion be believed or disbelieved, practised or not practised, protected and supported, or reproached, profaned and extinguished." Perkins countered, however, that individuals were "answerable at the bar of the public, and to civil society" for their personal religion. Society as a whole had a compelling interest in the religious life of its members, because either their faith would bless society or their amorality would curse it.[22] Perkins and established ministers like him possessed of their corporate ethic believed that only Christianity kept anarchy at bay.

Given the importance of religion to society, established ministers argued in the early 1800s that it was the duty of Christians to act in society, not flee from it. Their arguments drew on both the New Divinity concept of disinterested benevolence and a more rationalist idea of patriotism, which was another kind of benevolence. Matthew 22:34-40 records that Jesus had taught that one's highest obligation was to love God and his neighbor. From this scriptural injunction, Zebulon Ely of Lebanon, Connecticut, stated that the "object [which] must be uppermost in our minds, take the lead in our affections, and govern our practice . . . must be the good of the community." In the moral society, "each individual should feel responsible to each individual, and to the whole," asserted Nathan Perkins, an orthodox Calvinist of New Light sympathies. "No man may live for himself alone, but must look at the things of others, and that the public good may be advanced." Similarly, although coming from the opposite end of the theological spectrum, William Ellery Channing lauded patriotism as eminently Christian. In July 1812, he preached on Luke 19:41-42, which recounted Jesus' weeping over the impending doom of Jerusalem, "the metropolis of his country." From this text, he drew the lesson "that it is a part of our character and duty, as christians, to be affected by the prospect of national suffering. The miseries of our country, as far as they are unfolded to us, should arrest our attention, should draw tears from our eyes, and lamentation from our lips; should increase our interest in our native land, and rouse every effort for its security." Finally, Lyman Beecher, then of Litchfield, Connecticut, criticized the individualistic ethic of the acquisitive entrepreneur in 1812. Such a man disregarded "the general welfare," and his attitude was, "Society must take care of itself." This kind of unconcern for "the general good" flew in the face of the standing order's traditional desire to hold the community morally responsible and united.[23]

Ministers such as these would have known what to prescribe next within their conventional social ideology, but that option was no longer available to them. They would have implored the magistracy to combat vice and put forward a godly front, but, as we have seen, they had grown weary of this strategy by the latter half of the first decade of the nineteenth century. Even a few years before disestablishment, the realization had hit home that elected officials were not completely reliable partners in the effort to build a godly society. Added to this disappointment with the Federalist magistracy was the ministry's disillusionment with the national government and its repudiation of the Constitution. Nevertheless, they did not surrender the project of building the righteous community. Instead, Congregational clergymen of an evangelical bent began to construct an alternative model of the godly society in response to their alienation from the new political culture of the first party period. Indeed, by the War of 1812, the established ministry might have despaired utterly had it not been for some hopeful developments outside the political realm that offered new insight. Around 1810—the pivotal years for the story told in this book—these orthodox Congregationalists began to develop a new variation of their public Christianity that stressed the sanctifying influence of the church on society. Moving away from their initial, primarily conservative response, they entered a transitional period that was more creative. They saw as a favorable portent recent developments in the fields of missions and revivals. From these trends, they began to envision an optimistic scenario of the church renewing society. It was a strategy of achieving the establishment's traditional, overarching goal of the righteous society, at a time when the older methods had either vanished or proven impotent. Accordingly, the orthodox also launched new institutions to advance their gains, carry their new vision into reality, and raise their presence in society.

Orthodox Congregationalists celebrated the news of revivals and missions that reached them in the early nineteenth century. They thirstily imbibed the glad tidings that "the work and strivings of God's holy Spirit have, of late, been greater and more remarkable, in many parts of the land; and, gracious influences more copiously shed down, than at almost any former period within the memory of the oldest people among us." Not just revivals, but missionary initiatives, too, "challenge[d] our religious acknowledgements." Newburyport's Samuel Spring, for example, found "abundant reason to adore God for the late missionary spirit which has expanded so rapidly, and already obtained such extensive influence . . . on both sides [of] the ocean." "Gloomy and dreadful as is the aspect of the political horizon," added Timothy Dwight, "the Christian world has already roused itself from the slumbers of two centuries, and with a spirit of prayer, zeal, and liberality, scarcely exampled, has wafted the Bible to distant nations, and planted missions [Ps. 23:4] *in the region and shadow of death*."[24] In contrast to the bad news emanating from American politics, "the Christian world" produced encouraging reports.

These blessed developments evoked images of the millennium. As the French Revolution and America's apparently growing involvement with it had called forth visions of contamination and apocalypse, so the revivals and missionary movements of the early nineteenth century seemed to fulfill prophecies of divine showers of blessing and the Second Coming. Transatlantic missionary work seemed, to Samuel Spring at least, to "proclaim the near approach of Zion's God and King." Likewise, to Samuel West of Stockbridge, Massachusetts, the turn-of-the-century revivals throughout the United States and missionary projects were "happy omens—omens of good. The Lord grant, that Zion may soon hear the voice, [Isa. 60:1] *Arise, shine, for thy light is come*." Dan Huntington tied these ideas together better than anyone else. "That [millennial] day cannot be far distant," he said in 1814. "We have striking, and constantly increasing evidence, of its near approach, in precious revivals of religion; in a mighty spirit stirred up, in many parts of Christendom, to make the name of Emmanuel known and glorified in the earth; in the removal of those barriers, which have hitherto obstructed the blessed work; and in the general fulfillment of prophecy. 'The signs of the times' [Matt. 16:3] cannot be mistaken. The period in which we live forms an era, for Christian enterprize."[25] Here were sources of hope to counterbalance darker portents.

The orthodox wing of Congregationalism began to develop these signs of vitality into a new emphasis on the church as the critical institution in its goal of creating a righteous community. In the late 1790s, the standing order had already started to move toward a greater faith in the church, as opposed to the nation-state, as the enduring instrument in the plans of Providence. Now Congregational ministers completed this transition. Given the reverses dealt them in the early nineteenth century and the "astonishing changes and revolutions [that] have taken place among the nations of the earth," they eagerly grasped hold of the faith that "the God of Zion" was "watching over the interests of his church, and preparing the way for its enlargement." Stephen Stebbins of Stratford, Connecticut, added in 1811 "that while God's government tends to the good of the world, it is especially designed for the direction, support and defence of his church." The "church" spoken of in these terms did not refer to any single local congregation or denomination. Rather, it referred to the larger body of believers, whose boundaries were left indistinctly drawn, united together under the lordship of Jesus Christ. Sometimes, ministers used the church in this sense internationally, as when they praised Anglo-American missionary work. Describing the worldwide aspirations of missions, Samuel Spring remarked, "The Lord has promised, that his church shall embrace the nations; and while we suppress all unwarrantable confidence respecting the universal triumph of grace, the Prophets impel us to hail the approaching day when the temple of Christ will be commensurate with the habitable globe."[26] Amid parlous times, orthodox ministers took their stand on the rock of the church as their sure foundation.

This church, superintended by God, would have a profound and salutary influence on the surrounding society. Samuel West likened the body of American Christians, or the church, to Lot's family, who (Gen. 19) had temporarily saved Sodom from its deserved obliteration: "And, if God would have spared Sodom for the sake of ten righteous people, we may hope that the prayers of *many* will avail, through Christ, with the infinite merciful God, for averting the calamities, which we deserve, and which, in some respects, threaten us." Along these same lines, Timothy Dwight produced another provocative metaphor when he said that "the church of GOD is the safeguard of mankind; the *salt*, which keeps this putrid world from absolute corruption."[27] In other words, the church would preserve the republic, even one that had become as "putrid" as "Sodom," as they believed the United States had.

The Connecticut election sermon of 1810 shows these new ideas of the church in society beginning to coalesce. It was a transitional work, containing conventional elements but also pointing the way toward a new language. Its author, John Elliott, had a representative, if not exceptionally distinguished, ministry in the town of Guilford. The publisher of many sermons and a member of the Yale Corporation, Elliott's embedment in the culture and institutions of Connecticut Congregationalism makes him an authentic voice for its changing perceptions.[28] His election sermon straddled the shift taking place within the establishment's public Christianity between the standing order's emphasis on the cooperation of Moses and Aaron and an emerging evangelical social ideology.

Elliott's sermon struck many of the traditional chords of the standing order's social ideology. Its thesis was the sermon's title, *The Gracious Presence of God, The Highest Felicity and Security of Any People.* Elliott specified five ways that a people could detect the presence of God. His first two signs were the familiar ones of godly magistrates and ministers. "Godly CIVIL RULERS," he asserted, came from Providence's "invisible hand." The same was true of "a sound, faithful and evangelical ministry." He concluded familiarly, "in a community where God is graciously present, . . . Moses and Aaron walk hand in hand." Also reflecting the establishment's corporate ethic, he argued that Christianity influenced everything, "personal, social and moral," and that "the moral governor of the world would [not] grant the same smiles to an obedient and disobedient people."[29]

But more important to the point at hand were the newer emphases that Elliott wove into his sermon, because he outlined how a revitalized church radically transformed its community. The remaining signs of God's presence were "revivals of religion," "a missionary spirit," and "a spirit of love, unity and peace." In Elliott's conceptualization, revivals played a catalytic role. They touched off a three-stage chain reaction that moved from the Spirit's initial spark to the church and from there blazed outward to the community at large. As the first stage of the process, faithful preaching was the means by which the power of the Holy Spirit came upon a people, which ignited a revival. Reflecting good Calvinism, Elliott was scrupulous to point out that this was a work of grace, not the preacher's manipulation: "If a minister

THE GRACIOUS PRESENCE OF GOD, THE HIGHEST FELICITY
AND SECURITY OF ANY PEOPLE.

A

SERMON,

PREACHED BEFORE HIS EXCELLENCY

THE

GOVERNOR,

AND THE

HONORABLE LEGISLATURE

OF THE

STATE OF CONNECTICUT,

CONVENED AT HARTFORD,

ON THE

ANNIVERSARY ELECTION,

MAY 10th, 1810.

BY JOHN ELLIOTT, A. M.

PASTOR OF A CHURCH IN GUILFORD.

HARTFORD:
PRINTED BY HUDSON AND GOODWIN.
1810.

Title page of John Elliott, *The Gracious Presence of God* (Hartford, Conn., 1810).
Courtesy American Antiquarian Society.

preach the truth with apostolic purity and zeal for a longer or shorter period, he does no more towards converting and sanctifying sinners, than the husbandman does toward bringing showers from Heaven, and actually making his grass and grain grow, when he plows, plants and manures." Second, as the revival advanced, it swept into the church, which "was purged from great corruption" and "beautified and enlarged."[30] Within this renewed church, the "spirit of religious enterprize is roused, to spread the knowledge of the Redeemer to remote quarters of the globe, and gather subjects into his holy and spiritual kingdom." In other words, for Elliott the revivals did more than just save souls one by one. They also mobilized the saints and concentrated them into an institution for societal redemption and transformation. Third, this church then had a penetrating impact on its community and preserved it. As he described the result, "The face of community resembles the surface of the ocean in a summer's day. No wind ruffles. No wave rolls. All is tranquil and serene. What is wanting in the view of the profound statesman, the sound moralist, or the pious Christian, to render this community as happy as any on earth can be?" In Elliott's equation, therefore, the church would sanctify and shelter its host community. "The extent of rational expectation is, that although such a nation be *cast down*, it will not *be destroyed*; that it will experience such wonderful deliverances, as the records of New-England declare her to have experienced, or such as is recorded in the annals of this State." In short, Elliott had mapped out a way for the standing order still to foster a righteous community but now somewhat less reliant on the establishment and magistracy. As he concluded, "We learn what method those who love their country should pursue, as the most effectual to promote her real prosperity; earnestly pray for the welfare of Zion."[31]

Elliott's *Gracious Presence of God* additionally marked a clear break within the ranks of the standing order's public Christianity because his emphases on revivals and missions appealed to evangelical sympathies, not the Unitarian mind. In an obvious dig at Unitarianism, he said that "the real Gospel exalts both the Father and the Son: heresies dishonor them." Continuing this line of criticism, he distinguished between "revealed truths . . . accompanied with divine power" and the feckless "speculations" of uninspired philosophers. Referring to the latter, Elliott commented that "the light they diffuse is like that of the sun upon the bleak regions of the polar circle. They leave the heart cold and unaffected."[32] In other words, rationalistic, anti-Trinitarian preaching would abort the new model of social sanctification through the Spirit and church. A succession of crises between the 1750s and 1815 had forestalled this split between rationalists and evangelicals in the standing order's public Christianity along the lines first scored by the Great Awakening. But as Congregationalists formally hived off into two camps in the early nineteenth century, the establishment's unified front before society fell victim as well. After the Peace of Ghent removed their last common ground, orthodox and Unitarians were free to develop different social visions.

Elliott's sermon closed by surveying the manifestations of the hand of God in Connecticut. These included faithful statesmen like the recently deceased Governor Trumbull, a widespread belief in sound religion, revivals, blessings for the missionary society, and "the establishment of a Theological institution in a sister state for the express purpose of training young men for the service of the sanctuary." "The formation of a 'Religious Tract' and 'Bible Society,'" he added, "may be also noticed, as hopeful means for disseminating interesting truths where greatly needed, and saving souls from eternal perdition." Elliott's mention of Andover Seminary and the evangelistic societies pointed to another important development of the period around 1810: many of the institutions that so powerfully shaped "evangelical America" in the antebellum era had their roots in the first decade of the nineteenth century.[33] These voluntary societies for missions and reform also made this a transitional period.

Institutional Outgrowths

> Behold, how great a matter a little fire kindleth!
>
> —James 3:5

As John Elliott observed, the first fifteen years of the nineteenth century abounded with institutional innovations. Congregational ministers, either working among themselves or with laymen and laywomen, organized societies that sought to evangelize the unchurched at home and abroad, coordinate more effectively the disparate local churches and associations, educate the next generation of clergymen, and combat immorality. These new institutions embodied the Congregationalists' transformed corporate ethic, which emphasized the churches' impact on society. They also creatively substituted for the standing order's loss of influence with civil rulers and the widening circle of dissenters. Amid these developments, the local, regional, and national dimensions remained complexly intertwined. The exchange of information was vital to initiating and coordinating activity across the different levels, just as news of the local revivals had inspired the reconceptualization of the Congregationalists' regional public Christianity. Usually people working at the grassroots pioneered novel organizational forms, and then only later were regional or nationwide umbrella groups gathered. Although local organizers sometimes took their cue from larger regional groups above them, their activity was nonetheless indispensable to the achievement of the larger groups' goals. Once again the experience of Worcester County clergymen such as Samuel Austin and Joseph Goffe typified developments taking place throughout southern New England.

The post-Revolutionary out-migration of New Englanders to the new settlements in Maine, Vermont, New York, and Ohio brought the Congregationalists' need for missionary endeavor to the fore. News of British missionaries also set a pattern for emulation. In the early 1790s, Connecticut's General Association of Congregational clergy began to send missionaries to these regions and in 1798 organized itself as the Connecticut Missionary Society. Massachusetts ministers, led by Nathanael Emmons, aped the methods of their Connecticut coreligionists and formed the Massachusetts Missionary Society in 1799. Samuel Austin served for many years as a trustee of the Massachusetts society and was its first secretary.[34]

The missionary movement's spate of activity had mixed results. On the one hand, the missionaries could not reproduce the New England establishment on the frontier. They succeeded in planting churches in the newly settled areas and ministering to the populations of erstwhile New Englanders there, but the standing order in its totality of hierarchy, order, and tax support could not be replicated. Perhaps most relevant to the standing order's failure was the problem of ministerial supply. The Congregationalists could not generate college-educated clergymen as rapidly as, say, the Methodists could establish preaching circuits. Moreover, the New Divinity Congregationalists' pure-church scruples made them reluctant to gather converts without the prospect of being able to settle a regular pastor.[35]

On the other hand, the new missionary societies bore good fruit back home in southern New England. They served as a rallying point for the evangelical community. Among the laity, women especially responded to the call to support missions and formed auxiliary "cent societies" to raise funds. As a spin-off of missions, the clergy launched communications projects such as tract organizations and periodicals. The societies' publications gave the ministry an additional channel of public influence and fueled the evangelical movement by feeding people with narratives of missionary labors. For instance, on Sunday, May 19, 1805, Joseph Goffe "read the missionary society's address" before his congregation and "proposed a contribution next sabbath." Accordingly, on the following Sunday he took in $20 as "a contribution for the Massa. Miss. Society." During the next week, he journeyed to Boston, attended the society's annual meeting, and presumably delivered his church's contribution. The societies further provided another venue for the collaboration of the orthodox clergy. While Goffe was in Boston for the Massachusetts Missionary Society's meeting, he also attended the election sermon the next day and the ministers' convention. Finally, local and regional missionary societies served as a laboratory for the conception of further projects. Missions to the American frontier, for instance, spawned an interest in foreign ones. Goffe proudly noted in his autobiographical memoir that he had cast a vote in favor of organizing the American Board of Commissioners for Foreign Missions (A.B.C.F.M.).[36]

That vote to form the A.B.C.F.M. was taken at the 1810 meeting of the Massachusetts General Association. The General Association was conceived in 1802 as a statewide body to facilitate the closer coordination of the several local associations of orthodox Congregational clergymen. Ephraim Ward, the moderator of the Brookfield Association, summed up well the aims of the General Association. In conveying his association's desire to join the umbrella group then forming, Ward thought "that it may greatly subserve the Interest of the Redeemer[']s Kingdom, for the Ministers of the gospel to cultivate fraternal affection, Union, & christian harmony, & afford mutual aid & encouragement." In addition to boosting ministerial cooperation, Ward hoped "that it will tend to form a more powerful Barrier against infidelity, which is making awful strides in our Land; & also to promote the interests of christianity." By "infidelity" Ward more precisely may have meant Unitarianism, for the General Association was a gathering of the orthodox. Liberal associations had initially been invited to join, but they did not like the looks of the new statewide association. In declining to join, the Worcester Association, the one to which Aaron Bancroft belonged, cited both the impracticality of creating an association that encompassed all of the Congregational clergymen across the length of Massachusetts and the General Association's redundancy, given the preexistence of the annual ministers' convention. More important, the Worcester Association also feared that "the proposed plan may prove dangerous to the peace and liberty of congregational Chhs. It may lead to an attempt to establish an uniform system of Chh. discipline." In other words, the Unitarians were afraid that the General Association was a stalking-horse for orthodox domination. Under the benign banner of "Union," they were afraid that the General Association would become a steamroller for the Calvinists, so they passed on the opportunity to join. The formation of the Massachusetts General Association both reflected and propelled the emerging split between orthodox Congregationalists and Unitarians.[37]

Minus the Unitarians, the General Association served as a coordinator with other organizations, a disseminator of news and information, and an incubator for further projects. It provided a forum for ministerial associations from across the state to talk with one another and a formal way for the Congregational clergy to reach out beyond Massachusetts. It established ties with other Congregational state associations, starting with Connecticut in 1808, and even forged links to the Presbyterian General Assembly in 1814. Annual minutes publicized the General Association's doings. These first appeared in the *Panoplist* in 1807 and then as a separate pamphlet in 1811 and every year from 1813 on. The minutes related the General Association's initiatives, along with news from the local associations, such as the 1810 notice that revivals had that year touched seven Worcester County towns and garnered at least six hundred new church members. The General Association was, most important, a hive of activity, buzzing with yet more institution building. For example, in 1813 a "committee on the subject of ardent spirits . . . had procured to be instituted" the Massachusetts Society for the Suppression of Intemperance. That same year, the ministers of the Brookfield Association resolved to forgo liquor themselves and use "our preaching, our example, our conversation, and our whole influence" to curtail alcohol consumption among their people. This initiative "was adopted at the suggestion of the Gen. Ass. of Mass.," which shows how the statewide organization could line up the local associations to produce a united front. Likewise, in 1814 the General Association distributed to the local associations preprinted petitions on the subject of Sunday mail delivery. The local associations were to do the legwork of gathering signatures, while the General Association would collect the petitions and bundle them for delivery to Congress with maximum impact. In short, the Massachusetts General Association gave the orthodox clergy a new tool for better orchestrating its social engagement.[38]

More important than the General Association for developing the clergy itself was the founding by orthodox ministers of the Andover Theological Seminary in 1808. The "fall" of Harvard to Unitarian control provided the most direct catalyst for the organization of the new school, and it functioned as a theological arsenal in the war against Unitarianism. As an educational institution, Andover started a trend of replacing the traditional, eighteenth-century routine of studying for the ministry under a pastor after college with a three-year graduate program. The founding of Andover produced a number of important results in addition to its contribution to intellectual life. The seminary, as Williston Walker remarked, "was a focus of missionary zeal, and its successful foundation marked the union between Old Calvinism and Edward[s]eanism in eastern Massachusetts, a union which averted a very serious division in the evangelical forces at a time when all their strength was needed." Andover also served as a site for professionalization and ministerial networking, which often produced further institution building. The founders themselves recognized this important side effect. "The friendships, formed here, will, it is believed, spring from the best of all sources; Evangelical Virtue," argued Timothy Dwight in his sermon at Andover's opening. "They will, also, be strongly cemented by oneness of age, education, circumstances, and pursuits. They will, therefore, last through life; will have a powerful influence on the character and conduct; will extend their efficacy over every part of this land; and will effect, in the happiest manner, all the moral and religious interest of its inhabitants." In the town of Andover itself, a group of seven professors and town residents modeled the establishment's new institutional engagement. The group "had its finger in most of the benevolent projects centered around Boston," such as the A.B.C.F.M. and the American Temperance Society. Finally, Andover positioned the orthodox party within Congregationalism for renewed leadership. "More than eleven percent of Andover students in the first decade (twenty-six men) later became college or seminary professors," Natalie A. Naylor has discovered.[39] In short, the Andover Seminary provided the orthodox with another important base of operations. It brought ministers together out of the dispersed structure of New England Congregationalism and focused their initiatives. It gave the orthodox an intellectual resource center, a cadre of trained and systematized clergy, and an informal place for association and the exchange of new ideas.

The founding of Andover and the missionary societies prompted a group of Worcester County men in 1812 to organize a local fund-raising agency, the Religious Charitable Society. More specifically, these men were the same circle with whom Joseph Goffe had been collaborating through pulpit exchanges and the Worcester South Association since the early 1800s. Among the officers and directors chosen in the society's first year were the familiar names of Goffe, Samuel Austin, John Crane, Edmund Mills, and Upton's Benjamin Wood. The Religious Charitable Society supported three projects, all of which were evangelistic in nature: scholarships for ministerial students, funding for the A.B.C.F.M., and subsidies for struggling local churches. Appropriately, then, Benjamin Wood based his sermon at the society's organizational meeting on Luke 10:2, which describes how "the harvest truly is great, but the labourers are few." True to its purposes, the society's minutes record mostly mundane business matters in pursuit of these goals, as when the board voted on September 15, 1812, "that thirty Dollars be given to Mr. Hawes, a member in the Seignior [sic] Class, at Brown University . . . that Mr. Emerson Pain receive twenty Dollars . . . [and] that Doc. Crane and the Secretary be a Committee to inquire into the situation of Mr. Coleman, requesting the aid of the Society, and report at the next meeting of the Board." The money that the society dispersed came from a variety of sources. Four years after its founding, the society already boasted seventeen branches. It also claimed the patronage of wealthy individuals, such as the Waldo family of Worcester. Here, too, women's auxiliaries provided critical support. To cite just one example, at the annual meeting in September 1814, the board voted "that the Rev. James Murdock be requested to return the thanks of this Board to the Female Society in Harvard for their generous donation."[40]

Although the Religious Charitable Society was a local organization with modest means and influence, it nevertheless saw itself as engaged in much larger religious and political concerns. The society's *Constitution and Address* of 1812 cast this

Worcester County organization as no less than a preliminary "to the introduction of the millennial glory of the Church of Christ." It also situated the society amid the similar work "of christian people, both in Europe and America" toward "the great and good object of evangelizing the world." As the society had been inspired by this news of transatlantic missionary work, so it in turn broadcast its own doings to the world. After the annual meeting of 1818, for example, the board voted that its report "be published in the Panoplist, in the Missionary Herald, in the Boston Recorder, and in the Worcester papers." As with the missionary societies or the General Association, the Religious Charitable Society was engaged in an ongoing dialogue with the new religious news media. The society's directors were both informed by outside reports and motivated then to produce their own publicity. They also related their work to contemporary politics. The society's published message for 1814 familiarly juxtaposed the doleful state of the nation—from the perspective of New England Federalists, at least—with the promising outlook for the church. Although the authors confessed that "the aspects of Providence, relative to our country" were enough "to excite great apprehension," they nevertheless urged readers to take heart, because "Zion is in the safe keeping of its adorable Redeemer and King." Therefore, they urged everyone to "industriously work, with the mass of our fellow Christians, to prepare for the millennial glory." Clearly, clergymen such as those involved with the Religious Charitable Society were not advocating a withdrawal from social engagement but rather new strategies for the church to have an impact on the world.[41]

The moral societies organized throughout New England most directly reflected, on an institutional level, the standing order's continuing corporate ethic and its desire to broaden its public presence. Nathanael Emmons initiated the first such society for the improvement of morals in Franklin, Massachusetts, in 1790, and by 1810 moral societies "were a familiar feature on the New England social landscape." The moral society movement took on a statewide structure in Connecticut in 1812 with the founding of the Connecticut Society for the Promotion of Good Morals.[42] These societies sought to counteract a host of symptoms that seemed to indicate that rot had set into New England's communal moral fiber: a decline in respect for the Sabbath and religion in general; an increase in profanity, gambling, and intemperance; and an apparently pervasive and growing contempt for the law.[43] The established clergy's diagnosis of national sin had been growing bleaker during the early nineteenth century. It is no coincidence that as the clergy's denunciations reached a crescendo around 1812, the moral reform movement gathered momentum.[44] The moral societies amounted to an innovative strategy to combat the threat of innovation. At bottom, the societies had deeply conservative aims of preserving regional values and averting divine wrath. Yet, reflecting the betwixt-and-between nature of the period around 1810, they also represented a novel solution to conventional problems. With the recognition of the magistracy's unreliability, clergymen launched new institutions to do what magistrates no longer could. They rallied the faithful in a new mode to pursue their concern for the corporate welfare.

Fear, coming from several directions, called the moral societies into existence. For one, ministers argued that unless something was done, and done soon, the traditionally pious and ordered New England way of life would vanish. Nathanael Em-

mons mourned, "The time was, when we were distinguished among all other nations, *for purity of manners*. Our Fathers when they came to this land, were strict and
rigid in their notions of morality. . . . But alas! how is the gold become dim!" "If we
do neglect our duty, and suffer our laws and institutions to go down, we give them up
forever," warned Lyman Beecher in a similar burst of homage to his ancestors. "It is
easy to relax, easy to retreat, but impossible when [Matt. 24:15] the abomination of
desolation has once passed over New-England, to rear again the thrown down altars,
and gather again the fragments, and build up the ruins of demolished institutions.
. . . Another Connecticut will not arise upon the ruins of this happy State, if it be
given up to the empire of sin." Like modern historians, these clergymen recognized
the distinctiveness of New England's Puritan-rooted culture, and they wanted to preserve it. "New-England can retain her pre-eminence," argued Beecher, "only by upholding those institutions and habits which produced it. Divested of these, like
Sampson shorn of his locks, she will become as weak and contemptible as any other
land." Moreover, always undergirding the clergy's corporate vision was the threat to a
wicked society of "the judicial displeasure of God." To quote Beecher again, through
the action of the local moral societies, "the land is purified, the anger of the Lord is
turned away, and his blessing and protection restored."[45] Republicanism added to this
mix the fear of the decline of free government. Among the reasons to join the reform
movement listed by Heman Humphrey of Fairfield, Connecticut, were "the momentous interests of your country," "the blessings of good government," and "the security of life, liberty and property."[46] In their intentions at least, the moral societies
strove for nothing novel. They acted from prudential motives and dyed-in-the-wool
conservatism to arrest a perceived moral decline.

One leading reason for the moral crisis, as the ministry saw it, was the magistracy's failure in its assigned role. This complaint has been noted previously, but it
was especially pronounced in the moral society movement. Noah Porter of Farmington, Connecticut, flatly charged that "magistrates generally are answerable for the
sabbath-breaking, the profane swearing, the drunkenness, the lewdness, and all the
other open immoralities, which, by neglect of their official duty, they tolerate." Like
Porter, Beecher sought to understand why public officials seemed hesitant to crack
down on immorality. He recognized that "in a republican government, where so
much emolument and the gratification of so much ambition depend upon the suffrages of the people," unpopular policies, though essential and righteous, would not
be carried out. This situation Beecher depicted in stark terms: "When the toleration
of crimes becomes the price of public suffrage—when the people will not endure
the restraint of righteous laws, but reward magistrates who violate their oath and suffer them to sin with impunity; and when magistrates will sell their conscience and
the public good for a little brief authority, then the public suffrage is of but little
value, for the day of liberty is drawing to a close, and the night of despotism is at
hand."[47] It was time for clergymen to act to save the republic, and they would do so
independently of the magistracy, if need be.

Dire though the situation may have appeared, Beecher and his associates were
not ones to sit on their hands. Rather, they saw a possible remedy in a course of action developed in Britain. Emmons contended that the experience of the British Society for the Reformation of Manners showed "convincing evidence, that Unions in

virtue may be so formed and conducted, as to restrain, in some measure at least, the progress of vice." Others seconded his assessment.[48]

The societies sought to chart a new relationship with the civil leadership. According to some of their spokesmen, the moral societies would be committees that oversaw the magistrates. Acting as a political pressure group, the societies would encourage public officials to enforce the moral laws. If the societies could succeed in making "the faint hearted leave their hiding places and be found at their posts; . . . [then] soon, we should hear no more about the difficulty of executing the laws. Punishment would tread so uniformly and so closely upon the heels of transgression, that the enemy would no longer think of keeping the field. In a month, the whole main body of sabbath-breakers, tipplers, &c. would disappear, and it would only be necessary, to keep a watchful eye, upon a few stragglers."[49]

Alternately, the societies pursued strategies that were nongovernmental altogether. Recognizing that popularly elected officials might be reluctant to act, the societies "deliberately set about to try to disengage clerical public guardianship from the processes of politics." Instead of incessantly carping that the magistrates needed to act, ministers called upon their congregations to enlist in the cause of moral reform. Beecher hoped that by uniting "the wise and the good" "of all denominations" into "a sort of disciplined moral militia," the societies could change "public opinion."[50] "Every man, woman and child can do something—can do *much*," implored Ebenezer Porter, the Bartlett Professor of Sacred Rhetoric at Andover Seminary. He continued,

> Who cannot spare one cent, to buy a small tract? That tract, dropped on the high road, or given to a stranger, may carry comfort to some desponding, or conviction to some careless heart; may reclaim some profligate, awaken some drunkard to sobriety, some sabbath-breaker or swearer to saving reformation. The day is coming, when men will be accustomed to reckon the establishment of a tract or moral society, or a praying meeting, among the instruments of ushering in the glory of the church, and the salvation of the world.

These were concrete ways by which the church would act upon its surrounding community. Only its efforts could yield a godly society, since "the kingdom of God is a kingdom of means."[51]

The moral society founded in Worcester County in 1815 epitomized the broader regional movement of its time. The Worcester County organization was not one of the earliest to get started, so it borrowed from the example of moral societies already underway. As the society wrote to its local branches, "This Society is not a solitary instance in attempting a reformation of morals.—Within the United States, hundreds of Moral Societies now exist. . . . In the efforts you are making, you act in union with thousands who are associated for similar purposes. It must give you pleasure to cooperate with a host of useful men, who have the best interest of mankind at heart." This quotation suggests once more the central role played by the transmission of news and information in organizing the various new societies for missions, the ministry, and reform. Indeed, in order for people *to obtain an affecting sense of the necessity of reformation*," Brookfield's Micah Stone urged them to "meditate, converse, and read respecting the prevalent sins; . . . consider the evils thence resulting to the individuals and society; and the dangers which threaten all." Like societies elsewhere in southern New England, the Worcester County group also derived, in part, from a concern over the magistracy's weakness. In response, the society argued both for "the appointment of vigilant, faithful, discreet men" and for the branch societies "to supply the vacancy, so far as they can do it, in their private capacity." Other current events further prompted the Worcester society's formation. "Our late suffering and bleeding country demands our commiseration and calls aloud for a reformation," argued North Brookfield's Thomas Snell in 1816. "And since the scourge [of the War of 1812] is removed by a merciful God, his goodness should constrain us to repent." Regardless of these mentions of civil magistrates and the highly polarized war, the society contended that its goals were nonpartisan and sought only "to promote [Prov. 14:34] that righteousness which exalteth a nation, and to prevent that sin which is the reproach, degradation and ruin of any people." Whether or not this disavowal of partisanship convinced skeptical observers, the time had arrived, said Micah Stone, for people "TO ACT." He urged his listeners to seize every available opportunity to converse upon moral subjects, set a good example, "promote the circulation of useful publications," and see to it that only "judicious and faithful men should be chosen to all offices." In sum, Worcester County's Society for the Reformation of Morals embodied the prevailing idea in the clergy's public Christianity by 1815 that the faithful needed to unite and shoulder the load of building the godly society.[52]

The formation of moral societies across southern New England in the years around 1810 clearly signaled the dawn of a new phase for the establishment. Pursuing its traditional goal of a godly community, the clergy organized an array of novel institutions. Ebenezer Porter certainly captured the spirit of the times when he called it an "age of action."[53] Finding that it could no longer count on the cooperation of the magistracy as it once had, the ministry blazed alternative paths to link Christianity and society. These new connections developed both institutionally and ideologically. By 1815, the ministry had already begun to position itself for the better known campaign to sanctify society that would flourish in the 1820s.

The Congregational ministry's creative adaptations were rather remarkable. The transformations of southern New England culture in the years between 1800 and 1815 had divested the establishment of its close association with the region's political elite, deprived it of the allegiance of a sizable segment of the population, and divided it within. The boom of dissenters and the Unitarian controversy had negatively affected the standing order, but the most salient development was the advent of the first party competition. The contest between Federalists and Democratic-Republicans altered the ideology of both the establishment and dissenters. For the standing order, the Jeffersonian triumph inaugurated a period of drastic reevaluation. To established ministers, the War of 1812 formed only the tip of an iceberg of infidelity and sin that threatened to scuttle the national ship. They repudiated their providential reading of American history and spiraled into grim, apocalyptic nightmares of impending doom. But their response to the first party system did not stand alone. The years of partisan polarization produced a jarring diversity of opinions. Dissenters embraced the change. The Democratic-Republicans gave them not only concrete benefits such as electoral allies and some legislative access but also the less tangible advantage of more potent language. The dissenters' critique of the establishment became more mainstream, as they utilized popular Jeffersonian discourse. By joining with others who detested the standing order's political preaching, dissenters were able to weaken or even bring down the establishment.

Because of these changes, the established ministry had to conceive new strategies if it still wanted to link Christianity and society. Moving outside the realm of party politics, it built new institutional platforms for public engagement and found a new voice in the ideology of the church acting on the community. The critical question of this transitional period remained this: "if while we enjoy the highest degree of political liberty, and temporal prosperity, we are not a virtuous and religious people, shall we not provoke the most HIGH to withdraw these favors, and pour out his judgments upon us, and empty us from vessel to vessel?"[54] Interestingly, this was a question posed by the Baptist Asahel Morse. As the orthodox Congregationalists moved away from the magistracy and toward their new model of public engagement, they built bridges to some of the dissenting groups. Herein lay the foundations of an evangelical activism, which would have such significant consequences in the 1820s and 1830s. This process of rapprochement is a prime focus of the next chapter.

FIVE

‒‒◦○◦‒‒

Public Christianity's Renewal
and Realignment
1815–1833

THE RAGING STORMS of partisan and sectarian controversy that had racked southern New England during the two decades between the late 1790s and 1810s subsided as quickly as they had blown up. The decline of the first party competition, the end of the establishment as an issue in Connecticut politics, the return of international peace, and the rise of a spirit of evangelical interdenominationalism all combined by 1820 to clear the atmosphere of the frenzied polarization that had marked the first years of the nineteenth century. The abeyance of intense partisanship allowed a resurgence of patriotism. In contrast to the despair and hostility they had recently shown toward the national government, Congregational ministers reverted to the position that the United States would likely play some role in the providential renovation of the world. Yet, the return of more irenic days did not mean a simple reversion to the status quo antebellum. As the high winds and flood waters of a storm in the natural world alter the landscape, so, too, the political storm had reshaped relationships and beliefs among southern New England's political and religious factions.

The disappearance of a shared enemy—be it George III, the Jacobins, or Jefferson—meant that Unitarian and Trinitarian (or orthodox) Congregationalists were now free to go their separate ideological ways. The two sides had already begun to divide their institutional property in the decade after the controversy over Harvard's Hollis Chair of Divinity in 1805. In the 1820s, the two branches of the old Massachusetts standing order freely vented their disagreements. The full articulation of distinctive theological frameworks among Unitarians and Trinitarians also led to divergent understandings of the relationship between religion and society, whereas earlier the establishment had presented a more unified front. Just as the standing order was breaking up, the orthodox and the old dissenting denominations discovered a new convergence of interests at several points.

This realignment of denominational allies recast the debate over public Christianity. The traditional New England quest to build a godly society continued along both axes of providential interpretation and social prescription. Clergymen did not retreat from their conviction that society needed a religious influence, nor did their providential worldview collapse. However, the specific content of their public Christianity had changed. The Unitarians, despite their theological innovations, remained in some ways the most conventional in terms of their social beliefs. Like the standing order of the 1780s, they adhered the longest of any denomination to the traditional establishment of Congregationalism in Massachusetts. Orthodox Congregationalists, cut off from the establishment in both Connecticut and Massachusetts, had to find new ways by which to link their religion to society. They did so by cultivating the nascent developments outlined in chapter 4. The orthodox advocated an ideology focused on the revived and mobilized church as the institution that would act on its community. Such action ultimately carried millennial consequences. They also developed a model of political engagement that relied on a new concept of Christian citizenship. On these issues, the orthodox were able to build bridges to the old dissenting denominations, such as the Baptists and Episcopalians, creating a new evangelical coalition.[1] Therefore, both the Unitarians and evangelical groups remained committed to engaging their Christianity with social life, but from different perspectives.

The Resurrection of Patriotism

> God be merciful unto us, and bless us; and cause his face to shine upon us; Selah. That thy way may be known upon earth, thy saving health among all nations.
>
> —Ps. 67:1-2

In the years immediately following the War of 1812, prior antagonisms abated. The cessation of hostilities in 1815 dramatically decreased the level of acrimony in politics and public life. With the Peace of Ghent, the most divisive issue in domestic politics, the War of 1812, had come to a close; moreover, Napoleon no longer presented a threat abroad. Additionally, the contest between Federalists and Democratic-Republicans slackened during "the Era of Good Feelings." These changes had a significant impact on the clergy's public Christianity. They allowed ministers to reconsider their interpretation of the relationship between the nation and Providence. National sins seemed comparatively less alarming than previously, and Congregationalists who had recently been alienated from the nation-state came in from the cold. Several prominent clergymen began to reimagine how, borrowing the words of the Psalmist, the United States might help make the way of the Lord known among all nations.

As the first dozen years of the nineteenth century had been a period of partisan organizing and widening polarization, the decade and a half following the War of 1812 was a time of demobilization. Not only did the tone of political discourse soften but also voter turnout declined in conjunction with the decay of party organization. Even before the war ended, the first party struggle in Massachusetts had begun to lose its prewar vigor. As Ronald P. Formisano argues, "the Republican organization grew weak from defeat amid the war's unpopularity, while Federal organization withered away in success." Formisano also supports the notion of an Era of Good Feelings in Massachusetts that lasted from 1816 to between 1827 and 1831. "The end of the war accelerated the decline of organized competitive politics," he writes. For example, partisan labels became less significant in the gubernatorial race, with both Federalists and Republicans backing Levi Lincoln Jr. in 1825. In addition, when James Monroe visited Boston in July 1817, the *Independent Chronicle* editorialized that "the visit of the President seems wholly to have allayed the storms of party," and another paper even came up with the phrase "era of good feelings" for the occasion. In Connecticut, meanwhile, after the disappearance of the Federalist party in 1820, a period of nonpartisanship similarly reigned. Rhode Island politics also went through a "relatively placid decade" between 1818 and 1828. Thus, by the late 1810s, a period of lessened partisanship and comparative political harmony, the Era of Good Feelings, had flowered in southern New England.[2]

Congregational clergymen eagerly welcomed the new atmosphere of nonpartisanship and did what they could to support it. There had always been a salient strand of antiparty feeling among the clergy, as evidenced by the dissent of such ministers as Joseph McKeen and Samuel West.[3] Both men had regretted the standing order's political involvement in the first decade of the nineteenth century. The bulk of Congregational ministers now reemphasized unifying, nonpartisan themes in their preaching. Peter Eaton, a Unitarian from Boxford, Massachusetts, commenced the 1819 election sermon by noting that "a thick cloud [no longer] darkened our political horizon" and by promising "to avoid all political discussions." On the occasion of the end of the War of 1812, Hartford's Abel Flint urged his auditors to "avoid party spirit; cultivate union; and manifest towards each other an accommodating disposition." Borrowing a theme from Jefferson's first inaugural address, he concluded, "Let us adopt no names ourselves, nor give any to our fellow citizens, but that of AMERICANS; and let that name dispose us to cherish a love for one another, and to treat each other as friends and brothers." Samuel Austin, then pastoring Samuel Hopkins's former church in Newport, Rhode Island, contended in 1822 that "the people of these United States have never been really so divided in their political creed, or in their pursuits, in regard to the public welfare, as the professed organs of their opinions would have to be understood. Republicanism has been the doctrine, in which, at least, ninety-nine hundredths of them have acquiesced." This amounted to both a gilding of history and a personal change of heart.[4] Ministers like Austin had always claimed to be nonpartisan, even if they simultaneously staked out obviously Federalist positions in the public debate. When the political culture at large moved away from its polarized state in the late 1810s, clergymen gladly moved with it and avoided the awkwardly self-contradictory position that they had held in the first dozen years of the century.

This is not to say that the peace resolved the bifurcation of American public opinion regarding the war. Indeed, the critics and proponents of the War of 1812 remained as divided as ever in their postbellum assessments: both sides felt that the outcome of the conflict had vindicated their positions.[5] The words of John Smith of Salem, New Hampshire, just across the border from Massachusetts, provide a case in point. On the annual fast day in 1813, Smith had blasted the War of 1812 as a national sin that a providential God was punishing. "Must not every man among us," he asked, "who is influenced by the fear of God, disapprove the invasion of Canada, as unrighteous and cruel? and view the hand of Heaven in the defeat of three armies, as an awful frown on the enterprise?" In April 1815, in a sermon on the national thanksgiving for peace, he conceded nothing to the war's proponents, regardless of Jackson's victory at New Orleans or anything else. In Smith's reading of the war's outcome, God had prevailed on the side of the war's opponents. "In the revolutionary war," he noted in comparison, "the providence of God caused a general union among the people. In the late war, the same kind providence prevented a union." Providence also frustrated the aggressive strategies of both belligerents, and the end of the war meant peace between the United States and Britain, that "Christian nation, which is doing more than any other, if not more than all other nations on the globe, in spreading the gospel among the heathen."6 Nevertheless, even if prowar and antiwar factions could not agree on the necessity or justice of the war in hindsight, the war's end did remove a major bone of contention that had inflamed the body politic for the past three to five years.

Ministers of the standing order also celebrated the defeat of French arms. Since the late 1790s, Congregational clergymen had sounded the trumpet of warning to call attention to the threat of French subversion and infidelity. By 1815, the anti-Christian, Gallic conspiracy had apparently collapsed. According to the analysis, again, of John Smith, "The Roman beast or Antichrist, in that particular form, in which it existed for about twenty years past, seems for a time to have gone into perdition. The flame of war, which was last kindled by its contagious breath, has of late been extinguished by the breath of the Almighty. . . . Has there been a time since Christ was crucified, in which such wonderful things, in favour of the Christian religion, were accomplished, in the space of one year?" Likewise, Elijah Parish of Byfield, Massachusetts, practically breathed an audible sigh of relief at the defeat of Napoleonic France. Since the 1790s, Parish had been one of the New England clergy's most vociferous critics of French atheism, but in 1815 he could finally lower his guard. "The malignant vapors [of Enlightenment skepticism] are dissipated, by encreasing [sic] light, by the irresistable [sic] splendors of truth," he noted optimistically. "The intolerable plagues of infidelity have demonstrated the necessity of revelation; the world has been amazed and convinced. Daring infidels have become courageous champions of the cross. . . . An irresistable [sic] influence in favor of christianity is extending itself far and wide, even to the pagan nations."7 The end of the revolutionary and supposedly infidel regime in France allowed the clergy of southern New England to relax and lay aside its apocalyptic fears. God had dealt the forces of the Antichrist a stunning blow, and ministers could once again open their minds to more hopeful thoughts.

In short, the issues such as partisan competition, international crisis, and war that had propelled intense controversy and division in the two decades between the 1790s and 1810s had either lost a considerable amount of their momentum or vanished altogether. These developments opened a window of opportunity for the Congregational clergy; they gave ministers the chance to rethink their attitude toward the nation and its providential role. Congregational clergymen expressed a kind of national pride that had been absent since the 1780s and 1790s. Once again, they allowed themselves to speculate regarding the way in which God would use the United States to advance his plans. They confidently predicted that other nations would seek to imitate the peace and prosperity of the United States. As the Christian's ultimate hope for history lay in the millennium, a variety of clergymen asserted a national role in the fulfillment of millennial scenarios.

One noticeable shift of this period was that ministers quit their denunciations of the Constitution as a flawed and godless compact. The repudiations that rang out at the time of the War of 1812 disappeared from the ministry's pronouncements. In addition to the negative evidence of a lack of criticism, one can also detect a shift in the ministry's attitude on the basis of positive celebrations of American government. Samuel Austin's remarkable new praise for the national government captured the Congregational ministry's retreat from secessionist leanings. Eleven years after he had elevated the British constitution over the American on account of the former's explicit acknowledgment of a Christian foundation, Austin in 1822 gave thanks to God for having "graciously favored this country [the United States] with this form of government, and preserved it, to this day, unimpaired." He had made quite a turnaround by the time of this Fourth of July oration, concluding, "Wo to the man who shall touch this constitution with an impure design. Let him, who would wickedly seek its subversion, know, that it is treason of far greater turpitude than any which has hitherto brought a subject to the scaffold." Likewise, Eleazar T. Fitch, professor at Yale Divinity School, boasted that the United States, where government is "regulated by open compact," "is the dwelling of freedom."[8] Congregational clergymen once more defended and extolled the federal Constitution.

Along these same lines, ministers restated the case for the compatibility between Christianity and American patriotism. Around the time of the nation's semicentennial in 1826, some argued that not only did Christianity present no conflict with American patriotism but also it polished and completed that virtue. Perhaps the clergy wished to rid itself of any lingering odor of disloyalty that remained in the wake of the War of 1812 or the Hartford Convention. Nathaniel L. Frothingham of Boston's First Congregational (Unitarian) Church pointed out that the Bible contained numerous incidents that exhibited patriotism, or "love of one's country." One of these was Jacob's last command, "bury me with my fathers," found in Gen. 49:29, the chosen text for a sermon that Frothingham delivered in 1826, entitled *Christian Patriotism*. According to him, there was no contradiction between Christianity and patriotism; rather, patriotism was a subset of Christian benevolence. Whereas Christianity "commands us to think and act for the general welfare; to do good to all . . . to be interested in whatever concerns the improvement and happiness of man," patriotism merely focused this general sentiment on "those who are the nearest; . . . in the scenes that surround us, in the objects on which we can most readily act, in the persons with whom we stand anywise connected." Fourth of July celebrations served as an important occasion for the clergy to stitch Christianity and patriotism back together. In an 1825 July Fourth address also entitled *Christian Patriotism*, Nathaniel Bouton sang the praises of patriotism; "no attribute of the human character sooner awakens esteem and admiration. You love the man who loves his country; who endeavors to promote the civil happiness of the community to which he belongs." Bouton had graduated from Andover Seminary the year before and recently been installed as a Congregational minister over a church in Concord, New Hampshire. The type of civic patriotism he described was fine as far as it went but could only improve with the addition of Christianity. If one "let the love of God mingle with his love of country," Bouton said, then "soon it will shed a holy influence over all his actions. He will not relax his efforts for their temporal good, but the motive that actuates his will be purer, and the end in view more worthy of accomplishment."[9] In the 1820s, Christian patriotism no longer required one to reject the national government but to embrace it.

Some ministers also retold the tale of the guiding hand of Providence in the American Revolution. The 1826 and 1827 sermons of two Congregational ministers, Charles A. Boardman of New-Preston, Connecticut, and Joseph Dana of Ipswich, Massachusetts, read as if they could have been delivered in 1783. Both were replete with an analysis of God, "the Divine over-ruling favor," as the first cause behind such events as the colonists' unity and acquisition of supplies, the leadership of Washington, and the Americans' surprising victories over British arms.[10] Again, it appears that the occasion of the U.S. semicentennial fostered a return to Revolutionary-era themes. Although the clergy's providential discourse could also serve as an instrument of rebuke to national chauvinism, it is undeniable that some ministers at some times did, indeed, realign national and providential histories.

More significantly, clergymen of a variety of theological and denominational stripes enumerated the several facets of national greatness and optimistically discussed "the rising glory of this western world." Both Eleazar T. Fitch, the Yale Divinity School professor, and Nathaniel Thayer, the Unitarian minister of Lancaster, Massachusetts, came up with essentially the same list of characteristics that demonstrated "the goodness of God to this nation." Both named "favorable" geography, "equality" and economic "opportunity," freedom and good government, learning, and "religious freedom and toleration" as the hallmarks of the United States.[11] Given these endowments, the United States was bound to become a showcase for the world. As they had done in the 1780s, ministers predicted that American government and religion especially would become global models. On Independence Day, 1824, Loammi Ives Hoadly, an orthodox Congregationalist from Worcester, Massachusetts, expressed the hope that from the United States "the spirit of freedom will still be more and more diffused, till the pure elements of liberty and christian uprightness shall at length come forth, to constitute a national happiness as yet unknown in continental Europe and the rest of the Eastern world." The following year, New Haven's Leonard Bacon argued "that it is neither arrogance nor enthusiasm to say" that the United States "might send forth from its borders the institutions of freedom and the light of salvation, to the ends of the world."[12] The eyes of all nations, said Congregational ministers, would once again turn to the United States.

This American-inspired global transformation might ultimately connect to the millennium. Most mainstream American Protestants of this era were postmillennialists. They believed that the earth would be gradually readied to bring about a thousand-year reign of righteousness that would precede Christ's Second Coming. In light of their renewed sense of national promise, some ministers concluded that the nation was contributing to the millennium. William B. Sprague, for one, believed in the millennial role of the United States. "We know—for God has told us—that there is a period of universal moral renovation approaching," he remarked to a Fourth of July audience in Northampton, Massachusetts, in 1827, "and there is much in the aspect of

Francis Wayland. Courtesy Brown University Library.

Providence, which seems to indicate that our country is to have a prominent—may I not say—a principal instrumentality in the introduction of that period."[13]

In an interesting example of convergence of previously antagonistic Baptists and Congregationalists, both Francis Wayland and Lyman Beecher presented parallel scenarios during the mid-1820s of how the United States would contribute to the emancipation of other nations. These two prominent clergymen imagined that Europe would soon turn to the United States for tutelage in democracy and religious liberty. Wayland and Beecher each enjoyed careers at the top of their denominations, the Baptist and Congregational, respectively. From 1821 to 1826, Wayland held the prestigious pulpit of Boston's First Baptist Church and then went on to serve as president of Brown from 1827 to 1855. In 1826, Beecher had just concluded a sixteen-

Lyman Beecher. Courtesy American Antiquarian Society.

year pastorate over the First Congregational Church of Litchfield, Connecticut, and then moved to Boston's Hanover Congregational Church that March. An effective revivalist, he played a leading role in the evangelistic and reform projects of the era, helping to form moral, missionary, and publication societies.[14] Both Wayland and Beecher occupied places at the forefront of the debate over public Christianity in antebellum America.

According to Wayland's analysis, Europe had reached a crossroads by 1825. The continent was split between nations that were either despotic and Catholic or democratic and Protestant. He thought that something decisive was about to happen that would tilt the balance of power in favor of one side or the other, although he expressed confidence that the forces of liberalism would ultimately triumph. The United States figured importantly in this situation because it demonstrated to doubters that democracy could succeed and that the democratic-Protestant tandem produced the greatest amount of national happiness. "The moral influence, which nations are exerting upon each other," Wayland explained, "is greater than it has been at any antecedent period in the history of the world. The institutions of one country, are becoming known almost of necessity to every other country." The United States was now gaining such renown. "Our heroic struggle [of revolution], its perfect success, its virtuous termination have rivetted the eyes of the people of Europe specially upon us, and they cannot now be averted." Indeed, the time seemed ripe for the United States to point the way toward a social, political, and religious reorganization of the Old World. "Ancient constitutions having been abolished, new ones must be adopted by almost every nation in Europe," Wayland reasoned. "The old foundations will have been removed; it will still remain to be decided on what foundations the social edifice shall rest. From the relation we now sustain to the friends of free institutions, as well as from all the cases of revolution which have lately occurred, it is evident that to this nation they will all look for precedent and example."[15]

Beecher went further than Wayland, arguing that the United States would be a model not just for Europe, although perhaps most importantly so, but for the whole world. For the millennium to commence, Beecher said, three changes had to take place: a feudal system of land tenure, aristocratic government, and state-supported churches all had to give way in favor of yeoman control of the land, democratic government, and freedom of conscience in religion. The United States—and more specifically the part settled by the Puritans—manifested all three of these characteristics and "has been raised up by Providence to exert an efficient instrumentality in this moral renovation of the world." True to the ministry's providential outlook, Beecher found the highest proof for his hypothesis in history. "The history of our nation is indicative of some great design to be accomplished by it. It is a history of perils and deliverances and of strength ordained out of weakness." As examples, he pointed to the way that Providence had shielded the colonists from the Indians, French, and British. "These deliverances the enemy beheld often with wonder, and our fathers, always, with thanksgiving and praise. But, in the whole history of the world, God has not been accustomed to grant signal interpositions without ends of corresponding magnitude." In other words, because Providence had been so intimately concerned with American history in the past, it stood to reason that this was in preparation for something more significant still. And what could be a more important goal than the millennium? "Let this nation go on, then," Beecher concluded, "and multiply its millions and its resources, and bring the whole under the influence of our civil and religious institutions, and with the energies of its concentrated benevolence send out evangelical instruction; and who can calculate what our blessed instrumentality shall have accomplished, when He who sitteth upon the throne shall have made all things new."[16] In a section to follow, this chapter considers the way in which Beecher and like-minded men relied on the "concentrated benevolence" of evangelical institutions to remake the globe. Here, note the way that clergymen such as Beecher had reintegrated the United States within their providential framework in a positive—indeed, millennial—light.

That part of the clergy's public Christianity that dealt with the nation's relationship to a providential God underwent a positive reassessment. The Congregational clergy reunited with other denominations, including Francis Wayland's Baptists, to anticipate the spread of American civilization around the globe. Providence seemed to have fixed a significant role for the nation, perhaps in preparation for the millennium. This recrudescence of patriotism had been fostered by the atrophy of the first party competition, the decline of the Gallic threat, and the end of war. In the late 1810s and 1820s, there was a continuity with the early nineteenth century inasmuch as clergymen continued to interpret the meaning of corporate life within a providential framework. However, this tradition of providential analysis had shifted away from the Congregationalists' rejection of the United States and toward the more celebratory nationalism that the dissenters and Democratic-Republicans had maintained.

The ministry's budding nationalism provided a noticeable point of interdenominational consensus in the years following the War of 1812. Figures such as Lyman Beecher, Nathaniel Thayer, and Francis Wayland—an orthodox Congregationalist, Unitarian, and Baptist, respectively—diverged sharply in other matters but could all assent to the proposition "that America is destined by providence to distinction."[17] This agreement stood in contrast to the growing split that was developing between Unitarians and the orthodox in other aspects of their corporate ethic. The next two sections consider the emergence of differing social visions between the two branches of the old standing order.

The Unitarians' Public Christianity

> But we desire to hear of thee what thou thinkest: for as concerning this
> sect, we know that every where it is spoken against.
>
> — Acts 28:22

The same factors that encouraged a revival of providential patriotism, such as the end of war and the decline of party competition, also meant that Unitarian and orthodox Congregationalists had lost their common adversaries and were freed to quarrel among themselves. The label "standing order" became an anachronism by 1830 because the Connecticut establishment had been undone in 1818 and Massachusetts Congregationalists continued to move apart over the decade of the 1820s. As the Congregationalists split into Unitarian and orthodox wings with respect to theology and organization, the two branches also diverged with respect to their inherited corporate ethic. There remained, naturally, many points of overlap between the Unitarians and orthodox, in that the two groups were descended from a common lineage. Nevertheless, in the post-1815 period, Unitarians and Trinitarians developed outlooks on society that manifested their theological labels. Trinitarians emphasized the action of Jesus Christ and the Holy Spirit when they described the influence of revival upon the community, whereas the Unitarians explained the fatherhood of God as a reasonable model for men and women to follow.[18]

Two of the Unitarians' principles stand out as particularly relevant to the articulation of their distinctive public Christianity. Although full treatments of Unitarian thought have been provided elsewhere,[19] the Unitarian commitments to rationalism and liberalism require elaboration here. The Unitarians' rationalism and liberalism led them in directions different from the orthodox. For instance, the Unitarians scaled back their providential pronouncements; they seldom spoke of an interventionist Providence in human affairs or of a wrathful God demanding corporate repentance. However, on a number of points, the Unitarians adhered to the standing order's conventional public Christianity. They continued to stress that society needed religion, both from moral rulers and from the establishment of Congregationalism in Massachusetts. When everyone else had come to favor disestablishment, the Unitarians fought to preserve the government's support of religion into the 1830s.[20]

William Ellery Channing's 1819 sermon at the ordination of Jared Sparks, also known as his Baltimore sermon, demonstrated the salient position of reason in Unitarian thought. "We object strongly," explained Channing, taking on the role of spokesman for the Unitarians as a whole, "to the contemptuous manner in which human reason is often spoken of by our adversaries, because it leads, we believe, to universal skepticism. If reason be so dreadfully darkened by the fall, that its most decisive judgments on religion are unworthy of trust, then Christianity, and even natural theology, must be abandoned; for the existence and veracity of God, and the Divine original of Christianity, are conclusions of reason, and must stand or fall with it." Likewise, Worcester's Aaron Bancroft defended reason as "the peculiar excellence of the human constitution, and the more uniformly we are governed by reason, under the sanction of an enlightened conscience, the nearer shall we approach the goal of perfection." Christianity hinged on reason also, Channing continued, because there was not "a book which demands a more frequent exercise of reason than the Bible." The "passions" provided the greatest threat to reason and had to be guarded against. This constituted the crux of the problem with the Trinitarians: they were far too taken with passionate ideas like conversion. "We object strongly," Channing said, "to the idea of many Christians respecting man's impotence and God's irresistible agency on the heart, believing that they subvert our responsibility and the laws of our moral nature, that they make men machines, that they cast on God the blame of all evil deeds, that they discourage good minds, and inflate the fanatical with wild conceits of immediate and sensible inspiration." Instead, he proposed as the Unitarian model of "Christian virtue" something far more rationalistic: "We conceive, that the true love of God is a moral sentiment, founded on a clear perception, and consisting in a high esteem and veneration, of his moral perfections."[21] The doctrine of the Trinity clouded this "clear perception" "by dividing and distracting the mind in its communion with God."[22] The boast of Peter Whitney at the funeral of John Adams in 1826 epitomized this Unitarian stress upon reason. Whitney, the minister of Quincy, Massachusetts, said of Adams that "he was strictly a Unitarian; nor is it of little importance to that class of christians that a mind so capable of judging as *his*, and so critical in its inquiries in order to obtain satisfaction, should at length settle itself in the belief of that system, which Unitarians support." In other words, a discriminating genius such as Adams's would likely reach the conclusions of Unitarianism.[23]

Liberalism—defined as the defense of free inquiry and the rights of conscience against dogmatism—formed a second hallmark of the Unitarian movement. After

William Ellery Channing. Courtesy American Antiquarian Society.

all, a commitment to the development of reason required that one be free to follow the lead of rational consideration. Channing, once again, provided the clearest and most succinct statement of the position. "I call that mind free, which jealously guards its intellectual rights and powers, which calls no man master, which does not content itself with a passive or hereditary faith, which opens itself to light whencesoever it may come," he said during the Massachusetts election sermon of 1830. He continued, "Just as far as [religion] assumes an intolerant, exclusive, sectarian form, it subverts, instead of strengthening, the soul's freedom, and becomes the heaviest and most galling yoke which is laid on the intellect and conscience." According to the elder Henry Ware, Harvard's Hollis Professor of Divinity, the Unitarians were in the tradition of the Protestant Reformers, scraping away the accretions of erroneous tradition. Here he employed the image of Calvin against the nineteenth-century Calvinists: "The followers and successors of those great men [the Reformers], who first gave an impulse to the christian world, have satisfied themselves with indolently adopting the *peculiar opinions* of the Reformers, instead of asserting the great *principles* of the Reformation. They have only changed one human master for another, instead of renouncing all authority, but that of our common master, the great head of the church."[24]

Liberalism also functioned defensively, in that Unitarian ministers invoked the ideal of free inquiry as a shield against orthodox accusations of apostasy. In an 1816 sermon entitled *The Nature and Worth of Christian Liberty*, Aaron Bancroft argued in favor of "the unalienable nature and inestimable worth of Christian liberty" in terms that John Leland probably would have found acceptable. Bancroft feared the establishment of a consociation or "ecclesiastical tribunal" aimed at driving Unitarian ministers out of their pulpits, and he wanted to show "the evils which must ever result from the establishment of human formularies as the standard of orthodoxy, and the erection of human tribunals, before which men must account for their Christian opinions." Such a system of oversight, he warned, would have been deadly to the intellectual freedom of ministers. Should a minister experience "doubts respecting the dogmas of his party," Bancroft said, "then farewell to his peace and usefulness, to every pleasurable intercourse with the people of his charge, and to all the blessings of society. The crime of heresy will be fixed upon him . . . and to censure and revile him, to destroy his clerical respectability and influence, and to deprive him of his living, will be considered as Christian acts."[25] A profession of liberalism provided cover for theological irregularities. N. L. Frothingham objected to the kind of doctrinal "controversy" that occupied the orthodox and Unitarians in the 1820s because it succeeded only in "chaining up the mind, . . . narrowing the sphere of intellectual vision, [and] was unfriendly to truth." He said in exasperation, "Will it last forever, this cry of sectarian titles, this din of theological debate?"[26] In short, Unitarian liberalism could be both a principled stance in favor of the pursuit of knowledge and a defensive answer to critics of the Unitarians' theological innovations.

Like their Puritan forefathers, Unitarian ministers sought to relate their religious faith to life in society; therefore, their emphases upon rationality and liberalism inevitably intersected their corporate ethic at a few different points. The Unitarians' leadership in creating a public intellectual culture, for example, grew out of this kind of combination of their corporate ethic with their rationality. As Peter S. Field writes, "ministers argued that philanthropic support of literary activities promised one important way of satisfying civic duty." It is no coincidence that the Unitarians provided the moving force behind the Boston Athenaeum and the literary journal, the *Monthly Anthology*.[27] The commitment to reason also influenced the reforms that the Unitarians sought to promote in public life. They gravitated toward issues that dealt with man-in-society as a rational creature, such as the temperance movement, which sought to cure people of a maddening passion. For example, in an 1823 temperance address, Boston's Henry Ware Jr. asked his listeners to "consider how [intemperance] deforms and brutalizes the whole man; how it destroys the intellectual faculties; how it palsies the moral affections; how it unfits for duty, incapacitates for improvement, disqualifies for the pure and elevated sentiments of devotion, and renders one as little capable of religion as of reason."[28] As discussed more fully at the end of this section, both their rationalism and their liberalism contributed to the Unitarians' long-lasting support of the establishment. The establishment of Congregational (especially Unitarian Congregational) churches in Massachusetts was intended to create reasonable and responsible citizens. The Unitarians' liberalism also related to the establishment, because they considered their tolerance of diverse opinions to be the only strategy that would prevent the ministerial and parish factionalism that was tearing apart the Massachusetts standing order.[29]

Finally, the Unitarians' rationality undercut the habit of looking for the mysterious hand of Providence in human affairs. In one noticeable break with the traditional public Christianity of the southern New England clergy, the Unitarians tended not to dwell on the Providence of God in human affairs. This is not to say that they rejected the principle of providential superintendence—far from it. As seen in their predictions of the global destiny of the United States, they, too, argued that Providence was the overarching influence in history. In light of France's political upheavals of 1830 as well, the Boston Unitarian Francis Parkman vigorously restated the thesis that God controlled events: "the Scriptures present to us the most sublime and instructive views of God, as the great governor of the nations." However, Unitarians discussed and interpreted the actions of Providence less than the orthodox were apt to do. The Unitarians' rationalism probably played some role in this development. The providential perspective drew heavily on the Old Testament accounts of God's dealings with the nation of Israel and the prophets' announcements of judgment. For William Ellery Channing at least, the Unitarians' reasoned approach to the Bible reduced the significance of the Old Testament. As the dean of Boston Unitarians said, "Our religion, we believe, lies chiefly in the New Testament. The dispensation of Moses, compared with that of Jesus, we consider as adapted to the childhood of the human race, a preparation for a nobler system, and chiefly useful now as serving to confirm and illustrate the Christian Scriptures." The Unitarians' Arminianism, with its emphasis on human ability, also lessened their focus on the invisible hand of Providence.[30]

A cluster of sermons from 1832 revealed the Unitarians' difficulties with conventional providentialism. In that year, an outbreak of cholera threatened Boston, and accordingly a day of fasting was called. As Joseph Goffe recounted, "Christians knowing where their safety lay, fled to the throne of mercy." However, in three sermons, the Unitarian clergy argued against the supposition that an incensed God had caused the cholera epidemic. "Let no one dream of an angry Deity, pouring out vials of wrath on his creatures," remarked Boston's Samuel Barrett. "God is love, and whoever does not so regard him, alike in adversity and prosperity, has the elements of religion yet to learn." Rather, an event like the cholera was not a judgment, argued Christopher Thayer in a sermon at Beverly, Massachusetts, but a trial sent to produce maturity. "Every evil, which our heavenly Father permits to reach us, is a blessing to them who receive and improve it aright. None of his punishments are vindictive . . . but all of them disciplinary—assigned with no other view than our own and others' improvement and welfare." Somewhat unusually, these divines also cautioned that the intentions of Providence were difficult to interpret; as Thayer added, "What are judgments and what are mercies it is impossible for us with our limited faculties always to determine." Likewise, John G. Palfrey, Harvard's professor of biblical literature, acknowledged that nations, if they were going to be judged, had to be so in the present, because they had no existence in the hereafter. However, this epidemic, seemingly so random in its progress, defied the conventional reading of it as a judgment for any specific national sin. It was, Palfrey said, "utterly confounding us, if we will regard it as a rod of national punishment, in our conjectures about what we need first of all to know, in order for it to serve as punishment,—that is, what sins it is meant to punish."[31] At the end of the Revolutionary War, in contrast, New England ministers had expressed no such reservations about their ability to discern the providential meaning of events. This chariness about providential language signaled a departure from orthodoxy.

Otherwise, the Unitarians advocated many of the traditional prescriptions of the Congregational clergy's public Christianity. This traditionalism may seem paradoxical, given the Unitarians' theological liberalism, but the two tendencies coexisted nonetheless. "Enlightenment rationalism," as Daniel Walker Howe writes, "was intermingled with Puritan moralism in Unitarian political views."[32] Unitarian ministers often enjoyed the privilege of giving the Massachusetts election sermon, so we have a clear record of their reflections. Throughout the 1820s, they made the same argument for the establishment of Congregationalism that had been conventional since the 1780s at least: the fabric of society required religion to keep it knit together, thus government, in a self-preserving act, should support religion.

The Unitarians shared with the orthodox the conviction that society needed religion for a variety of reasons. According to the elder Henry Ware, the idea of the fatherhood of God over all mankind would unify society. "Not to separate but to combine, not to drive men asunder, but to unite them together, and bind them by new ties of interest and affection is its tendency. Breathing kindness and good will all around, it produces, not hatred and hostility, not mutual injuries and deeds of violence, but love, and harmony, and peace." Christianity was also the only reliable source of social morality. As Peter Eaton argued, "France has taught Christian nations, a practical lesson, upon this subject; and, by a melancholy experiment, has shown, how feeble are the restraints of moral virtue, separate from religious principle." This was especially the case with regard to the masses, or so Eaton said in a typical and also traditional display of Unitarian elitism. "What interest will the mass of the community take in philosophical discussions of the nature of virtue? Incapable of reasoning themselves, they will listen with no interest to a strain of reasoning from others, which they do not readily comprehend. . . . That the obligation to virtue may be felt, it must be enforced by the high authority of Him who made us."[33] Furthermore, Christianity played a critically important role in the support of government. Nathaniel Thayer banked on religion and education to support the republic. "In the establishment of schools and seminaries of learning, and in the erection of temples, the most effectual means were devised for attaching permanency to our civil privileges. . . . A well informed and religious people are in no danger of losing their liberties." Unitarian ministers also affirmed the conventional case for the religion of society's governors. Religion, said Peter Eaton, "is one of the firmest pillars and most effectual supports of civil government. Religious principle has the best effect upon rulers; it secures their faithful services, and is a guard and preservative from intentional error."[34] In brief, Unitarian ministers continued to believe, during the first third of the nineteenth century at least, that society had natural inclinations toward anarchy and/or tyranny, which could be counteracted only by the diffusion of Christian morality among rulers and the populace.

Therefore, in light of the importance of Christianity to government and social life more generally, the Unitarian clergy concluded that government should still come to the support of the Congregational establishment. Eaton "earnestly entreat[ed]" legislators to give the establishment their "countenance and patronage." Thayer, too, called on the legislature to continue its support of religion and education, exhorting its members to "use your influence then in securing for your destitute brethren the means of religious knowledge." The senior Ware painted a picture of social and governmental decline in the event of disestablishment. If Massachusetts were to abandon the establishment, he argued, then the younger generation would "grow up in ignorance and irreligion," the eventual result of which would be chaos. "Throwing off their allegiance to God, what is to be expected, but that [our children] will throw off their subjection to parental authority; having learned to trample upon the laws of Heaven, that they will not be slow in casting off their respect for human laws?"[35] The Unitarian clergy abided by the old syllogism, which read that because society needed morality and morality came from religion, therefore, the state should support religion.

William Ellery Channing once more provided the most penetrating exposition of the Unitarians' establishmentarian position in an 1820 sermon entitled *Religion a Social Principle*. His analysis revealed that the standing order's corporate ethic was alive and well within the Unitarian fold. He justified the establishment of Congregational churches as a key means by which a community's interdependent members could perpetuate societal harmony. Religion, he said, was not individualistic but "is the gift of society. You received it from parents, and still more from the community; for did not Christianity flourish in the community, were it not made visible by publick institutions and continual observances, how few of us would possess it." Here his argument was both very modern in its notion of how knowledge is propagated within communities and conservative in its organic conception of social interconnectedness. He also said that religion was "social," as opposed to strictly private, because it bound people together; all were the children of the same Father and worshiped him corporately. In addition, he argued that religion "is the best support of the virtues and principles on which social order rests." He made the familiar argument that, if the belief in God expired, there would be no check to human wickedness. Therefore, Channing came to the same conclusion as the rest of his Unitarian colleagues: government should support the churches in the same way it supported the schools. "God, we have seen is the author of Society, and a sense of this Great Being is its strength, support, and the life of its freedom; and shall not then a community, as such, acknowledge God, and provide as far as it has power for spreading a reverence for his authority?"[36] His argument directly confronted the dissenters' individualism and rejected it.

Religion, we are told, is a private, personal thing, a concern between the individual and God. His neighbour or the community must not meddle with it. Whether he have any religion or not, or a good or a bad one, is no one's business but his own. — Vague language of this kind, which carries no definite meaning, but gives the general idea, that a man's religion is a subject in which society has no interest, and no right to use its influence, may do much injury; and in opposition to it, I would maintain that religion is eminently *a social principle*, entering into social life, having most important bearings on the public weal, and that society has a deep concern in it, and cannot without violation of what is due to itself overlook or disparage it.[37]

Despite the Unitarians' endorsement of the establishment, Congregationalism's privileged status did not survive beyond 1833.[38] The Unitarians, laymen and clergy, formed its last major bloc of supporters. At the same time as this Unitarian support propped up the establishment, that support ironically also contributed to its downfall. Once it became clear to the orthodox during the 1820s that the establishment belonged not to them but to the Unitarians, the orthodox withdrew. Without both branches of Congregationalism undergirding it, the establishment of religion in Massachusetts could not withstand the combined weight of its opponents, which continued to grow.[39]

The Unitarian controversy had been dividing Congregationalists in eastern Massachusetts for at least fifteen years before the state Supreme Court weighed in on the legalities of separation in the case of *Baker v. Fales* in 1821.[40] In that decision, the Unitarian-dominated court seemingly gave a one-sided victory to its coreligionists. The case originated in Dedham and thus took on the name of "the Dedham case." There a conflict arose, as had occurred in Princeton, Massachusetts, between Unitarians and Trinitarians over the issue of settling a new minister. The church, composed of the full members of Dedham's First Congregational Church, opposed the settlement of Alvan Lamson, a Unitarian; the full church members tended to be orthodox in their religion. The parish, made up of the town's ecclesiastical taxpayers, supported Lamson, however, and overrode the church's vote against him, and thus ensued a lawsuit between the church and parish. In *Baker v. Fales*, the Supreme Court gave the right to call a minister, among other powers, to the parish, which was the legally recognized entity. The orthodox felt cheated and realized that the establishment, at least in heavily Unitarian areas, did them no good. They who fancied themselves the godly ones, the true church members, suddenly were under the control of the unconverted and theologically unorthodox parish. The court had decided according to the logic of the establishment: the state had supported religion in general as a means to stabilize society, and therefore the taxpayers in general, not just the orthodox ones, should have a say in how their money was spent. To the orthodox, though, the dissenters' arguments against the establishment as a godless thing began to make some sense. William G. McLoughlin summarized the consequences of the Dedham decision for the minds of orthodox Congregationalists.

For years the Trinitarians (and Unitarians) had argued against the dissenters that Massachusetts had no establishment because the parish minister was really a civil servant. And they had insisted that the minority of dissenters in any parish had no just complaint against taxes levied by the majority for the benefit of the general welfare (because these were civil taxes and not, as the dissenters claimed, religious taxes). But now that the Supreme Court had ruled that the majority of the parish could overrule the "Orthodox" church members and that the church's only role in the parish was that of inculcating morality, the Trinitarians suddenly began to see what the dissenters had been driving at all along. Now *they* were a minority forced to support (or at least to leave its property in the hands of) a parish church which they considered unorthodox.... The minority, said [Chief Justice] Parker, as earlier judges had said to the Baptists, could not claim liberty of conscience against the parish majority.[41]

Unitarian ministers were not oblivious to the way that the Unitarian-orthodox split threatened the establishment of Congregationalism. They pleaded for harmony, fearing that without government support, vast swaths of the Massachusetts countryside would be "destitute of the blessing of a settled ministry." In a demonstration of Unitarian liberalism, Abiel Abbot called for mutual forbearance between the factions in the wake of the Dedham decision. "Nothing can be more important in the religious and civil community than to prevent the rising of jealousies between *the church and parish*," he said. Aaron Bancroft agreed with Abbot about the danger of bankrupt parishes resulting from the Unitarian controversy: "Ministers have high influence over the religious feelings and sentiments of the public; and if they appear to be alienated in their affections, if they manage their disputes with sectarian animosity, and in the spirit of reprobation, if they struggle for superiour authority, . . . their contentions and parties will be carried into our societies; . . . [and] our parishes will be frittered into shreds, and no party will possess the means effectually to maintain a preached gospel." Part of Bancroft's concern also arose from the Unitarians' commitment to rationalism. He warned that "destitute parishes will be left open to impressions from ignorant and enthusiastic itinerants; and the worst evils of party, and the most extravagant excesses of fanaticism, it must be expected will prevail."[42]

In the dozen years after the Dedham decision, the establishment gradually lost most of its last supporters and was excised from the state constitution in 1833. It is not necessary here to recapitulate all of the various petitions, legislative maneuvers, and votes that finally led to the disestablishment of Congregationalism; McLoughlin provided the exhaustive account. Suffice it to say that, once the Trinitarians stopped defending the system of parish taxation, it had the support of only the Unitarians behind it. The orthodox did not immediately forsake the establishment after *Baker v. Fales* because some vainly hoped for a few years for a reversal of the decision. However, the Religious Liberties Act of 1824 accelerated the erosion of the standing order. It allowed church members to leave their churches and join another just by handing in a certificate, which meant that in many towns the minority of Trinitarians or Unitarians left the old Congregational church to form a separate one. For example, the orthodox living in Unitarian-controlled parishes now became another dissenting group, free to leave the established church. The act formalized the separation of Unitarian and orthodox congregations encouraged by *Baker*. By about 1828 or 1830, the orthodox could not see much point in hanging on to this shell of the establishment. In the final push to amend the state constitution and remove article 3's sanction for religious taxation, the Universalists led in the needed publicizing and petitioning; the Baptists had dropped out of the dissenting vanguard. Typically, the Universalists took up the cry of "Christ's kingdom is not of this world." Finally, on November 11,

1833, Massachusetts voters overwhelmingly ratified the eleventh amendment of the state constitution, which put all churches on a basis of voluntary support.[43]

The Unitarians' public Christianity, therefore, was a complicated blend of novel and conservative elements. Theological developments, especially their emphases on rationalism and liberalism, carried the Unitarians away from Calvinism and led to a parting of ways with more conservative Congregationalists. During the 1820s, Massachusetts Congregationalists completed the process of splitting into two denominations. The Unitarians' rationalism led them to a new circumspection regarding their ability to interpret the intentions of Providence in history. Paradoxically, however, they preserved a significant part of the old standing order's corporate ethic. The Unitarians maintained a traditional view on the societal and governmental need for religion. A democratic society needed the kind of informed and reasonable citizenry that Unitarianism could produce, and only Unitarian liberalism could keep the contention among disagreeing congregations at a low boil. Throughout the 1820s and into the 1830s, the Unitarians were the most committed and ultimately the last defenders of government support of the Congregational churches.

As the movement for disestablishment in Massachusetts showed, a denominational realignment broke up the old standing order. The next section considers both how the orthodox half of the standing order reacted to disestablishment and how it advantageously adapted its public Christianity to the new denominational landscape.

Evangelicals for Christ the Transformer of Culture

> Then I said unto them, Ye see the distress that we are in, how Jerusalem
> lieth waste, and the gates thereof are burned with fire: come, and let us
> build up the wall of Jerusalem, that we be no more a reproach.
>
> —Neh. 2:17

Like the Unitarians, Trinitarian Congregationalists carried into the 1820s a public Christianity that combined elements of tradition and innovation. They shared with the Unitarians a conventional commitment to relating their religion to life in early republican society. However, the breakdown of the standing order in both Connecticut and Massachusetts occasioned from the orthodox a different response than that from the Unitarians. About a decade before the Unitarians were forced to do so, orthodox Congregationalists forsook the establishment. They had to develop new strategies to respond to their old belief in a corporate relationship with a providential God and their abiding conviction that society could not exist without religion.

Orthodox divines—led by a younger generation of spokesmen such as Lyman Beecher (b. 1775, Yale 1797), Heman Humphrey (b. 1779, Yale 1805), and Ebenezer Porter (b. 1772, Dartmouth 1792)—initiated a pair of strategies for connecting Christianity and corporate life.[44] The first called for a Christian electorate to oversee the political process and, hopefully, inject a godly voice therein. The second portrayed the churches as the primary instruments in the work of Christianizing and purifying society. In both strategies, the orthodox earned their synonymous label of Trinitarians because, unlike the Unitarians, they emphasized the triune nature of the deity; in addition to the fatherhood of God and the atonement of Jesus, they highlighted the action of the Holy Spirit in producing revivals. This revivalism would both help create a Christian electorate and revitalize the churches, equipping them for their new social ministry.

The Trinitarians' move away from the establishment and toward purified churches facilitated a denominational realignment. The orthodox built bridges to the old dissenting groups, such as the Baptists, a principal spokesman of which was Francis Wayland. The resulting evangelical coalition organized new institutions to carry out the churches' vision of evangelization and moral renewal. This coalition had its limits and precipitated a countercoalition of challengers but nevertheless constituted an important part in the development of antebellum culture. It also formed a key pathway between the corporate ethic of the old, eighteenth-century standing order and the social activism of antebellum reformers.

Whatever may have led the Unitarians to lessen their providential pronouncements, orthodox Congregationalists experienced no similar loss of boldness. Throughout the period under study, they continually held that God ruled in terms that would have been familiar to their congregations back in the 1780s. As Diodate Brockway of Ellington, Connecticut, flatly stated, "The success of all human efforts depends entirely, and exclusively, upon the providential and all-powerful influence of God." Even in the bloody conquests of Napoleon, he asserted, "we discover the footsteps of a mysterious and righteous Providence. The wars in which he was so successfully engaged, were the Lord's, in which he was pouring out the vials of his wrath upon those nations which had received the mark of the *Beast*." John Bartlett, a Congregational minister from Windsor, Connecticut, explained in a common analysis how God acted in a threefold manner, through creation, providence, and redemption. For the orthodox, this last category of God's redemptive work played a particularly important role theologically. They anticipated, as the Unitarians did not emphasize, the active workings of God in conversions. "We behold God coming down from the highest heavens," Bartlett said, "in the person of his Son and Spirit, to dwell with men; we behold him setting up his kingdom within them, and in the greatness of his condescension, manifesting himself to them as their Father, . . . and communing with them from above the mercy seat! In these wondrous works of grace, God has declared himself near, and has graciously manifested his presence, in one place or another, in every age of the world."[45] In titanic events like wars, as well as in individual ones like conversions, Congregational ministers noted the hand of God at work.

As a natural corollary to the axiom of providential direction, ministers pointed to "the Divine agency in the affairs of nations." William B. Sprague gave one typical illustration of this doctrine in his 1827 July Fourth address: "We should devoutly recognise our dependance on God for the *continuance* of our freedom, and all our national blessings; should commit our country, anew, with all its interests, to His special protection. . . . We should humble ourselves in view of our national sins, for which we so justly deserve the frown of the Almighty."[46] American and New England history demonstrated how this hand of Providence guided national affairs. For instance, on the two-hundredth anniversary of the Plymouth landing, Gardiner Spring showed how the Pilgrims' enterprise had been directed and protected by God. "How obvious to the most superficial observer, that the whole course of our venerable forefathers was the result of the divine purpose, lay under the divine inspection, and was directed by a divine and omnipotent hand." Spring was the pastor of the Brick Presbyterian Church in New York City and the son of Newburyport's Samuel Spring. God had shepherded the national history, he said, in order "that the work of redemption should ultimately be carried forward on the largest scale in the western world."[47] The clergy's providential viewpoint continued to link society to a cosmic framework.

Orthodox ministers did not hesitate to warn of impending judgments. This formed another contrast with the Unitarians, who were much more uncomfortable with, if not outright repulsed by, the idea of divine punishments. Orthodox and Baptist ministers perpetuated the ancient New England tradition of the jeremiad, exposing and denouncing the nation's sins. In a typical and quotable remark from 1831, Ebenezer Porter cried, "*God is angry with us.* He looks down upon this great and guilty nation, which his own right hand has planted and prospered, and sees us [Isa. 1:4] 'a people laden with iniquity.' Oh, what idolatry of wealth; — what profanation of his Sabbath; — what scenes of out-breaking, depravity, brutality, blasphemy, does he witness every week in our towns and cities?" Similarly, Francis Wayland cautioned that if Americans were to squander their abundant opportunities to further the gospel, they would face the "avenging majesty" of God.[48] Calvinist clergymen made the conventional observation that because nations could not face judgment in the hereafter, they would have to be punished for sins in the present.[49] Ministers' jeremiads provided a check to their other, more patriotically bombastic predictions of how God would use the United States for millennial ends.

The orthodox also absolutely believed that the future of the republic depended on Christianity's permeation of society. On this point, at least, they agreed with the Unitarians. Into the 1830s, they argued for the social necessity of religion for as many as four distinguishable reasons. In the first place, a righteous community would avoid the scourges of providential displeasure. According to Samuel Austin, "Religion, universally embraced, would avert the judgments of God, and secure, in the ordinary course of things, and by a particular blessing, an abundance of all the comforts of life."[50] Ministers also claimed that Christianity assuaged contentions and fostered social tranquility. "The spirit inculcated by the gospel is friendly to human happiness," said Andrew Eliot. "It sanctifies every relation of life, by demanding the constant interchange of benevolent affections and kind offices."[51] In addition, Christianity led to good government. For example, ministers restated that an officeholder's piety would lead him to act justly.[52]

Finally, and most important, religion yielded the morality needed to maintain democratic government. "The Christian patriot well knows that religion and morality are essential to the preservation of the inestimable blessings of civil liberty," summarized John Codman of Dorchester, Massachusetts. "He feels no other security for the continuance of these blessings, than as they are guarded by virtuous and correct principles."[53] Not governed by might, a free society depended on informal methods to control its population. As Heman Humphrey, the president of Amherst College, explained in 1823, "the freer any state is, the more virtue is necessary to secure private rights, and to preserve the public tranquility. A government of opinion, founded on the morality of the Gospel, exerts a silent and invisible influence, which like the great law of attraction keeps every thing in its place, without seeming to exert any influence at all." The American republic needed Christianity to avert a plunge into licentiousness; law enforcement could never substitute to suppress the kind of criminal behavior that would tear apart the social fabric. "What woes does that nation embosom in itself," asked Eleazar T. Fitch, "that is corrupted in its own sins? A nation in which neither the fear of God, respect for an oath, nor regard for a future state, stand as barriers against crime or securities for truth and justice?" For men living in the 1820s, the recent experience of revolutionary France furnished historical proof of the danger society faced from atheistic amorality.[54]

At this point, orthodox Congregationalists faced an obstacle to their traditional ways of thinking. During the last two decades of the eighteenth century, they, like the Unitarians, would have followed the statement of the social necessity of Christianity with a defense of the government's support of the Congregational churches and a charge to the magistrates to fulfill their duties vigorously. However, for reasons already discussed, this avenue was closed to them. Standing order ministers had had something of a falling out with the magistracy during the years around 1810. Furthermore, the Connecticut standing order had been overthrown in 1818, and the Massachusetts establishment had been abandoned to the Unitarians during the mid-1820s. Disestablishment presented an intellectual challenge to the orthodox. Trinitarian Congregational ministers candidly recognized the establishment's problems but voiced their unhappiness in its absence. They responded with two solutions. They developed an ideal of Christian citizenship, in which conscientious voters would assume a new oversight of the state, and they called on the church to take an active role in transforming society. In both ways, orthodox ministers sought to relate their faith to life in society in a new era of evangelical pluralism.

In the 1820s, orthodox Congregationalists disavowed the establishment. The chronologies of this development differed by a few years in Connecticut and Massachusetts. In Connecticut, the Congregational establishment ended abruptly in 1818, whereas it limped along for another fifteen years in Massachusetts. However, by the mid-1820s, a consensus was emerging among southern New England's orthodox Congregationalists. They agreed that the establishment was a thing of the past, but its passing left them disquieted as well.[55] Nathaniel W. Taylor's 1823 election sermon manifested the Congregational clergy's mixed feelings. Taylor, professor at Yale Divinity School, thought that the fight over disestablishment in Connecticut had been a function of and contributed to a "declining estimate of the value of religious institutions." He accepted the verdict of disestablishment but thought the churches increasingly vulnerable: "Neither the necessity of the change adverted to, nor the wisdom and the integrity of many who were active in producing it, is called in question. There were dangers and evils without the change, it is believed, greater than exist with it. All that is asserted is, that these perils have not wholly ceased." The lingering problem, Taylor feared, was a "withdraw[al] [of] patronage and support from religious institutions." Loammi Ives Hoadly also rejected "a religious establishment," saying, "we want nothing of this sort." And yet, something was missing. As Hoadly pointed out, "nothing can be plainer, however, than our duty to guard our politics by religion. What I mean is, that the religious principle should operate in politics as well as in every thing else. . . . From the nature of our government, thus elective and free, it must come to be the case, except as men are governed by moral obligation and religious principle, that demagogues will rise here and there, and party spirit will prevail."[56] How could the ministry continue to uphold the needed social presence of Christianity, given the reality of disestablishment?

Lyman Beecher limned one of the two answers to this problem. In the mid-1820s, he laid out a new paradigm of Christian citizenship. In this instance, Beecher merited the appellation of "religious virtuoso" bestowed on him by the historian Robert H. Abzug. Beecher's 1823 sermon, *The Faith Once Delivered to the Saints*, was primarily a theological critique of Unitarianism. He based it on Jude 3, which reads in part, "ye should earnestly contend for the faith which was once delivered unto the saints." By the faith "once delivered unto the saints," Beecher meant Calvinist orthodoxy as opposed to Unitarian liberalism. As one part of defending the ancient faith, Beecher called for Christians to use "a proper exercise of their civil influence."[57] He thereby discussed at length the relationship between Christianity and politics in the postestablishment age. Two and a half years later, Beecher repeated many of the same prescriptions in his Connecticut election-day sermon. He pioneered new rules of engagement between Christianity and politics and was an articulate spokesman for his ideas.

Beecher recognized that by the third decade of the nineteenth century, denominational pluralism had rendered the old standing order anachronistic. "For two hundred years the religious institutions of our land were secured by law. But as our numbers increased, and liberty of conscience resulted in many denominations of Christians, it became impossible to secure by law the universal application of religious and moral influence." As a result of disestablishment, "christians are perplexed, and know not what to do. They are afraid to withhold their efforts, to benefit religion through the medium of government; and environed by difficulties and dangers, they are afraid to exert it."[58]

Into this state of confusion and anxiety, Beecher stepped with his new proposals. He realized that the mixing of religion and politics was a sticky wicket. Therefore, he specified four ways in which Christians were to try not to become entangled in politics. First of all, he advised Christians not to take stands *as Christians* on mundane political issues; rather, they should reserve their witness for exceptional circumstances. "When great questions of national morality are about to be decided, such as the declaration of War; or as in England the abolition of the slave trade, or the permission to introduce christianity into India by Missionaries; it becomes christians to lift up their voice, and exert their united influence. But, with the annual detail of secular policy, it does not become christians to intermeddle." Beecher warned, second, against aligning Christianity with any one political party. Clearly, this was a lesson learned during the acrimonious era of the first party competition and the War of 1812. "A spirit of party zeal," he reminded his listeners, "creates also a powerful diversion of interest and effort from the cause of Christ: creates prejudices in christians one against another: and in the community against the cause itself. Annihilates spirituality of mind; prevents a spirit of prayer, and efforts for revivals of religion: and renders christians the mere dupes, and tools, of unprincipled, ambitious men." Third,

Beecher made clear that he did not want special privileges or favors from the government on behalf of the Congregationalists; rather, he stood by the principle of a level playing field for all denominations. "The end of heaven has been answered, in the powerful and direct aid given to the churches, by the civil fathers of New-England. Then, it was needed, to lay foundations, to form habits, to surmount obstacles, and to carry the churches through the wilderness. But now it is not needed, and cannot be bestowed, in the manner it has been." Fourth, Beecher denied that he was calling for any kind of doctrinal or denominational test for office. Instead, he said that office seekers should merely be men of morality and "integrity."[59] Beecher was a veteran of the battle for disestablishment in Connecticut. He was aware that a potential minefield lay ahead in formulating a public Christianity, so he was careful to avoid missteps.

Having cautioned against inappropriate linkages between religion and politics, Beecher then detailed his vision of a Christian influence over public affairs. Christians were to engage politics by acting as a conscientious voting bloc, thus counteracting partisanship and injecting a measure of morality into the democratic process.

> In all the competitions for political elevation, of which there will always be many in free governments; the suffrage of a Christian community, held in reserve, to be exercised under the influence of conscience, and a cool uncommitted discretion, would have an influence highly salutary to the state, and to the interests of piety and morality. As long as Christians are divided, and will vote blindly, under the influence of a political mania; no individual fears the consequence of irreligion, or immorality; and no party, fears the consequence in their candidates for office.
>
> But if Christians retire from unhallowed competitions, to bestow their suffrage by the dictation of an enlightened conscience, they will hold an amount of suffrage, not to be lightly regarded or despised on either side. In this, there is no electioneering, no officious meddling, and no violence. Christians exercise their own civil rights, under the guidance of their own consciences, enlightened by the word of God; and in doing it, allay the violence of party, elevate the standard of morality, and secure to religion, all the protections that it needs, and to their country, so far as their influence can avail, an administration of the government, devoted to the public good, and not to the interests of a party.[60]

Christians would form an independent force in American politics, Beecher hoped. They would cast their votes not out of party loyalty but based on "conscience" and would thus hold in their righteous hands the balance of power between the two parties.

By 1830, Beecher's model of Christian political action seemed to have taken root within the ministry. Other leaders among the orthodox such as Heman Humphrey and Ebenezer Porter, the presidents of Amherst College and Andover Theological Seminary, respectively, echoed Beecher's analysis. Like Beecher, Humphrey repudiated the establishment; indeed, he sounded like a Baptist dissenter from the standing order in his rejection.[61] However, Humphrey added that an acceptance of disestablishment did not mean that religion should make no contribution to political matters. As Congregational clergymen had been doing for at least the past fifty years, Humphrey denied that John 18:36 meant either "that those who become the subjects of [Christ's] kingdom, thereby forfeit all, or any, of their civil rights" or "that Chris-

tian teachers shall never allude in their discourses to the principles of civil government—to the qualifications of rulers, or to the political rights and duties of private
citizens." "Most obviously, then," he concluded, "the text was never intended to be
put into the hands of infidels and demagogues, as a political talisman, to dissever religion from legislation, to fasten suspicion upon every friend of the Bible and the
Sabbath, and to rebuke every whisper of remonstrance, which may have the temer-
ity to enter into the ears of governments." Porter shared this disestablishmentarian
viewpoint and also advocated, as had Beecher, Christian activism at the ballot box.
"While Christians have liberty to speak, they will say that he who spurns the obligations of religion, is not fit to be the ruler of a Christian country. While they have liberty to vote, they will not vote for that man; because there is in him no adequate
ground of confidence."[62]

This emphasis on Christian citizenship and political participation coincided
with an inconspicuous abandonment of the standing order's old hierarchicalism.
Generally speaking, the Unitarians appealed to an elite, eastern segment of the Massachusetts population. Corresponding to this constituency, and also in keeping with
their support of the establishment, Unitarian ministers tended to stress the importance of society's leaders, as had been traditional.[63] The orthodox, however, adjusted
more rapidly to the democratic tides shaping nineteenth-century America. A number of Congregational ministers highlighted the popular dimension of their social
prescriptions. Christianity, according to Andover professor Moses Stuart, "is the genuine, unadulterated doctrine of liberty and equality. To all men it gives a liberty to
exercise their efforts and desires without restraint, so far as consists with the public
good. . . . None are too high to be made the subjects of these laws [of heaven]; none
too low to be affected by their controul. Consequently all men are, by the nature of
their subjection to the same laws, placed on the ground of equality by the Christian
religion." Likewise, in Lyman Beecher's portrayal, the coming "moral renovation" of
the world would "not be partial in its influence, like the sun shining through clouds
on favoured spots, but co-extensive with the ruin. Nor shall its results be that national
glory, which gilds only the palace, and cheers only the dwellings of the noble. It shall
bring down the mountains and exalt the valleys. It shall send liberty and equality to
the dwellings of men."[64] Orthodox ministers underscored the egalitarian aspects of
their doctrines.

The vision of a grassroots Christian electoral force gained credence from the re-
current revivals that rolled through New England over the first third of the nineteenth century because the revivals were bringing large numbers of people into the
churches and creating a pool of converts potentially available for mobilization. The
revivals of the 1820s and 1830s displayed a morphology that was for the most part similar to those of 1800. Even though he was sixty-five years old by late 1831, Joseph
Goffe was still actively engaged in reviving religion through an exhausting schedule
of preaching, holding meetings, and calling upon people in their homes. Likewise,
the ministers of the Brookfield Association voted on January 7, 1829, "to assist each
other, by an interchange of labor, in sustaining" "the plan of frequent meetings in
our respective churches for devotional purposes."[65] One innovation introduced by
the Brookfield Association was the employment of an evangelist specifically dedicated to the job "of aiding feeble churches and assisting in revivals of religion" within

the association's territory. Regardless of whatever strategies they employed to foment revival, orthodox ministers always insisted on the agency of the Holy Spirit in producing conversions; this understanding further marked off the orthodox from the Unitarians.[66] These revivals, along with the aforementioned fall of Napoleon, assuaged the ministry's earlier fears of infidelity; they appeared, to the clergy's eyes, as harbingers of the millennium.[67] The revivals were also significant as part of the ministry's public Christianity because they were believed to change society. They produced a state of society, in the words of Noah Porter of Farmington, Connecticut, "in which the principles of envy, discord, and contention are supplanted by mutual good-will; in which intemperance, profaneness and riot are exchanged for sobriety, reverence for God, and peacefulness of life."[68] Congregational clergymen believed that society needed religion; for the orthodox, revivals were one important means by which to disseminate godliness.

If the revivals helped spawn the idea of a Christian voting bloc, they also led ministers to envision the revitalized church as an institution of social transformation. The churches and their voluntary adjuncts would be active in the evangelization and moral uplift of society. Congregational clergymen relied on the church as a second answer to the problem of penetrating society with Christianity in the period after the dissolution of the partnership of Moses and Aaron. The plan for a Christian electorate sought to connect religion and society within the political system, while this new program acted from without. Both addressed society's recognized need for Christianity and morality. In this new scenario, ministers brought to full flower the seeds planted in the first decade of the nineteenth century. Works such as John Elliott's 1810 election sermon, *The Gracious Presence of God*, had begun to suggest how revivals in the churches would influence society. In this vision, orthodox Congregationalists would be joined by other evangelical ministers. Ministers specified how the United States would play its anticipated role in inaugurating the millennium. A principal voice for the idea of the American churches and their parachurch organizations as torchbearers of the millennium was Heman Humphrey. As Lyman Beecher had led the call for a Christian electorate, so the church theme ran through Humphrey's sermons over the entire chronological span of this chapter.

Throughout the first third of the nineteenth century, ministers exhorted their congregations to work toward national and international evangelization. "Let the church sing and shout for joy," trumpeted Heman Humphrey. "Let her arise and shake herself from the dust, and put on her beautiful garments. Strong in faith and nothing wavering, let her redouble her efforts and prayers in behalf of the heathen. . . . Let her think how rapidly the kingdom of darkness is waning, and how fast the walls of Jerusalem are rising."[69] The clergy's evangelistic thrust developed out of the missionary movement that had begun at the end of the eighteenth century and pushed it even higher. "In modern times," as John Bartlett recounted the history, "a missionary spirit has been again enkindled in the christian church, and it is probable that this spirit will not be extinguished so long as there remains an immortal in our world, unacquainted with the way of life through a crucified Saviour: it is probable that this spirit will prevail, till that pleasing dawn of the Millenium [*sic*] which we may now, perhaps, faintly discern, shall have brightened and advanced to the full

Heman Humphrey. Courtesy Amherst College Archives and Special Collections.

blaze of meridian glory." Ministers expressed confidence that God's Providence would protect and prosper the church.[70]

Millennialism acted as both an endorsement of and motivation for the churches' activities. As Bartlett commented, initiatives like those on behalf of missions "faintly" revealed the millennium. In other words, the clergy validated missionary and reform activity by saying that such activity foreshadowed the millennium. For example, Daniel Crosby of Conway, Massachusetts, said, with reference to temperance and other benevolent reform projects, "There is a predicted glory which has not yet come. . . . So far and so brightly has its light stretched itself into the future, that the universal triumphs of truth and holiness are already seen by the eye of faith, rising in the distance, and pouring on the mountain-tops their golden light. . . . A period of complete redemption is on its way. And do you not see its precursors?"[71] In addition, the millennial promise called forth not only praise but also pleas for further exertion. If more people pushed history along, ministers contended, the final transformation might come about. In an unusually blunt declaration of this principle, Francis Wayland thundered, "It is for us to say whether the present religious movement, shall be onward until it terminate in the universal triumph of Messiah, or whether all shall go back again, and the generations to come after us suffer for ages the divine indignation, for our neglect of the gospel of the grace of God." In an 1832 speech on behalf of Cincinnati's Lane Seminary, Lyman Beecher, too, told listeners to work actively to inaugurate the millennium. He depicted a chain reaction leading up to the millennium. The millennium was surely coming, Beecher noted, but it needed liberty to flourish. Liberty depended on the United States, as he had said earlier, and the fate of the nation hinged on the west. Because the destiny of the west depended on education, his audience should support Lane Seminary. In short, support for Lane could make or break the millennium.[72]

This millennially inspired activity on the part of the churches would strongly influence American society. The churches' initiatives would multiply conversions and also produce a salutary change of morals among those affected. As Nathaniel Bouton explained to "Christian Patriots" gathered on July 4, 1825, "Let us consecrate our hearts to God. In our intercourse with our fellow-citizens, let us ever regard the interests of their immortality; do nothing which will diffuse a baleful influence over the soul; reflect that he does most for his country, whose life best accords with the principles of religion, and who is most efficient in removing moral evils, the principal source both of national calamity and national ruin." Five years earlier, Asa Cummings had urged his fast-day listeners to make "determined exertions" "to put a stop, if possible, to the progress of degeneracy." He voiced a cautious optimism that the churches' benevolent and moral reform societies could succeed, concluding, "Till these pious charities, and these truly christian exertions begin to fail, we will believe that God has mercies in reserve for us; and this belief will be strengthened in proportion as these charities increase, and these exertions multiply." Ebenezer Porter also feared for the impending "wreck of those moral institutions and habits, which have been the safety and glory of the land." He called on the faithful to unite and "to engage in building up the cause of Christian piety and morals."[73]

Preaching from Neh. 2:17, the verse that heads this section, Porter wanted to inspire his listeners to be like Nehemiah, the man who restored Jerusalem's walls, and to step forward in rebuilding America's moral foundations. Other ministers joined Porter and gravitated toward the biblical figure of Nehemiah as a new typological identity. The image of Moses and Aaron had epitomized the ministry's close bond with the magistracy under the establishment, but, given the altered political situation, that image no longer accurately reflected reality. Instead, ministers by the 1810s began to refer to the examples of Nehemiah and Ezra, the men who had rebuilt Jerusalem and reinstated worship at the temple there after the Babylonian captivity. Since the seventeenth century, as Harry S. Stout writes, "the Old Testament had always served as New England's 'ancient constitution,' and each generation had read and interpreted it from their own unique vantage point." Thus, this new typology of

Ebenezer Porter. Courtesy American Antiquarian Society.

Nehemiah and Ezra better comported with the churches' role in the early republic as the restorers of American culture.[74]

Lyman Beecher, once again, concisely captured the situation. We have already seen in the first section of this chapter how Beecher envisioned a millennial role for the United States. The churches would fulfill a large part of that national destiny by using "the energies of [America's] concentrated benevolence [to] send out evangelical instruction." Not only would this benevolent activism influence other nations, but it would also play an important function domestically. As Beecher said in a memorable phrase, "our charitable institutions . . . are the providential substitutes for the legal provisions of our fathers, now inapplicable by change of circumstances. . . . Now, unless the salt of the earth contained in christian institutions, can be diffused through the land, the mass will putrify [*sic*]."[75] In other words, Beecher also concurred with the vision of the American church sanctifying society. He played an important part in conceiving both strategies that evangelical Congregationalists used to connect Christianity and society in the 1820s.

This emphasis on the role of the churches reached back to that facet of covenant language that identified the church as the true focus of providential action in history. As in the 1780s, there was in the 1820s a certain unresolved ambiguity regarding the relationship of Providence to the nation-state and the church. In the crisis of the 1790s and through the dark first decade of the 1800s, ministers had stressed the theme that the church would endure, no matter what. During the War of 1812, they had seemingly clarified the confusion surrounding Providence, the United States, and the church, as they had rejected the national government. In the late 1810s and the 1820s, however, with the revival of patriotism discussed at the beginning of this chapter, the issue became muddled again. Orthodox ministers spoke both of how the United States was an instrument of Providence and of how the American churches were contributing to the millennium. In the great providentially conducted orchestra of redemption, so to speak, the church may have sat in the first chair, but other instruments contributed to the symphony as well.

The ministry did not leave its new model of the church in society floating in the air, a verbal construct of its pronouncements alone. Rather, ministers worked to organize concrete institutions to put their vision into practice. As the ideal of the partnership of Moses and Aaron had been embodied in the laws of the establishment and the rituals of the election day, so the new concept of an active church developed a set of its own organizations. The years after 1815 witnessed the consolidation and expansion of earlier institutional initiatives. Many of the local evangelistic and reform agencies that had been planted in the first dozen years of the nineteenth century blossomed into national societies. At the same time, their local auxiliaries remained essential for the actual functioning of the new nationwide societies. Worcester County, Massachusetts, once again provides a case in point.

The trickle of institutions and initiatives from the first dozen years of the nineteenth century, such as Andover Seminary, state missionary agencies, and local moral societies, became a torrent of national societies in the dozen years after the War of 1812. Ebenezer Porter gave voice to the spirit of the era when he declared in 1823, "Surely this is not the time to talk of remitting our efforts. No, —they must be increased a hundred fold. New enterprises must be undertaken, new societies formed, new sources of revenue for the church devised. Every heart must beat with a higher impulse, every arm be braced with increased strength."[76] These national organizations are well known and have not gone wanting for their historians, so they are only briefly mentioned here. The church developed different types of agencies to carry out its missions of evangelism and benevolence: missionary societies to coordinate and fund evangelists, educational charities to train aspiring clergymen and pay for their studies, and publishing enterprises to propagate the Scriptures and other godly tracts. The American Board of Commissioners for Foreign Missions (A.B.C.F.M.), organized in 1810 at the prodding of a group of Andover Seminary students with a desire for undertaking a mission to India, expanded its range to include not only India but also Polynesia, the Near and Far East, and the Cherokee and Choctaw lands of the American Southeast. In 1826, the American Home Missionary Society formed for the purpose of domestic evangelism. The American Education Society, founded in 1815, addressed the problem of a "want of *preachers*" in spreading the gospel by supplying "pecuniary aid to pious young men, whose own resources were inadequate to the expense of their studies." The American Bible Society, established 1816, and the American Tract Society, founded nine years later, armed the evangelists with printed materials for distribution. It is noteworthy that all of these organizations were interdenominational in character, combining the initiatives of the Congregationalists with the Presbyterian and Dutch Reformed denominations in particular. This nexus of evangelical missionary and reform societies the historian Charles I. Foster dubbed "the Evangelical united front." As the national organizations expanded, they appeared at first to gobble up their smaller predecessors. For instance, "in view of the rise & progress of some of the great national institutions of the day," the Religious Charitable Society in the County of Worcester decided to "recede from our independent stand, & assume the place of an *auxiliary* to some one or more of these national Societies." Therefore, rather than fund scholarships for ministerial students on its own, the Worcester society would henceforward turn its money over to the American Education Society.[77]

Nevertheless, midlevel organizations, standing above the local churches and beneath the statewide or national societies, played a critical intermediary role. The records of two Worcester County ministerial groups, the Brookfield Association and the Harmony Conference, reveal how such groups were indispensable to the work of the national organizations. The Harmony Conference formed at a meeting at Joseph Goffe's house in Millbury on June 17, 1828. It consisted of many of the same churches and clergymen with whom Goffe had collaborated during his first revival season back in 1800, including John Crane of Northbridge, Benjamin Wood of Upton, and Sutton's John Maltby, the successor to the late Edmund Mills. Right away, the new conference set about promoting the causes of larger benevolent societies. At its meeting of September 15, 1829, the Harmony Conference voted to establish its own Sunday school organization that would be an auxiliary of the Massachusetts Sunday School Union. It also dispatched "messengers" to the local Sunday schools to communicate the conference's initiatives and report back to the Massachusetts union. In this way, the Harmony Conference formed a critical link between the state body and the local churches. Likewise, the Brookfield Association voted to assist the A.B.C.F.M. in setting up auxiliaries within its territory and to raise money on behalf of the American Tract Society. Indeed, so enmeshed were the Brookfield Association and the Harmony Conference in the work of the national organizations that each eventually passed resolutions that divided the calendar among the several benevolent causes. For example, in 1833 the Harmony Conference apportioned the year like so: "the months of Jan. & Feb. be devoted to the A. Tract Society—March & Apr. to Amer. Ed. Socy.—May & June, to A. Home Mis. Socy. July to A. Col[onization]. Socy.—Aug. & Sept. to A.B.C.F.M. Socy.—Oct. & Nov. to A. Bible Socy." Thus, even if the national benevolent societies grabbed the headlines and the subsequent attention of historians, local and midlevel organizations of ministers and laymen were key cogs in the institutional implementation of the clergy's vision of the church in society.[78]

The new conception of the church and its institutions as the vehicles for renewing society marked a profound shift in the Congregational clergy's public Christianity. In the late eighteenth century, the standing order had stood for the ideal of "Christ above culture," to use the categorization of H. Richard Niebuhr. It had sought a neat synthesis of church and state. Now, during the 1820s, the orthodox came to advocate the vision of "Christ the transformer of culture." In this new type, the emphasis moved from religiopolitical harmonization to "the divine possibility of a present renewal." In this "*conversionist* solution," Niebuhr wrote, "Christ is seen as the converter of man in his culture and society, not apart from these." That is, the orthodox clergy positioned the churches not as the stewards of New England society but as the society's redeemers.[79]

The Baptists joined as well in this new ideal of churchly transformation, as typified by the quotations from Francis Wayland that are sprinkled throughout the foregoing discussion. The Baptists were coming to this position from the opposite direction than the orthodox, but the two former antagonists were now converging. As the orthodox retreated from the establishment, the Baptists were moving away from their separatist stance of John 18:36 and beginning to express a more assertive opinion on Christianity and social life. By the early nineteenth century, the Baptists were becoming a more self-consciously secure social group, no longer bound to a separatist rejection of the world. The Baptists had earlier shown points of agreement with the standing order on issues of social morality and a providential interpretation of history; however, the fights over disestablishment and the first party conflict had overshadowed these natural similarities. By the 1820s, these controversies had faded into the past, and an opportunity for an evangelical rapprochement around the position of "Christ the transformer of culture" presented itself. In their ascent to denominational maturity and "respectability," the Baptists copied the Congregationalists' missionary, educational, and reform organizations. For example, Jonathan Going, pastor of Worcester's Baptist Church from 1815 to 1831 and himself an 1809 graduate of Brown, "insisted upon the importance of an educated ministry," and "to the establishment of the Theological Seminary in Newton he contributed in no small degree." Francis Wayland embraced the idea of evangelical cooperation aimed at mutual goals. "Notwithstanding the multiplicity of our sects," he said in 1830, "a greater degree of good fellowship, in promoting the eternal welfare of men, is discoverable here [in the United States], than has been commonly witnessed, at least in the latter ages of the Christian church." The American Sunday School Union, before which Wayland spoke on this occasion, exemplified such interdenominationalism.[80] The Baptists also saw themselves as part of a new evangelical majority with considerable political clout. "By 1828 [the Baptists] began to modify their strict apolitical stance and to anticipate before too long that orthodox, evangelical Christians would control the political actions of the nation." Moreover, "Baptists could see no danger of a new kind of establishment of religion because this time they were themselves to be part of that establishment."[81]

Orthodox Congregationalists likewise tried to reach out to their former adversaries among the dissenters by downplaying theological particularities and highlighting the interdenominational agenda they shared with other evangelical groups. Lyman Beecher moved at the forefront of this initiative, as he did in so many others. In 1823, he tried to recast the precedent of two centuries of New England history. Rather than depicting the fundamental religious fault line as dividing the standing order and the dissenters, Beecher drew a new line between *"the Evangelical System"* and *"the Liberal System."* He arrayed like-minded orthodox Congregationalists and Baptists, perhaps along with some Methodists and Episcopalians, too, against the liberalism of the Unitarians and Universalists. Beecher employed the umbrella term of "the evangelical system," he said, "not only because I believe [its doctrines] to be the Gospel; but because no man, or denomination, has held them so exclusively, as to render it proper to designate them by the name of an individual or a sect." In the same year, Ebenezer Porter interpreted "the increase of candour and fraternal feeling among different denominations of Christians" as one of the first hopeful rays of the millennial dawn. He also noted in his sermon before the American Education Society back in 1820 that that organization served students from different denominations.[82]

One of the few remaining areas where evangelicals and Unitarians could still work together in the 1820s was in the cause of Bible distribution. The goal of supplying every family with a copy of the Scriptures in the vernacular had general appeal for Protestants. For example, the orthodox ministers of the Brookfield Association considered it their "indispensible [*sic*] duty immediately, to take measures to aid the American Bible Society, in their special effort to 'supply every destitute family in the United States within two years.'" They and their brethren in the Harmony Conference both resolved to take a census in 1829–1830 of every household within their purview to find out who lacked a Bible. Likewise, Unitarians provided much of the membership, financial support, and leadership for the Worcester County auxiliary of the American Bible Society. Aaron Bancroft served as president for a number of years. However, a spokesman for the auxiliary pointed out that there was "nothing sectarian in its character, its objects, or its operations," and it enjoyed a broad basis of support. The auxiliary's membership book listed many Unitarian clergymen from their traditional base in the eastern part of the county, from towns such as Lancaster, Lunenburg, and Northborough, but it also included Micah Stone, orthodox minister of Brookfield. Records also show that the Branch Baptist church in Fitchburg contributed $12 in 1833. However, the collaboration between Calvinists and Unitarians that was found in the Auxiliary Bible Society of Worcester County was the exception that proves the rule. More typically at this time, orthodox Congregationalists aligned with the Baptists against Unitarian liberalism.[83]

In a revealing remark, William Ellery Channing testified in his 1830 election sermon to the latent power of this new evangelical coalition. Channing came not to praise this coalition but to sound a warning regarding its potential for abuse.

> We say we have no Inquisition. But a sect skilfully organized, trained to utter one cry, combined to cover with reproach whoever may differ from themselves, to drown the free expression of opinion by denunciations of heresy, and to strike terror into the multitude by joint and perpetual menace, — such a sect is as perilous and palsying to the intellect as the Inquisition. It strikes the ministers as effectually as the sword. The present age is notoriously sectarian, and therefore hostile to liberty. . . . We have in-

deed no small protection against this evil, in the multiplicity of sects. But let us not forget, that coalitions are as practicable and as perilous in church as in state; and that minor differences, as they are called, may be sunk, for the purpose of joint exertion against a common foe.

Channing clearly felt threatened by the prospect of the orthodox clergy whipping up a frenzy and organizing a posse to hunt down their "common foe," namely, the Unitarians. His nervous warning provides backhanded confirmation of the success that the orthodox were having in building bridges to other evangelical denominations.[84]

Even the Episcopalians partook of the new feeling of Christian cooperation. The honor of giving the 1828 election sermon in Connecticut was bestowed on Nathaniel S. Wheaton, rector of Christ Church, Hartford. His sermon was remarkable in its utter lack of remarkability: the Episcopalian advocated the same principles as the Congregationalists. Wheaton's sermon addressed the importance of public morality in the sight of an overruling Providence. "We are no advocates for a political alliance between religion and the state," he averred, "but let it never be supposed, that the magistrate can rule or the laws be obeyed, without the support of religion. The church needs not the protection of the state; but the state has great need of support from the church." Just ten years earlier, at the time of disestablishment in Connecticut, the Episcopalians would have been warier of linking religion and society as closely as Wheaton did in this sermon.[85] Wheaton also endorsed the idea of a conscientious, Christian electorate. As he concluded,

> What has a contemner of God, and of every thing holy, to do with legislating for a christian people! Should it ever happen, that important public trusts shall be confided to men of this stamp, in preference to those of long tried experience and sterling integrity; should the fear of God, and the love of truth, no longer be thought important in the legislator or the magistrate; should offices be sought, and sought successfully, by adopting the prejudices, and flattering the self-love of the lowest of the people, instead of studying to win their confidence by the allurements of intellectual worth and blameless integrity; there will be reason to suspect that the pillars of social order are already beginning to decay.

In Wheaton's estimation, the people of Connecticut—whether Episcopal, Congregational, Baptist, or Methodist—were "a christian people," which is indicative of the kind of interdenominational spirit that was blossoming in the 1820s.[86]

Beyond Wheaton's Connecticut or even just southern New England, an evangelical social engagement was emerging nationwide. The dozen or so years after 1815 saw the formation of a variety of national benevolent and reform organizations. All of these agencies took root in the South as well, with the exception of abolitionist groups in the 1830s. Like those in New England, southern "evangelicals contended that religion was vital to the preservation of the American republic." In the middle states, Ezra Stiles Ely, a Philadelphia Presbyterian minister, called in 1827 for "a Christian party in politics." Ely's idea for an evangelical electoral force sounded very much like the formulation that Lyman Beecher had articulated in the previous four years.[87] As the Congregationalists abandoned their anomalous, regional attachment to the standing order, they preserved their corporate ethic by joining a more denominationally and territorially broad-based coalition of evangelical activists.

The interdenominationalism of the 1820s—sort of a religious analogue to the Era of Good Feelings in politics—had definite limits. As a general rule, nineteenth-century denominations jealously guarded their separate identities. The degree of interdenominational cooperation, though an important development, should not be overstated.[88] Joseph Goffe, for example, had generally cordial relations with Baptists, as was noted in the last chapter. He preached, for instance, in Boston's First Baptist Church during a revival in 1803. Still, when his daughter was away in the deep South and could attend only Baptist or Methodist preaching, Goffe warned her not to be misled. "Some of both these classes are doubtless good men, & say many good things, but they are not to be relied on. They are *sectarians*, & like others of the kind they seek their own, & not the things of Jesus Christ. You can hear them, perhaps, but compare what they say with God's word of truth & grace, & receive or reject it according to that unerring oracle." Moreover, the evangelical in-groups considered certain denominations to be beyond the pale of fellowship, and the out-groups repaid the evangelicals' hostility with interest. Ebenezer Porter indicated in 1823 that interdenominationalism should go only so far. He gave thanks to God "that the hostility respecting minor subjects, which has so long armed the disciples of Christ against each other, and disgraced the religion they profess, is passing away; and that ages of angry speculation are succeeded at length by an age of fraternal feeling and action. Every step in the advance of genuine catholicism, I would hail as auspicious to the cause of Zion." However, the Andover Seminary professor and future president also warned that there was a danger inherent in the principle of denominational "union," namely, that "we should not give up the *gospel* for the sake of union." "A compromise, call it what we will, that rests on the basis of an indefinite charity, and that overlooks or deliberately sacrifices the grand essentials of Christianity, is a building of hay, wood, and stubble; it will not stand fire."[89] Clearly, Porter's last remark referred to the Unitarians' pleas for charity, liberalism, and an end to doctrinal conflict. For the orthodox, fundamental doctrines weighed more heavily than the goal of preserving the establishment and the standing order. Men like Porter, after all, had founded Andover Seminary when they could no longer compromise with the theology emanating from Harvard.

A bitter exchange arising out of the 1827 Massachusetts election sermon exposed the new configuration of denominational alliances. In the course of his sermon, Moses Stuart opined that the Universalists, although he did not mention them by name, should be disallowed from either holding office or giving courtroom testimony because they "deny the doctrine of future retribution for crimes committed in the present world." In other words, because the Universalists did not believe in the possibility of judgment and damnation, they would have no disincentive to keep them from lying, cheating, stealing, or committing any other immoral act. This line of reasoning drew on the familiar argument that only Christianity could ensure virtue and prevent crimes from being committed beyond the eye of the law. Stuart did not stand alone in his attack on the Universalists; that new denomination formed a common target for evangelicals.[90]

Hosea Ballou, pastor of Boston's Second Universalist Society and a denominational leader, responded to Stuart's remarks the same year in a sermon entitled *Orthodoxy Unmasked*. Ballou turned Stuart's reasoning around. He said that if anyone

Hosea Ballou. Courtesy American Antiquarian Society.

should be disbarred from giving an oath, it should be the Calvinists, because members of the elect had no reason not to perjure themselves, knowing that their salvation was assured in any case! Ballou concluded his sermon by gleefully recalling the reverses the Congregationalists had been suffering during the 1820s on account of the Unitarian controversy. "Look through New England, and you at once realize the assertion in the text [Jer. 10:21], 'all their flocks shall be scattered!' How many country towns within a very few years have been reduced to the necessity of dismissing their regular clergymen; how many parishes have been scattered, part to one denomination and part to another; how many are partly supplied from missionary funds; how many entirely destitute."[91]

The flare-up between Stuart and Ballou illuminated the contours of the emerging denominational landscape. Evangelical groups like the orthodox Congregationalists and Baptists, along with some Methodists and Episcopalians, were finding common ground both ideologically and organizationally. Those outside this evangelical union resisted its reach and resented its pretensions to pronounce a shared public Christianity. For their resistance, the out-groups such as the Universalists and Unitarians functioned for the evangelicals as a negative referent, standing in sharp contrast to the comparatively small disagreements dividing the evangelicals. The Baptists, wrote William McLoughlin, "were as loud as Morse and Beecher in denouncing Harvard's infidelity." The "evangelical united front" thrived on the anti-evangelical opposition.[92]

Abraham Bishop was another one of those who stood outside the new evangelical coalition and viewed its emergence with suspicion and hostility. He was a leading spokesman for the Connecticut Democratic-Republicans, a position he cemented when he delivered the speech *Connecticut Republicanism* in 1800. *Connecticut Republicanism* had lambasted the state's standing order as an integral part of Federalist tyranny and vilified the clergy as self-serving hypocrites. Bishop essentially repeated these same criticisms two dozen years later. The calculation of Edward D. Griffin, president of Williams College, that the evangelization of the world required 700,000 clergymen, provoked Bishop's diatribe against the evangelical coalition. Bishop launched his assault in a series of newspaper articles in 1824 that were republished together in the same year. He was then serving as collector of the Port of New Haven, an appointed post that he had gained in return for his services to the Republican party. Bishop ridiculed the Presbyterian Education Society, like the American Education Society an organization for subsidizing the education of ministerial students, as a rich men's club, which he contrasted with the "poverty and humility" of Jesus' disciples. He also sneered that such an organization had more than benevolent motives in mind; he warned that it was part of a neo-Federalist conspiracy against the common man. "Every friend of civil and religious liberty in this country ought to be on the watch, when he sees an alliance offensive and defensive actually formed between the *pretended religion and real wealth* of the country, the hierarchy and oligarchy combined. If it is difficult to ascertain the course by which the men are to compass dominion over the people, it is perfectly obvious and certain, that their ostensible object is not their real object."[93] Bishop was intent on making the charges of priestcraft and fraud stick to the Calvinist clergy.

Yet, in spite of the mocking derision Bishop heaped on the interdenominational coalition, his abuse revealed both that the coalition's message was getting across and that it was gaining influence. Bishop's criticism revealed a comprehension of the evangelical coalition's two main programs: he had gotten the message about the power of the Christian electorate and a coalition of churches. But whereas ministers like Humphrey or Beecher cast these two ideas in a positive light as means to save the nation, Bishop countered that religion in politics inevitably led to tyranny and that the evangelicals' interdenominationalism was a sham, concocted by the old standing order to conceal its dark machinations.

> And now, men, brethren, and fathers, for what purpose are all these things? . . . It is to associate and consociate all the natural enemies of the church, those who are declared such in the New-Testament, under the popular name of religion; the main body to be presbyterian, orthodox and federal, and to draw into their circle now and then a republican, now and then a priest of one of the minor orders, so that he may

draw in as many of his people, as can be *duped to pay*, and so as to give to the whole the appearance of catholicism and toleration, and to go on smoothly so as not to alarm the people.

And what are these mighty people to gain by all this? Nothing more or less than the control of your civil and religious rights, the power of appointing all the great officers of the nation, and of changing the form of your government at their pleasure. Look to the hundred millions of papal Christendom. There the same game has been played by a like class of Pharisees with perfect success, because it was not resisted. There the people are in the dust, where you will be, if you will follow their example of indifference.[94]

Abraham Bishop was nothing if not a perceptive observer of the contemporary scene. Although he cast orthodox clergymen in the most nefarious light, he nevertheless correctly understood the outlines of their plan to maintain the connection between Christianity and society. While the orthodox celebrated their gains, Bishop wailed and gnashed his teeth. He wanted to arouse the American public to the threat he saw in the new programs launched by the evangelical clergy. To maximize the apparent danger, Bishop reached back to the vocabulary of the first party competition. He tried to resurrect the linguistic potency of the Republican-dissenter coalition by portraying benevolent societies as a front for the reestablishment of the standing order. By the late 1810s, Bishop wrote,

> Moses [had] lost all his power, and Aaron had the best possible chance of atoning for his past errors by devoting the remainder of his days to the care of souls; but such Aarons, when they have once tasted [Ps. 133:1] how good and pleasant it is for federal brethren to dwell together in unity, felt, like an old coachman, a great relish for the crack of the whip, and they cried with a loud voice, Moses, Moses! and from the north Missionary Moses, from the south Bible Moses, and from the interior Education Moses, answered: and the parties met, embraced and formed articles, the main object of which was the raising of money by the admission of members and by all manner of addresses to the ambition, the piety, enthusiasm or hypocrisy, the fears and hopes, the joys and sorrows of this great community.[95]

Although Bishop's attacks were just as caustic in 1824 as they had been in 1800, they somehow seemed less biting that before. Without a bitter two-party competition and the living issue of the establishment to provoke antagonism, Bishop's remarks came across as toothless and irrelevant. His attack on Moses and Aaron rang hollow by 1824; by then, even the orthodox ministry had forsaken that platform.

In conclusion, Bishop's criticisms cast into sharp relief the evolution of the clergy's public Christianity. Orthodox Congregationalists continued to adhere to their beliefs that God ruled the nations and that society needed religion. By the 1820s, however, they had given up the establishment in southern New England. They hoped still to address corporate life with their religious faith, as Bishop had observed, by relying on a Christian voting bloc and socially engaged churches. This shift on the part of the orthodox toward the position of "Christ the transformer of culture" led to a new coalition with other evangelical denominations. In turn, the interdenominational coalition precipitated an antievangelical opposition, too. The "evangelical united front" organized an array of new institutions to achieve the goals of societal Christianization, moral purification, and perhaps the inauguration of the millennium. Despite Abraham Bishop's claims to the contrary, the interdenominational coalition was real, although he was certainly correct to detect its potential to alter the American church and state. The revivals of the Second Great Awakening did not just convert men and women individually and in isolation but fired a vision among their leaders of taking their Christianity to society. Ministers sought a social transformation; they wanted someone to be like Nehemiah in rebuilding the walls of Jerusalem.

We are finally in the position, as promised, to interpret and set in context Samuel Austin's 1825 July Fourth address, which framed some of the questions for this book in the opening pages of the introduction. Austin's address was not anything exceptional, but it was representative. Likewise, Austin's long career covered most of this study's time span, making him a fitting symbol for his generation. He had served with the American army in 1776 and had gone on to laud George Washington and warn of the dangers of France in the 1790s, to edit the works of Jonathan Edwards and oppose the Jeffersonians in the next decade, and to organize Congregational missionary and ministerial associations. His 1825 address epitomized the foregoing discussion of the public Christianity of the orthodox in the 1820s. The elderly Austin concurred with the younger generation, to whom the Revolutionary generation had now passed the baton of leadership, as to the role of the churches as "transformer of culture." This oration amounted to Austin's valedictory, in that illness overtook him shortly thereafter. Perhaps his physical ailments were apparent when Austin ascended the pulpit on the Fourth of July, 1825. Perhaps the "tall, stately" frame of his youth stooped beneath his sixty-four years and his failing health. The speech would be one of Austin's last performances before he sadly sank into a depression that lasted the final five years of his life, from which he would not emerge until death released him in 1830.[96]

Austin's message was that the American churches would renew the world. He advocated, as did other colleagues in the 1820s, the position that the revived churches would carry the load of evangelizing the globe, elevating American society, and forwarding the millennium. He praised the Revolution on its forty-ninth anniversary for vanquishing the forces of tyranny, but more important were the Revolution's ramifications for Christian progress. Placing himself within the long tradition of providential interpretation, Austin depicted the American Revolution as "not a casual, but a providential, event." Typically, he mingled his providential pronouncements with American nationalism; like the rest of the clergy discussed at the beginning of this chapter, Austin had reconciled himself with American patriotism. No longer did he scorn the Constitution as a godless document as he had done in 1811, but he termed it "a mere civil institution." More significant than the state in Austin's estimation was the church. As he continued, "The Church appears to have been perpetuated through every age as the special charge of the Almighty. . . . Can we doubt a moment, my brethren, that the extension of the boundaries, and the increase of the spiritual glory, of the Church was the specific object her King and her God had in view, in placing us in a situation in which we might, relying upon his protection, control our own interests, and put at defiance the oppressors of mankind?" In other words, Austin portrayed the American Revolution instrumentally, as subsidiary to American Christianity. The Revolution had liberated religion in the United States, such that

Austin could say, "The gospel has . . . been here perfectly unmanacled." This opened the way for the pure gospel's spread and enabled American Christians to play a role of global dimensions by way of "the numerous societies that have been formed among ourselves, the circulation we have given to the scriptures, and the many efficient and faithful missionaries that have gone out from us." They would help bring about the millennium: "I simply ask the question, — Have not the numerous Christians in this country had, and what hinders but they should have — must they not have, till this grand spiritual occupation of the earth is effected, an important instrumental agency in bringing it to pass? Can we bring such a stigma upon our reputation, or deprive ourselves of the honours of such an achievement, by drowsily losing sight of the object, or suspending, for a moment, our efforts?" In light of this last remark, Austin closed by calling on his hearers to act on society. "And by all means let us *live* as well as speak [the Lord's] praise. Let us put our religion, which is his most reasonable service, into its full influence over ourselves, over those committed to our care, and, as far as we can, over the favoured country we enjoy. O that it had its genuine dominion over all the population of these United States, and were cherished both by the high and the low, as the grand, vivifying power by which individuals and communities are to live."[97] With that, Samuel Austin rested his public voice.

As Austin had called for action, ministers and churches engaged American society along several fronts. It remains to briefly consider how the activities of American Christians contributed in the first third of the nineteenth century to a variety of reform campaigns.

SIX

⚊⚊⚊⚊⚊⚊

Public Christianity's Relevance to
Understanding Reform

Wisdom crieth without; she uttereth her voice in the streets.

—Prov. 1:20

IN THE YEARS FROM 1815 into the 1830s, the standing order had finally broken asunder, in part from the internal strains of trying to hold Trinitarians and Unitarians together within the establishment, and in part from the external blows of its enemies. In the aftermath of the standing order's disintegration, ministers reassembled the separate pieces into new configurations. Former antagonists among different denominations worked to overcome their differences and forge a new, evangelical coalition. The disparate groups on the outside of the "evangelical united front"—whether they were Unitarians, Universalists, anticlerical secularists, or Roman Catholics—were not united among themselves, except in their common suspicion of the evangelicals' aims.

At the same time as these denominational realignments were taking place, the southern New England clergymen were also undergoing a structural change vis-à-vis the governing authorities. The end of the establishment and the first party competition both separated the Congregational clergy from the civil leadership. The widening gap between the clergy and the governing class also derived from the former's less hierarchical view of the social order. Both the revivals and the locally grounded reform and benevolent enterprises had given ministers a new appreciation for grassroots action that did not rely on a trickle-down mode of influence. The ministry's old partnership with the magistracy was now a thing of the past. In its place, the clergy and its lay allies had created a host of new organizations to act on society in a way that was more independent of the state. The president of Brown, Francis Wayland, mentioned some of these organizations and their societal impact when he exhorted, "Christian men and women, in the Sabbath School, in the Bible Class, and in the use of all the means which God has placed in our power, let us labour to bring this world into immediate subjection to the Redeemer—or let us cease to pray [Matt. 6:10] 'Thy kingdom come.'"[1] Indeed, so detached were ministers from the region's civil rulers that political pressure had replaced partnership as the operative under-

185

standing of their relationship. Moral reform organizations prodded magistrates to vigilance in suppressing vice, and ministers such as Lyman Beecher spoke of mobilizing the evangelical electorate. In other words, Moses and Aaron no longer walked hand-in-hand; rather, Aaron was trying to twist Moses' arm.

Yet amid these profound alterations in the religious and political landscapes, a continuity endured at the foundations of the region's public Christianity. Into the 1830s and beyond, ministers continued to comment on the providential status of the United States. They also insisted that society needed an infusion of Christian values, although they sharply disagreed over how that was to occur. Both Unitarian and evangelical divines offered their perspective on public life. They both earned the label of "the proprietary Protestants" or "those groups that saw themselves as the protectors of an American Christian heritage and the builders of a distinctly Protestant society."[2] Southern New England's ongoing public Christianity, nourished by the clergy over the preceding two centuries, fueled a vital debate over social morality in the early republic and formed an integral component in the development of antebellum American culture.

The ministers who are the focus of this study contributed significantly to the development of several of the leading reform campaigns in nineteenth-century America. Their carefully cultivated public Christianity embodied a living tradition of beliefs and warnings about the community's meaning and purpose that was distinct from secular ideologies such as republicanism, liberalism, or romantic nationalism, positing a religious perspective. As Robert H. Abzug has written, "it was the sacred communal identity forged by the founders and later generations of New Englanders that allowed some to create a broad religious vision conducive to reform."[3] Obviously, the ministry's public Christianity did not always appear in a confrontational mode. Instances of accommodation abound. For example, in speculating about the global mission of the United States, ministers drew upon and fed a bumptious nationalism. They employed liberal values in their exaltation of political liberty and in their professed opposition to hierarchy. Moreover, reform had other sources besides public Christianity; historians too numerous to mention have located the roots of reform in factors ranging from changing social relations and gender roles to innovations in communications technology. Nevertheless, the clergy's public Christianity showed itself to be protean in its assaults on contemporary social practices. The clergymen under study criticized what they regarded as the excesses of jingoism and the market revolution. They also took on social customs at variance with their corporate ethic, such as intemperance and violations of the Sabbath. Perhaps most significantly, they stepped up their denunciations of slavery. In all of these ways, southern New England ministers demonstrated the relevance of their ongoing public Christianity, and their greater detachment from the civil leadership gave them the freedom to speak their minds. Historians have carefully recounted all of these reform initiatives, but they are briefly mentioned here to show the wide-ranging impact of the New England clergy's public Christianity.

Using the language of their public Christianity, ministers challenged the spread-eagle nationalism of the United States in the 1820s. The ministry's relationship with nationalism had been an ongoing issue since the 1780s at least and one that had never been fully resolved. The question boiled down to this: how much patriotism was too much of a good thing? Ministers had for the most part returned the United States to a favorable light after the War of 1812. One way in which they dealt with the issue of rising nationalism was to show the complementarity between Christianity and patriotism; piety perfected the virtue of patriotism, so they said. Ministers had joined in the celebration of national greatness and high prospects but began to wonder if they had gone too far. They tried to rein in their praise for the new nation and its providential role, which they thought Americans were putting in jeopardy.

A number of ministers did not approve of the way that the Fourth of July had evolved, either in its celebrations or in the attendant orations. These festivities abraded both sides of the clergy's public Christianity, namely, the corporate identity of a people in relationship with a providential God and the definition of a godly community. One could find the highest octane of nationalism available at Fourth of July commemorations. By the third decade of the nineteenth century, the day's orations had become formulaic. They usually followed the pattern of the Whig interpretation of the American Revolution, retelling the story of how virtuous and liberty-loving Americans overcame debased and tyrannical Britons, and then forecasting how the victorious Americans would set a pattern for the world to emulate. "Citizens glorified the mythic past, hyperbolized the contemporary, and breathlessly imagined America's future."[4] The pride and chauvinism of this oratory exceeded the bounds of the nation's providential identity. Americans seemed to be burning incense to their own image, which raised the old concept of ingratitude again. As Asa Cummings, a Bowdoin College tutor and recently a student at the Andover Theological Seminary, remarked in 1820, "We have boasted of *American prowess*, of the *unconquerable spirit of freemen*, without remembering, that [1 Sam. 17:47] 'the battle is the Lord's, and that [Ps. 22:28] he is governour among the nations.' What is the language of our publick celebrations and festivals? . . . Are these anniversaries employed in recounting the wonderful works of God towards us, as motives to excite our gratitude? By how many is the Author of our blessings once thought of? How grossly are these festivals perverted!" New Haven's Leonard Bacon put the problem mildly but firmly: "We might dwell in our thoughts, on those topics of exultation, which the occasion [of July Fourth] affords—on the unrivalled prosperity of our country, and the perfect beauty of our political institutions—on the bright memory of the past, and the still brighter prospect of the future;—and from all these contemplations learn no holier lesson, than to indulge the unhallowed exultation of national pride, or to cherish the bloody fanaticism of national ambition."[5] An appropriate celebration of Independence Day, from the clergy's point of view, would have been humbly framed in the context of the nation's dependence on providential guidance.

The vices exhibited on the national holiday further conflicted with the clergy's pronouncements about the moral boundaries of liberty and with the corporate concern for the behavior of others. July Fourth celebrations, several ministers thought, were encouraging people to toss their morality to the wind. Asa Cummings lamented that "the manner, in which the day is now celebrated, destroys many, and, we fear, makes no patriots. Exulting in freedom, we prove ourselves the slaves of appetite." In particular, the demagogic oratory, the "promiscuous" mingling of the sexes, and the drinking to intoxication all disgusted him. Likewise, William B. Sprague, Congregational minister of West Springfield, Massachusetts, charged "that *vice* has stalked abroad, on this day, with a more than commonly shameless front; as if the freedom, which the day commemorates, were only the liberty of doing wrong." Partisanship, another species of vice, further frustrated the program to create a disinterested, Christian electorate. "Not unfrequently [*sic*]," Sprague complained, the celebration of the Fourth of July "has been perverted to purposes of political jangling; —for brandishing, even in the sanctuary of God, the carnal weapons of party spirit;— for stirring up the worst passions of human nature." Ministers wanted the Fourth of July to be a reverent day for remembering God's goodness to the nation, not a bacchanalia for celebrating national vanity. However, "on a day with thousands of citizens on the loose, insufficient police, and a high level of consciously encouraged excitement, perfect order was perfectly impossible." Given the problems of partisanship and disorderliness on the Fourth of July, there appeared specifically "religious celebration[s] of Independence" that were designed to commemorate the day properly.[6]

In an interesting pattern of co-optation, ministers incorporated national ideals as part of their jeremiads. In other words, they rendered their patriotism in a prophetic voice. William Lloyd Garrison chose the Fourth of July, not insignificantly, to begin his campaign for the abolition of slavery in 1829. Although a layman himself—a journalist, to be more precise—Garrison used biblical language to confront the nation. The evil of slavery, he said, "should make this a day of fasting and prayer, not of boisterous merriment and idle pageantry, a day of great lamentation, not of congratulatory joy. It should spike every cannon, and haul down every banner. Our garb should be sackcloth, our heads bowed in the dust, our supplications for the pardon and assistance of Heaven." "I am sick of our unmeaning declamation in praise of liberty and equality," he added, "of our hypocritical cant about the unalienable rights of man."[7]

Heman Humphrey exploited the same contradiction between American ideals and practice in a jeremiad he issued against Andrew Jackson's policy of Indian removal in 1829. He pointed his finger in shame that such a policy was being carried out "in the 19th century, and under the sanction of the most enlightened and christian republic on earth!" The fact that the Five Tribes were moving "rapidly from pagan darkness and coming into the light of well regulated, civil and Christian communities," in Humphrey's eyes, made matters only worse. He closed with a warning about the threat of divine wrath, saying that "there is a just God in heaven and that sooner or later his wrath will wax hot against the nation that tramples upon the rights of its defenceless and imploring neighbors."[8] He concluded, amplifying this theme,

> The Cherokees and Choctaws cannot, indeed, resist our arms. They lie at the mercy of their white neighbors. . . . But though they are too weak to meet us in the field, they are not too weak to lift up their cries to heaven against us. . . . Their members are more than sufficient to bring down the judgments of God upon their cruel oppressors. Who then will [Ezek. 22:30] "make up the hedge and stand in the gap before Him for the land that He should not destroy it?" The crisis is awful, and the responsibilities of our rulers and of the whole nation are tremendous! The Lord is a holy God, and he is jealous![9]

In short, the public Christianity of southern New England's clergymen — especially in its capacities to warn of providential rebuke and to denounce public sins — gave ministers the rhetorical tools with which to challenge self-congratulatory nationalism. In this way, ministers used their Christian perspective to open a fundamental debate over public life and morality that had wide-ranging implications for politics, identity, and reform.

Ministers likewise tapped their public Christianity for the purpose of defending Sunday as a day devoted to attending worship and cultivating one's religion. The Sabbath issue had concerned the ministry from the colonial period to the 1790s, but it took on new urgency in the 1810s and 1820s.[10] In 1810, Congress mandated that post offices open on Sunday at "those offices where the mails actually arrived." Moreover, advances in highway and canal transportation in the years after the War of 1812 added to the pace of activity on Sundays. The historian Richard R. John has perceptively described how the issue of business on the Sabbath "violate[d] what one might term the moral geography of the Sabbath." Opening the post office, for instance, created a distraction from the day's supposedly singular focus on church and other pious devotions. "Rather than being set apart as a day sacred to God," John writes, "the Sabbath was fast becoming no different from the rest of the week." Clergymen thought that for their strategies of social sanctification to have any chance of success, there needed to be a time set apart for corporate worship and instruction. Ebenezer Porter, a member of the faculty at Andover Theological Seminary, advanced this line of argument in typical fashion: "Divine revelation and general experience concur in the testimony, that social and civil institutions cannot be preserved, unless the public manners are formed on the basis of sound morality; that such morality cannot be maintained among a people, without the active sense of religious obligation; and that neither can long exist when the sabbath ceases to be regarded as an ordinance of heaven."[11]

Porter's reasoning was essentially the same as that reasoning that had been used to uphold the establishment. Here ministers tried to walk a fine line as to the limits of legislative involvement in religious matters. Although they had abandoned the establishment of Congregationalism, they tried to claim that the issue of enforcing the Sabbath was something different entirely. "You will deeply regret the want of discernment," said Zephaniah Swift Moore to the members of the legislative and executive branches of Massachusetts in the election sermon of 1818, "in those who can see no difference between a national religious establishment and the legislative protection of an institution, appointed by the benevolent Sovereign of the universe, for the happiness of the whole human family." "Do we encroach upon any man's rights," Thomas Snell of North Brookfield, Massachusetts, asked rhetorically, "by restraining him from crimes injurious to individuals or to the commonwealth? How then are the rights of men infringed when they are restrained from treading down an institution most precious to our fathers, most conducive to civilization and christian virtue, necessary to maintain a sense of God, of moral obligation, and personal responsibility, and on whose support and sacred observance, essentially depend the safety and glory of the state?" The Sabbath was something so benign and so conducive to social well-being, these clergymen argued, that they acted as if opposition to Sabbatarian laws was utterly unfathomable.[12]

With this logic, ministers led two petition campaigns in 1814–1815 and 1828–1830 to halt the delivery of mail on Sundays. Although both were initiated by Presbyterians from the mid-Atlantic region, the New England clergy joined enthusiastically, providing much support. For example, the Massachusetts General Association petitioned Congress on its own in both 1815 and 1816. The same "interdenominational and nonsectarian" coalition organized in 1828 the General Union for the Promotion of the Christian Sabbath (GUPCS), a voluntary society modeled after those already discussed for missions and evangelization. However, the failure of petitioning and the anti-Sabbatarian backlash belied ministers' contention that the issue of the Sabbath would be completely noncontroversial.[13] Nonetheless, the petition drives and the GUPCS form another instance of the impact of the ministry's public Christianity on reform.

Sabbatarianism was just one of the issues of public morality that generated controversy in the quarter century after the War of 1812. In May 1828, for example, Joseph Goffe attended a town meeting in Millbury, Massachusetts, at which the agenda concerned a variety of "customs & abuses of long standing, & pernicious influence upon the order & morals of the town." Those in attendance voted to crack down on violators of the Sabbath laws, sumptuary excesses at funerals, and "public show-men, circus-riders, & all species of juggling & witchcraft, which have recently increased to a great degree." At funerals and elsewhere, the citizens of Millbury also resolved "to promote the cause of temperance." The temperance campaign was probably the most widespread and successful reform movement to come out of the clergy's public Christianity in the early republic.[14]

Admittedly, the temperance movement drew on many aspects of its nineteenth-century milieu. Temperance omnivorously fed on a diverse diet of cultural materials, including medical literature, millennialism, patriotism, and the rage for statistics.[15] The revivalists' concern for the conversion of the individual's soul also carried implications for the temperance campaign; how could the Holy Spirit penetrate a soul soaked with rum?[16] Nevertheless, the clergy's corporate ethic also fired the temperance campaign in at least two ways. Playing the role of social scientists, ministers analyzed the societal costs of alcohol consumption. They also denounced intemperance as contrary to the Christian duties to exercise love and responsibility for others. The ministry's corporate concern for the public welfare and its traditional belief in the interdependence of society made no small contribution to the effort to reform America's drinking habits.

Ministers almost always assailed the pecuniary burden intemperance entailed. Their emphasis on the social costs of drinking grew, in part, out of their corporate concern for society as a whole. They proffered an array of figures to document the monetary drag intemperance placed on the national community. On the annual fast of 1827, William B. Sprague offered this typical estimate.

> In the United States, it is calculated that more than thirty millions of dollars are expended annually for intoxicating liquors; and the pauperism occasioned by them, costs upwards of twelve millions more; so that, allowing three-fourths of the first mentioned sum to be set to the account of intemperance, it appears that the nation is taxed for the support of this vice, more than thirty-four millions of dollars. It is calculated, moreover, that ten thousand lives are annually sacrificed to it; that more

than two hundred thousand persons are diseased and impoverished by it; and that it is the occasion of far the greater part of all the crimes committed in the country.[17]

When Heman Humphrey and two associates penned one of the first temperance addresses in 1813, they cast the social costs of drinking in another light. They depicted the opportunity costs of intemperance, or what could have been had if all the money spent on liquor had gone toward more socially worthwhile purposes, such as "building colleges, supporting schools, improving roads, encouraging manufactures, extinguishing the national debt, increasing our navy, fortifying our seaboard, sending out missionaries, and disseminating the Scriptures." Along these same lines of the toll intemperance took on society, a few ministers added the republican note of a depreciation of virtue. "If intemperance should increase as it has done and go on to corrupt the public morals, and set the laws at defiance our government cannot stand," Humphrey warned on another occasion. "A sober people may possibly be enslaved; but an intemperate people cannot long remain free."[18]

Ministers additionally portrayed intemperance as a dereliction of social duty and a violation of people's corporate responsibilities to love and serve one another. In this criticism, Unitarians and Trinitarians agreed. Henry Ware Jr., a Boston Unitarian, denounced intemperance "as *a habit of gross self-indulgence*," adding "that life was not intended to be, and ought not to be, a season of mere self-indulgence." Echoing William Ellery Channing's sermon, *Religion a Social Principle*, Ware argued that society had an organic interconnectedness. He labeled intemperance a sin, because "*unfaithfulness to the social relations of life* is criminal. We are made to live with one another and help one another. The Creator has interwoven the interest and happiness of every man with the interest and happiness of some others. He has parents, or consort, or children, or friends, for whose peace and happiness he is bound to consult, no less than for his own." William B. Sprague, an orthodox Congregationalist, concurred with Ware's position that no man is an island. He suggested many ways by which people could bring others to the temperance pledge, such as by not offering alcoholic drinks when entertaining, by not compensating employees with a provision of liquor, by selling alcohol responsibly, by teaching children to avoid drinking, "by circulating tracts which are fitted to direct public attention to this object; and more generally, by their efforts to promote the cause of christian education, and to extend the influence of the gospel." One should do these things, Sprague said, because the drunkard "is thy brother still; and as such, thou hast no right to shut up thy bowels of compassion against him."[19]

In light of intemperance's social price and everyone's duty to aid one another, clergymen called for action against the alcoholic threat. As Humphrey concluded, "let every *christian*, every *patriot*, every *philanthropist*, gird himself up to the great work of reform, and never cease from it till it shall be accomplished." Sprague also employed the prospect of the millennium as a reason to support the temperance campaign. "In suppressing intemperance, you actually unclench the hand of avarice; you pour contributions into every treasury of the Lord; you increase the amount of that influence by which the kingdom of Christ is to become universal. Let the wealth which is now wasted in the support of this vice, even in our own country, be consecrated to this great object, and songs of thanksgiving, breaking from every land and every dwelling, would soon announce that the grand jubilee of the church had come." In other words, temperance would fund the churches in their strategy of sanctifying society. Congregational ministers took the lead in founding both the Massachusetts Society for the Suppression of Intemperance in 1813 and the more successful American Temperance Society in 1826.[20] The clergy's public Christianity, with its society-wide field of vision, attacked intemperance as not just a private but a social sin. Intemperance contradicted the ministry's benevolent concern for others and its belief in the social nature of mankind. By challenging society's values regarding alcohol, the ministry fostered reform in nineteenth-century America.

The ministry also raised for debate the threat posed to social morality by the ever-expanding influence of commerce. The market's expansion drove the Sabbatarian and temperance campaigns in complex and contradictory ways, as various scholars have argued. On the one hand, the growth of the market economy fostered an entrepreneurial frame of mind. This modernizing outlook was open to changes not only in business practices but also in societal customs, and hence could imagine reform. On the other hand, the market's relentlessness elbowed its way into Sundays and made liquor more readily available.[21] By the late 1820s and 1830s, ministers began to voice their reservations about U.S. material prosperity. Unitarians and evangelicals alike feared the power of mammon to produce selfishness, materialism, and the fraying of their corporate ethic. *"The strong, and increasing love of money,"* warned the New Haven Congregationalist Charles A. Boardman in 1830, "indicated by the spirit of adventure and speculation . . . as it is a selfish affection, is incompatible with that lofty patriotism which renders the work of government easy and effectual." In the same year, Boston's William Ellery Channing, a leading Unitarian, feared "that various causes are acting powerfully among ourselves, to inflame and madden that enslaving and degrading principle, the passion for property."[22]

However, these anxieties existed side by side with the clergy's usually lavish praise for American prosperity. The country's wealth often factored into ministers' calculations of national greatness and providential blessing. For instance, also from 1830, Francis Wayland interpreted rising national wealth and technological innovations as favorable to the spread of the Gospel.[23] An uneasy tension existed in the clergy's attitude toward wealth, with millennial optimism giving way to wariness. Nowhere was this tension more apparent than in the 1827 thanksgiving sermon of Eleazar T. Fitch, professor of homiletics at the Yale Divinity School. In his listing of America's blessings, Fitch offered this paean to the expanding commercial economy.

> She has established her populous and busy marts; that vie in elegance and wealth with foreign cities and far surpass them in their rapidly increasing prosperity. From her hills and vallies [sic], she annually rolls into these confluent marts, the products and fabrics of trade, to the amount in value of more than a hundred millions; yet leaving the granaries of the farmer full, and permitting, as does no other nation, the laborer to detain enough in his possession to furnish himself and his household with the necessaries and luxuries of life.

Yet, later in the same sermon, Fitch cautioned that "this is the crisis of her [the nation's] prosperity." Employing the jeremiad, Fitch warned that the Almighty would not ignore the nation's commercial binge: "But if we withdraw our confidence from him; if we ungratefully merge the thought of his goodness in our own worldliness and pride and lust; the scourges of vengeance are in his storehouse, and he will no doubt draw them forth for our punishment."[24] In sum, the clergy's public Christianity could add to the debate in nineteenth-century culture over the merits of capitalism. Although the ministry's pronouncements clearly divided on the issue, they nevertheless provided a basis for dissent from and criticism of the national culture.

No aspect of America's money-hungry, market-driven way of life came in for more damning criticism than the buying and selling of human beings, the "peculiar institution" of chattel slavery. It took the outside factor of religion to challenge American slavery. African Americans, given their experiences of slavery and racism, could arrive at abolitionism apart from religious conviction, but the same was not true of whites. "No man, no family, no state, no nation is to live merely for individual and private ends. It is incumbent on all to help their fellows, and thus themselves." So claimed Loammi Ives Hoadly of Worcester's Calvinist Church in a quintessential statement of the Congregational clergy's corporate ethic during a July Fourth address in 1824.[25] Hoadly was not spreading the blanket of clerical benevolence over dissipated Fourth of July revelers, aggressive traducers of the Sabbath, prodigal drunks, or the enticing entrepreneurs of the market economy. Rather, he referred to African American slaves as another object of Christian paternalism.

The critique of slavery in the 1820s mined the same conglomeration of motives as had propelled the antislavery movement in the 1790s. Early New England antislavery drew upon the contradictions slavery presented to disinterested benevolence and to the Revolution's claims to liberty, the danger posed by such patent sinfulness in the eyes of a vengeful God, and the contamination of virtue that contact with slaveholding threatened. Ministers especially highlighted the contrast between the Fourth of July and chattel slavery, which relates back to their criticism of excessive nationalism. "It is just cause for grief and humiliation," mourned William B. Sprague, "that while we are chanting the praises of national liberty, there are more than two millions among us, who are groaning under the most abject bondage."[26] Asa Cummings warned that God's justice would avenge slavery, noting that nations had to be punished in this world. "Have we not the cause for trembling? When the Almighty shall make inquisition for blood, what shall we answer him? Verily we shall, in our turn, feel the weight of his uplifted rod. This outrage upon justice and humanity, this traffick in human flesh, this oppression of the poor and friendless, will certainly sink the nation that authorizes it, unless their doom be averted by speedy repentance."[27] Both their providentialism and prescriptions for societal righteousness gave ministers the independent point of view from which to challenge the justice of slavery.

However, many *antislavery* clergymen were not thorough *abolitionists* in the 1820s. They, too, compromised their principles, namely, by qualifying their antislavery stance in the face of racism. The American Colonization Society's professedly moderate solution to the problem of slavery—the transportation of freed blacks to an independent colony on the African coast or elsewhere—appealed to a number of southern New England ministers. It promised a way to deal with the problem of slavery, a social sin with serious consequences, while not threatening the political or racial orders with dangerous upheaval. According to Loammi Ives Hoadly, only three potential solutions to slavery in the United States offered themselves: "a nauseous amalgamation, removal by colonization, or the dismemberment and ruin of these flourishing States." Given that choice, colonization was obviously the only viable option. Nathaniel Bouton of Concord, New Hampshire, agreed. Emancipation without any strings attached would never do because free blacks were "the most ignorant, degraded and vicious class in the community." Bouton endorsed the program of the American Colonization Society (A.C.S.) as "the only judicious plan" available. "By colonizing the free blacks," he argued hopefully in 1825, "you open the door for gradual emancipation. Many slave-holders stand ready to give up their slaves, the moment they can be removed out of the country." Of course, the folly of that pie-in-the-sky optimism would soon become apparent.[28]

Leonard Bacon proposed one more set of motives to support the A.C.S. He contended that the colonization of freed African Americans would partially fulfill the millennial destiny of the United States. Specifically, the United States would be the seedbed for the germination of a free black vanguard that would civilize and Christianize Africa. "How can you imagine a more splendid contribution to the cause of human happiness," Bacon asked his New Haven audience on the Fourth of July, 1825, "than you might make, if you would train up and send to Africa such men as were the Pilgrims of Plymouth, or the Puritans of New-Haven?"[29] In other words, Bacon envisioned a scenario whereby the United States would renovate the globe, as ministers like Ezra Stiles had foretold in the 1780s.

It remained for a layman to apply the ministry's public Christianity most fully and uncompromisingly to the problem of slavery. That man was William Lloyd Garrison. Garrison rejected the racial separatism of the A.C.S. He launched his abolition campaign by modeling it after other reform projects, specifically the temperance drive. "Can we not operate upon public sentiment (the lever that can move the moral world)," he asked on the Fourth of July, 1829, "by way of remonstrance, advice, or entreaty?" He continued, "We have seen how readily, and with what ease, that horrid gorgon, Intemperance, has been checked in his ravages. Let us take courage. Moral influence, when in vigorous exercise, is irresistible." Garrison had entered the temperance ranks under the influence of Lyman Beecher's preaching in Boston during the latter half of the 1820s, and he knew the power of a reforming crusade. Garrison argued that among all the other benevolent campaigns underway in the public sphere, abolitionism should take the first rank. He appropriated the clergy's public Christianity in two more ways. First, he challenged the churches to take up the issue. "I call upon the churches of the living God to lead in this great enterprise," he said, speaking from that evangelical bastion, Boston's Park Street Church. "Let them combine their energies, and systematize their plans, for the rescue of suffering humanity. Let them pour out their supplications to Heaven in behalf of the slave. Prayer is omnipotent: its breath can melt adamantine rocks, its touch can break the stoutest chains. Let anti-slavery charity-boxes stand uppermost among those for missionary, tract, and educational purposes." Second, Garrison preached in the classic tradition of the jeremiad. He predicted a slave insurrection if nothing were done and concluded that "the terrible judgments of an incensed God will complete the catastrophe of republican America."[30] In a sense, abolitionism represents the full flowering of this study's subject and a fitting point at which to conclude. It was a call to redeem

American society, using the churches and the language of the jeremiad. Garrison had linked American society with Christianity along the two lines of providential interpretation and social prescription that the ministry had built and maintained since the Revolution. Like Abraham Bishop, Garrison was an astute, outside observer of the clergy's corporate stance, but, unlike Bishop, he held it up as something positive and useful.

There existed, therefore, a considerable amount of continuity between the clergy's public Christianity of 1783 and 1833. Fifty years later, ministers and laymen still speculated on the U.S. relationship to the millennium, as Ezra Stiles had descanted upon in his 1783 election sermon, *The United States elevated to Glory and Honor*. In other ways, however, a visitor from 1783 would have found the denominational landscape all but unrecognizable. The standing order was gone, replaced by an unpredicted new coalition of Trinitarian Congregationalists and former dissenters. Ministers no longer preached about the model partnership of Moses and Aaron, except among a few Unitarian holdovers. Their pronouncements contained much less of the earlier hierarchy and deference. Instead, ministers focused on revivals, church organizations, and Christian political activism as means by which to connect religion and society.

Epilogue

... ye should earnestly contend for the faith which was once delivered unto the saints.

— Jude 3

WHEN THE IDEA for this study first germinated almost ten years ago, the initial impetus came from two outstanding books. In *The New England Soul*, Harry S. Stout details how the Puritans' national covenant remained an important and meaningful social ideology from the Great Migration of the 1630s to the American Revolution of 1776. In *The Democratization of American Christianity*, Nathan O. Hatch paints a fascinating picture of how radical Christians seized on the egalitarianism of the American Revolution to create new, independent, and antielite denominations in the early republic. I wanted to explore the implicit intersection of these two works: I sought to understand the national covenant's dissolution in post-Revolutionary America, to which Stout alludes in his epilogue, amid the turbulent environment described by Hatch. I also hoped to provide a coherent interpretation of a time period, 1783 to 1833, that is often divided between students of the Revolution and scholars of antebellum America.

In contrast to Hatch's portrayal of them, I quickly learned that neither had the traditional clerical leaders been stripped of all their authority in the early nineteenth century nor had they atrophied and lost their initiative. Rather, they remained an important element in the overlapping histories of the development of politics, culture, and national identity in the new nation. Over time, through my engagement with the primary and secondary literature, I also came to understand that the "national covenant" was not the organizing principle I had thought it to be. True, the Puritans' post-Revolutionary descendants had a vital religiosocial ideology, but to refer to it as their "national covenant" both confines it within too narrow a definition and confuses it with its seventeenth-century antecedents. Instead, I have chosen to refer to the southern New England clergy's social ideology as its "public Christianity." This public Christianity combined the heritage of the national covenant with elements of republicanism, nationalism, millennialism, and social organicism. The clergy—especially the established Congregational clergy—consistently tried to relate its religious faith to social experience. Rather than tracing the collapse of the clergy's public Christianity—as I expected and as the secondary literature purports —I found that it endured and adapted to events in the half-century following the American Revolution.

Although this study concludes in 1833, the story of the clergy's public Christianity and its legacy does not end there. The final disestablishment of Massachusetts Congregationalism in 1833 certainly marked a watershed event and constitutes a legitimate place at which to close this account. Yet, the public Christianity of the southern New England clergy made a significant impact on antebellum America, during the Civil War years, and into the first part of the twentieth century. In the years after 1833, ministers continued to contend earnestly in the public sphere for the faith once delivered unto the saints.

After disestablishment, the Unitarians were faced with the same dilemma the orthodox had confronted a decade earlier. The Unitarians, the establishment's last defenders, scrambled to find new strategies by which to connect religion and society in the years around 1833. They shifted from politics to social and cultural endeavors. Whereas Lyman Beecher and company spoke of revivals and a Christian electorate, the Unitarians devoted themselves to projects like education, writing, and charity. To cite just one example, Joseph Tuckerman developed a novel ministry to Boston's poor that embodied Unitarianism's social conscience without relying on the state. The Unitarians kept alive a variant of their corporate ethic in antebellum eastern Massachusetts.[1]

In the years leading up to the Civil War, the public Christianity of the southern New England clergy, particularly the evangelical clergy, exerted a growing national influence. For purposes of clarity and regional specificity, the focus of this study has been on the discrete area of southern New England. However, that region was never isolated from its neighbors. National and international political events impinged on it, and the ministry's voluntary associations took on nationwide scope in the 1820s by forming alliances with mid-Atlantic Presbyterians and the Dutch Reformed especially. With the post-Revolutionary out-migration from New England, the first missionary societies formed to reach transplanted New Englanders. Beginning in the 1820s, ministers increasingly turned their eyes to the west with a mixture of excitement and trepidation. "When it is considered that the inhabitants of the new states will soon be the majority of the American people," warned the president of Williams College, Edward Dorr Griffin, in 1824, "and will have in their hands the government of all our institutions, every friend of his country, every friend of free government, if he has no pity for the immortal soul, ought to be roused to this concern."[2] Lyman Beecher called for New England to be to the west what Europe had been to the east in providing funds and personnel for its colleges. The founding of Iowa College provided an interesting case of the actualization of Beecher's vision. A group of eleven graduates of the Andover Theological Seminary class of 1843 conceived a plan to go west after graduation and establish a college in Iowa, then at the frontier's edge. They did so to carry New England's brand of Christian civilization across the plains. Moreover, as New England emigrants fanned out across the northern tier of the old northwest, they packed the culture of their homeland with them. This New England diaspora carried the seeds of the region's public Christianity into fresh soil.[3]

As New England culture expanded in antebellum America, it exercised a formative influence on the second party competition between Jacksonian Democrats and Whigs. The clergy's public Christianity dovetailed with the Whig party's culture at a number of points. As the standing order had always championed the vigorous magistrate, so the Whigs advocated activist government, along the lines of internal improvements, tariffs, and a national bank. The Whigs also had a deeply moral streak that was indebted to the Unitarian and evangelical reformers discussed in the foregoing pages. As early as 1813, Heman Humphrey sounded proto-Whig themes in one of the first salvos fired in the war against intemperance. He asked his readers to "think how much good might be done by expending this money [spent on alcohol,] which is so many thousand times worse than wasted, in building colleges, supporting schools, improving roads, encouraging manufactures, extinguishing the national debt, increasing our navy, fortifying our seaboard, sending out missionaries, and disseminating the Scriptures."[4] Humphrey's mixture of civic, economic, and moral "improvements" typified the later Whig agenda. The evangelicals' "organizing process" was similar to the Whigs' American System, in that both relied on national institutions for social development. Although the clergy never fully realized the dream of Lyman Beecher to create a disciplined bloc of Christian voters that could tip the balance in any close election toward the side of morality, Christian values did thoroughly infuse the political culture of the second party period.[5]

This is not to suggest that the clergy's public Christianity marched triumphantly and uninterruptedly through the ensuing decades. Rather, as had been the case from 1783 to 1833, the issue of public Christianity remained a wellspring of contention. In addition to the external criticism of anticlerical types like Abraham Bishop, there remained a significant cluster of denominations outside the evangelical coalition. Roman Catholics, Old School Presbyterians, and Antimission Baptists, for example, were determined steadfastly to go their own ways, resisting the evangelicals' amalgamating embrace, which they regarded as "religious imperialism."[6]

Disagreements internal to evangelicalism also presented occasions for controversy. In the 1810s, revivalism had come to occupy a central place in the evangelicals' public Christianity. However, the nature of revivalism itself provoked disagreement by the late 1820s. A younger generation of ministers introduced new strategies designed to systematize revivals and to yield more converts. One of these was "the protracted meeting," a revival gathering that lasted every evening for days on end in order to convince wavering converts to make a decision for Christ. These meetings bore results in Worcester County as elsewhere in the nation in the early 1830s. The Harmony Conference reported in June 1832 that protracted meetings had produced revivals in all of its churches; the year before, the ministers of the Brookfield Association "discussed the subject of *protracted Meetings*, and were happily united in favour of such meetings." However, some ministers of the old guard were skeptical of these newfangled measures. Millbury's Joseph Goffe, a Worcester County revivalist since 1800, feared that these revivals "look too much like the work of men, — a movement upon the feelings & passions; & I fear that a large proportion of the supposed conversions that are made will prove delusive & spurious, & the Chhs be filled up with hypocritical members." And he knew who was to blame, namely, the "new set of ministers, from N[ew] Haven & Andover schools," whose "tone of sentiment & preaching is very much altered & *lowered*." "To that plain, pointed & rousing tone of sentiment & preaching, which used to be heard," he lamented, "has succeeded a *smooth & easy* system & manner, which may be pleasing to the ear, but which leaves untouched the conscience & heart." Goffe longed for "the days of Dr [Samuel]

Austin, Dr [John] Crane, & their contemporaries," who had preached more to his standards back in his heyday in the first quarter of the century. Goffe's dissent was indicative of a broader division within southern New England evangelical ranks that eventually produced a rival, conservative seminary at East Windsor, Connecticut, to check Yale's influence. Goffe spoke for those who worried that the church was so wrapped up in "laudable enterprize & benevolent action" and "schemes for evangelizing the world" that old-fashioned Calvinist preaching, the kind with "plainness & point, so as to prick the heart & cut like a two edged sword," would fall by the wayside.[7]

Even among those who focused upon "enterprize & benevolent action," repeated disputes cropped up between moderates and radicals. The historian Robert H. Abzug has brought this fissiparous tendency within reform most clearly to light. He titled his study of antebellum reformers *Cosmos Crumbling* to highlight the way in which reformers constantly pushed beyond the boundaries even of evangelical reformers like Lyman Beecher. In Abzug's retelling, radical reformers always became frustrated with the slow pace of the churches and their institutions. The radicals wanted immediate, uncompromising action against evils such as intemperance, which brought them into conflict with ecclesiastical leaders more concerned with revivals and with maintaining the unified witness of the church. As a result, "those who were comrades-in-arms in 1827 in many cases became enemies by 1834."[8] One famous instance of this radical-conservative split occurred at the Lane Seminary in Cincinnati, Ohio. Lyman Beecher had gone there in 1832 to become president. When the trustees voted to clamp down on student antislavery discussion in 1834— for fear that the students were antagonizing the residents of the border city of Cincinnati—the bulk of the student body abandoned Lane in favor of Oberlin. Charles Grandison Finney then became the new professor of theology at Oberlin at the request of the erstwhile Lane students. Even Finney, himself the target of conservatives within the Presbyterian denomination, tried to rein in the reform radicals, who he thought were losing sight of the primary goal, revivalism.[9] Evangelicalism powerfully fueled reform movements in antebellum America, but it was also a highly volatile compound that tended to create explosive divisions.

No issue proved more divisive to the clergy's public Christianity than that of slavery. William Lloyd Garrison had challenged the churches to move beyond colonization and to embrace abolitionism. That 1829 address at Boston's Park Street Church proved to be only the opening shot in a protracted exchange. Garrison and his followers quickly moved toward a more extreme abolitionist position, scorning the evangelical churches for their lack of enthusiasm. Likewise, slavery eventually rent the Unitarians' public Christianity. Unitarian ministers condemned slavery on principle but were unable to decide what to do about the problem; slavery presented a turbulent issue to men averse to rocking the boat. For one thing, Unitarian divines inclined to denounce slavery ran afoul of their mercantile parishioners. Ultimately, slavery utterly divided Unitarian moral philosophy, as it also split the Massachusetts Whig party into antislavery "Conscience" and pro-Southern, "Cotton" factions.[10] As the issue of slavery undid the Union, it also proved greater than the tensile strength of the clergy's public Christianity.

A convention of Worcester County ministers in December 1837 and January

1838 showed the ability of the slavery issue to cleave the clergy. The convention was held so that ministers could try to hammer out a united platform on this most contentious question. On a 58–14 vote, the assembled divines denounced slavery as a violation of free labor and the golden rule, as a debasement of the morals of both slaves and masters, and as an unjustifiable denial to slaves of the ability to acquire religious knowledge through literacy. The majority therefore called for immediate emancipation in the conventional yet stirring tones of its public Christianity: "Believing Slavery, therefore, to be both a SIN in itself, and a prolific parent of Sin, we believe also in the DUTY of its *removal*, and that without delay. And because we believe in the *duty*, we believe likewise in the *safety* of the measure; for under the government of God, 'righteousness' has no tendency to subvert, but only to 'exalt a nation.'" The minority, however, demurred, arguing that ministers should not "take the lead in political movements," especially one that "threaten[ed] to dissolve the Union in the conflict of geographical parties." Therefore, the convention's goal of discerning "correct opinion and right feeling" on the topic of slavery proved elusive. The convention is finally worthy of note because old adversaries, Aaron Bancroft and Joseph Goffe, once more lined up on opposite sides. Both men were in the twilight of long and remarkable careers that have woven their way through the pages of this book from chapter 1; indeed, for both men, participation in this convention was one of their last major public acts. Goffe voted with the majority, which was true to his form as someone who was not afraid to step forward in defense of controversial principles, whether they were human depravity, Federalism, public morality, or antislavery. Bancroft, in siding with the minority, once more showed a liberal's reluctance to stir controversy, preferring instead a pacific moderation. The different stances taken by Bancroft and Goffe in 1838 epitomized slavery's dividing nature, for the New England clergy as for the nation.[11]

Abolitionism may have been exceeded in the amount of turmoil it precipitated only by the related debate over women's rights. The two contentious issues were doubly connected. First, many early feminists came to espouse women's rights after involvement in the abolitionist movement. Second, in his epistle to the Ephesians, 5:22-33 and 6:5-9, St. Paul had used similar language to call upon wives to "submit" to their husbands and slaves to be "obedient" to their masters. As female abolitionists challenged slavery, they likewise confronted their own prescribed submission and rejected Pauline arguments that they submit and be silent. The role of women divided reformist, evangelical ranks in the late 1830s. Catharine Beecher, the educator, and her father, Lyman, rejected women's leadership, limiting women's role to the domestic sphere. Sarah and Angelina Grimké, disciples of Garrisonian abolitionism, countered with a biblical defense of women's equality and public roles. Robert Abzug has well assessed the significance of this controversy: "Reform had thus moved from changing habits such as drinking to rethinking the basic theological and social foundations of Western culture. For a significant number of radical reformers, nearly two decades of metahistorical tinkering had led to the collapse of the evangelical Christian cosmos."[12] The clash between the Beechers and the Grimkés demonstrates how the public Christianity of the southern New England clergy could slip beyond clerical control.

Despite its contentious quality, the relevance and vitality of southern New England's public Christianity are demonstrated by the very fact that people continued to fight over it. If evangelical reform crumbled at the edges, its main body continued to hold together, at least in the North. One recognizes the legacy of the New England clergy's public Christianity in antebellum America's best-seller, *Uncle Tom's Cabin.* In the novel's last sentence, Harriet Beecher Stowe addressed her readers: "Not by combining together, to protect injustice and cruelty, and making a common capital of sin, is this Union to be saved, — but by repentance, justice and mercy; for, not surer is the eternal law by which the millstone sinks in the ocean, than that stronger law, by which injustice and cruelty shall bring on nations the wrath of Almighty God!"[13] Clearly, one hears in this remark the echoes of the New England ministry, which since the 1780s and before had loved to quote Prov. 14:34, "Righteousness exalteth a nation: but sin is a reproach to any people." In this regard, Harriet Beecher Stowe was the true offspring of Lyman Beecher, her father.

The public Christianity analyzed in this book loomed very large indeed for the generation that witnessed the Civil War. As James H. Moorhead has shown, Northern Protestants interpreted the conflict within their providential framework. Many clergymen, employing the jeremiad tradition, attributed disunion and the outbreak of war to the nation's sins, as they had done during the War of 1812. The total war aspect of the Civil War also led many to draw on millennial language for meaning. The Puritans' descendants, among other Northerners, thought they were witnessing a final battle against the powers of evil, represented by the slave power, prior to the onset of the millennium. The United States, purged of slavery, would reassume its status as worldwide model for pure Christianity and democracy.[14]

Beyond the Civil War, the clergy's public Christianity received powerful new articulations. In June 1865, an assembly of Congregationalists meeting at Plymouth, Massachusetts, issued the Burial Hill Declaration. In part, it reaffirmed that the founders of New England "held this gospel, not merely as the ground of their personal salvation, but . . . applied its principles to elevate society, to regulate education, to civilize humanity, to purify law, to reform the Church and the State, and to assert and defend liberty; in short, to mold and redeem, by its all-transforming energy, everything that belongs to man in his individual and social relations." In other words, the Congregationalists entered the postwar era still committed to making their religious faith speak to life in society.[15]

Twenty-one years later, another best-selling book, Josiah Strong's *Our Country,* likewise restated the New England clergy's early-nineteenth-century public Christianity and reformulated it for the Gilded Age. In the introduction, Austin Phelps, professor emeritus at Andover Seminary, explicitly noted the parallel between *Our Country*'s focus on immigration and the west and Lyman Beecher's 1835 *A Plea for the West.* Indeed, at the time of the book's publication, Strong was pastor of the Central Congregational Church in Cincinnati, the city where Beecher had resided when he issued his *Plea.* Beyond that introductory similarity, several of Strong's themes directly drew on arguments made by New England divines seventy-five or a hundred years earlier. Echoing an idea that dated back to Ezra Stiles's 1783 *The United States elevated to Glory and Honor,* Strong argued that "the two great needs of mankind, that all men may be lifted up into the light of the highest Christian civilization, are, first, a pure, spiritual Christianity, and second, civil liberty." But whereas Stiles, reflecting the first blush of post-Revolutionary enthusiasm, had seen it as the new *nation's* destiny to bring about liberty and pure Christianity, Strong contended that the Anglo-Saxon *race* would do so, reflecting the influence of the nineteenth century's "scientific" racialism. "It seems to me," Strong concluded, invoking Providence to cement his thesis, "that God, with infinite wisdom and skill, is training the Anglo-Saxon race for an hour sure to come in the world's future." Strong also employed an image used by both Timothy Dwight and Lyman Beecher when he said that "the Anglo-Saxon race would speedily decay but for the salt of Christianity." And like Francis Wayland and numerous other messengers for the missionary cause before him, Strong asserted that it was "fully in the hands of the Christians of the United States, during the next ten or fifteen years, to hasten or retard the coming of Christ's kingdom in the world by hundreds, and perhaps thousands, of years." In brief, Josiah Strong's *Our Country*, a book that sold more than 175,000 copies in its first thirty years of publication, was simply a restatement of classic New England public Christianity, albeit in an updated style that featured its era's concern over urbanization and racial thinking, and a nascent Progressive's preoccupation with quantitative expertise.[16]

The early republic's public Christianity also fed into the Social Gospel movement in the late nineteenth and early twentieth centuries. Obviously, the social context had changed dramatically. The industrialization of America compelled clergymen to rethink the relevance of Christianity to an urban and largely immigrant audience.[17] Nevertheless, one detects an ongoing attempt to link Christianity to life in society that harked back to the concerns of the eighteenth-century standing order. Therefore, the public Christianity of the southern New England clergy did not expire quietly in Jeffersonian America. Rather, it continued to exert an influence into the early years of the twentieth century.

Does it continue to speak today? That is a question that I will leave to scholars who are more deeply immersed in studying the contemporary religious scene. As I have said, this study did not begin as a tract for the times, searching for a usable past to deploy in present controversies. Nonetheless, the role of religion in American public life continues to provoke sharp debate and to stimulate activism. I hope the analysis in *A Republic of Righteousness* will provide historical perspective from the early republic for the participants in today's debates.

Notes

Introduction

1. Samuel Austin, *An Address, Pronounced in Worcester, (Mass.) on the Fourth of July, 1825, being the Forty-Ninth Anniversary of the Independence of the United States, before an Assembly Convened for the Purpose of Celebrating this Event Religiously* (Worcester, Mass., 1825), 6, 10–12. Regarding Austin's background, see Franklin Bowditch Dexter, *Biographical Sketches of the Graduates of Yale College: With Annals of the College History*, 6 vols. (New York, 1885–1912), 4:248–251.

2. Austin, *An Address, Pronounced . . . on the Fourth of July*, 1825, 17, 22.

3. Among many possible choices, see, e.g., Gordon S. Wood, "The Significance of the Early Republic," *JER* 8 (1988): 1–20; idem, *The Radicalism of the American Revolution* (New York: Knopf, 1992); Joyce Appleby, *Inheriting the Revolution: The First Generation of Americans* (Cambridge: Harvard University Press, Belknap Press, 2000).

4. Edwin S. Gaustad, "Religious Tests, Constitutions, and 'Christian Nation,'" in *Religion in a Revolutionary Age*, ed. Ronald Hoffman and Peter J. Albert (Charlottesville: University Press of Virginia, 1994), 218–235; Stephen Botein, "Religious Dimensions of the Early American State," in *Beyond Confederation: Origins of the Constitution and American National Identity*, ed. Richard Beeman, Stephen Botein, and Edward C. Carter II (Chapel Hill: University of North Carolina Press, 1987), 317–320.

5. Robert H. Abzug, *Cosmos Crumbling: American Reform and the Religious Imagination*

(New York: Oxford University Press, 1994); Richard Carwardine, *Evangelicals and Politics in Antebellum America* (New Haven: Yale University Press, 1993); Nathan O. Hatch, *The Democratization of American Christianity* (New Haven: Yale University Press, 1989); Christine Leigh Heyrman, *Southern Cross: The Beginnings of the Bible Belt* (New York: Knopf, 1997); John G. West Jr., *The Politics of Revelation and Reason: Religion and Civic Life in the New Nation* (Lawrence: University Press of Kansas, 1996).

6. James R. Rohrer gives an insightful critique of the secondary literature's "caricatures" of the Congregational clergy in *Keepers of the Covenant: Frontier Missions and the Decline of Congregationalism, 1774–1818* (New York: Oxford University Press, 1995), 8.

7. Richard J. Purcell, *Connecticut in Transition: 1775–1818* (Washington, D.C.: American Historical Association, 1918; Middletown, Conn.: Wesleyan University Press, 1963), 3.

8. Ibid., 91, taking a cue from a fellow Progressive, Frederick Jackson Turner.

9. Ibid., 16, 191–192, 195–207; Vernon Louis Parrington, *Main Currents in American Thought: An Interpretation of American Literature from the Beginnings to 1920*, vol. 1, *The Colonial Mind, 1620–1800* (New York: Harcourt, Brace, 1927), 360–363, quote on 361.

10. John R. Bodo, *The Protestant Clergy and Public Issues, 1812–1848* (Princeton, N.J.: Princeton University Press, 1954), 9–10; Clifford S. Griffin, *Their Brothers' Keepers: Moral Stewardship in the United States, 1800–1865* (New Brunswick, N.J.: Rutgers University Press, 1960), x, xii. See also Joseph R. Gusfield, "Temperance, Status Control, and Mobility, 1826–60," in *Ante-Bellum Reform*, ed. David Brion Davis (New York: Harper & Row, 1967), 120–139; Charles I. Foster, *An Errand of Mercy: The Evangelical United Front, 1790–1837* (Chapel Hill: University of North Carolina Press, 1960). The premier work utilizing this approach is, of course, Richard Hofstadter, *The Age of Reform: From Bryan to F.D.R.* (New York: Vintage-Random, 1955). This privileging of social structure over values resulted from a bastardization of Parsonian functionalism; see Jeffrey C. Alexander, "Analytic Debates: Understanding the Relative Autonomy of Culture," in *Culture and Society: Contemporary Debates*, ed. Jeffrey C. Alexander and Steven Seidman (New York: Cambridge University Press, 1990), 4–6. For a recent use of "social status in decline" as an explanation of the clergy's motivation, see Peter S. Field, *The Crisis of the Standing Order: Clerical Intellectuals and Cultural Authority in Massachusetts, 1780–1833* (Amherst: University of Massachusetts Press, 1998), 142.

11. Lois W. Banner, "Religious Benevolence as Social Control: A Critique of an Interpretation," *JAH* 60 (1973): 23–41, quote on 23; Richard D. Shiels, "The Second Great Awakening in Connecticut: Critique of the Traditional Interpretation," *CH* 49 (1980): 401–415. For further problems with the definition of "social control" and its connotations as "elitist, conservative, and repressive," see Lawrence Frederick Kohl, "The Concept of Social Control and the History of Jacksonian America," *JER* 5 (1985): 21–34.

12. Perry Miller, "From the Covenant to the Revival," in *Religion in American Life*, ed. James Ward Smith and A. Leland Jamison, vol. 1, *The Shaping of American Religion* (Princeton, N.J.: Princeton University Press, 1961), 336, n. 20, 323. I refer to this essay rather than Miller's posthumously published book, *The Life of the Mind in America: From the Revolution to the Civil War* (New York: Harcourt, Brace & World, 1965), because the former's time frame is closer to my own. *The Life of the Mind* deals mainly with the antebellum years from the 1830s to the 1850s. Moreover, in the book Miller tended to be uncharacteristically dismissive toward New England. The region's revivals he characterized as only (p. 6) "a local phenomenon" compared with those held on the frontier or led by Charles Grandison Finney, and the persistence of the Congregational establishment into the nineteenth century he brushed aside as (p. 36) "vestigial." Nevertheless, the book made the same overall argument about the triumph of revivalism.

13. Perry Miller, "From the Covenant to the Revival," 328, 343.

14. Ibid., 350, 353, 367. In *The Life of the Mind*, Miller emphasized revivalism's goals of societal preservation rather than its individualizing tendencies.

15. For example, as Mary P. Ryan found in her study of Utica, New York, "those who joined the evangelical churches and reform crusades along the route of the Erie Canal were responding to the inducements of their kin as much as of their employers and were often involved in an exercise in 'self-control' rather than 'social control'" (*Cradle of the Middle Class: The Family in Oneida County, New York, 1790–1865* [New York: Cambridge University Press, 1981], 13).

16. Alan Heimert, *Religion and the American Mind: From the Great Awakening to the Revolution* (Cambridge: Harvard University Press, 1966). On republicanism, millennialism, and Hopkinsian disinterested benevolence, see respectively, Nathan O. Hatch, *The Sacred Cause of Liberty: Republican Thought and the Millennium in Revolutionary New England* (New Haven: Yale University Press, 1977); Ruth H. Bloch, *Visionary Republic: Millennial Themes in American Thought, 1756–1800* (New York: Cambridge University Press, 1985); Joseph A. Conforti, *Samuel Hopkins and the New Divinity Movement: Calvinism, the Congregational Ministry, and Reform in New England between the Great Awakenings* (Grand Rapids, Mich.: Christian University Press, Eerdmans, 1981). The following two historiographical essays also insightfully survey the literature: Philip F. Gura, "The Role of the 'Black Regiment': Religion and the American Revolution," *NEQ* 61 (1988): 439–454; Philip Goff, "Revivals and Revolution: Historiographic Turns since Alan Heimert's *Religion and the American Mind,*" *CH* 67 (1998): 695–721.

17. "The separation of church and state together with the new orthodoxy of inviolable individual rights meant that the sermon, in its occasional form as a coercive ritual of social order, could not survive the transition to independent nationhood. . . . In place of the occasional sermon other, more secular rituals emerged to organize, direct, and revitalize the collective ideals of the community and the nation. Fourth of July orations, inaugural ceremonies, and Memorial Day observances did for the American republic what fast and election sermons had done for colonial New England" (Harry S. Stout, *The New England Soul: Preaching and Religious Culture in Colonial New England* [New York: Oxford University Press, 1986], 312–331, quote on 316).

More recently, Stout has retreated somewhat from this epilogue. "What lessons can we take from the persistence of Puritan rhetoric in the early republic?" he asks. "For one, we are cautioned against completing intellectual revolutions in religious thought too quickly. . . . The triumph of an individualistic, egalitarian evangelicalism with its antihistoricism and commonsense realism was a more gradual transition than historians have generally allowed. In many ways the transition is still incomplete. Lying beneath the new evangelicalism of nineteenth-century America was an older rhetorical world, one that was corporate, coercive, providential, deductive, and elitist" ("Rhetoric and Reality in the Early Republic: The Case of the Federalist Clergy," in *Religion and American Politics: From the Colonial Period to the 1980s*, ed. Mark A. Noll [New York: Oxford University Press, 1990], 73). In this essay, Stout does not track the phenomenon of a lingering Puritan rhetoric in any detail.

18. Donald Weber, *Rhetoric and History in Revolutionary New England* (New York: Oxford University Press, 1988), 149. Likewise, although Barry Alan Shain advances a strong case that Revolutionary American political thought was "reformed Protestant and communal," he nevertheless suggests that this ideology was rapidly eclipsed after 1790 (*The Myth of American Individualism: The Protestant Origins of American Political Thought* [Princeton, N.J.: Princeton University Press, 1994], 4).

19. Emerson, writing in 1852, quoted in Lewis P. Simpson, ed., *The Federalist Literary Mind: Selections from the "Monthly Anthology and Boston Review," 1803–1811, Including Documents Relating to the Boston Athenaeum* (Baton Rouge: Louisiana State University Press,

1962), 6; Wood, "Significance of the Early Republic," 5. I thank Daniel W. Howe for alerting me to the Emerson quotation.

20. Hatch, *Democratization*, 8, 21; Jon Butler, *Awash in a Sea of Faith: Christianizing the American People* (Cambridge: Harvard University Press, 1990), 225–256, quote on 226.

21. Michael Zuckerman encapsulates the shift from republicanism to liberalism: "After the Revolution, Americans . . . came to aspire to a character they had previously scorned, as free individuals rather than as virtuous communards. After decades of devotion to the self-denying norms of republicanism, they moved with remarkable rapidity toward the ideology that the nineteenth century would know as liberalism" ("A Different Thermidor: The Revolution beyond the American Revolution," in *The Transformation of Early American History: Society, Authority, and Ideology*, ed. James A. Henretta, Michael Kammen, and Stanley N. Katz [New York: Knopf, 1991], 185). For a very similar interpretation, see Wood, "Significance of the Early Republic," 18. However, at the end of the essay (pp. 191–193), Zuckerman toned down this bold position and recognized the persistence of community: "The continuity of the values of virtuous community in the teeth of the triumph of liberalism was already the defining dilemma of American life in the years after the Revolution" (193).

22. Wood, *Radicalism of the American Revolution*, 333; Joyce Oldham Appleby, *Without Resolution: The Jeffersonian Tensions in American Nationalism: An Inaugural Lecture delivered before the University of Oxford on 25 April 1991* (Oxford: Clarendon, 1992), 16.

23. David W. Kling, *A Field of Divine Wonders: The New Divinity and Village Revivals in Northwestern Connecticut, 1792–1822* (University Park: Pennsylvania State University Press, 1993); Rohrer, *Keepers of the Covenant*, 118. Another work that shows the relevance of New Divinity Calvinism to contemporary social life is Mark Valeri, *Law and Providence in Joseph Bellamy's New England: The Origins of the New Divinity in Revolutionary America* (New York: Oxford University Press, 1994).

24. Kling, *A Field of Divine Wonders*, 54–57; Rohrer, *Keepers of the Covenant*, 62–69. Likewise, Field, *Crisis of the Standing Order*, 91–92, argues that the Unitarian clergy of Boston decided "to avoid soiling themselves with political activism" around 1800.

25. James M. Banner Jr., "Afterword: The Federalists—Still in Need of Reconsideration," in *Federalists Reconsidered*, ed. Doron Ben-Atar and Barbara B. Oberg (Charlottesville: University Press of Virginia, 1998), 248.

26. Doron Ben-Atar and Barbara B. Oberg, "Introduction: The Paradoxical Legacy of the Federalists," in *Federalists Reconsidered*, ed. Ben-Atar and Oberg, 3.

27. Paul G. E. Clemens hopes that "by creating more challenging interpretative linkages between the colonial period and the nineteenth century, Mid-Atlantic scholarship can become paradigmatic for early American studies" ("Introduction," *WMQ* 51 [1994]: 353). Both Abzug, *Cosmos Crumbling*, 38–56, and West, *Politics of Revelation and Reason*, 79–100, offer interpretations of the developments in the New England clergy's public Christianity for the period between the 1780s and 1820s. However, both base their conclusions on a few sermons by one minister, Lyman Beecher.

28. Edwin Scott Gaustad, *Historical Atlas of Religion in America*, rev. ed. (New York: Harper & Row, 1976), 16; Mark Y. Hanley, *Beyond a Christian Commonwealth: The Protestant Quarrel with the American Republic, 1830–1860* (Chapel Hill: University of North Carolina Press, 1994).

29. In *The Democratization of American Christianity*, in contrast, they are the passive victims of abuse who merely form a static backdrop to the unfolding drama of the rise of populist religion. Hatch (p. 34) describes the established clergy as "confounded" and "without a ready defense" in the face of the populist uprising.

30. John Winthrop, "A Modell of Christian Charity," in *The Puritans*, ed. Perry Miller and Thomas H. Johnson, 2 vols., rev. ed. (New York: Harper Torchbooks, 1963), 1:198–199.

31. For a recent interpretation of these themes for eighteenth-century Connecticut, see Christopher Grasso, *A Speaking Aristocracy: Transforming Public Discourse in Eighteenth-Century Connecticut* (Chapel Hill: University of North Carolina Press, 1999). For seventeenth- and eighteenth-century Massachusetts, there is a convenient summary of the secondary literature regarding the Congregational clergy's sociopolitical thought in Dale S. Kuehne, *Massachusetts Congregationalist Political Thought, 1760–1790: The Design of Heaven* (Columbia: University of Missouri Press, 1996).

32. H. Richard Niebuhr, *Christ and Culture* (New York: Harper & Brothers, 1951).

33. Mark A. Noll, "'And the Lion Shall Lie Down with the Lamb': The Social Sciences and Religious History," *Fides et Historia* 20 (1988): 10–11; Miller, "From the Covenant to the Revival," 333. Similarly, Robert H. Abzug writes that "we can only understand reformers if we try to comprehend the sacred significance they bestowed upon these worldly arenas [of society, politics, and economics]" (*Cosmos Crumbling*, viii).

34. Clifford Geertz, "Ideology as a Cultural System," in *The Interpretation of Cultures* (New York: Basic Books, 1973), 201.

35. Clifford Geertz, "Religion as a Cultural System," in *Interpretation of Cultures*, 91–93.

36. Stout, *New England Soul*, 4–7, quotes on 4 and 6.

37. This division of labor, emphasizing the importance of both content and context, I derive from Robert Wuthnow, *Rediscovering the Sacred: Perspectives on Religion in Contemporary Society* (Grand Rapids, Mich.: Eerdmans, 1992), especially 44–57 and 122–126. See also Mark A. Noll, "Evaluating North Atlantic Religious History, 1640–1859. A Review Article," *Comparative Studies in Society and History* 33 (1991): 415–425.

38. Jerald C. Brauer, "Regionalism and Religion in America," *CH* 54 (1985): 366–378. Cf. Nathan Hatch, who focuses *Democratization* (p. 12) on themes that are national in scope.

39. Mark A. Noll, *Princeton and the Republic, 1768–1822: The Search for a Christian Enlightenment in the Era of Samuel Stanhope Smith* (Princeton, N.J.: Princeton University Press, 1989), 5. As Noll's book shows, mid-Atlantic Presbyterians formed the group perhaps closest in ideological affinity to the southern New England standing order. For instance, the New Jersey Presbyterian layman Elias Boudinot shared many of the New England clergy's religious, social, and political attitudes. See George Adams Boyd, *Elias Boudinot: Patriot and Statesman, 1740–1821* (Princeton, N.J.: Princeton University Press, 1952), 252–262.

40. James M. Banner Jr., *To the Hartford Convention: The Federalists and the Origins of Party Politics in Massachusetts, 1789–1815* (New York: Knopf, 1970), 6–12.

41. Patricia U. Bonomi, *Under the Cope of Heaven: Religion, Society, and Politics in Colonial America* (New York: Oxford University Press, 1986), 19, 65–72, quote on 72.

42. Heyrman, *Southern Cross*, 6–27; John H. Wigger, *Taking Heaven by Storm: Methodism and the Rise of Popular Christianity in America* (New York: Oxford University Press, 1998), 9–11.

43. On the importance of this distinction, see Banner, *To the Hartford Convention*, 170–173; Stephen A. Marini, *Radical Sects of Revolutionary New England* (Cambridge: Harvard University Press, 1982), 27–39.

44. Donald M. Scott, *From Office to Profession: The New England Ministry, 1750–1850* (Philadelphia: University of Pennsylvania Press, 1978), 1.

45. William G. McLoughlin, *New England Dissent, 1630–1833: The Baptists and the Separation of Church and State*, 2 vols. (Cambridge: Harvard University Press, 1971), 1:xvii. For the ways in which ministers coordinated their energies to promote revival, see Kling, *A Field of Divine Wonders*, 62–72. For the local struggles involved with the Unitarian controversy, see Conrad Wright, "Institutional Reconstruction in the Unitarian Controversy," in *American Unitarianism, 1805–1865*, ed. Conrad Edick Wright, Massachusetts Historical Society Studies in American History and Culture, no. 1 (Boston: Massachusetts Historical Society and Northeastern University Press, 1989), 3–29.

46. John L. Brooke, *The Heart of the Commonwealth: Society and Political Culture in Worcester County, Massachusetts, 1713–1861* (New York: Cambridge University Press, 1989; Amherst: University of Massachusetts Press, 1992), xv, and see also 117–121.

47. Information on these and other ministers is taken from E[lam] Smalley, *The Worcester Pulpit; With Notices Historical and Biographical* (Boston, 1851).

48. In his dissertation on antislavery in Worcester County, James Eugene Mooney contended that "the variety and number of sources in print and manuscript to support such a case study of this county are the best of any county in the nation, Essex in Massachusetts not excepted" ("Antislavery in Worcester County, Massachusetts: A Case Study" [Ph.D. diss., Clark University, 1971], 1).

49. This interpretation contrasts with both Bernard Bailyn, "Religion and Revolution: Three Biographical Studies," *Perspectives in American History* 4 (1970): 85–169, and Hatch, *Sacred Cause*.

50. For the argument that the New England clergy did attach the national covenant to the United States, see Stout, *New England Soul*, 7–9, 293–311; Sacvan Bercovitch, *The American Jeremiad* (Madison: University of Wisconsin Press, 1978), 119–137.

51. To take one example, in *An Errand of Mercy*, Charles I. Foster begins the story of the evangelical benevolent societies in the United States in 1816, the year of the founding of the American Bible Society. By doing so, he uproots the societies from their early national background and casts them as politically motivated British imports. However, a longer perspective that reaches back to the Revolution enables one to view these societies as a more organic development.

52. Hatch, *Democratization*, 14.

Chapter One

1. Peter Thacher, *Observations upon the Present State of the Clergy of New-England, with strictures Upon the Power of Dismissing Them, usurped by Some Churches* (Boston, 1783), 3–6.

2. Douglass Adair and John A. Schutz, eds., *Peter Oliver's Origin & Progress of the American Rebellion: A Tory View* (San Marino, Calif.: Huntington Library, 1961), 41; Patricia U. Bonomi, *Under the Cope of Heaven: Religion, Society, and Politics in Colonial America* (New York: Oxford University Press, 1986), 209–216.

3. Bonomi, *Under the Cope of Heaven*, 96.

4. Isaac Morrill, *Faith in Divine Providence the Great Support of God's People. A Sermon, Preached at Lexington, April 19, 1780. In Memory of the Commencement of the unnatural War between Great-Britain and America; which took place in said Town April 19, 1775* (Boston, 1780), 9, 6.

5. Leonard Woolsey Bacon, *A History of American Christianity* (New York, 1897), 230, quoted in Douglas H. Sweet, "Church Vitality and the American Revolution: Historiographical Consensus and Thoughts Towards a New Perspective," *CH* 45 (1976): 342. Other luminaries listed by Douglas Sweet, pp. 343–344, include William Warren Sweet, Sydney E. Ahlstrom, and Martin E. Marty. The same scenario of infidelity on the march can be found in Richard J. Purcell, *Connecticut in Transition: 1775–1818* (Washington, D.C.: American Historical Association, 1918; Middletown, Conn.: Wesleyan University Press, 1963), 7–23.

6. Sweet, "Church Vitality," 345–346.

7. P. H. Welshimer, *Concerning the Disciples: A Brief Resume of the Movement to Restore the New Testament Church* (Cincinnati: Standard Publishing, 1935), 31–33, set his account of the rise of the Disciples of Christ against a backdrop of a "dark pall of infidelity" over Amer-

ica around 1800. The significance of that denomination appears all the more dramatic when compared with the fatalistic and befuddling Calvinism that had supposedly prevailed.

"The American Revolution is the most crucial event in American history . . . the fault line that separates an older world, premised on standards of deference, patronage, and ordered succession, from a newer one that continues to shape our values" (Nathan O. Hatch, *The Democratization of American Christianity* [New Haven: Yale University Press, 1989], 5–6). "Before the Revolution, New England's religious establishments helped spin a web of daily ritual and belief that connected individual, society, and Heaven into a comprehensible cosmos. . . . The American Revolution changed all that" (Robert H. Abzug, *Cosmos Crumbling: American Reform and the Religious Imagination* [New York: Oxford University Press, 1994], 5).

8. Cf. Hatch, *Democratization*, 59, who writes, "What is striking about the period after the Revolution in America is not disestablishment per se but the impotence of Congregational, Presbyterian, and Episcopalian churches in the face of dissent. At the turn of the century, their own houses lay in such disarray that movements such as the Methodists, Baptists, and Christians were given free rein to experiment."

9. As John D. Cushing points out, this "establishment" was not rigidly structured in Massachusetts but had a great degree of congregational autonomy and only the loose doctrinal commonality of a Puritan heritage ("Notes on Disestablishment in Massachusetts, 1780–1833," *WMQ* 26 [1969]: 169). Charles H. Lippy argues that the Massachusetts Constitution did not create an establishment properly defined because "rather than organizing an official or semi-official state church, Article 3 of the 1780 Massachusetts Constitution was designed to create an ethos within which civil religion could flourish" ("The 1780 Massachusetts Constitution: Religious Establishment or Civil Religion?" *Journal of Church and State* 20 [1978]: 533–549, quote on 549). Lippy's argument overreaches because clearly the constitution empowered more than a mere "ethos." The dissenters he cites objected strongly to the taxation allowed by the constitution. As William G. McLoughlin wrote, "whether the New England system was an establishment or not, the Baptists opposed it" (*New England Dissent, 1630–1833: The Baptists and the Separation of Church and State*, 2 vols. [Cambridge: Harvard University Press, 1971], 1:617).

10. The Massachusetts Constitution of 1780 is reprinted in Charles Kettleborough, comp. and ed., *The State Constitutions and the Federal Constitution and Organic Laws of the Territories and Other Colonial Dependencies of the United States of America* (Indianapolis: B. F. Bowen, 1918); articles 2 and 3 are found on pp. 654–655. On the adoption of the 1780 constitution, see McLoughlin, *New England Dissent*, 1:591–635; he reprinted articles 2 and 3 in their entirety on pp. 1:603–604. Urban churches were an exception to this system and did not enjoy tax support. See McLoughlin, *New England Dissent*, 2:1072; Peter S. Field, *The Crisis of the Standing Order: Clerical Intellectuals and Cultural Authority in Massachusetts, 1780–1833* (Amherst: University of Massachusetts Press, 1998), 55–65.

11. Cushing, "Notes on Disestablishment," 172.

12. Ibid., 173–189; McLoughlin, *New England Dissent*, 1:636–684, quote on 1:646.

13. Gordon S. Wood, *The Creation of the American Republic, 1776–1787* (Chapel Hill: University of North Carolina Press, 1969; New York: Norton, 1972), 276–277. The other state was Rhode Island.

14. McLoughlin, *New England Dissent*, 2:921–937, 962–984.

15. Bonomi, *Under the Cope of Heaven*, 19–21; Barry Alan Shain, *The Myth of American Individualism: The Protestant Origins of American Political Thought* (Princeton, N.J.: Princeton University Press, 1994), 7, n. 11.

16. McLoughlin, *New England Dissent*, 1:8, 2:920, 1:503, quote on 1:8.

17. Joseph S. Clark, *A Historical Sketch of the Congregational Churches in Massachusetts, from 1620 to 1858. With an Appendix* (Boston, 1858), 218, 226. Referring to the Congregation-

alists as a "denomination" is, I am aware, anachronistic for this time period, due to their lack of central authority. "Congregationalists held aloof from this rush of American churchmen [in the post-Revolutionary period] to create denominations. They did not hold a national convention until 1852, and the formation of a Congregational National Council with a permanent organization and staff did not take place until 1871" (Samuel C. Pearson Jr., "From Church to Denomination: American Congregationalism in the Nineteenth Century," *CH* 38 [1969]: 67). However, I use the term here as convenient shorthand for that family of churches in New England that shared a common history.

18. McLoughlin, *New England Dissent*, 2:919. The totals for each denomination's churches in 1792 were: 168 Congregational, 30 Episcopal, 10 Separate, and 1 Methodist. The Baptists had 55 in 1795. Combining the Baptist total with the others from 1792 shows that the Congregational churches represented 168 out of 264, or 63.6%. David W. Kling, *A Field of Divine Wonders: The New Divinity and Village Revivals in Northwestern Connecticut, 1792–1822* (University Park: Pennsylvania State University Press, 1993), 183, n. 46, gives somewhat different figures for the numbers of churches each denomination had in 1790, but he likewise reports that the Congregationalists made up about two-thirds of the total.

19. Conrad Wright, *The Beginnings of Unitarianism in America* (Boston: Starr King Press, 1955), quote on 252. For the New Divinity, see William Breitenbach, "The Consistent Calvinism of the New Divinity Movement," *WMQ* 41 (1984): 241–264; Joseph A. Conforti, *Samuel Hopkins and the New Divinity Movement: Calvinism, the Congregational Ministry, and Reform in New England between the Great Awakenings* (Grand Rapids, Mich.: Christian University Press, Eerdmans, 1981); Mark Valeri, "The New Divinity and the American Revolution," *WMQ* 46 (1989): 741–769; idem, *Law and Providence in Joseph Bellamy's New England: The Origins of the New Divinity in Revolutionary America* (New York: Oxford University Press, 1994).

20. Nathan O. Hatch, *The Sacred Cause of Liberty: Republican Thought and the Millennium in Revolutionary New England* (New Haven: Yale University Press, 1977), 6–9, quote on 6–7; Harry S. Stout, *The New England Soul: Preaching and Religious Culture in Colonial New England* (New York: Oxford University Press, 1986), 232–236.

21. Jon Butler, *Awash in a Sea of Faith: Christianizing the American People* (Cambridge: Harvard University Press, 1990), 104–105, 174–175. On the Church of England's missionary effort in colonial Connecticut, including the (in)famous 1722 conversion to Anglicanism of Timothy Cutler, rector of Yale, and three of the college's tutors, see Nelson Rollin Burr, *The Story of the Diocese of Connecticut: A New Branch of the Vine* (Hartford, Conn.: Church Missions Publishing Co., 1962), 16–34, 40–62.

22. Clara O. Loveland, *The Critical Years: The Reconstitution of the Anglican Church in the United States of America: 1780–1789* (Greenwich, Conn.: Seabury, 1956), 3–6. "Reporting on the situation in New England [in the 1780s], Samuel Parker wrote that he was alone in Boston, with only three other clergymen left in Massachusetts. Rhode Island had three churches, but no clergy; New Hampshire, two churches with one minister. Connecticut was the strongest, with fourteen of twenty missionaries still there, as well as seven other clergymen" (ibid., 19). On the Anglican clergy's difficulties during the Revolution in Connecticut, see also Burr, *Diocese of Connecticut*, 121–126.

23. Loveland, *Critical Years*, 3–288; M. L. Bradbury, "Structures of Nationalism," in *Religion in a Revolutionary Age*, ed. Ronald Hoffman and Peter J. Albert (Charlottesville: University Press of Virginia, 1994), 244–246; Charles C. Tiffany, *A History of the Protestant Episcopal Church in the United States of America*, The American Church History Series, vol. 7, ed. Philip Schaff et al. (New York, 1895), 385. Likewise, James Thayer Addison termed these the years of "the Church Convalescent," during which "the Church showed few symptoms of vitality and made little progress" (*The Episcopal Church in the United States, 1789–1931* [New York: Charles Scribner's Sons, 1951], 76–77).

24. Sydney V. James, *A People among Peoples: Quaker Benevolence in Eighteenth-Century America* (Cambridge: Harvard University Press, 1963), 280–281, quote on 281; George A. Selleck, *Quakers in Boston, 1656–1964: Three Centuries of Friends in Boston and Cambridge* (Cambridge, Mass.: Friends Meeting at Cambridge, 1976), 71–83, quote on 73. Regarding the Quakers in Massachusetts at the end of the eighteenth century, William G. McLoughlin wrote that "the sect was declining in numbers and influence and seemed to be devoting its energies primarily to benevolence and philanthropy rather than to evangelism" (*New England Dissent*, 1:651). McLoughlin also noted that in 1780 "there were no other significant sects [aside from the Baptists] at this time in Massachusetts. Small numbers of Rogerenes, Sandemanians, Universalists, and Shakers existed but none of these took stands on the constitution. . . . The Quakers, Episcopalians, and Presbyterians voiced no known opposition to Article Three and even the Separates had become so few and inconsequential in Massachusetts by this time that they are not known to have taken any stand" (ibid., 1:607, n. 33).

25. George Claude Baker Jr., *An Introduction to the History of Early New England Methodism, 1789–1839* (Durham, N.C.: Duke University Press, 1941), 7–10; C. C. Goss, *Statistical History of the First Century of American Methodism: with a Summary of the Origin and Present Operations of Other Denominations* (New York, 1866), 41–61; Leroy M. Lee, *The Life and Times of the Rev. Jesse Lee* (Richmond, Va., 1848), 215–268, 288–315.

26. Wade Crawford Barclay, *Early American Methodism, 1769–1844*, vol. 1, *Missionary Motivation and Expansion*, History of Methodist Missions (New York: Board of Missions and Church Extension of the Methodist Church, 1949), 131–140. Specifically, Barclay writes (p. 137) that in 1796, "Methodists in New England numbered 2,999: Connecticut, 1,201; Massachusetts, 913; Rhode Island, 177; Province of Maine, 616; New Hampshire, 92."

27. Purcell, *Connecticut in Transition*, 47.

28. This is the overarching theme of McLoughlin, *New England Dissent*.

29. The names of the trustees for 1800 are printed in *Connecticut Evangelical Magazine* 1 (July 1800): 14. A similarly integrated group of prominent ministers and laymen formed the officers of the Connecticut Society for the Promotion of Freedom. The timing of this antislavery group's two annual meetings provides another instance of the interlocking character of clerical and political power in Connecticut: "The Society shall meet at New-Haven on the day succeeding the Commencement in Yale-College, and at Hartford on the day of the anniversary Election." This was when ministers and magistrates convened from throughout the state (*The Constitution of the Connecticut Society for the Promotion of Freedom, and the Relief of Persons unlawfully holden in Bondage, as revised and enlarged on the 13th Day of September 1792* [New Haven, Conn., 1792]).

30. For most of the individuals discussed next, the information is taken from Franklin Bowditch Dexter, *Biographical Sketches of the Graduates of Yale College: With Annals of the College History*, 6 vols. (New York, 1885–1912). Specifically, it is found at the following volume and page numbers: John Treadwell, 3:247–251; Jonathan Brace, 4:101–103; John Davenport, 3:376–378; Nathan Williams, 2:395–397; Benjamin Trumbull, 2:621–623; Levi Hart, 2:656–658; Cyprian Strong, 3:49–52; Nathan Strong, 3:357–360; Charles Backus, 3:310–312. Information on Heman Swift comes from Francis S. Drake, *Dictionary of American Biography* (Boston, 1874), 887–888. The Roger Newberry listed as a member of the board of trustees is probably the son of Roger Newberry, Yale Class of 1726, described in Dexter, *Biographical Sketches*, 1:333. Dexter wrote that "one of the sons received the honorary degree of Master of Arts from the College in 1793, being then a member of the Corporation by virtue of his office as one of the six Senior Assistants in the Council." Since from the list in *Connecticut Evangelical Magazine* we know that the Roger Newberry on the board of trustees also sat on the council, it seems likely that he was the son described by Dexter. I have been unable to locate any further information regarding Dr. Joshua Lathrop; the list of board members simply de-

scribes him as a merchant. On the composition of the board, see also James R. Rohrer, *Keepers of the Covenant: Frontier Missions and the Decline of Congregationalism, 1774–1818* (New York: Oxford University Press, 1995), 61–63, 165.

31. Donald M. Scott, *From Office to Profession: The New England Ministry, 1750–1850* (Philadelphia: University of Pennsylvania Press, 1978), 3–9.

32. James C. Welling, *Connecticut Federalism, or Aristocratic Politics in a Social Democracy, An Address delivered before the New York Historical Society on its Eighty-Sixth Anniversary, Tuesday, November 18, 1890* (New York, 1890), 40–41. Welling also noted how the ruling elite not only held several positions at once but also hung onto them. "The annals of Connecticut office-holding read like an abstract from the chronicles before the Flood," in that men served lengthy terms that ended only in death at a ripe old age. As David Hackett Fischer writes regarding Jonathan Brace, "it will be noted, [he] simultaneously held high executive, legislative, and judicial offices in his state, where pluralism was prevalent during the Federalist era. . . . The transcendent holism of the old school, the consciousness of social and political interdependency which was articulated with increasing clarity by older Federalists as the Jeffersonian movement gathered strength and power, reinforced a determination that power should not be divided but rather united in the hands of 'natural rulers,' who would remain ultimately responsible to the people but more directly responsive to a certain self-evident sense of the 'public good'" (*The Revolution of American Conservatism: The Federalist Party in the Era of Jeffersonian Democracy* [New York: Harper & Row, 1965], 284–285). Also indicative of this concentration of power is John Adams's exaggeration that "the state of Connecticut has always been governed by an aristocracy, more decisively than the empire of Great Britain is. Half a dozen, or, at most a dozen families, have controlled that country when a colony, as well as since it has been a state" (Adams quoted in S. Hugh Brockunier, "Foreword," in Purcell, *Connecticut in Transition,* x).

33. On the deferential character of eighteenth-century politics in Massachusetts, stretching from the colonial era into the 1790s, see Ronald P. Formisano, *The Transformation of Political Culture: Massachusetts Parties, 1790s–1840s* (New York: Oxford University Press, 1983), 25–33.

34. Lee, *Life and Times,* 259; Garrettson's journal quoted in Alfred S. Roe, "The Beginnings of Methodism in Worcester," *Collections of the Worcester Society of Antiquity* 9 (1891), 45.

35. Formisano, *Transformation of Political Culture,* 86–87, quotes on 86. In Connecticut, moreover, there was a tradition of an "election night dinner" following the day's governmental affairs and election sermon. William G. McLoughlin summarized the dinner and its significance: "All of the Standing ministers were invited to this dinner, as were the newly elected legislators; there they dined at public expense, a fitting symbol of the unity of church and state" (*New England Dissent,* 2:1018).

36. David Tappan, *A Sermon Preached before His Excellency John Hancock, Esq. Governour; His Honor Samuel Adams, Esq. Lieutenant-Governour; the Honourable the Council, Senate, and House of Representatives, of the Commonwealth of Massachusetts, May 30, 1792. Being the Day of General Election* (Boston, 1792), 7; David D. Hall, *Worlds of Wonder, Days of Judgment: Popular Religious Belief in Early New England* (New York: Knopf, 1989), 166–172, quote on 167. See also Scott, *From Office to Profession,* 13.

37. J. William T. Youngs Jr., *God's Messengers: Religious Leadership in Colonial New England, 1700–1750* (Baltimore: Johns Hopkins University Press, 1976), 69–73; Kling, *A Field of Divine Wonders,* 63–64; Ephraim Abbot, Autobiography, 1779–1827, p. 15, Ephraim Abbot Papers, 1801–1904, box 2, folder 6, AAS.

38. Youngs, *God's Messengers,* 98–99. For a summary of the secondary literature's unflattering "caricature" of the Congregational clergy, see Rohrer, *Keepers of the Covenant,* 5–8.

39. *An Historical Sketch of the Convention of the Congregational Ministers in Massachu-*

setts; with an Account of its Funds; its connexion with the Massachusetts Congregational Charitable Society; and its Rules and Regulations. MDCCCXXI (Cambridge, Mass., 1821), 15–16; Harold Field Worthley, "An Historical Essay: The Massachusetts Convention of Congregational Ministers," *Proceedings of the Unitarian Historical Society* 12 (1958): 49–55; Ephraim Ward, Diary 1787, AAS; Youngs, *God's Messengers*, 78. On Ward's background, see Clifford K. Shipton, *Biographical Sketches of those who Attended Harvard College in the Classes 1761–1763 with Bibliographical and other Notes*, Sibley's Harvard Graduates, vol. 15 (Boston: Massachusetts Historical Society, 1970), 502–504. The "Mr. Prince" of Salem mentioned in Ward's diary on October 14, 1787, is identified as John Prince in William B. Sprague, *Annals of the American Pulpit; or, Commemorative Notices of Distinguished American Clergymen of Various Denominations, from the early settlement of the country to the close of the year eighteen hundred and fifty-five*, 9 vols. (New York, 1857–1869), 8:128–132. With the exception of the postal system, Richard R. John points out, the early American republic had few large-scale institutions (*Spreading the News: The American Postal System from Franklin to Morse* [Cambridge: Harvard University Press, 1995], 3–6).

40. Brookfield Association, 22 June 1757, Records, 1757–1837, CL.

41. Joseph Goffe, Autobiography, Joseph Goffe Papers, 1789–1846, box 3, folder 3, AAS; Youngs, *God's Messengers*, 30–37, 74, quote on 30; Joseph Goffe, Diary, 15 Oct. 1800, Joseph Goffe Papers, 1721–1846, AAS; Brookfield Association, Records, 7 Oct. 1773.

42. Brookfield Association, Records, 3 Oct. 1781, 2 May 1792. For further examples of associations dispensing "advice," see Youngs, *God's Messengers*, 75.

43. Goffe, Autobiography; idem, Diary, 7 and 20 Dec. 1796; Aaron Bancroft, *A Sermon Delivered in Worcester, January 31, 1836, by Aaron Bancroft, D.D. at the Termination of Fifty Years of His Ministry* (Worcester, Mass., 1836), 18–19, 24–25, 41, n. K; E[lam] Smalley, *The Worcester Pulpit; With Notices Historical and Biographical* (Boston, 1851), 234.

44. Ward, Diary, July 1787; Brookfield Association, Records, 4 Sept. 1782, 13 Aug. 1794, 2 Jan. 1799. The Brookfield Association was not alone in discussing *Salvation for All Men*. According to Edward M. Griffin, the biographer of Charles Chauncy, the pamphlet, "consisting of a preface by Chauncy condemning Murrayism and a collection by [assistant pastor John] Clarke of scriptural texts and selections from theologians supporting universal salvation[,] . . . drew a crossfire of pamphlets, sermons, and letters-to-the-editor" (*Old Brick: Charles Chauncy of Boston, 1705–1787*, Minnesota Monographs in the Humanities, vol. 11 [Minneapolis: University of Minnesota Press, 1980], 173–174).

45. Brookfield Association, Records, 28 Feb. 1776, 27 Feb. 1782, 1 May 1799.

46. Scott, *From Office to Profession*, 7.

47. As Josiah Whitney of Brooklyn, Connecticut, explained matters, "That there is a living, intelligent author of universal nature, a Being called GOD, is a truth, which shines gloriously in the splendor of the sun—vegitates [*sic*] in every plant—lives in every animal, and diffuses itself throughout all nature. That [Dan. 4:35] *this glorious Being does according to his will, in the army of heaven, and among the inhabitants of the earth*; and that his dominion is absolute, yet wise and reasonable, are also truths agreeable both to natural and revealed religion" (*The essential requisites to form the good Ruler's Character, illustrated and urged. A Sermon, Preached in the Audience of His Excellency Samuel Huntington, Esq. L.L.D. Governor, and Commander in Chief; His Honor Oliver Wolcott, Esq. Lieutenant-Governor, and the Honourable the Counsellors and House of Representatives of the State of Connecticut, At Hartford, on the Day of the Anniversary Election, May 8th 1788* [Hartford, Conn., 1788], 5). North Haven's Benjamin Trumbull made the same point when he rejoiced, "Omnipotent and glorious is the arm upon which rests universal nature! Large and bountiful is the hand which openeth itself and supplieth the wants of every living thing" (*God is to be praised for the Glory of his Majesty, and for his mighty Works. A Sermon Delivered at North-Haven, December 11,*

1783. The day appointed by the United-States for a General Thanksgiving on Account of the Peace Concluded with Great-Britain [New-Haven, Conn., 1784], 10). "Could we comprehend the divine plan—could we look through the scheme of Heaven," commented Hartford's Nathan Strong, "we should doubtless see that all natural events, all political events, and all the wisdom of this world, are permitted and designed by the Most High, for the benefit of his moral government, to display his own glory, and bring eventual perfection and blessedness to the universe" (*The Agency and Providence of God acknowledged, in the Preservation of the American States. A Sermon Preached at the Annual Thanksgiving, December 7th, 1780* [Hartford, Conn., 1780], 5). See also Ammi R. Robbins, *The Empires and Dominions of this World, made subservient to the Kingdom of CHRIST; who ruleth over all. A Sermon, delivered in presence of His Excellency Samuel Huntington, Esq. L.L.D. Governor, And the Honorable the General Assembly of the State of Connecticut, Convened at Hartford, on the Day of the Anniversary Election. May 14th, 1789* (Hartford, Conn., 1789), 10.

48. Eliphalet Porter, *A Sermon, Delivered to the First Religious Society in Roxbury, December 11, 1783; Being the First Day of Public Thanksgiving, In America, after the Restoration of Peace, and the Ultimate Acknowledgment of her Independence* (Boston, 1784), 7. "Here God appears inhabiting eternity, and having in his own infinite mind a most glorious and perfect plan, relating to all the future inhabitants of the world; the situation, numbers, rise and fall, of the various states and empires that were to overspread the earth. God determined all these things, in his boundless wisdom and goodness, before he began to operate in his providence; that point in the vast round of eternity cannot be conceived of, when he had not so decreed" (Joseph Huntington, *God ruling the Nations for the most glorious end. A Sermon, In presence of his Excellency, and both Houses of Assembly. Hartford, May 13th, 1784* [Hartford, Conn., 1784], 6–7).

49. According to Conrad Wright, "This general concept of [a providential] God was shared by Calvinists and Arminians" (*Beginnings of Unitarianism*, 163–170, quote on 170). Note also the similarities between Warren Association of Baptists, *Minutes of the Warren Association, at their Meeting, in Middleboro', Sept. 7 and 8, 1784* (n.p., 1784), 5; and John Tyler (an Episcopalian), *The Blessing of Peace: A Sermon Preached at Norwich, on the Continental Thanksgiving, February 19, 1795* (Norwich, Conn., 1795), 8–9.

50. Butler, *Awash in a Sea of Faith*, 218–219. As Thomas Brockway of Lebanon, Connecticut, pointed out, "When events are brought about, in the ordinary course of nature, the world is apt to be regardless of a superintending providence, and nature, without the God of nature, is the idol they worship. But when God, in his providence, steps out of this common track, his hand is more easily seen and readily acknowledged, even by the world. God often, in this way, breaks the chain of Deistical reasoning; confounds the bold Atheist, and gets to himself glory, even from such enemies as these" (*America saved, or Divine Glory displayed, in the late War with Great-Britain. A Thanksgiving Sermon, Preached in Lebanon, Second Society, And now offered to the Public, at the Desire of a Number of the Hearers* [Hartford, Conn., 1784], 12).

51. Nathan Williams, *Carefully to observe the signatures of Divine Providence, a mark of wisdom. Illustrated in a Sermon, Delivered in Stafford on the Anniversary of American Independence, July 4th, A.D. 1793* (Hartford, Conn., 1793), 14. "Mankind are exceedingly apt in a time of prosperity, and under any signal success, to sacrifice to their own skill, and burn incense to their own valour," agreed Eliphalet Porter. "Like the stout hearted king of Assyria, they are prone to arrogate to themselves that honour which is due to God" (*A Sermon, Delivered . . . December 11, 1783*, 6). Joseph Willard, president of Harvard, added another good illustration of this point: "It becomes us to acknowledge a divine providence, when we are partakers of peculiar favors; for however the blessings we enjoy may appear to have been in any measure procured by ourselves, or by any of our fellow men, we or they are but second causes. God is

the first cause, and without him nothing can be brought to pass" (*A Thanksgiving Sermon Delivered at Boston December 11, 1783, to the Religious Society in Brattle Street, under the Pastoral Care of the Rev. Samuel Cooper, D.D.* [Boston, 1784], 19).

52. Citing Ezek. 3:17, Jedidiah Morse of Charlestown, Massachusetts, said that "it would be criminal in me to be silent" (*A Sermon, Exhibiting the Present Dangers, and Consequent Duties of the Citizens of the United States of America. Delivered at Charlestown, April 25, 1799. The Day of the National Fast* [Charlestown, Mass., 1799], 9). Joseph Lathrop, *Christ's Warning to the Churches, to beware of False Prophets, who come as Wolves in Sheep's Clothing: And the Marks by which they are known: illustrated in Two Discourses* (Springfield, Mass., 1789), 3; Samuel Austin, *The Manner in Which the Gospel Should be Heard, and the Importance of Hearing it Rightly, Illustrated and Urged, in a Discourse, Preached by Samuel Austin, M.A. in Worcester, on the Lord's Day immediately succeeding his Installation, September 29th, MDC-CXC* (Worcester, Mass., 1791), 30; Willard, *A Thanksgiving Sermon*, 9–11; Whitney, *Essential requisites*, 7; David Osgood, *The Wonderful Works of GOD are to be remembered. A Sermon, delivered on the Day of the Annual Thanksgiving, November 20, 1794* (Boston, 1794), 7; Ruth H. Bloch, *Visionary Republic: Millennial Themes in American Thought, 1756–1800* (New York: Cambridge University Press, 1985), xi.

53. Huntington, *God ruling the Nations*, 6. See also Williams, *Carefully to observe*, 9. Non-Congregationalists, too, affirmed the providential direction of nations; see Tyler, *Blessing of Peace*, 12–13; Thomas Baldwin, *A Sermon, delivered February 19, 1795: being the day of Public Thanksgiving throughout the United States* (Boston, 1795), 6–8.

54. Timothy Stone of Lebanon, Connecticut, elaborated: "Communities, have their existence in, and from, this glorious personage [Jesus Christ]. The kingdom is his, and he ruleth among the nations. Through his bounty, and special providence, it is, that a people enjoy the inestimable liberties and numerous advantages of a well regulated civil society: through his influence, they are inspired with understanding to adopt, with strength and public spirit to maintain, a righteous constitution: He gives able impartial rulers, to guide in paths of virtue and peace; or sets up over them the basest of men. By his invisible hand, states are preserved from internal convulsions, and shielded by his Almighty arm from external violence: or, through his providential displeasure, they are given as a prey to their own vices; or to the lusts and passions of other states, to be destroyed" (*A Sermon, Preached before his Excellency Samuel Huntington, Esq. L.L.D. Governor, and the Honorable the General Assembly of the State of Connecticut, Convened at Hartford, on the Day of the Anniversary Election. May 10th, 1792* [Hartford, Conn., 1792], 21–22). The same point is made in Andrew Lee, *The origin and ends of civil Government; with reflections on the distinguished happiness of the United States. A Sermon, Preached Before His Excellency Samuel Huntington, Esq. L.L.D. Governor, and the Honorable General Assembly of the State of Connecticut, at Hartford, on the Day of the Anniversary Election, May 14, 1795* (Hartford, Conn., 1795), 7–12.

Henry Cumings of Billerica, Massachusetts, framed the providential control of events in similar terms: "As rational and dependant [*sic*] creatures, it behoves us to cultivate the most exalted ideas of God's universal government and dominion, and to endeavour to possess our minds with an habitual realizing persuasion, that his providence presides over all the affairs of the world, and guides all the movements of nature; that he pulls down one nation and sets up another, as he pleases, and superintends all the revolutions that take place in the kingdoms of men; that he determines the (to us uncertain) issues of war, and over-rules the passions of men, and the free motions of their wills, in such a manner, as to make them subservient to his purposes of judgment or mercy; that he forms the warrior and the statesman, the hero, patriot and politician, bestowing accomplishments, abilities, wisdom, skill, prowess and resolution, on whom he pleases, for answering the designs of his providence; and lastly, that although his interpositions may seldom be miraculous, in a strict sense, yet his agency is really and truly concerned in deciding the event of all human undertakings" (A *Sermon Preached in Billerica, December 11, 1783, The Day recommended by Congress to All The States, To be observed as a Day of Public Thanksgiving, and Appointed to be observed accordingly, throughout The Commonwealth of Massachusetts, By the Authority of the same* [Boston, 1784], 6–7).

55. Commonwealth of Massachusetts, *By His Excellency John Hancock . . . A Proclamation, For a Day of Thanksgiving* (Boston, 1784). For further discussion of the importance of marking the providential direction of public events through these annual rituals, see also Osgood, *Wonderful Works of GOD*, 10–11; Porter, A *Sermon, Delivered . . . December 11, 1783*, 3–4; Samuel Spring, A *Discourse, Delivered at the North Church in Newburyport, November 7th, 1793. Being the day appointed for a General Thanksgiving, by the authority of Massachusetts* (Newburyport, Mass., 1794), 5.

56. Rozel Cook, A *Sermon, Delivered at New-London, North-Parish, Upon the Anniversary Thanksgiving, December 11, 1783* (New London, Conn., 1784), 11. See also Strong, *Agency and Providence of God*, 6. Warren Association, *Minutes . . . 1784*, 6. Indeed, the association's 1784 circular letter linked the Revolution to the millennium. The Revolution, by unlocking freedom of thought and communication, would contribute the the the destruction of "error" and hence "Antichrist" (ibid., 6–7).

57. "And, above all, it becomes us to take notice, and adore the kind and wonderful interpositions of divine providence towards us as a people, the year past," Rozel Cook argued, "in that it hath pleased God, in his free and unmerited goodness, to rain down a rain of righteousness upon some parts of our land: that he hath been pouring out his spirit in plentiful effusions; which hath caused great seriousness, and an attention to divine things: that there hath been, and still are, many enquiring what they shall do to be saved" (A *Sermon, Delivered at New-London*, 21). John Marsh, minister at Wethersfield, Connecticut, likewise prayed in the language of revival that God "would be graciously pleased to pour down his spirit upon the inhabitants of these states, and unite them in giving glory to his name in such a manner as will secure his preference, protection and blessing" (A *Discourse Delivered at Wethersfield, December 11th, 1783. Being a Day of Public Thanksgiving, Throughout the United States of America* [Hartford, Conn., 1784], 22). The same prayer appears in David Osgood, *Reflections on the goodness of God in supporting the People of the United States through the late war, and giving them so advantageous and honourable a peace. A Sermon Preached on the Day of annual and national Thanksgiving December 11, 1783* (Boston, 1784), 34–35. See also Samuel Wales, *The Dangers of our national Prosperity; and the Way to avoid them. A Sermon, Preached before the General Assembly of the State of Connecticut, at Hartford, May 12th, 1785* (Hartford, Conn., 1785), 25–26.

58. Zabdiel Adams, *The evil designs of men made subservient by God to the public good; particularly illustrated in the rise, progress and conclusion of the American war. A Sermon Preached at Lexington, on the Nineteenth of April, 1783; Being the Anniversary of the Commencement of the War between Britain and America, which broke out in that Town on the 19th of April, 1775* (Boston, 1783), 14; Cook, A *Sermon, Delivered at New-London*, 25. "We must be stupid," Henry Cumings commented bluntly, "if we do not *rejoice in the God of our salvation,* and adore his providence, which has wrought so great deliverance for us, and raised us to a conspicuous place, upon the theatre of nations" (A *Sermon Preached . . . December 11, 1783*, 10). Eliphalet Porter concurred with Cook and Cumings: "Whoever attends to the American revolution, in the rise, the progress, and the completion of it, cannot but discern the clear footsteps of that Providence, whose purpose and design no human wisdom or power can defeat" (A *Sermon, Delivered . . . December 11, 1783*, 10). For dissenters' agreement with the standing order on this point, see Baldwin, A *Sermon, delivered February 19, 1795*, 12–15; John Murray, *The Substance of a Thanksgiving Sermon, Delivered at the Universal Meeting-House, in Boston, February 19, 1795* (Boston, 1795), 16; Samuel Stillman, *An Oration, Delivered July 4th,*

1789, at the Request of the Inhabitants of the Town of Boston, in Celebration of the Anniversary of American Independence (Boston, 1789), 15.

59. John Lathrop, *A Discourse on the Peace; Preached on the day of Public Thanksgiving, November 25, 1784* (Boston, 1784), 19. Henry Cumings, too, stressed the providential gift of unity: "That a people, so distant from one another; and so different, in many respects, in their manners, customs and modes of living, from whence strong local prejudices commonly arise; should be so generally inspired, as it were with one soul, and breathe the same spirit; and, regardless of the frowns and insidious flatteries of Britain, should bind themselves together in the closest alliance, to oppose her as a common enemy, and resist her even to blood; and should have the courage to erect themselves into a national state, and to adhere to their independence and sovereignty, amidst the greatest discouragements and difficulties, and most alarming dangers; cannot be accounted for, without acknowledging the interposing agency of that almighty Being" (*A Sermon Preached . . . December 11, 1783*, 14–15). See also the remarks of Marsh, *A Discourse Delivered at Wethersfield*, 7–8; Osgood, *Reflections on the goodness of God*, 18–19; Strong, *Agency and Providence of God*, 16.

60. Marsh, *A Discourse Delivered at Wethersfield*, 14. See also Cumings, *A Sermon Preached . . . December 11, 1783*, 20–27; Porter, *A Sermon, Delivered . . . December 11, 1783*, 16–19; Lathrop, *A Discourse on the Peace*, 20.

61. Cook, *A Sermon, Delivered at New-London*, 16; Marsh, *A Discourse Delivered at Wethersfield*, 10; Strong, *Agency and Providence of God*, 17–18.

62. "Nothing could more pointedly mark the watchful care of Heaven for the preservation of these infant States," said David Osgood, "than the manner of bringing to light, at so critical a juncture, the dark treachery and deep laid plot of the *infamous Arnold*" (*Reflections on the goodness of God*, 19). See also Willard, *A Thanksgiving Sermon*, 26.

63. Cumings, *A Sermon Preached . . . December 11, 1783*, 17. Eliphalet Porter applied Zech. 4:6—part of which reads, "Not by might, nor by power, but by my Spirit, saith the LORD of hosts"—to the Revolution. "The greatest exertions and most powerful efforts, independent of the divine blessing, will prove ineffectual, and end in disappointment and defeat. Not by might nor by power can any accomplish their designs, if God see fit to counteract the natural tendency of their exertions, and deny them success" (*A Sermon, Delivered . . . December 11, 1783*, 9). Regarding Lexington and Concord, Zabdiel Adams explained, basing himself upon Gen. 50:20, that "as the great Jehovah overruled the *malice* and *envy* of *Joseph's* brethren for the good of the whole family and Jewish nation; so the *unprecedented massacre* of *this day*, and the subsequent ravages of the British troops, through the country, though 'meant by them for evil, yet the great Jehovah has overruled for good,' not only to *this* and the United States of America, but also to *some other kingdoms* of the world!" In other words, "The *king* of *Britain* meant one thing, but the KING OF HEAVEN another" (*The evil designs of men*, 8, 17). See also, Osgood, *Reflections on the goodness of God*, 26–28.

64. Cook, *A Sermon, Delivered at New-London*, 13–15. He was drawing upon 2 Sam. 15:31, the second half of which reads, "And David said, O LORD, I pray thee, turn the counsel of Ahithophel into foolishness."

65. Marsh, *A Discourse Delivered at Wethersfield*, 9. See also Huntington, *God ruling the Nations*, 29–30; Brockway, *America saved*, 17.

66. Daniel Foster, *A Sermon preached before His Excellency John Hancock, Esq. Governour; His Honor Samuel Adams, Esq. Lieutenant-Governour; the Honourable the Council, Senate, and House of Representatives, of the Commonwealth of Massachusetts, May 26, 1790. Being the Day of General Election* (Boston, 1790), 10; Whitney, *Essential requisites*, 8; Willard, *A Thanksgiving Sermon*, 11–13.

67. Ezra Stiles, "The United States elevated to Glory and Honor. A Sermon, Preached before His Excellency Jonathan Trumbull, Esq. L.L.D. Governor and Commander in Chief,

And the Honorable The General Assembly of The State of Connecticut, Convened at Hartford, At the Anniversary Election, May 8th, 1783," in *The Pulpit of the American Revolution: or, the Political Sermons of the Period of 1776*, ed. John Wingate Thornton (Boston, 1860), 442. For more on this point, see Robert P. Hay, "George Washington: American Moses," *American Quarterly* 21 (1969): 780–791. Hay concludes, p. 789, "Like their Puritan forebears, these New Englanders still thought that the American people were the covenant people, that God had raised up his American Israel to be the example to the rest of mankind." However, as discussed later, the New England clergy was far from unanimous in the assertion that Americans were a "covenant people."

68. Cumings, *A Sermon Preached . . . December 11, 1783*, 29. See also Trumbull, *God is to be praised*, 6. Samuel Langdon, *The Republic of the Israelites an Example to the American States. A Sermon, Preached at Concord, in the State of New-Hampshire; before the Honorable General Court at the Annual Election. June 5, 1788* (Exeter, N.H., 1788), 31. For his background, see Drake, *Dictionary of American Biography*, 527.

69. Samuel Cooper, *A Sermon Preached Before his Excellency John Hancock, Esq; Governor, the Honourable the Senate, and House of Representatives of the Commonwealth of Massachusetts, October 25, 1780. Being the Day of the Commencement of the Constitution, and Inauguration of the New Government* (Boston, 1780), 2. David Osgood also pointed out the Old Testament parallel. "With what holy joy should we praise the divine goodness for this inestimable blessing, and for bringing about a peace so highly advantageous and honourable to our country! The Egyptian Pharaoh was not more loth to part with his Hebrew slaves, than the British court to give up their once American subjects. By a series of miracles were the Israelites rescued from the house of bondage. And by a series of providential wonders have the Americans emerged from oppression, and risen to liberty and independence" (*Reflections on the goodness of God*, 20). See also Samuel Deane, *A Sermon, preached before His Honour Samuel Adams, Esq. Lieutenant Governor; the Honourable the Council, Senate, and House of Representatives of the Commonwealth of Massachusetts, May 28th, 1794. Being the Day of General Election* (Boston, 1794), 19.

70. Perry Miller, *The New England Mind: The Seventeenth Century* (1939; Cambridge: Harvard University Press, 1963), 398; idem, *The New England Mind: From Colony to Province* (Cambridge: Harvard University Press, Belknap Press, 1953); Stout, *New England Soul*.

71. My emphasis on the clergy's divided position contrasts with the interpretation of Nathan O. Hatch, who writes that "the American republic actually became the primary agent of redemptive history" (*Sacred Cause*, 17). He also contends that "one theme above all others maintained its hold on the clergy. It was the solid conviction that their own community had been chosen as a special people of God" (ibid., 59).

My awareness of the differences between covenantal and providential language, and of the clergy's own divided stance, has been raised by two scholars in particular: Christopher Grasso, *A Speaking Aristocracy: Transforming Public Discourse in Eighteenth-Century Connecticut* (Chapel Hill: University of North Carolina Press, 1999), 24–85; Valeri, "New Divinity," 743–745, 751–752, 759–762; idem, *Law and Providence*, 26–29, 114–117.

72. For instance, Harry S. Stout writes, "The idea of a national covenant supplied the 'liberties' New Englanders would die protecting as well as the 'conditions' that promised deliverance and victory over all enemies" (*New England Soul*, 7 and passim). Likewise, Dale S. Kuehne concludes that "the covenant remained as important to the Congregationalists as it was to the Puritans, and it continued to form the basis of their political vision" (*Massachusetts Congregationalist Political Thought, 1760–1790: The Design of Heaven* [Columbia: University of Missouri Press, 1996], 145).

73. John Murray, *Jerubbaal, or Tyranny's Grove Destroyed, and the Altar of Liberty Finished. A Discourse on America's Duty and Danger, Delivered at the Presbyterian Church in*

Newbury-Port, December 11, 1783. On Occasion of the Public Thanksgiving for Peace (Newbury-Port, Mass., 1784), 8–22, 32, quote on 32.

Similarly, William Symmes of Andover, Massachusetts, the 1785 election preacher, used rhetorical questions to make the case for an American covenant. His chosen text was 1 Chron. 28:8, in which, he explained, "[David] reminds the 'assembly of the mighty' of the peculiar presence of the Deity; gives him the attractive title of the 'Lord our God,' which imports parental affection, and covenant privileges: And then fixes their attention to the main point, endeavouring to persuade them to 'keep and seek for all the commandments of the Lord their God.'" Having sketched the meaning of the chosen text, Symmes then argued that it was as applicable today as it was to the ancient people of God. "In some instances there is a similarity of circumstances betwixt the ancient congregation of the Lord and us. Were they a people nigh unto God; since their rejection we have been taken into a like visible relation to him? Were their long and arduous contests for freedom happily terminated? our redemption from the hand of the enemy is completed by the establishment of 'peace in our borders.' Did their civil constitution secure the rights and privileges of the people, ours is like to theirs before they trespassed in asking a king? Our religious advantages are greatly superior, and our land is perhaps as good and fertile as theirs, were it equally cultivated. And the late revolution in America, tho' not effected by the wonder-working rod of a Moses, was accomplished in the course of the divine administration under the auspices of a leader, great and good next to him: And in a manner which carries evident marks, and signatures of his hand, who 'changes the times and the seasons, who removeth kings and setteth up kings,' and possesses all perfections in their highest exaltation. Thus circumstanced:—The advice given in the text to the rulers and people of Israel, is as fruitful and proper for us as it was for them" (*A Sermon, Preached Before His Honor Thomas Cushing, Esq; Lieutenant-Governor, The Honorable the Council, and the Two Branches of the General Court, of the Commonwealth of Massachusetts, May 25, 1785: Being the Anniversary of General Election* [Boston, 1785], 7–8).

74. Samuel Austin, *A Sermon, Delivered at Worcester, on the Day of Public Thanksgiving, observed throughout the Commonwealth of Massachusetts, December 15th, MDCCXCVI* (Worcester, Mass., 1797), 8–10; Wales, *Dangers of our national Prosperity*, 25, 5, quote on 25. On the universalizing tendencies of arguments based in moral government, see Valeri, "New Divinity," 744–745, 759. Brockway, *America saved*, 7.

75. Marsh, *A Discourse Delivered at Wethersfield*, 17; Henry Ware, *The Continuance of Peace and increasing Prosperity a Source of Consolation and just Cause of Gratitude to the Inhabitants of the United States. A Sermon, Delivered February 19, 1795; Being a Day Set Apart by The President, for Thanksgiving and Prayer through the United States* (Boston, 1795), 5.

Eliphalet Porter also added the United States and a republican interpretation of politics into his text from Ps. 124: "'If it had not been the Lord who was on our side, now may' America 'say; if it had not been the Lord who was on our side, when men rose up against us; then they had swallowed us up quick when their wrath was kindled against us. Then the waters' of calamity and ruin 'had overwhelmed us, the stream' of affliction 'had gone over our soul.' Then the proud waters' of tyranny and oppression 'had gone over our soul'—Imperious and unreasonable men had executed their arbitrary designs against us, and our vaunting adversaries had triumphed over us, and stripped us of our dearest enjoyments. 'Blessed be the Lord, who hath not' delivered us up to the will of our enemies—'who hath not give us as a prey to their teeth. Our soul'—our dear country, with its valued rights and privileges, of a civil and religious nature, 'is escaped' out of the hand of those who sought her ruin, 'as a bird out of the snare of the fowlers; the snare is broken,'—the designs and attempts of our enemies are effectually defeated, 'and we are escaped. Our help is in the name of the Lord, who made heaven and earth.'" Somewhat more clearly than Marsh, Porter seemed to say that the United States, too, was a covenant nation. "That support and protection which have been afforded our land during the late contest, and the signal deliverance we have at length obtained, will well bear a comparison with the memorable interposition of Providence on the behalf of ancient Israel, and the remarkable political salvation experienced by that highly-favoured people. And the psalm we have selected for the theme of the present discourse, though originally designed as a song of praise for some great deliverance granted the Jewish nation, is yet very applicable to the present occasion, and may with all propriety be adopted by the American Israel this day" (*A Sermon, Delivered . . . December 11, 1783,* 4–5).

76. Huntington, *God ruling the Nations,* 18, 23; Jonathan Edwards Jr., *The Necessity of the Belief of Christianity by the Citizens of the State, in order to our political Prosperity; Illustrated in a Sermon, Preached before His Excellency Samuel Huntington, Esq. L.L.D. Governor, and the Honorable the General Assembly of the State of Connecticut, Convened at Hartford on the Day of the Anniversary Election. May 8th, 1794* (Hartford, Conn., 1794), 5.

77. David Osgood, *A Sermon, Preached at the Request of the Ancient and Honourable Artillery Company, in Boston, June 2, 1788, Being the Anniversary of their Election of Officers* (Boston, 1788), 4, 12–13.

78. Stiles, "United States elevated," 402–403; Edmund S. Morgan, *The Gentle Puritan: A Life of Ezra Stiles, 1727–1795* (New Haven: Yale University Press, 1962), vii, 56, 73, 134–157, quote on vii. Huntington, *God ruling the Nations,* 24, gave a similar list of parallels; his is another example, like Osgood's, of the blurring of the line between church and nation.

79. Stiles, "United States elevated," 464, 485–486. Stiles detailed the full scenario in these words: "In this country, out of sight of mitres and the purple, and removed from systems of corruption confirmed for ages and supported by the spiritual janizaries of an ecclesiastical hierarchy, aided and armed by the secular power, religion may be examined with the noble Berean freedom, the freedom of American-born minds. And revelation, both as to the true evangelical doctrines and church polity, may be settled here before they shall have undergone a thorough discussion, and been weighed with a calm and unprejudiced candor elsewhere. Great things are to be effected in the world before the millennium, which I do not expect to commence under seven or eight hundred years hence; and perhaps the liberal and candid disquisitions in America are to be rendered extensively subservient to some of the most glorious designs of Providence, and particularly in the propagation and diffusion of religion through the earth, in filling the whole earth with the knowledge of the glory of the Lord. A time will come when six hundred millions of the human race shall be ready to drop their idolatry and all false religion, when Christianity shall triumph over superstition, as well as Deism, and Gentilism, and Mohammedanism. They will then search all Christendom for the best model, the purest exemplification of the Christian church, with the fewest human mixtures. And when God in his providence shall convert the world, should the newly Christianized nations assume our form of religion, should American missionaries be blessed to succeed in the work of Christianizing the heathen,—in which the Romanists and foreign Protestants have very much failed,—it would be an unexpected wonder, and a great honor to the United States. And thus the American Republic, by illuminating the world with truth and liberty, would be exalted and made high among the nations, in praise, and in name, and in honor. I doubt not this is the honor reserved for us; I had almost said, in the spirit of prophecy, the zeal of the Lord of Hosts will accomplish this."

80. Wright, *Beginnings of Unitarianism,* 161–176. Boston's Jeremy Belknap, to take an extreme example, confided in a letter to his friend Ebenezer Hazard that he found the interpretation of Cotton Mather's *Wonders of the Invisible World,* with its discussion of satanic forces at work in the world, to be laughable. As Belknap's most recent biographer writes, "While Belknap did not entirely remove God from the historical stage, he placed Him far from the main flow of human action. God was not the dominant force in Belknap's exposition. The minister wrote almost purely secular history. He did not offer religious answers to ques-

tions about historical causation. He posited reason as the determinate force in history and rejected omens, portents, superstition, and miracles. In this sense, he was an anomaly for his age" (Louis Leonard Tucker, *Clio's Consort: Jeremy Belknap and the Founding of the Massachusetts Historical Society* [Boston: Massachusetts Historical Society, 1990], 39).

81. McLoughlin, *New England Dissent*, 1:341–354, quote on 349; Grasso, *Speaking Aristocracy*, 68; Mark A. Noll, "The American Revolution and Protestant Evangelicalism," *Journal of Interdisciplinary History* 23 (1993): 626–627.

82. Valeri, "New Divinity," 745; idem, *Law and Providence*, 3–75, 110–139. Yet, adherence to the idea of a national covenant did not follow the lines of theological factionalism simply. For example, the ardent New Divinity preacher Samuel Austin espoused it as much as Samuel Wales, who at least had New Divinity leanings, denied it. On the identification of Austin as a participant in the New Divinity movement, see Conforti, *Samuel Hopkins*, 228. Regarding Wales's tendency toward the New Divinity, see Morgan, *Gentle Puritan*, 377.

83. As Valeri points out, even for the New Divinity, "the notion of a divine covenant . . . remained an implicit foundation" ("New Divinity," 751).

84. Langdon, *Republic of the Israelites*, 32. In 1788, Connecticut's election preacher, Josiah Whitney, also attributed the Constitution to "the footsteps of a kind, almighty Providence" (*Essential requisites*, 35). See also Robbins, *Empires and Dominions*, 25; Williams, *Carefully to observe*, 18.

85. Spring, *A Discourse, Delivered . . . November 7th*, 1793, 14; Jonathan French, *A Sermon, Delivered on the Anniversary Thanksgiving November 29, 1798* (Andover, Mass., 1799), 8, 12, 23. In November 1794, both Henry Channing of New London, Connecticut, and David Osgood gave thanks for the evident hand of Providence in the suppression of the Whiskey Rebellion (Henry Channing, *The Consideration of divine Goodness an argument for religious gratitude and obedience. A Sermon, Delivered at New-London, November 27, 1794. Being the day appointed by Authority, For public Thanksgiving in the State of Connecticut* [New-London, Conn., 1794], 20–22; Osgood, *Wonderful Works of GOD*, 20).

86. Cumings, *A Sermon Preached . . . December 11, 1783*, 31–32; Osgood, *Reflections on the goodness of God*, 25. See also Joseph Lathrop, *The Happiness of a Free Government, and the Means of Preserving it: Illustrated in a Sermon, delivered in West-Springfield, On July 4th, 1794, in Commemoration of American Independence!* (Springfield, Mass., 1794), 14–15, 22–23.

87. Cooper, *A Sermon Preached . . . October 25, 1780*, 52. For lists similar to Cooper's, see Adams, *The evil designs of men*, 27, and Willard, *A Thanksgiving Sermon*, 33. In the same vein, Benjamin Trumbull predicted millennial consequences from the American experiment. "As the nations make themselves acquainted with our wisdom, liberty and happiness they will more and more aspire after and adopt them into their own systems, and so it will tend to diffuse knowledge, liberty, religion and happiness through the earth, and to prepare mankind for the universal reign of the Son of God, in the glories of the latter day" (*God is to be praised*, 22). For more on predictions of "American greatness," see Bloch, *Visionary Republic*, 47–49, 94–95.

88. Enos Hitchcock, *An Oration: Delivered July 4, 1788, at the Request of the Inhabitants of the Town of Providence, in Celebration of the Anniversary of American Independence, and of the Accession of Nine States to the Federal Constitution* (Providence, R.I., 1788), 16–17.

89. Huntington, *God ruling the Nations*, 31–32; for a similar scenario, see Stillman, *An Oration, Delivered July 4th, 1789*, 29. Robbins, *Empires and Dominions*, 23–24; see also Foster, *A Sermon preached . . . May 26, 1790*, 23–25. Brockway, *America saved*, 23.

90. Simeon Baldwin, *An Oration pronounced before the Citizens of New-Haven, July 4, 1788; in commemoration of the Declaration of Independence and Establisment [sic] of the Constitution of the United States of America* (New-Haven, Conn., 1788), 6. See also Jonathan L.

Austin, *An Oration, delivered July 4, 1786, at the Request of the Inhabitants of the Town of Boston, in Celebration of the Anniversary of American Independence* (Boston, 1786), 5; Joel Barlow, *An Oration, Delivered at the North Church in Hartford, at the Meeting of the Connecticut Society of the Cincinnati, July 4th, 1787. In Commemoration of the Independence of the United States* (Hartford, Conn., 1787), 11.

91. Hatch, *Sacred Cause*, 145. See also John F. Berens, *Providence and Patriotism in Early America 1640–1815* (Charlottesville: University Press of Virginia, 1978), 5–9, 112–128; Sacvan Bercovitch, *The American Jeremiad* (Madison: University of Wisconsin Press, 1978).

92. Samuel Cooper called for "a warm and passionate patriotism" to cement people's attachment to the Massachusetts constitution of 1780 (*A Sermon Preached . . . October 25, 1780*, 31). Ministers leaned more heavily toward this position during the 1790s, as the ministry called for allegiance to the embattled Adams administration. See chapter 2, and in the primary sources see especially John Lathrop, *Patriotism and Religion. A Sermon, Preached on the 25th of April, 1799, the Day Recommended by the President of the United States, to be Observed as a National Fast* (Boston, 1799).

93. Edmund S. Morgan concisely defines the *jeremiad* as "a lament for the loss of virtue and a warning of divine displeasure and desolation to come" ("The Puritan Ethic and the American Revolution," in *In Search of Early America: The William & Mary Quarterly, 1943–1993*, ed. Michael McGiffert [Williamsburg, Va.: Institute for Early American History and Culture, 1993], 80. [This essay was orig. published in *WMQ* 24 (1967): 3–43]). See also Miller, *New England Mind: From Colony to Province*, 27–37; James M. Banner Jr., *To the Hartford Convention: The Federalists and the Origins of Party Politics in Massachusetts, 1789–1815* (New York: Knopf, 1970), 32–35; Scott, *From Office to Profession*, 14–15.

94. For examples, Murray, *Jerubbaal*, 75; Osgood, *Reflections on the goodness of God*, 33; Porter, *A Sermon, Delivered . . . December 11, 1783*, 24; Huntington, *God ruling the Nations*, 24; Nathanael Emmons, *A Discourse, Delivered November 3, 1790, at the particular request of a number of respectable men in Franklin, who were forming a Society, for the Reformation of Morals* (Providence, R.I., 1790), text; Timothy Dwight, *Virtuous Rulers a National Blessing. A Sermon, Preached at the General Election, May 12th, 1791* (Hartford, Conn., 1791), 17; Stone, *A Sermon, Preached . . . May 10th, 1792*, 17; Lathrop, *Happiness of a Free Government*, 20; Lee, *The origin and ends of civil Government*, 24; John Marsh, *A Sermon, Preached before His Honor Oliver Wolcott, Esq. L.L.D. Lieutenant-Governor and Commander in Chief, and the Honorable the General Assembly of the State of Connecticut, Convened at Hartford, on the Day of the Anniversary Election, May 12th, 1796* (Hartford, Conn., 1796), 19.

95. Adams, *The evil designs of men*, 26. Likewise, Samuel West, the 1786 Massachusetts election preacher from Needham, said, "No man therefore can better evidence his public virtue, than by endeavouring in his proper sphere, to prevent the contagious spread of vice; or to promote the influence of morality and religion" (*A Sermon, preached before His Excellency James Bowdoin, Esq. Governour; His Honour Thomas Cushing, Esq. Lieutenant-Governour; the Honourable the Council, Senate, and House of Representatives, of the Commonwealth of Massachusetts, May 31, 1786: Being the Day of General Election* [Boston, 1786], 21–22).

96. Murray, *Jerubbaal*, 70. Leonard Woods used similar language to characterize the problem of profanity in society in 1799. "The prophet says, [Jer. 23:10] *because of swearing the land mourneth.* — Have not we reason to adopt the same plaintive strain? Is not this one of the prevailing iniquities of the present day? Does not our land lie, as it seems, pressed down with the ponderous load and groaning to be delivered from it?" (*Two Sermons On Profane Swearing, Delivered April 4, 1799; The Day Appointed By The Governor of Massachusetts For Humiliation, Fasting and Prayer* [Newburyport, Mass., 1799], 34). See also Emmons, *A Discourse, Delivered November 3, 1790*, 23; Trumbull, *God is to be praised*, 35.

97. Murray, *Jerubbaal*, 56; Osgood, *Reflections on the goodness of God*, 18; Wales, *Dangers of our national Prosperity*, 16; Charles Backus, *A Sermon, Preached in Long-Meadow, at the Publick Fast, April 17th, MDCCLXXXVIII* (Springfield, Mass., 1788), 6–7.

98. Emmons, *A Discourse, Delivered November 3, 1790*, 12; Woods, *Two Sermons On Profane Swearing*, 38. Isaac Morrill stated the relationship this way: "If we turn to the Lord, in the way of our duty, he will turn to us in ways of mercy, and cause his face to shine upon us. But so long as we love our sins, we must expect trouble" (*Faith in Divine Providence*, 29). See also Symmes, *A Sermon, Preached . . . May 25, 1785*, 20; Joseph McKeen, *A Sermon, Preached on the Public Fast in the Commonwealth of Massachusetts, April 11, 1793* (Salem, Mass., 1793), 18.

99. James Dana, *The African Slave Trade. A Discourse Delivered in the City of New-Haven, September 9, 1790, before the Connecticut Society for the Promotion of Freedom* (New-Haven, Conn., 1791), 24.

100. Shain, *Myth of American Individualism*, 3, 24–47, quote on 24; Banner, *To the Hartford Convention*, 53; Levi Hart, *The Description of a GOOD CHARACTER attempted and applied to the subject of Jurisprudence and civil Government. A Discourse, addressed to his Excellency the Governor, and the Honourable Legislature in the State of Connecticut, convened at Hartford on the General Election, May 11th, M.DCC.LXXXVI* (Hartford, Conn., 1786), 16; Deane, *A Sermon, preached . . . May 28th, 1794*, 13. See also Scott, *From Office to Profession*, 24–27; Stone, *A Sermon, Preached . . . May 10th, 1792*, 7; Lathrop, *Happiness of a Free Government*, 10; Timothy Dwight, *The True Means of Establishing Public Happiness. A Sermon, Delivered on the 7th of July, 1795, before the Connecticut Society of Cincinnati, and published at their request* (New Haven, Conn., 1795), 5.

101. Isaac Lewis, *The Political Advantages of Godliness. A Sermon, Preached before His Excellency the Governor, and the Honorable Legislature of the State of Connecticut, Convened at Hartford on the Anniversary Election. May 11, 1797* (Hartford, Conn., 1797), 10; Stone, *A Sermon, Preached . . . May 10th, 1792*, 18.

102. Elizur Goodrich, *The Principles of civil Union and Happiness considered and recommended. A Sermon, Preached before his Excellency Samuel Huntington, Esq. L.L.D. Governor and Commander in Chief, and the Honorable the General Assembly of the State of Connecticut. Convened at Hartford, on the Day of the Anniversary Election, May 10th, 1787* (Hartford, Conn., 1787), 7; Whitney, *Essential requisites*, 36. Samuel Deane concluded, similar to Whitney, that "complainers and fault-finders, who vent their gall against publick characters and measures, should always be discountenanced by every friend to the Republick. For persons should not be hasty in concluding that their rulers have erred in any instance. They should rather consider that the collected wisdom of the State or Nation, and the superior advantages for information, possessed by political assemblies, render it probable that their decisions are more wise and fit than the opinions even of an enlightened individual" (*A Sermon, preached . . . May 28th, 1794*, 28). On the illegitimacy of the Jeffersonian opposition in Federalist eyes, see Banner, *To the Hartford Convention*, 75–83.

103. For more on disinterested benevolence, see Conforti, *Samuel Hopkins*, 117–124; Rohrer, *Keepers of the Covenant*, 19–21.

104. Samuel Austin, *Disinterested Love, the Ornament of the Christian, and the Duty of Man. A Sermon Delivered at New-York, June 5, 1790* (New York, 1791), 3. He added, p. 11, "His [the man of disinterested love's] hand will be open to relieve the distressed. The hungry, the naked, the widow and the orphan; the family of sickness and affliction, will be the objects of his tenderness and charity. . . . The good of the public, of useful societies, and institutions he will endeavour to advance; and above all, the eternal salvation of his fellow creatures [will occupy him]."

105. Jonathan Edwards Jr., *The Injustice and Impolicy of the Slave Trade, and of the Slavery of the Africans: Illustrated in a Sermon Preached before the Connecticut Society for the Pro-*

motion of Freedom, and for the Relief of Persons unlawfully holden in Bondage, At their annual Meeting in New-Haven, September 15, 1791 (New Haven, Conn., 1791), 3–4. See also Samuel Hopkins, *A Discourse upon the Slave-Trade, and the Slavery of the Africans. Delivered in the Baptist Meeting-House at Providence, before the Providence Society for abolishing the Slave-Trade, &c. At their Annual Meeting, on May 17, 1793* (Providence, R.I., 1793), 4–9; Conforti, *Samuel Hopkins*, 125–141; David S. Lovejoy, "Samuel Hopkins: Religion, Slavery, and the Revolution," *NEQ* 40 (1967): 227–243.

106. Whitney, *Essential requisites*, 9. The same point was made by John Marsh: "Man is formed for society. Such are his faculties—his natural desires, inclinations and capacities, that he would be uneasy without an intercourse with his fellow-creatures. Such his weakness and his wants, that without their aid, he could not exist comfortably, if he could exist at all. And such are the lusts of men, from whence come wars and fightings, that the weaker would always be in danger from the stronger, without the protection of laws, which numbers agree to adopt and support, for their mutual safety and advantage" (*A Sermon, Preached . . . May 12th, 1796*, 7). See also Foster, *A Sermon preached . . . May 26, 1790*, 8.

107. As Moses Hemmenway of Wells, Massachusetts (now Maine), explained in the 1784 election sermon, the purpose of that annual ritual was to enable "a CHRISTIAN STATE to [worship] the supreme King of nations, whose ordinance civil government is; from whom all the authority of rulers and all the rights of subjects are originally derived; to whom the mutual duties of all orders of men are to be ultimately referred; and by whose blessing alone, communities, as well as individuals, can be happy" (*A Sermon, Preached before His Excellency John Hancock, Esq; Governor; His Honor Thomas Cushing, Esq; Lieutenant-Governor; the Honorable the Council, and the Honorable the Senate, and House of Representatives, of the Commonwealth of Massachusetts, May 26, 1784. Being the Day of General Election* [Boston, 1784], 6).

108. Cyprian Strong, *The Kingdom Is the Lord's. A Sermon, Preached at Hartford, on the Day of the Anniversary Election, May 9, 1799* (Hartford, Conn., 1799), 9; Nathan Strong, *A Sermon, delivered in presence of His Excellency Samuel Huntington, Esq. L.L.D. Governor, And the Honorable the General Assembly of the State of Connecticut, Convened at Hartford, on the Day of the Anniversary Election. May 13th, 1790* (Hartford, Conn., 1790), 22; Hemmenway, *A Sermon, Preached . . . May 26, 1784*, 21. According to Elizur Goodrich, the good society was one in which "every member of the community, will be found, fixed in his proper place, and discharging the duties of it" (*Principles of civil Union*, 57–58). Chandler Robbins of Plymouth, Massachusetts, conveyed this idea through a biological metaphor. "The most happy and perfect state of the human body, results from the due order of its various members and parts, each performing regularly, the several offices assigned them by the great Creator. . . . So in collective bodies, or societies—as they are composed of various orders and individuals, each connected with, and subservient to the other; the health and prosperity of the whole, is then only maintained, when the several parts and members of the body politic preserve their proper places, and regularly and faithfully perform the duties of their various stations" (*A Sermon, Preached before His Excellency John Hancock, Esq. Governour; His Honor Samuel Adams Esq. Lieutenant-Governour; The Honourable the Council, and the Honourable the Senate and House of Representatives, of the Commonwealth of Massachusetts, May 25, 1791. Being the Day of General Election* [Boston, 1791], 8). See also Stone, *A Sermon, Preached . . . May 10th, 1792*, 20.

109. As Robert E. Shalhope has noted, "the exclusive purpose of republican government" was "the public good" ("Republicanism and Early American Historiography," *WMQ* 39 [1982]: 335).

110. Noll, "American Revolution and Protestant Evangelicalism," 628–631. For instance, Ezra Stiles, in a famous remark, argued that New England had "realized the capital ideas of

Harrington's Oceana" ("United States elevated," 404). See also Lathrop, *A Discourse on the Peace*, 8–9.

111. Osgood, *A Sermon, Preached . . . June 2, 1788*, 8. In the words of Henry Cumings, "If we submitted, it was obvious, that our lives, liberties and estates were at once subjected to [Britain's] arbitrary disposal; and that we should become slaves ourselves, and entail slavery on our posterity" (*A Sermon Preached . . . December 11, 1783*, 13). See also Osgood, *Reflections on the goodness of God*, 7–8, 21–22; Huntington, *God ruling the Nations*, 11–12; Brockway, *America saved*, 8; Hitchcock, *An Oration: Delivered July 4, 1788*, 9; William Emerson, *A Discourse, delivered in Harvard, July 4, 1794, at the Request of the Military Officers in that Place, Who, with the militia under their command, were then assembled to commemorate the Anniversary of the American Independence* (Boston, 1794), 8.

112. Porter, *A Sermon, Delivered . . . December 11, 1783*, 3–4; Hitchcock, *An Oration: Delivered July 4, 1788*, 22; Osgood, *Reflections on the goodness of God*, 29–30; Stiles, "United States elevated," 454; Trumbull, *God is to be praised*, 12–13, 22; Bloch, *Visionary Republic*, 85–86.

113. Edwards, *Injustice and Impolicy*, 23. See also, from a Connecticut lawyer, Zephaniah Swift, *An Oration on Domestic Slavery. Delivered at the North Meeting-House in Hartford, on the 12th Day of May*, A.D. 1791. *At the Meeting of the Connecticut Society for the Promotion of Freedom, and the Relief of Persons unlawfully holden in Bondage* (Hartford, Conn., 1791), 4.

114. Hitchcock, *An Oration: Delivered July 4, 1788*, 5; Baldwin, *A Sermon, delivered February 19, 1795*, 13. Jonathan Maxcy, the Baptist president of Rhode Island College, used scriptural terminology such as "every tongue," "resurrection," and "regeneration" to describe the importance of the Revolution: "The citizens of America celebrate that day which gave birth to their liberties. The recollection of this event, replete with consequences so beneficial to mankind, swells every heart with joy, and fills every tongue with praise. We celebrate . . . the resurrection of liberty, the emancipation of mankind, the regeneration of the world . . . we love liberty, we glory in the rights of men, we glory in independence" (*An Oration, Delivered in the Baptist Meeting-House in Providence, July 4*, A.D. 1795, *at the Celebration of the Nineteenth Anniversary of American Independence* [Providence, R.I., 1795], 5).

115. Emerson, *A Discourse, delivered in Harvard*. As Bloch writes in this regard, "Not only did ministers respond to the imperial crisis by preaching about liberty and tyranny in the language of the radical whigs, but the very terms 'liberty' and 'tyranny' were deeply infused with religious, even spiritual, meaning" (*Visionary Republic*, 63).

116. "Our ancestors," asserted William Emerson in a familiar myth, "abandoned the shores of Britain: they sought the rights of conscience and of man amid Columbian wilds" (*A Discourse, delivered in Harvard*, 6). Timothy Stone described the government of the Israelites in terms that would make any republican proud: "It was a free constitution, in which, all the valuable rights of the community were most happily secured. The public good, was the great object in view, and, the most effectual care was taken to preserve the rights of individuals" (*A Sermon, Preached . . . May 10th, 1792*, 5–6). Samuel Cooper also depicted Old Testament government as "a free republic" (*A Sermon Preached . . . October 25, 1780*, 8). See also Lathrop, *Happiness of a Free Government*, 6–9; Huntington, *God ruling the Nations*, 24. In the secondary literature, see Hatch, *Sacred Cause*, 16, 46, 61–62, 77; Stout, *New England Soul*, 293–295.

117. Bernard Bailyn, "Religion and Revolution: Three Biographical Studies," *Perspectives in American History* 4 (1970): 85–169; Hatch, *Sacred Cause*, especially pp. 92–95.

118. Bloch, *Visionary Republic*, 45. See also Stout, *New England Soul*, 297–299; James T. Kloppenberg, "The Virtues of Liberalism: Christianity, Republicanism, and Ethics in Early American Political Discourse," *JAH* 74 (1987): 9–33; and Noll, "American Revolution and Protestant Evangelicalism," 624–632. Samuel Cooper provided an excellent example of lib-

erty's multiplicity when he said that Americans had drawn their liberal ideas of government from "the immortal writings of Sidney and Locke, and other glorious defenders of the liberties of human nature," the Glorious Revolution, and "reason and scripture" (*A Sermon Preached . . . October 25, 1780*, 18).

119. Hatch, *Sacred Cause*, 63. Cf. Shain, *Myth of American Individualism*, 270, who writes, "Evidence of a powerful classical or Renaissance republican presence in the thought or actions of Revolutionary-era Americans should therefore be hard to discover. And it is." On the diminishing explanatory power of republicanism, see Daniel T. Rodgers, "Republicanism: The Career of a Concept," *JAH* 79 (1992): 11–38. The crux of my difference with Hatch on this point reflects the shift over the last two decades in historiographical sensibility detailed by Rodgers.

120. "I find that in early Americans' writings, they assigned to liberty eight different meanings that cut across the various regions. They are: philosophical (freedom of the will), political, spiritual (or Christian), prescriptive, familial (economic independence or autonomy), natural, civil, and individualistic (modern individual autonomy)" (Shain, *Myth of American Individualism*, 169).

121. "If we now turn our eye to the oracles of DIVINE REVELATION, we shall find clear and manifold evidence that God approves and favors the cause of liberty, and that tyranny is most offensive to him—This appears in his delivering the Israelites from a state of miserable bondage, and punishing their oppressors with a mighty hand, and stretched-out arm. It appears in the laws and form of government he gave them; whereby liberty and property were secured to every one. It appears in the awful threatnings denounced by the prophets against the enslavers and oppressors of mankind; and which have been terribly executed. It appears in the whole strain, spirit, and tendency of the doctrine and religion taught and inculcated throughout the scriptures; which is to promote the practice of goodness, righteousness and truth, with all other divine and social virtues; and to dissuade men from all acts of injustice or unkindness, whereby the rights or liberties of any might be violated. It appears further, from express directions and exhortations to christians, that they stand fast in their liberty, and be not entangled with a yoke of bondage; nor be the servants of men; nor call any man master upon earth; nor exercise lordly dominion over one another. Finally, it appears from the example of Christ, and the apostles, prophets, and holy men, whose characters and conduct are recorded for our imitation; who spoke and acted with the most ingenuous freedom, and most reverse to a base servile spirit" (Hemmenway, *A Sermon, Preached . . . May 26, 1784*, 8, 27–28). For a similar list, see John Mellen, *The Great and Happy Doctrine of Liberty. A Discourse, delivered at Hanover, Commonwealth of Massachusetts, February 19, 1795, on the day of Public Thanksgiving and Prayer, appointed by the President, to be observed throughout all the United States of America* (Boston, 1795), 9.

122. Hemmenway, *A Sermon, Preached . . . May 26, 1784*, 8. Chandler Robbins drew the same distinction as Hemmenway when he rejoiced that the Constitution had secured Americans' "natural, civil and religious rights" (*A Sermon, Preached . . . May 25, 1791*, 33). Likewise, Mellen, minister at Hanover, Massachusetts, divided his discussion of liberty into "the three following heads. I. Natural, common liberty. II. Political, civil liberty. III. Moral, religious liberty" (*Great and Happy Doctrine*, 11). See also Dana, *African Slave Trade*, 32.

123. Hemmenway, *A Sermon, Preached . . . May 26, 1784*, 10, 24–25, 52. Mellen denominated these two types of Christian liberty "*moral* liberty," and "*religious* liberty," or freedom from "the *coercion* of human laws" (*Great and Happy Doctrine*, 17). The former type Shain calls "Revolutionary-era Americans' most fundamental understanding of liberty" (*Myth of American Individualism*, 193, 199–206, quote on 193). James Dana, pastor of New Haven's First Congregational Church, also defined Christian liberty as freedom from sin. "Christian freedom, being alike the privilege of converts from Judaism and heathenism, primarily in-

tends, on the part of the former, the abolition of the encumbered ritual of Moses; and, on the part of the latter, liberation from idolatrous superstition, to which they were in servile subjection: On the part of both it intends deliverance from the slavery of vicious passions" (*African Slave Trade*, 7).

124. Stiles, "United States elevated," 503; Morrill, *Faith in Divine Providence*, 27–28. On the Lexington anniversary three years later, Zabdiel Adams likewise concluded by exhorting his audience to "seek peace with God through Jesus Christ, the great peace-maker; *who has made both Jew and Gentile one, and [Col.* 1:20] *made peace by the blood of the cross*;—that so when we are called away from the enjoyments of American citizens, we may be made free of the city of the *New-Jerusalem*, and become the denisons [*sic*] of the Zion that is above" (*The evil designs of men*, 35).

125. Lathrop, *A Discourse on the Peace*, 29. Nineteenth-century Unitarianism made much of these same themes of liberty, reason, and theological progress, as we shall see in chapter 5.

126. Bonomi, *Under the Cope of Heaven*, 199–209. It is interesting that as late as 1784, John Murray of Newburyport, Massachusetts, still expressed concern over the issue of an Episcopal bishop, should Washington act in favor of his denomination (*Jerubbaal*, 46).

127. Cumings, *A Sermon Preached . . . December* 11, 1783, 36; David Osgood, *The signal Advantages derived to the Nations of Christendom from their Religion, illustrated in a Discourse delivered before the Annual Convention of the Congregational Ministers of Massachusetts, in Boston, May* 31, 1798 (Boston, 1798), 27; Tappan, *A Sermon Preached . . . May* 30, 1792, 11; Lathrop, *Patriotism and Religion*, 12; Strong, *A Sermon, delivered . . . May* 13th, 1790, 16. For more on the conventional New England wisdom that popery and tyranny went hand in hand, see Charles P. Hanson, *Necessary Virtue: The Pragmatic Origins of Religious Liberty in New England* (Charlottesville: University Press of Virginia, 1998), 10–11.

128. As Shain concludes, the interests of society took priority over "idiosyncratic behavior on the part of the individual or the valorization of the immediate needs of the individual" (*Myth of American Individualism*, 174).

129. Whitney, *Essential requisites*, 11; the italicized phrases denote two biblical quotations, from Judg. 21:25 and Gen. 6:11, respectively. Samuel Wales voiced a common warning about not letting liberty run amok when he said, "Tyranny and despotism are undoubtedly very great evils, but greater still are the dangers of anarchy" (*Dangers of our national Prosperity*, 22). Timothy Stone likewise explained that liberty became operative only in a social context and therefore had to have bounds. "That liberty consists in freedom from restraint, leaving each one to act as seemeth right to himself, is a most unwise mistaken apprehension. Civil liberty, consists in the being and administration of such a system of laws, as doth bind all classes of men, rulers and subjects, to unite their exertions for the promotion of virtue and public happiness" (*A Sermon, Preached . . . May* 10th, 1792, 9–10). For other attacks upon "licentious" liberty, see Backus, *A Sermon, Preached in Long-Meadow*, 11–13; Robbins, *Empires and Dominions*, 14; Enos Hitchcock, *A Discourse on Education, Delivered at the Meeting-House on the West Side of the River, in Providence, November* 16, 1785 (Providence, R.I., 1785).

130. Mellen, *Great and Happy Doctrine*, 11–12. "Creatures, who have risen in rebellion, against the holy and perfect government of JEHOVAH," pronounced Timothy Stone, "have partial connections, selfish interests, passions and lusts, which often interfere with each other, and which, will not always be controlled by reason, and the mild influence of moral motives, however great: but these in their external expressions, must be under the restraint of law, or there can be no peace, no safety among men" (Stone, *A Sermon, Preached . . . May* 10th, 1792, 9). On the "formative American influence" of the doctrine of original sin, see Shain, *Myth of American Individualism*, 218–233.

131. David Hackett Fischer, *Albion's Seed: Four British Folkways in America* (New York: Oxford University Press, 1989), 199–205.

132. Hemmenway, *A Sermon, Preached . . . May 26, 1784*, 6–7, 33–34.
133. Ibid., 12.
134. Trumbull, *God is to be praised*, 6.
135. Dwight, *True Means*, 6; Randolph A. Roth, *The Democratic Dilemma: Religion, Reform, and the Social Order in the Connecticut River Valley of Vermont, 1791–1850* (New York: Cambridge University Press, 1987), 5–6, 14.

Chapter Two

1. H. Richard Niebuhr, *Christ and Culture* (New York: Harper & Brothers, 1951), 2.
2. Gordon S. Wood, *The Radicalism of the American Revolution* (New York: Knopf, 1992), 180, 229. Donald M. Scott also describes eighteenth-century New England as a deference society. "The ministry was a public office and shared a common character and idiom with magistracy. . . . Once a person was 'elevated' to a 'chief office,' it was the obligation of those who conferred the office (and retained the power of removal) to grant him respect and obedience and cheerfully to acquiesce in his exercise of his office" (*From Office to Profession: The New England Ministry, 1750–1850* [Philadelphia: University of Pennsylvania Press, 1978], 9).
3. Niebuhr, *Christ and Culture*, 40–44, 117–122. As he wrote, the typical synthesizer "combined without confusing philosophy and theology, state and church, civic and Christian virtues, natural and divine laws, Christ and culture" (ibid., 130). Mark A. Noll, *One Nation under God? Christian Faith and Political Action in America* (San Francisco: Harper & Row, 1988), 29–30, 25. While I have profited from Noll's discussion of the styles of Christian political activity, I also differ with him on this point. He sees (p. 31) the one "dominant religious outlook toward public life throughout American history" to have been the "Reformed" tradition. He is correct to a large extent but in his overview does not notice the way in which the religious establishments of New England had departed from their Reformed (and reforming) roots.
4. David Osgood, *Reflections on the goodness of God in supporting the People of the United States through the late war, and giving them so advantageous and honourable a peace. A Sermon Preached on the Day of annual and national Thanksgiving December 11, 1783* (Boston, 1784), 31–32. Timothy Dwight agreed with Osgood as to what was riding on the national experiment. Shortly prior to his installation as president of Yale in 1795, Dwight said, "To establish on firm foundations the Happiness of Society is evidently one of the most important concerns of man. If the attainment of that happiness be highly desirable, the perpetuation of it must be more desirable. . . . The attainment is usually not a difficult task, the establishment a Herculean one. A free government has been always, and justly, supposed to be a primary source of national happiness. To form such a government has been found sufficiently easy; but to render it durable has been ever considered as a problem of very difficult solution. . . . Should we fall, the fairest hopes of wise and good men will be blasted; the maxim, That mankind cannot be governed without force and violence, will stand on higher proof, and be advanced with new and triumphant confidence; and the great body of civilized men will probably sit down in sullen and melancholy conviction, that nations cannot, unless circumscribed by Alps, or oceans, be permanently free" (*The True Means of Establishing Public Happiness. A Sermon, Delivered on the 7th of July, 1795, before the Connecticut Society of Cincinnati, and published at their request* [New Haven, Conn., 1795], 5–6).
5. Joel Barlow, *An Oration, Delivered at the North Church in Hartford, at the Meeting of the Connecticut Society of the Cincinnati, July 4th, 1787. In Commemoration of the Independence of the United States* (Hartford, Conn., 1787), 3, 8–12, quote on 3. See also Simeon Baldwin, *An Oration pronounced before the Citizens of New-Haven, July 4, 1788; in commemoration*

of the Declaration of Independence and Establishment [sic] *of the Constitution of the United States of America* (New-Haven, Conn., 1788), 8–13; Enos Hitchcock, *An Oration: Delivered July 4, 1788, at the Request of the Inhabitants of the Town of Providence, in Celebration of the Anniversary of American Independence, and of the Accession of Nine States to the Federal Constitution* (Providence, R.I., 1788), 9–15; William Hull, *An Oration delivered to the Society of the Cincinnati in the Commonwealth of Massachusetts. July 4, 1788* (Boston, 1788), 12–15. On Barlow's background, see Francis S. Drake, *Dictionary of American Biography* (Boston, 1874), 62–63.

6. Gordon S. Wood, *The Creation of the American Republic, 1776–1787* (Chapel Hill: University of North Carolina Press, 1969; New York: Norton, 1972), 471–475; Bernard Bailyn, *The Ideological Origins of the American Revolution*, enlarged ed. (1967; Cambridge: Harvard University Press, Belknap Press, 1992), 65, 368–379.

7. Charles Backus, *A Sermon, Preached in Long-Meadow, at the Publick Fast, April 17th, MDCCLXXXVIII* (Springfield, Mass., 1788), 7–10. Very similarly, Thomas Brockway of Lebanon, Connecticut, admonished his listeners in 1784, "If in gaining our liberty and independence, we looked for a paradise, or a total exemption from expence [sic] and trouble, the idea was frantic; it is what this world does not afford: for under all revolutions, however interesting, it will still be a world of trouble. But if we have been contending to have our legislative and executive authority at our own election, . . . then we have gained the point—this is ours—and this is liberty—yea, all the civil liberty that in the present state of the world we can rationally desire" (*America saved, or Divine Glory displayed, in the late War with Great-Britain. A Thanksgiving Sermon, Preached in Lebanon, Second Society, And now offered to the Public, at the Desire of a Number of the Hearers* [Hartford, Conn., 1784], 21). Both Backus and Brockway probably had in mind a text like John 16:33, where Jesus said, "In the world ye shall have tribulation." For more on the dangers of "unreasonable expectations," see Joseph Lathrop, *National Happiness, illustrated in a Sermon, delivered at West-Springfield, on the Nineteenth of February, 1795. Being a Day of General Thanksgiving* (Springfield, Mass., 1795), 6; Samuel Wales, *The Dangers of our national Prosperity; and the Way to avoid them. A Sermon, Preached before the General Assembly of the State of Connecticut, at Hartford, May 12th, 1785* (Hartford, Conn., 1785), 26–27.

8. Levi Hart, *The Description of a GOOD CHARACTER attempted and applied to the subject of Jurisprudence and civil Government. A Discourse, addressed to his Excellency the Governor, and the Honourable Legislature in the State of Connecticut, convened at Hartford on the General Election, May 11th, M.DCC.LXXXVI* (Hartford, Conn., 1786), 24; Samuel West, *A Sermon, preached before His Excellency James Bowdoin, Esq. Governour; His Honour Thomas Cushing, Esq. Lieutenant-Governour; the Honourable the Council, Senate, and House of Representatives, of the Commonwealth of Massachusetts, May 31, 1786: Being the Day of General Election* (Boston, 1786), 25; Nathanael Emmons, *A Discourse, Delivered November 3, 1790, at the particular request of a number of respectable men in Franklin, who were forming a Society, for the Reformation of Morals* (Providence, R.I., 1790), 17, 20–22; Daniel Foster, *A Sermon preached before His Excellency John Hancock, Esq. Governour; His Honor Samuel Adams, Esq. Lieutenant-Governour; the Honourable the Council, Senate, and House of Representatives, of the Commonwealth of Massachusetts, May 26, 1790. Being the Day of General Election* (Boston, 1790), 26.

9. Isaac Morrill, *Faith in Divine Providence the Great Support of God's People. A Sermon, Preached at Lexington, April 19, 1780. In Memory of the Commencement of the unnatural War between Great-Britain and America; which took place in said Town April 19, 1775* (Boston, 1780), 29; Joseph Huntington, *God ruling the Nations for the most glorious end. A Sermon, In presence of his Excellency, and both Houses of Assembly. Hartford, May 13th, 1784* (Hartford, Conn., 1784), 26; Wales, *Dangers of our national Prosperity*, 13–22.

10. Samuel Spring, *A Discourse, Delivered at the North Church in Newburyport, November 7th, 1793. Being the day appointed for a General Thanksgiving, by the authority of Massachusetts* (Newburyport, Mass., 1794), 10–11; Samuel Hopkins, *A Discourse upon the Slave-Trade, and the Slavery of the Africans. Delivered in the Baptist Meeting-House at Providence, before the Providence Society for abolishing the Slave-Trade, &c. At their Annual Meeting, on May 17, 1793* (Providence, R.I., 1793), 15.

11. Backus, *A Sermon, Preached in Long-Meadow*, 15–16. Here Backus cited Prov. 22:6, "Train up a child in the way he should go: and when he is old, he will not depart from it." On the issue of a decline in Sabbath observance, see Thomas Barnard, *A Sermon, Delivered at Salem, on March 31, 1796, the Day of General Fasting through the State of Massachusetts* (Newburyport, Mass., 1796), 13.

12. Backus, *A Sermon, Preached in Long-Meadow*, 19–20, 23. Nathanael Emmons of Franklin, Massachusetts, employed the same reasoning as Backus. "We have more reason than any other nation, to expect that our vices will speedily awaken the displeasure of the Almighty, and draw down his judgments upon us. Heaven has favoured us with great and distinguishing privileges. We have been indulged with more instructions and examples of virtue and religion, than any other nation on earth. . . . Add to all this, the great and marvellous deliverances, which God has, from age to age, and especially of late, granted to our nation. These will amazingly aggravate our guilt, if we forsake the author of our mercies and the God of our Fathers, and defile the land which he hath taken from the Heathens, and given to us" (*A Discourse, Delivered November 3, 1790*, 23). See also Wales, *Dangers of our national Prosperity*, 11–13.

13. Hopkins, *A Discourse upon the Slave-Trade*, 17–18.

14. Wales, *Dangers of our national Prosperity*, 10; Joseph Lathrop, *Christ's Warning to the Churches, to beware of False Prophets, who come as Wolves in Sheep's Clothing: And the Marks by which they are known: illustrated in Two Discourses* (Springfield, Mass., 1789), 4; Morrill, *Faith in Divine Providence*, 29. Likewise, a year earlier Charles Backus remarked, "Licentiousness in thinking, is a fruitful source of evils in the present day. Shameful abuses have been made of our rare opportunity, to push our enquiries into every subject with unreserved freedom." He elaborated, "Self-evident moral principles are treated as great uncertainties:— Attempts are made to take off the restraints of the self-denying lessons of Christianity; and infidelity lifts up it's [*sic*] head" (*A Sermon, Preached in Long-Meadow*, 11, 13). See also Emmons, *A Discourse, Delivered November 3, 1790*, 17–18.

15. Ammi R. Robbins, *The Empires and Dominions of this World, made subservient to the Kingdom of CHRIST; who ruleth over all. A Sermon, delivered in presence of His Excellency Samuel Huntington, Esq. L.L.D. Governor, And the Honorable the General Assembly of the State of Connecticut, Convened at Hartford, on the Day of the Anniversary Election. May 14th, 1789* (Hartford, Conn., 1789), 38. See also John Murray, *Jerubbaal, or Tyranny's Grove Destroyed, and the Altar of Liberty Finished. A Discourse on America's Duty and Danger, Delivered at the Presbyterian Church in Newbury-Port, December 11, 1783. On Occasion of the Public Thanksgiving for Peace* (Newbury-Port, Mass., 1784), 48–50, 55–56.

16. For example, in 1796 Thomas Barnard of Salem, Massachusetts, protested that "while there is great indifference to those excellent writings which establish the truth of Natural, and Revealed Religion upon an immoveable foundation; those treatises are read with great avidity which represent them as the whimsies of affrighted minds, or the fictions of politicians to keep mankind in awe" (*A Sermon, Delivered at Salem*, 17). See also John Mellen, *The Great and Happy Doctrine of Liberty. A Discourse, delivered at Hanover, Commonwealth of Massachusetts, February 19, 1795, on the day of Public Thanksgiving and Prayer, appointed by the President, to be observed throughout all the United States of America* (Boston, 1795), 32.

17. Emmons, *A Discourse, Delivered November 3, 1790*, 22. For a discussion of the Congregational clergy's understanding of the problem of virtue in terms of republicanism, upon

which this and the following paragraphs draw, see Nathan O. Hatch, *The Sacred Cause of Liberty: Republican Thought and the Millennium in Revolutionary New England* (New Haven: Yale University Press, 1977), 103–113. See also Mark A. Noll, "The American Revolution and Protestant Evangelicalism," *Journal of Interdisciplinary History* 23 (1993): 625–630; James M. Banner Jr., *To the Hartford Convention: The Federalists and the Origins of Party Politics in Massachusetts, 1789–1815* (New York: Knopf, 1970), 25–32.

18. Benjamin Hichborn, *An Oration, delivered July 5th, 1784 at the Request of the Inhabitants of the Town of Boston; in Celebration of the Anniversary of American Independence* (Boston, 1784), 19; Henry Cumings, *A Sermon Preached in Billerica, December 11, 1783, The Day recommended by Congress to All The States, To be observed as a Day of Public Thanksgiving, and Appointed to be observed accordingly, throughout The Commonwealth of Massachusetts, By the Authority of the same* (Boston, 1784), 35.

19. Ruth H. Bloch, *Visionary Republic: Millennial Themes in American Thought, 1756–1800* (New York: Cambridge University Press, 1985), 3–4, 109. As Bloch writes, p. 4, "The very words 'corruption,' 'virtue,' and 'vice,' which so infused radical whig rhetoric, were laden with religious connotations. Even the qualities thought to be inherent in the civic virtue of the body politic—self-sufficiency, industriousness, frugality, public responsibility—were cornerstones of the Puritan ethic."

20. Dwight, *True Means*, 13; Murray, *Jerubbaal*, 75. John Lathrop made an identical amalgamation of Christianity and virtue. "We must be *wise* and *virtuous*, we must be governed by that religion which we profess, we must be influenced by those doctrines which we say we believe, as we hope to be a happy people" (*A Discourse on the Peace; Preached on the day of Public Thanksgiving, November 25, 1784* [Boston, 1784], 30).

21. Osgood, *Reflections on the goodness of God*, 32. See also John Marsh, *A Discourse Delivered at Wethersfield, December 11th, 1783. Being a Day of Public Thanksgiving, Throughout the United States of America* (Hartford, Conn., 1784), 21; Henry Ware, *The Continuance of Peace and increasing Prosperity a Source of Consolation and just Cause of Gratitude to the Inhabitants of the United States. A Sermon, Delivered February 19, 1795; Being a Day Set Apart by The President, for Thanksgiving and Prayer through the United States* (Boston, 1795), 23–24.

22. Wales, *Dangers of our national Prosperity*, 25; Mark Valeri, "The New Divinity and the American Revolution," *WMQ* 46 (1989): 749–753, 759. William Symmes of Andover concurred with Wales in his Massachusetts election sermon of the same year: "the general prevalancy [*sic*] of vice in a nation has never failed sooner or later to involve it in national calamities and ruin." (*A Sermon, Preached Before His Honor Thomas Cushing, Esq; Lieutenant-Governor, The Honorable the Council, and the Two Branches of the General Court, of the Commonwealth of Massachusetts, May 25, 1785: Being the Anniversary of General Election* [Boston, 1785], 19). Those outside the realm of the establishment voiced this opinion as well. John Tyler, an Episcopal rector from Norwich, Connecticut, described the "natural" effects of virtue and vice: "The natural Effect or Tendency of sincere Religion, upon Nations, is, to make them industrious, frugal, healthy, rich, populous, public spirited, unanimous, and brave. . . . But the natural Tendency of Wickedness, is, to make them idle, dissipated, enfeebled; to impoverish, depopulate, to render them mean-spiritedly selfish, disunited, and dispirited; to make them impudent, injurious, unfriendly, and malevolent; to extinguish their Concern for the common Good. . . . And, in general, it seems scarce necessary for divine Providence to interpose, otherwise than by the original Constitution of Things, to exalt a People, of good Morals and sincere Piety, to a State of Prosperity, Peace, and Happiness; or to depress and chastise a vicious People; because it seems as though they would do this effectually themselves" (*The Blessing of Peace: A Sermon Preached at Norwich, on the Continental Thanksgiving, February 19, 1795* [Norwich, Conn., 1795], 12–13).

23. Jonathan Edwards Jr., *The Injustice and Impolicy of the Slave Trade, and of the Slav-*

ery of the Africans: Illustrated in a Sermon Preached before the Connecticut Society for the Promotion of Freedom, and for the Relief of Persons unlawfully holden in Bondage, At their annual
Meeting in New-Haven, September 15, 1791 (New Haven, Conn., 1791), 10–12; Theodore
Dwight, An Oration, spoken before "The Connecticut Society, for the Promotion of Freedom and
the Relief of Persons Unlawfully Holden in Bondage." Convened in Hartford, On the 8th day
of May, A.D. 1794 (Hartford, Conn., 1794), 14–16; John Chester Miller, The Wolf by the Ears:
Thomas Jefferson and Slavery (New York: Free Press, 1977; Charlottesville: University Press of
Virginia, 1991), 31–45. Theodore Dwight was a Hartford lawyer and brother of Timothy
Dwight; Drake, Dictionary of American Biography, 291. Because New Englanders attacked the
effects of slavery on its victims' morality, one objective of early antislavery societies was to in-
still virtue in emancipated slaves. See Hopkins, A Discourse upon the Slave-Trade, 20; The
Constitution of the Connecticut Society for the Promotion of Freedom, and the Relief of Persons
unlawfully holden in Bondage, as revised and enlarged on the 13th Day of September 1792 (New
Haven, Conn., 1792), 1.

24. Elizur Goodrich, The Principles of civil Union and Happiness considered and recommended. A Sermon, Preached before his Excellency Samuel Huntington, Esq. L.L.D. Governor
and Commander in Chief, and the Honorable the General Assembly of the State of Connecticut. Convened at Hartford, on the Day of the Anniversary Election, May 10th, 1787 (Hartford,
Conn., 1787), 17. As Hatch acknowledges, "they sought to build republican liberty upon a
foundation far more Hebraic and Puritan than classical and humanist" (Sacred Cause, 109).

25. Ezra Stiles, "The United States elevated to Glory and Honor. A Sermon, Preached before His Excellency Jonathan Trumbull, Esq. L.L.D. Governor and Commander in Chief,
And the Honorable The General Assembly of The State of Connecticut, Convened at Hartford, At the Anniversary Election, May 8th, 1783," in The Pulpit of the American Revolution: or,
the Political Sermons of the Period of 1776, ed. John Wingate Thornton (Boston, 1860),
502–503; Jonathan Edwards Jr., The Necessity of the Belief of Christianity by the Citizens of
the State, in order to our political Prosperity; Illustrated in a Sermon, Preached before His Excellency Samuel Huntington, Esq. L.L.D. Governor, and the Honorable the General Assembly
of the State of Connecticut, Convened at Hartford on the Day of the Anniversary Election. May
8th, 1794 (Hartford, Conn., 1794), 10, 15–16. Like Edwards, Charles Backus attacked merely
natural, deistic religion: "Amongst those who profess to believe the Bible, there are many in
this day, on both sides of the Atlantick, who are for reducing all its doctrines to a level with
the religion of nature. Publick discourses of this kind, are in reality nothing more than lectures
borrowed from Pagan moralists, christened in modern times. Many smart things, dignified by
the use of Scripture phrases, may be said, consistently with an undisturbed conscience. . . .
When the restraints of evangelical preaching are gone, we have the highest reason to fear, that
men[']s consciences will be hardened in sin, and that loose morals will prove the ruin of society" (A Sermon, Preached in Long-Meadow, 14–15). See also David Tappan, A Sermon
Preached before His Excellency John Hancock, Esq. Governour; His Honor Samuel Adams, Esq.
Lieutenant-Governour; the Honourable the Council, Senate, and House of Representatives, of
the Commonwealth of Massachusetts, May 30, 1792. Being the Day of General Election
(Boston, 1792), 9–10.

26. Nathan Strong, A Sermon, delivered in presence of His Excellency Samuel Huntington,
Esq. L.L.D. Governor, And the Honorable the General Assembly of the State of Connecticut,
Convened at Hartford, on the Day of the Anniversary Election. May 13th, 1790 (Hartford,
Conn., 1790), 13–14. See also Dwight, True Means, 6–11.

27. Edwards, Necessity of the Belief of Christianity, 7–8. In 1796, the ministerial association of Cambridge, Massachusetts, made the same argument: "Should the middling and lower
classes among a people abandon the principles of religion, and cease to fear God, there would
be no restraints, upon which we could depend, as effectual, for holding them back from the

greatest crimes, and thereby bringing the greatest miseries both upon themselves and their country. The best political constitutions, and the utmost vigor of human laws, would be found but feeble barriers against the ungovernable passions of multitudes of unprincipled men" (Cambridge Association, *To the Public. An Address from the Ministers of the Association in and about Cambridge, at their stated Meeting on the second Tuesday in October, 1796* [Boston, 1796]). See also Joseph McKeen, *A Sermon, Preached on the Public Fast in the Commonwealth of Massachusetts, April 11, 1793* (Salem, Mass., 1793), 15–18; Isaac Lewis, *The Political Advantages of Godliness. A Sermon, Preached before His Excellency the Governor, and the Honorable Legislature of the State of Connecticut, Convened at Hartford on the Anniversary Election. May 11, 1797* (Hartford, Conn., 1797), 22. See also Hatch, *Sacred Cause*, 110, where he writes, "it was asserted that nothing less than a belief in God's moral government and the approaching state of reward and punishment would effectively check the unruly passions of men."

28. Hart, *The Description of a GOOD CHARACTER*, 28; Robbins, *Empires and Dominions*, 16–17. Timothy Stone of Lebanon, Connecticut, also clearly explained why a converted Christian was most likely to be virtuous. "The holy religion of the Son of GOD, hath a most powerful and benign influence upon moral beings in society," he said. "It not only restrains malicious revengeful passions, and curbs unruly lusts; but will in event, eradicate them all from the human breast—it implants all the divine graces and social virtues in the heart—it sweetens the dispositions of men, and fits them for all the pleasing satisfactions, of rational friendship—teaches them self denial—inspires them with a generous public spirit—fills them with love to others, to righteousness and mercy—makes them careful to discharge the duties of their stations—diligent and contented in their callings" (*A Sermon, Preached before his Excellency Samuel Huntington, Esq. L.L.D. Governor, and the Honorable the General Assembly of the State of Connecticut, Convened at Hartford, on the Day of the Anniversary Election. May 10th, 1792* [Hartford, Conn., 1792], 22–23). See also Osgood, *Reflections on the goodness of God*, 33–34; West, *A Sermon, preached . . . May 31, 1786*, 12–14; Samuel Austin, *The Manner in Which the Gospel Should be Heard, and the Importance of Hearing it Rightly, Illustrated and Urged, in a Discourse, Preached by Samuel Austin, M.A. in Worcester, on the Lord's Day immediately succeeding his Installation, September 29th, MDCCXC* (Worcester, Mass., 1791), 20; Dwight, *True Means*, 12–22; Lathrop, *National Happiness, illustrated*, 14; Lewis, *Political Advantages of Godliness*, 18.

29. Josiah Whitney, *The essential requisites to form the good Ruler's Character, illustrated and urged. A Sermon, Preached in the Audience of His Excellency Samuel Huntington, Esq. L.L.D. Governor, and Commander in Chief; His Honor Oliver Wolcott, Esq. Lieutenant-Governor, and the Honourable the Counsellors and House of Representatives of the State of Connecticut, At Hartford, on the Day of the Anniversary Election, May 8th 1788* (Hartford, Conn., 1788), 23.

30. David Parsons, *A Sermon, Preached before His Excellency John Hancock, Esq. Governour; The Honourable the Council, And the Honourable the Senate, and House of Representatives, Of the Commonwealth of Massachusetts, May 28, 1788. Being the Day of General Election* (Boston, 1788). Proverbs 29:2 was also quoted in Stone, *A Sermon, Preached . . . May 10th, 1792*, 17; Andrew Lee, *The origin and ends of civil Government; with reflections on the distinguished happiness of the United States. A Sermon, Preached Before His Excellency Samuel Huntington, Esq. L.L.D. Governor, and the Honorable General Assembly of the State of Connecticut, at Hartford, on the Day of the Anniversary Election, May 14, 1795* (Hartford, Conn., 1795), 11.

31. Timothy Dwight, *Virtuous Rulers a National Blessing. A Sermon, Preached at the General Election, May 12th, 1791* (Hartford, Conn., 1791), 15. Similarly, in the 1785 Massachusetts election sermon, William Symmes called for Christian morality as the surest basis of a ruler's

virtue. "A submissive respect paid to all God's commandments, at the same time that it raises a ruler above the pursuits of injustice, and a faulty ambition, is perfectly consistent with the greatest degrees of political wisdom that are subservient to the honor, preservation and support of society" (*A Sermon, Preached . . . May 25, 1785,* 11).

32. Chandler Robbins, *A Sermon, Preached before His Excellency John Hancock, Esq. Governour; His Honor Samuel Adams Esq. Lieutenant-Governour; The Honourable the Council, and the Honourable the Senate and House of Representatives, of the Commonwealth of Massachusetts, May 25, 1791. Being the Day of General Election* (Boston, 1791), 22.

33. Huntington, *God ruling the Nations,* 24.

34. Scott, *From Office to Profession,* 1. The following section generally concurs with and builds on Hatch, *Sacred Cause,* 114–117, where he writes, (p. 115) "history and experience offered only one clear solution, a tight bond between the civil and sacred orders." See also Joseph W. Phillips, *Jedidiah Morse and New England Congregationalism* (New Brunswick, N.J.: Rutgers University Press, 1983), 62–64. The section also amplifies this brief sketch by Robert Kelley: "The Congregational New Englanders were sharply distinctive in their *moralistic* republicanism. Fervently religious, they believed church and state—as in their Puritan colonies—must work closely together to keep the community pure and godly. Government must be constantly active, supervising the people's public and private virtue. . . . This led to the conception of the new United States as a virtuous and God-fearing Christian Sparta, to use Sam Adams' terminology. Its citizens must learn to sacrifice their individual welfare to the needs of the whole community. In such a republic, the common people would choose and follow those godly leaders, generally of good family and suitable substance, who best exemplified God's elect. Despite the general aura of political radicalism that hung about them, Puritans had never been comfortable with democracy" (*The Cultural Pattern in American Politics: The First Century* [New York: Random House, 1979; Lanham, Md.: University Press of America, n.d.], 83).

35. Declared Enos Hitchcock, "If the means of education should be neglected, the rising generation would grow up uninformed and without principle; their ideas of freedom would degenerate into licentious independence; and they would fall a prey to their own animosities and contentions" (*A Discourse on Education, Delivered at the Meeting-House on the West Side of the River, in Providence, November 16, 1785* [Providence, R.I., 1785], 10); Samuel Langdon, *The Republic of the Israelites an Example to the American States. A Sermon, Preached at Concord, in the State of New-Hampshire; before the Honorable General Court at the Annual Election. June 5, 1788* (Exeter, N.H., 1788), 39. "There cannot be too much care and attention paid to the education of youth," warned David Osgood, "that their hands may be early inured to the practice of the useful arts of life, their minds furnished with useful knowledge, and their tempers formed to early habits of virtue and piety" (*Reflections on the goodness of God,* 33). See also Goodrich, *Principles of civil Union,* 16; William Emerson, *A Discourse, delivered in Harvard, July 4, 1794, at the Request of the Military Officers in that Place, Who, with the militia under their command, were then assembled to commemorate the Anniversary of the American Independence* (Boston, 1794), 10–12; Samuel Deane, *A Sermon, preached before His Honour Samuel Adams, Esq. Lieutenant Governor; the Honourable the Council, Senate, and House of Representatives of the Commonwealth of Massachusetts, May 28th, 1794. Being the Day of General Election* (Boston, 1794), 17; Dwight, *True Means,* 23; Ware, *Continuance of Peace,* 30. On Langdon's background, Drake, *Dictionary of American Biography,* 527.

36. Emmons, *A Discourse, Delivered November 3, 1790,* 20. See also Phillips, *Jedidiah Morse,* 63, who writes, "In keeping with traditional New England values, Congregational ministers assigned responsibility for implanting virtue in the people to the institutions of family and school as well as the church." Edmund S. Morgan, *The Puritan Family: Religion and Do-*

mestic Relations in Seventeenth-Century New England, rev. and enlarged ed. (1944; New York: Harper & Row, 1966), 87–108.

37. Tappan, *A Sermon Preached . . . May 30, 1792*, 19–20. Tappan was then pastor of Newbury, just prior to being made Harvard's Hollis Professor of Divinity. Isaac Lewis of Greenwich, Connecticut, issued a word of caution similar to Tappan's: "It is not however our wish that any thing similar to the religious establishments of Europe, should be introduced into our country. We hope never to see our magistrates employed, in prescribing articles of faith; nor in the exercise of the least coercive power to compel men to adopt this, or that creed, or submit to any one mode of worship in preference to another. May liberty of conscience, in this land, be never violated" (*Political Advantages of Godliness*, 27). See also Dwight, *Virtuous Rulers*, 18.

38. Huntington, *God ruling the Nations*, 35. David Parsons, the 1788 Massachusetts election preacher, employed the same metaphor. "God requires that [rulers] co-operate with him in his designs to effect the best interest of his people—that they should be hearty friends to religion—devout worshippers of God—afford protection and encouragement to his servants—that they should be patrons, and nursing Fathers to the church of Christ; and use their utmost endeavours to advance his kingdom" (*A Sermon, Preached . . . May 28, 1788*, 12). For other references to this text, see Foster, *A Sermon preached . . . May 26, 1790*, 33; Deane, *A Sermon, preached . . . May 28th, 1794*, 18; Lee, *The origin and ends of civil Government*, 16.

39. Tappan, *A Sermon Preached . . . May 30, 1792*, 7. Tappan also called for the cooperation of the civil and ecclesiastical leadership on the basis of tradition: "The same union of friendship, of counsel and exertion in the public cause, which characterized the Hebrew Lawgiver and High-Priest, distinguished the political and religious Fathers of Massachusetts." However, he did admit that because of "the complexion of the age" the founders of Massachusetts had "carried this union of Church and State, to an unwarrantable length" (ibid., 25).

40. John Marsh, *A Sermon, Preached before His Honor Oliver Wolcott, Esq. L.L.D. Lieutenant-Governor and Commander in Chief, and the Honorable the General Assembly of the State of Connecticut, Convened at Hartford, on the Day of the Anniversary Election, May 12th, 1796* (Hartford, Conn., 1796), 28. Ezra Stiles raised the same biblical type when he declared that "it would greatly conduce to [making Americans the happiest people on earth] if Moses and Aaron, if the magistracy and priesthood, should coöperate and walk together in union and harmony" ("United States elevated," 487).

41. Goodrich, *Principles of civil Union*, 46; Lee, *The origin and ends of civil Government*, 12. Nathanael Emmons added that, from studying the scriptures, the prophet Daniel would have learned that "the Church of God, [w]as the great object, to which all human governments ought to be subservient" (*A Sermon, Preached Before His Excellency Increase Sumner, Esq. Governor; His Honor Moses Gill, Esq. Lieutenant-Governor; The Honorable the Council, Senate, and House of Representatives, of the Commonwealth of Massachusetts, May 30, 1798. Being the Day of General Election* [Boston, 1798], 10).

42. Cyprian Strong, *The Kingdom Is the Lord's. A Sermon, Preached at Hartford, on the Day of the Anniversary Election, May 9, 1799* (Hartford, Conn., 1799), 14–15. Nathan Strong put the relationship similarly: "There is not an idea, in the world, more dangerous to society, or more debasing to civil government, than this, that it stands on a basis of human wisdom and will, apart from those great religious obligations, which direct the manner and duties of intercourse in all worlds." Government and religion, in his view, were mutually beneficial. "Tho a distinction is made in the state, between the civil and Ecclesiastical departments, neither of them is independent of the other. Civility and the good order of political regulations are a great advantage to religion; religion and its institutions are the best aid of government, by strengthening the ruler's hand, and making the subject faithful in his place, and obedient to the general laws" (*A Sermon, delivered . . . May 13th, 1790*, 8, 15).

43. Strong, *Kingdom Is the Lord's*, 40; Marsh, *A Sermon, Preached . . . May 12th, 1796*, 18, emphasis added.

44. Emmons, *A Sermon, Preached . . . May 30, 1798*, 22; Tappan, *A Sermon Preached . . . May 30, 1792*, 20. Chandler Robbins advised his 1791 election-day audience to set a good example, because of the "peculiar fondness in the lower orders of life, to copy after their superiors" (*A Sermon, Preached . . . May 25, 1791*, 23). John Marsh lauded the godly example set by Connecticut's chief magistrate: "By his public profession of religion, for many years, his steady attendance on the institutions of christianity, and his exemplary good conversation, GOVERNOR HUNTINGTON made it manifest to all, that he was not ashamed of the Gospel of CHRIST" (*A Sermon, Preached . . . May 12th, 1796*, 22). See also Symmes, *A Sermon, Preached . . . May 25, 1785*, 16; Whitney, *Essential requisites*, 18; Dwight, *Virtuous Rulers*, 24; Deane, *A Sermon, preached . . . May 28th, 1794*, 13; Lee, *The origin and ends of civil Government*, 15; Ware, *Continuance of Peace*, 24; Banner, *To the Hartford Convention*, 53–57.

45. Huntington, *God ruling the Nations*, 35; Parsons, *A Sermon, Preached . . . May 28, 1788*, 13. The text reads, "for he is the minister of God to thee for good. But if thou do that which is evil, be afraid; for he beareth not the sword in vain: for he is the minister of God, a revenger to execute wrath upon him that doeth evil." Nathanael Emmons, in addition to calling for a local society to check vice, implored the magistrates to do their duty using this same text. "We have strict and severe laws against profane swearing, sabbath-breaking, gaming, tavern-haunting, drunkenness, lewdness, and debauchery. But have these laws against these public and pernicious vices been duly executed? . . . Can those who wear the sword of justice, wear it in vain, and yet be blameless? Or can they answer for their negligence, before the Supreme Ruler, whose ministers they are, and before whom they have lifted up their hand to be faithful?" (*A Discourse, Delivered November 3, 1790*, 28–29).

46. Dwight, *Virtuous Rulers*, 18–19; Connecticut General Assembly, *At a General Assembly of the State of Connecticut, holden at New-Haven, on the second Thursday of October, A.D. 1798* (1798). Levi Hart called on Connecticut's rulers to combat "needless lawsuits, and"—this as early as 1786—"the intemperate use of strong drinks" (*The Description of a GOOD CHARACTER*, 24).

47. Stone, *A Sermon, Preached . . . May 10th, 1792*, 13. "The clergy continued a long-standing tradition of assigning the magistrate qualities of moral wisdom and disinterested oversight of the public good" (Hatch, *Sacred Cause*, 116).

48. Backus, *A Sermon, Preached in Long-Meadow*, 22–23. "To leave the paths of sin—to forsake the ways of the destroyer—to become friends to the LORD JESUS, and lovers of mankind," argued Ammi Robbins similarly, "this will secure the favor of GOD—will make us a happy people. This will make us good citizens and good subjects. . . . Then shall we strive together to promote the general good" (*Empires and Dominions*, 39). See also Hopkins, *A Discourse upon the Slave-Trade*, 18. For calls to repent based on the hope of salvation, not a threat of damnation, see Rozel Cook, *A Sermon, Delivered at New-London, North-Parish, Upon the Anniversary Thanksgiving, December 11, 1783* (New London, Conn., 1784), 26; Murray, *Jerubbaal*, 70.

49. Barnard, *A Sermon, Delivered at Salem*, 19. "Exert yourselves therefore, Ye Pious, by your instructions, your examples, your prayers, and strict family government! Exert yourselves, Ye Magistrates, to restrain vice, and bring on a desirable reformation! Exert yourselves ye ingenious and able Defenders of the Faith! Then we might expect God would hear us when we called upon him, and never leave nor forsake us" (ibid.).

50. Whitney, *Essential requisites*, 30–31. David Tappan's 1792 Massachusetts election sermon also described how the ministry would preach subordination: "He [the minister] studies that his whole deportment respecting the Rulers and the laws, may express and promote a spirit of decent subjection and obedience, and he enforces such submission by all the author-

ity and sanction of religion. . . . His public discourses too, all tend either directly or remotely, to form his hearers into good citizens and subjects, as well as holy christians" (*A Sermon Preached . . . May 30, 1792*, 24). As Hatch notes, "the pulpit echoed with Pauline texts" on the themes of submission and obedience (*Sacred Cause*, 114).

51. Lewis, *Political Advantages of Godliness*, 30; Dwight, *True Means*, 29.

52. Cambridge Association, *To the Public*. The Connecticut General Assembly similarly noted that the Sabbath laws were "wisely calculated to form the habits of virtue, to promote social order, and of consequence, to support our free and happy constitution of government" (*At a General Assembly of the State of Connecticut*).

53. Dwight, *Virtuous Rulers*, 6; Parsons, *A Sermon, Preached . . . May 28, 1788*, 5. See also Foster, *A Sermon preached . . . May 26, 1790*, 5; Tappan, *A Sermon Preached . . . May 30, 1792*, 7.

54. Edwards, *Injustice and Impolicy*, 3–4.

55. Moses Hemmenway, *A Sermon, Preached before His Excellency John Hancock, Esq; Governor; His Honor Thomas Cushing, Esq; Lieutenant-Governor; the Honorable the Council, and the Honorable the Senate, and House of Representatives, of the Commonwealth of Massachusetts, May 26, 1784. Being the Day of General Election* (Boston, 1784), 21–22; Parsons, *A Sermon, Preached . . . May 28, 1788*, 25. As John Mellen of Hanover, Massachusetts, phrased matters, "All rule and government supposes subordination and degrees of standing. There must be some to govern, and others to be governed—Some to command and some to obey—Some to be employed in one part of the administration, and some in another—Some in one kind of service of the commonwealth, and some in another. But [1 Cor. 12:20–21] yet they are all one body, and neither the head or eye can say to the hand or the foot, I have no need of thee" (*Great and Happy Doctrine*, 15). See also Robbins, *Empires and Dominions*, 13.

56. Hemmenway, *A Sermon, Preached . . . May 26, 1784*, 18–19; Whitney, *Essential requisites*, 24. For one egalitarian complaint, see Michael Merrill and Sean Wilentz, eds., *The Key of Liberty: The Life and Democratic Writings of William Manning, "A Laborer," 1747–1814*, John Harvard Library (Cambridge: Harvard University Press, 1993), 175.

57. Emmons, *A Sermon, Preached . . . May 30, 1798*, 9; Tappan, *A Sermon Preached . . . May 30, 1792*, 8–9; Whitney, *Essential requisites*, 15. According to Timothy Stone, "The interests of society are always important, they are many times involved in extreme difficulty, through the weakness of some, and the wickedness of others; and there is need of the most extensive knowledge, wisdom and prudence, to direct the various opposing interests of individuals into one channel, and guide them all to a single object, the public good" (*A Sermon, Preached . . . May 10th, 1792*, 14). On this theme, see also John Marsh: "The care of those things which respect the welfare of a great people requires the close and unintermitted attention of the civil ruler. To attend to their situation with regard to other powers—to provide for their defence against foreign invasion and internal sedition—to secure those advantages that may justly be derived from an intercourse with other nations—to attend to the internal state of the commonwealth—to its finances—to its agriculture—commerce—manufactures—morals—learning and religion; to make such alteration in the laws, or such new ones, as the varying circumstances of the country, state, towns and corporations, may render expedient, and take effectual care to have them executed, is a most laborious and difficult employment" (*A Sermon, Preached . . . May 12th, 1796*, 10). See also Hart, *The Description of a GOOD CHARACTER*, 16–17.

58. Strong, *A Sermon, delivered . . . May 13th, 1790*, 9. This idea of temptation is also found in Robbins, *A Sermon, Preached . . . May 25, 1791*, 22–23; Deane, *A Sermon, preached . . . May 28th, 1794*, 9–10.

59. William G. McLoughlin, *New England Dissent, 1630–1833: The Baptists and the Separation of Church and State*, 2 vols. (Cambridge: Harvard University Press, 1971), 1:387;

Lee, *The origin and ends of civil Government*, 16. Samuel West typified the established ministry's professed attachment to religious freedom when he said, "We wish not to see our civil rulers officially interfering in matters of religion. Sacred be the rights of conscience!" (*A Sermon, preached . . . May 31, 1786*, 27). Taken out of context, such pronouncements sound anti-establishment.

60. Symmes, *A Sermon, Preached . . . May 25, 1785*, 16; Hart, *The Description of a GOOD CHARACTER*, 23; Edwards, *Necessity of the Belief of Christianity*, 40. As William G. McLoughlin wrote, "The defense of Article Three, in other words, was prudential and utilitarian: the safety of the state and the security of private property required the state to utilize the supernatural power of religion, as embodied in the Protestant churches, to enforce good citizenship in a free republic. Religious taxes were 'the price of protection' of life, liberty, and property" (*New England Dissent*, 1:611). "Entering into society, we deposit our property, lives, friends and happiness, in the hand of the public; the public recommit this trust to the care of rulers, and give them a right and power to see it inviolably preserved," added Nathan Strong. "If religion and its institutions be the most certain means to preserve, is it not their duty to protect and encourage virtue and piety" (*A Sermon, delivered . . . May 13th, 1790*, 19)? See also Phillips, *Jedidiah Morse*, 63, who writes, "Congregational ministers . . . insisted that these laws [for the public support of the Congregational churches] were wise policy because they insured that there would always exist a pious, learned ministry to inculcate morality in the people. The work of the clergy was too socially important to depend on the vagaries of voluntary support."

61. "The question of support for religion was often compared to the responsibility of the state toward all institutions concerning the general welfare — the courts, the roads, the schools, the armed forces. . . . It was no more inconsistent in the minds of most New Englanders to require a general tax for the support of religion than to require, as Jefferson advocated, a general tax for the creation and maintenance of a public school system" (McLoughlin, *New England Dissent*, 1:610).

62. Langdon, *Republic of the Israelites*, 47; Deane, *A Sermon, preached . . . May 28th, 1794*, 18; McLoughlin, *New England Dissent*, 1:597. Andrew Lee employed the same basic language and reasoning as Langdon. "But while each one judgeth for himself respecting the nature of religion, it is of importance that public worship should be kept up, and it is the duty of all, according to their ability, to contribute to its support. . . . And though God is pleased to bless those means, and render them effectual to spiritual advantages, it is on political principles that such regulations call for the civil ruler's support. For order, harmony and general happiness have, from time immemorial, been found to be their fruits" (*The origin and ends of civil Government*, 17–18).

63. Tappan, *A Sermon Preached . . . May 30, 1792*, 15–16; Deane, *A Sermon, preached . . . May 28th, 1794*, 18–19.

64. Parsons, *A Sermon, Preached . . . May 28, 1788*, 13. Along the lines of Parsons's accusation, Noah Worcester, a Congregational minister from Thornton, New Hampshire, asked, "May not covetousness, with regard to supporting the gospel, account for some of the additions made to the baptist denomination? . . . And have not some baptist teachers embraced such characters, and furnished them with certificates, without any rational evidence, that those persons were governed by any thing better than a covetous or contentious spirit?" (*Impartial Inquiries, respecting the Progress of the Baptist Denomination* [Worcester, Mass., 1794], 17). Regarding Worcester's *Impartial Inquiries*, see also McLoughlin, *New England Dissent*, 2:699–700.

65. Worcester, *Impartial Inquiries*, 19; West quoted in McLoughlin, *New England Dissent*, 1:624.

66. Symmes, *A Sermon, Preached . . . May 25, 1785*, 16. Nathan Strong argued too that religious liberty certainly did not have to be absolutely protected. "But while we speak of a lib-

eral spirit, let not immorality and irreligion think they have a right to our tenderness. Liberality is a divine affection of the heart, a love of the truth and of men, and cannot be pleased with vice. . . . If there be who speak with lightness of a most perfect and glorious providence; if there be, who think they may treat the religion of their brethren with lightness; if there be a few, either so odd or weak in their way of thinking, as not to see in our sacred books, truths most favorable to society, and a most glorious description of the Almighty, his justice and goodness; if there be, who live wicked and immoral lives, they ought not to think it consistent either with the dignity or safety of the state to protect their sins" (*A Sermon, delivered . . . May 13th, 1790*, 21–22). See also Robbins, *A Sermon, Preached . . . May 25, 1791*, 37–38.

67. Lathrop, *Christ's Warning*, 11, 6, 27. See also Nathan Williams, *Order and Harmony in the Churches of Christ, agreeable to GOD's Will. Illustrated in a Sermon, Delivered in Tolland, on the Public Fast, April 17th, 1793* (Hartford, Conn., 1793), 15. The Methodist itinerant, Jesse Lee, had a typical encounter with the standing order in the person of Newburyport's John Murray. Murray refused Lee his pulpit in 1790 not only on the grounds of Lee's Wesleyan theology but also on account of the fact that Lee seemed to run roughshod over any and all parish boundaries. See Leroy M. Lee, *The Life and Times of the Rev. Jesse Lee* (Richmond, Va., 1848), 245.

68. Cambridge Association, *To the Public*.

69. Symmes, *A Sermon, Preached . . . May 25, 1785*, 16. The same point is found in Lewis, *Political Advantages of Godliness*, 27–28.

70. Tappan, *A Sermon Preached . . . May 30, 1792*, 23. See also McLoughlin, *New England Dissent*, 1:621–622. Like Tappan, Henry Channing of New London, Connecticut, also denied that New England had an established religion: "We cannot but be deeply sensible to our inestimable privileges, in the enjoyment of religious liberty, and the security of the rights of conscience. —Here the members of every religious denomination, while they do not disturb the peace of the community, nor infringe upon the rights of others, are equally under the protection of the laws. No one is suffered to *dictate* articles of faith to another; or controul [*sic*] his conscience in the worship of God" (*The Consideration of divine Goodness an argument for religious gratitude and obedience. A Sermon, Delivered at New-London, November 27, 1794. Being the day appointed by Authority, For public Thanksgiving in the State of Connecticut* [New-London, Conn., 1794], 22–23).

71. Jon Butler has pointed out the common ground between evangelicals of different denominations, as opposed to religious liberals, on issues of social morality: "An Enlightenment writer like New York's William Livingston (a nominal Presbyterian) was more likely to describe religion as an individual and personal matter beyond the government's interest, while evangelicals evidenced more concern for linkages among piety, morality, and society" ("Coercion, Miracle, Reason: Rethinking the American Religious Experience in the Revolutionary Age," in *Religion in a Revolutionary Age*, ed. Ronald Hoffman and Peter J. Albert [Charlottesville: University Press of Virginia, 1994], 23).

72. Warren Association of Baptists, *Minutes of the Warren Association, At their annual Convention, held at Mr. Williams's Meeting-House, in Wrentham, 1785* (Boston, 1785), 5, 7–8; Samuel Stillman, *An Oration, Delivered July 4th, 1789, at the Request of the Inhabitants of the Town of Boston, in Celebration of the Anniversary of American Independence* (Boston, 1789), 25–27; Jonathan Maxcy, *An Oration, Delivered in the Baptist Meeting-House in Providence, July 4, A.D. 1795, at the Celebration of the Nineteenth Anniversary of American Independence* (Providence, R.I., 1795), 18. Wrote Baldwin, "As a nation we form a particular character, in distinction from that of individuals. As such, we may exhibit the amiable features of virtue and religion; or the base picture of vice and infidelity. In this character we may receive temporal blessings, as the fruits and reward of virtue, and also suffer national calamities as the punishment of our vice and impiety" (*A Sermon, delivered February 19, 1795: being the day of Public*

Thanksgiving throughout the United States [Boston, 1795], 6). Baldwin's appears to be an anomalous text. Most Baptists took a more localist stance, leaving such statements of corporate unity to the Congregationalists.

73. McLoughlin, *New England Dissent*, 1:605. For more on the Baptists and morality, see ibid., 2:751–761.

74. Jonathan Maxcy, *An Oration, delivered in the First Congregational Meeting-House, in Providence, on the Fourth of July, 1799* (Providence, R.I., 1799), 5; Samuel Stillman, *A Sermon, Preached at Boston, April 25, 1799; the Day Recommended by the President of the United States for a National Fast* (Boston, 1799).

75. Warren Association of Baptists, *Minutes of the Warren Association, at their Meeting, in Middleboro', Sept. 7 and 8, 1784* (n.p.: 1784), 7. The same point is made in Warren Association of Baptists, *Minutes of the Warren Association, held at the Baptist Meeting-House in Harvard. M,DCC,XCII* (Boston, 1792), 10. Defending the faith of the saints (against Unitarianism) became a leading cause of Lyman Beecher; see *The Faith Once Delivered to the Saints. A Sermon, delivered at Worcester, Mass. Oct. 15, 1823, at the Ordination of the Rev. Loammi Ives Hoadly, to the Pastoral Office over the Calvinistic Church and Society in that Place* (Boston, 1823).

76. Samuel Seabury, *A Sermon delivered before the Boston Episcopal Charitable Society, in Trinity Church; at their Anniversary Meeting on Easter Tuesday March 25, 1788* (Boston, 1788), 2; Nelson Rollin Burr, *The Story of the Diocese of Connecticut: A New Branch of the Vine* (Hartford, Conn.: Church Missions Publishing Co., 1962), 119, 439–444; McLoughlin, *New England Dissent*, 2:1026; Samuel Parker, *A Sermon, preached before His Honor the Lieutenant-Governor, the Honorable the Council, and the Honorable the Senate, and House of Representatives, of the Commonwealth of Massachusetts, May 29, 1793; being the day of General Election* (Boston, 1793), 11; Tyler, *Blessing of Peace*, 8–9; John Murray, *The Substance of a Thanksgiving Sermon, Delivered at the Universal Meeting-House, in Boston, February 19, 1795* (Boston, 1795), 16–18, 22.

77. John L. Brooke, *The Heart of the Commonwealth: Society and Political Culture in Worcester County, Massachusetts, 1713–1861* (New York: Cambridge University Press, 1989; Amherst: University of Massachusetts Press, 1992), 81–83, 158–188, quote on 81; Warren Association, *Minutes . . . 1784*, 4; Isaac Backus, "An Appeal to the Public for Religious Liberty, Against the Oppressions of the present Day," in *Isaac Backus on Church, State, and Calvinism*, ed. William G. McLoughlin, John Harvard Library (Cambridge: Harvard University Press, Belknap Press, 1968), 339; Maxcy, *An Oration, Delivered . . . July 4, A.D. 1795*, 17. Backus's *Appeal* was originally published in 1773; according to William G. McLoughlin, it "was the most complete and well-rounded exposition of the Baptist principles of church and state in the eighteenth century" ("Introduction," in *Isaac Backus on Church, State, and Calvinism*, 41–42).

78. John Leland, "The Rights of Conscience Inalienable, and, therefore, Religious Opinions not Cognizable by Law; or, the High-Flying Churchman, Stripped of his Legal Robe, Appears a Yaho," in *The Writings of the Late Elder John Leland, including some Events in his Life, written by himself, with Additional Sketches, &c*, ed. L. F. Greene (1845; reprint, New York: Arno Press and the New York Times, 1969), 181–182, 185–186. *The Rights of Conscience Inalienable* was first printed in New London, Connecticut, in 1791. See also Nathan O. Hatch, *The Democratization of American Christianity* (New Haven: Yale University Press, 1989), 96–101; Lyman H. Butterfield, "Elder John Leland, Jeffersonian Itinerant," *Proceedings of the American Antiquarian Society* 62 (1952): 155–242; McLoughlin, *New England Dissent*, 2:928–935. It should be noted that McLoughlin (p. 929) emphasized the atypicality of Leland's position: "Leland was considered a scandal within the denomination both for the eccentricity of his language and for his behavior. He was admired as a dedicated preacher and

opponent of religious tyranny, but his views on theology, church discipline, Baptist institutional aims, and church-state relations were often deplored by his brethren. His years in Virginia had put him out of touch with most of his New England brethren. . . . However much of a hero he was to Virginians and to his local partisans in western Massachusetts, he was a distinct embarrassment to most of the denominational leaders in New England."

79. "About twelve months ago as he [the author] was enusing [?] upon the great outcry in the world, with respect to Monarchy and Republicanism; he felt determined in himself, to give these two terms, a thorough investigation. When he had done this he compared them together to see how they would agree, and being satisfied in this this [*sic*] point he compared both with scripture, and compared a multitude of scripture passages, together. He then consulted the general good of mankind so far as abilities and circumstances would allow and also turned his thoughts to the situation of things in Church and State, as they had been managed in times past, and as they then stood in many nations in the world, so far as he had any knowledge of them. Then turning his attention to the present movement of things in a Revolutionary line, and comparing the whole together he came at length to this conclusion that there was a necessity of a universal revolution or a disappointment of scripture prophecy" (Elias Lee, *The Dissolution of Earthly Monarchies; the Downfall of Antichrist; and the Full Display of Zion's King. A Sermon, Delivered to the Baptist Church in Ridgfield, March 1, 1794* [Danbury, Conn.: 1794], preface).

80. Ibid., 8, 14, 25, 16. See also Bloch, *Visionary Republic*, 156–157.

81. Stillman, *A Sermon, Preached . . . April 25, 1799*, 19, 21.

82. McLoughlin, "Introduction," in *Isaac Backus on Church, State, and Calvinism*, 17–18.

83. "From Calvin the Puritans inherited an understanding of the church that made it both kingdom of the godly and comprehensive means of grace" (David D. Hall, *The Faithful Shepherd: A History of the New England Ministry in the Seventeenth Century* [Chapel Hill: University of North Carolina Press, 1972], 23). At least that was the *original* justification for the tax-supported establishment, but the New Divinity theologians were moving away from it in their campaign against the half-way covenant. See Valeri, "New Divinity," 751.

84. Isaac Backus, *The Kingdom of God, Described by His Word, with its Infinite Benefits to Human Society* (Boston, 1792), 20; Warren Association of Baptists, *Minutes of the Warren Association, at their Annual Convention, Held at Mr. Blood's Meeting-House, In Newton, 1786* (Charlestown, Mass., 1786), 7; Isaac Backus, *Godliness Excludes Slavery* (Boston, 1785), 3–4. "No national church," wrote John Leland in 1790, "can in its organization, be the Gospel Church. A national church takes in the whole nation, and no more; whereas, the Gospel Church, takes in no nation, but those who fear God, and work righteousness in every nation. The notion of a Christian commonwealth, should be exploded forever" (Leland, quoted in Butterfield, "Elder John Leland," 163).

85. Warren Association of Baptists, *Minutes of the Warren Association, held at the Baptist Meeting-House in New-Rowley, MDCCXCI* (Boston, 1791), 10; Backus, "An Appeal to the Public," in *Isaac Backus on Church, State, and Calvinism*, 315; Niebuhr, *Christ and Culture*, 66–67. See also Noll, *One Nation under God?* 27–28.

86. Jeremiah Leaming, *Dissertations upon Various Subjects, which may be well worth the Attention of every Christian; and of Real service to the sincere Inquirer after true Religion* (New-Haven, Conn., 1788), 6–11, 13; Burr, *Diocese of Connecticut*, 121–122; Noll, *One Nation under God?* 20–22, 26–27.

87. Simon Hough, *An Alarm to the World: Dedicated to All Ranks of Men; by a professed Friend to all Mankind—begging they would prepare for Christ's second coming, which is near, even at the doors* (Stockbridge, Mass., 1792), 6, 8; Bloch, *Visionary Republic*, 138; Leland, "Rights of Conscience Inalienable," in *Writings of the Late Elder John Leland*, 185.

88. That New England's Congregational clergy reacted with fear and hostility is a familiar story. This section draws on the overlapping, if sometimes jostling, insights of Gary B. Nash, "The American Clergy and the French Revolution," *WMQ* 22 (1965): 392–412; Hatch, *Sacred Cause*, 99–102, 120–138; Phillips, *Jedidiah Morse*, 39–84.

89. Initially, most New Englanders greeted the French Revolution with optimism. In 1792, for example, David Tappan contended that "the new world [already has] diffused the light and warmth of freedom across the Atlantic, into the old; which has given birth to a surprising and glorious revolution." "Let us especially labour and pray," he continued favorably, "that these political struggles and changes, may, under the divine agency, introduce new and brighter scenes of christian knowledge and piety, till the whole world shall be covered with divine glory and human bliss" (*A Sermon Preached . . . May 30, 1792*, 38–39). As late as July 4, 1794, Joseph Lathrop still equated the American and French Revolutions as struggles for "the common rights of mankind" (*The Happiness of a Free Government, and the Means of Preserving it: Illustrated in a Sermon, delivered in West-Springfield, On July 4th, 1794, in Commemoration of American Independence!* [Springfield, Mass., 1794], 14). However, ministers would soon do all they could to distinguish between the two. See also Phillips, *Jedidiah Morse*, 42–44; Banner, *To the Hartford Convention*, 17–18.

90. Noah Webster, *The Revolution in France, considered in respect to its Progress and Effects* (New York, 1794), 8, 19–20, 32, 4, 41–42, 71.

91. Phillips, *Jedidiah Morse*, 50. Adding to the sermon's significance, Hatch notes that it "ran through six pamphlet editions" (*Sacred Cause*, 127, n. 90).

92. David Osgood, *The Wonderful Works of GOD are to be remembered. A Sermon, delivered on the Day of the Annual Thanksgiving, November 20, 1794* (Boston, 1794), 16–20, 26–29.

93. James Sullivan, *The Altar of Baal Thrown Down: or, the French Nation Defended, against the Pulpit Slander of David Osgood, A.M. Pastor of the Church in Medford* (Boston, 1795), 7, 30. For Sullivan's background, see Ronald P. Formisano, *The Transformation of Political Culture: Massachusetts Parties 1790s–1840s* (New York: Oxford University Press, 1983), 68–72. Phillips, *Jedidiah Morse*, 51, also discusses criticism of Osgood in the pages of Boston's *Independent Chronicle*.

94. Azel Backus, *Absalom's Conspiracy: A Sermon, Preached at the General Election, at Hartford in the State of Connecticut, May 10th, 1798* (Hartford, Conn., 1798), 41.

95. Ibid., 5; John Prince, *A Discourse, Delivered at Salem, on the Day of the National Fast, May 9, 1798; appointed by President Adams, On account of the difficulties subsisting between the United States and France* (Salem, Mass., 1798), 28; Joseph Eckley, *A Discourse, delivered on the Public Thanksgiving Day, November 29, 1798* (Boston, 1798), 17; Jedidiah Morse, *A Sermon, Exhibiting the Present Dangers, and Consequent Duties of the Citizens of the United States of America. Delivered at Charlestown, April 25, 1799. The Day of the National Fast* (Charlestown, Mass., 1799), 12.

96. Nathanael Emmons, *A Discourse, Delivered on the National Fast, April 25, 1799* (Wrentham, Mass., 1799), 23; Backus, *Absalom's Conspiracy*, 24. Like Emmons and Backus, Jonathan French, minister of the South Church in Andover, Massachusetts, prayed for protection from "the men of treachery, slander and falsehood, of our own nation, who have been so busily employed in fomenting difficulties and divisions among ourselves; who, by wicked artifice, falshood [*sic*] and misrepresentation, have left no stone unturned, to bring us under foreign influence" (*A Sermon, Delivered on the Anniversary Thanksgiving November 29, 1798* [Andover, Mass., 1799], 23). On the pervasiveness of such conspiratorial reasoning in eighteenth-century thought, see Gordon S. Wood, "Conspiracy and the Paranoid Style: Causality and Deceit in the Eighteenth Century," *WMQ* 39 (1982): 401–441. In a further illustration of the way in which the standing order denied legitimacy to political dissenters, Samuel Austin of Worcester, Massachusetts, hoped that his preaching could contribute "to the convalescence

of any individual . . . from a political paroxysm" (*An Oration, Pronounced at Worcester, on the Fourth of July, 1798; the Anniversary of the Independence of the United States of America* [Worcester, Mass., 1798], 2).

97. *An Address, From the Convention of Congregational Ministers in the Commonwealth of Massachusetts, to their Christian Brethren of the several* Associations, *and others not associated throughout this State* (Boston, 1799); Warren Association of Baptists, *Minutes of the Warren Association, held at the First Baptist Meeting-House in Boston, September 12 and 13, 1797* (Boston, 1797), 8. Likewise, in 1799, Jonathan Maxcy declared that "efforts have been made to discredit the doctrines of natural and revealed religion. Hence it is, that cargoes of infidelity have been imported into our country, and industriously circulated to corrupt the minds and morals of the rising generation. . . . Let us then guard with the utmost vigilance against those domineering, abandoned and arrogant philosophists, who consider themselves as the asylums of wisdom, and the oracles of truth; who assert that there is no standard of moral rectitude; and are striving to persuade man, that to be perfect, he needs only forget every thing exterior to himself" (*An Oration, delivered . . . on the Fourth of July, 1799,* 14).

98. Eckley, *A Discourse, delivered . . . November 29, 1798,* 12; Emmons, *A Sermon, Preached . . . May 30, 1798,* 25. See also Nathan Strong, *Political Instruction From the Prophecies of God's Word. A Sermon, Preached on the State Thanksgiving, November 29, 1798,* reprinted ed. (New York, 1799), 20–21.

99. French, *A Sermon, Delivered . . . November 29, 1798,* 28–29. For a similar analysis, see David Osgood, *The Devil Let Loose, or The Wo [sic] occasioned to the Inhabitants of the Earth by his wrathful Appearance among them, illustrated in a Discourse delivered on the Day of the National Fast, April 25, 1799* (Boston, 1799), 9–13.

100. Bloch, *Visionary Republic,* 53–87; Patricia U. Bonomi, *Under the Cope of Heaven: Religion, Society, and Politics in Colonial America* (New York: Oxford University Press, 1986), 187–216. "To the Federalist mind," writes Nathan Hatch, "the plot by the Bavarian Illuminati was generated by the same two-pronged attack against liberty—civil and religious—which had been responsible for the simultaneous schemes of the Quebec Act and the tax on tea" (*Sacred Cause,* 131).

101. Prince, *A Discourse, Delivered at Salem,* 14. See also Backus, *Absalom's Conspiracy,* 45–46.

102. Morse, *A Sermon, Exhibiting the Present Dangers,* 7, 10–11. A 1798 proclamation of the Connecticut General Assembly presented a similar analysis. The "anarchy and despotism" in France resulted from "a corruption of the christian religion, and has been consummated by infidelity, atheism, and the total abolition of the Sabbath, and of such other institutions as serve to maintain the belief of a God, and obedience to his laws" (*At a General Assembly of the State of Connecticut*). A Baptist, Jonathan Maxcy, agreed. "The enemies of our own and of all other established governments, in order to give complete success to their schemes of destruction, have attempted to exterminate all religious and moral principles. They well knew, that if men would not fear and obey the Supreme Being, they would not any subordinate being" (*An Oration, delivered . . . on the Fourth of July, 1799,* 14).

103. Austin, *An Oration . . . on the Fourth of July, 1798,* 14–15. See also Lewis, *Political Advantages of Godliness,* 28–29.

104. Nathan Strong thought that "there is but a little period to come compared with the past" before the end times commenced (*Political Instruction,* 6). See also Osgood, *The Devil Let Loose,* 13–14; Timothy Dwight, *The Duty of Americans, at the Present Crisis, Illustrated in a Discourse, Preached on the Fourth of July, 1798* (New Haven, Conn., 1798), 7–8, 30–31.

105. Bloch, *Visionary Republic,* 203–205; Phillips, *Jedidiah Morse,* 74–84. For the full account of the Illuminati scare, see Vernon Stauffer, *New England and the Bavarian Illuminati,*

Studies in History, Economics, and Public Law, 82, no. 1 (1918; reprint, New York: Russell & Russell, 1967).

106. French, *A Sermon, Delivered . . . November 29, 1798*, 24. According to Elijah Parish of Byfield, Massachusetts, the Illuminati "taught that conjugal faithfulness, chastity and all the moral virtues, were mere prejudices of education; that modesty was refined voluptuousness; that self-murder was no crime; that the possession of property infringed on human rights, that the motive justifies the means; that civil government is the only fall of man; that there is no future state — no God." He continued, "These dens of impiety [the lodges of the Illuminati] vomit forth their contents, and in one day a million of men start up in arms to overturn altars and thrones, to destroy government and religion" (*An Oration Delivered at Byfield July 4, 1799* [Newburyport, Mass., 1799], 8–9). For a fuller discussion of the Illuminati's origins and tenets, see Dwight, *Duty of Americans*, 10–13. As Robert Kelley noted, "Moralists were convinced that American civilization was disintegrating sexually, ethically, and politically" (*Cultural Pattern*, 121).

107. Morse, *A Sermon, Exhibiting the Present Dangers*, 15–17, quote on 17.

108. Joseph Goffe, Diary, 3 and 5 Nov. 1798, 9 Aug. 1799, Joseph Goffe Papers, 1721–1846, AAS. Two of the books he referred to were John Robison, *Proofs of a Conspiracy against all the Religions and Governments of Europe, carried on in the secret meetings of Free Masons, Illuminati, and Reading Societies*, 3d ed. (Philadelphia, 1798), and [Augustin de Barruel], *Memoirs, illustrating the History of Jacobinism. A Translation from the French of the Abbe Barruel*, vol. 1, *The Antichristian Conspiracy* (Hartford, Conn., 1799).

109. Goffe, Diary, 9 May 1798, 25 April 1799, and 15 Jan. 1797.

110. Nathan Strong, *A Sermon, Preached at the Annual Thanksgiving, November 16th, 1797* (Hartford, Conn., 1797), 14; Eckley, *A Discourse, delivered . . . November 29, 1798*, 20. Samuel Austin made the same point as Strong. "Does it not behove us," he asked, "and especially at this crisis, when the spirit of intrigue is so insinuating, when faction is so daring, and convulsions are so frequent, to extend the eye of the most unremitted vigilance, over our established, and fortunate Constitution of Government?" (*An Oration . . . on the Fourth of July, 1798*, 29). "Suspect not an Adams, or Washington," admonished Elijah Parish, "but those, who blaspheme their unspotted virtues. To be jealous of your Rulers would be, as if a person were to choose him a bride from all the beauties of the world, and then, instantly, without cause, be jealous of her alone" (*An Oration Delivered at Byfield*, 15). As John Prince also concluded, "Let us avoid all party spirit and contention; treat each other with mildness in the discussion of political opinions, and our rulers with respect; and be of one mind with regard to our government, THAT WE WILL OPPOSE ALL FOREIGN INFLUENCE AND INNOVATION IN IT" (*A Discourse, Delivered at Salem*, 43). Finally, Nathanael Emmons advised his listeners to "speak well of their [rulers'] characters and duly appreciate their late noble and spirited measures. Reflect upon the plain and obvious reasons, upon which the Sedition and Alien Laws are founded, and upon the urgent necessity of heavy taxes for the public defence" (*A Discourse, Delivered . . . April 25, 1799*, 30). See also Cyprian Strong, *A Discourse, Delivered at Hebron, at the Celebration of the Anniversary of American Independence, July 4th, 1799* (Hartford, Conn., 1799), 17–18.

111. The president gave "sincere and hearty thanks to the Great Ruler of Nations" for America's governments, "which unite and by their union establish liberty with order," for the defeat of the Whiskey Rebellion and avoidance of the European war, and for prosperity (James D. Richardson, ed., *A Compilation of the Messages and Papers of the Presidents*, 10 vols. [New York: Bureau of National Literature, 1911], 1:171–172). For more on that day's sermons, see Phillips, *Jedidiah Morse*, 52–55; David Waldstreicher, *In the Midst of Perpetual Fetes: The Making of American Nationalism, 1776–1820* (Chapel Hill: University of North Carolina Press, 1997), 145–152. The sermons of both Jedidiah Morse and his future theological antagonist Henry Ware, to cite an interesting example, toed the administration line, praising the sta-

tus quo. Morse described Washington as America's "venerable political Leader and Father — who, in respect to his talents as a general in war, and a chief Magistrate in civil affairs — his success in exercising these talents — his prudence, sagacity, and paternal care, vigilance and so- licitude for the safety, peace and happiness of the people, and his possessing their entire con- fidence and esteem, may with singular propriety be compared to Moses" (*The present Situa- tion of other Nations of the World, contrasted with our own. A Sermon, delivered at Charlestown, in the Commonwealth of Massachusetts, February 19, 1795; being the day recom- mended by George Washington, President of the United States of America, for Publick Thanks- giving and Prayer* [Boston, 1795], 7). See also Ware, *Continuance of Peace.*

112. These were the chosen texts, respectively, of Emmons, *A Discourse, Delivered . . . April 25, 1799,* and Prince, *A Discourse, Delivered at Salem.* Emmons quote on p. 21.

113. John Lathrop, *Patriotism and Religion. A Sermon, Preached on the 25th of April, 1799, the Day Recommended by the President of the United States, to be Observed as a National Fast* (Boston, 1799), 8; Phillips, *Jedidiah Morse,* 50. Lathrop's Boston neighbor, Joseph Eckley, also made the case for Christian patriotism, because, he reasoned, "from the constant lectures de- livered by this Divine Teacher, on the subject of *Philanthropy,* the sincere attachment to the political, as well as moral advantages of the nation in which we live, is fully to be inferred as a necessary appendage to the true Christian's virtue" (*A Discourse, delivered . . . November 29, 1798,* 6).

114. Strong, *A Sermon, Preached . . . November 16th, 1797,* 13; Prince, *A Discourse, Deliv- ered at Salem,* 34. See also Strong, *Political Instruction,* 14; Emmons, *A Discourse, Delivered . . . April 25, 1799,* 27–28; *An Address, From the Convention of Congregational Ministers,* 1–2.

115. Dwight, *Duty of Americans,* 15, 18. Samuel Austin, too, said that it was time for Chris- tian virtue to come to the fore. "Let us feel the importance of a deep respect for the infinite moral Governor of the world; cultivate an unalterable reverence for the institutions of his wor- ship; and adopt, in our practice, that virtue, which the laws of the universe prescribe; giving full credence to the maxim of wisdom, that 'Righteousness exalteth a nation; but, that sin is the reproach of any people'" (*An Oration . . . on the Fourth of July, 1798,* 37). See also Eckley, *A Discourse, delivered . . . November 29, 1798,* 17–20. The somewhat uncharacteristic thing about Dwight's plan of action, however, was that it eschewed hierarchy, instead calling on everyone to play a role: "Few persons can be concerned in settling systems of faith, moulding forms of government, regulating nations, or establishing empires. But almost all can train up a family for God, instill piety, justice, kindness and truth, distribute peace and comfort around a neighborhood, receive the poor and the outcast into their houses, tend the bed of sickness, pour balm into the wounds of pain, and awaken a smile in the aspect of sorrow. . . . When an- gels became the visitors, and the guests, of Abraham, he was a simple husbandman" (*Duty of Americans,* 17).

116. As Cyprian Strong concluded, "Let *infidelity* and modern *liberality* find no counte- nance, nor have any hand in the administration of government. Avoid them, as you would avoid that plague, which has already interrupted the *peace* — unhinged the *government* — de- stroyed the *order* — and *bathed* the plains of almost all Europe with *human blood*" (*A Dis- course, Delivered . . . July 4th, 1799,* 45). For instances of the invocation of Rev. 18:4, see Dwight, *Duty of Americans,* 19–22; *An Address, From the Convention of Congregational Min- isters,* 3; Morse, *A Sermon, Exhibiting the Present Dangers,* 31.

117. Strong, *Political Instruction,* 5, 22; Parish, *An Oration Delivered at Byfield,* 13.

118. Timothy Stone said, for instance, in his 1792 election sermon, that "changes [in the laws] however, should be few as possible; for the strength and reputation of government, doth not a little depend upon the uniformity and stability observed in its administration" (*A Sermon, Preached . . . May 10th, 1792,* 12). In 1787, Elizur Goodrich voiced the same idea in *Principles of civil Union,* 16.

119. Backus, *Absalom's Conspiracy*, 33; David Daggett, *Sun-Beams may be extracted from Cucumbers, but the process is tedious. An Oration, Pronounced on the Fourth of July, 1799. At the Request of the Citizens of New-Haven* (New-Haven, Conn., 1799), 5–11, 15, 24–25, 27. Likewise, Noah Webster concluded, "Never, my fellow citizens, let us exchange our civil and religious institutions for the wild theories of crazy projectors; or the sober, industrious moral habits of our country, for experiments in atheism and lawless democracy. *Experience* is a safe pilot; but *experiment* is a dangerous ocean, full of rocks and shoals" (*An Oration pronounced before the Citizens of New-Haven on the Anniversary of the Independence of the United States, July 4th, 1798; and published at their request!* [New Haven, Conn., 1798], 15).

120. Dwight, *Duty of Americans*, 29–30.

121. Strong, *A Sermon, Preached . . . November 16th, 1797*, 13; idem, *Political Instruction*, 3–4. David Osgood, too, expressed confidence in the fate of the church: "It appears, that during these troublesome times, amidst the wreck of all temporal interests, and the constant jeopardy of life—to them who [Isa. 26:9-10] *learn righteousness, while these judgments are abroad in the earth*, an asylum will be presented. For the lovers of order and peace, while the deluge of ruin is rising and extending, an ark of safety is provided. By laying hold on the gospel hope, and seeking refuge in this strong hold, their most important interests will be effectually secured" (*The Devil Let Loose*, 15). Even some Baptists joined in this analysis. Amidst the "tumultuous commotions of the world" of the late 1790s, the Warren Association assured the readers of its circular letter that Christ's church would prevail. "The same kind Providence which has watched over and protected the church of Christ hitherto, has said, [Heb. 13:5] 'I will never leave nor forsake you.' The people of God, amidst all these varied and trying events, rest assured, that under the wise and perfect administration of the moral government of God, all will be favourable in the issue" (*Minutes . . . 1797*, 8, 10).

122. Morse, *A Sermon, Exhibiting the Present Dangers*, 27; Strong, *Kingdom Is the Lord's*, 31–32.

123. Eckley, *A Discourse, delivered . . . November 29, 1798*, 21.

Chapter Three

1. Abiel Holmes, *A Sermon, Preached at Cambridge, January 4, 1801, The First Lord's Day in the Nineteenth Century* (Cambridge, Mass., 1801); Timothy Alden, *The Glory of America. A Century Sermon Delivered at the South Church, in Portsmouth, New Hampshire, IV January, MDCCCI* (Portsmouth, N.H., 1801), 24; Joseph Lathrop, *The Works of God in Relation to the Church in General, and Our Own Land in Particular, Especially in the Last Century, Considered in a Sermon, Delivered in West-Springfield, on the 1st day of the Nineteenth Century* (Springfield, Mass., 1801), 17. See also Benjamin Trumbull, *A Century Sermon, or Sketches of The History of the Eighteenth Century. Interspersed and Closed with Serious Practical Remarks. Delivered at North-Haven, January 1, 1801* (New Haven, Conn., 1801); Moses Cook Welch, *A Century Sermon, Preached at Mansfield, January 1, 1801* (Hartford, Conn., 1801).

2. Elijah Parish, *Ruin or Separation from Anti-Christ. A Sermon Preached at Byfield, April 7, 1808, on the Annual Fast in the Commonwealth of Massachusetts* (Newburyport, Mass., 1808), 17, 11, 23. Regarding his "piercing eye," see the description in William B. Sprague, *Annals of the American Pulpit; or, Commemorative Notices of Distinguished American Clergymen of Various Denominations, from the early settlement of the country to the close of the year eighteen hundred and fifty-five*, 9 vols. (New York, 1857–1869), 2:268–269.

3. Elias Smith, *The Loving Kindness of God Displayed in the Triumph of Republicanism in America; Being a Discourse, delivered at Taunton, (Mass.) July Fourth, 1809; at the Celebration of American Independence* (n.p., 1809), quotes on 26–27, 32. Regarding Smith's back-

ground, see Nathan O. Hatch, *The Democratization of American Christianity* (New Haven: Yale University Press, 1989), 42, 68–70, 128–130; Michael G. Kenny, *The Perfect Law of Liberty: Elias Smith and the Providential History of America* (Washington, D.C.: Smithsonian Institution Press, 1994).

4. Henry Adams, *History of the United States of America during the Administration of Thomas Jefferson* (1889; New York: Albert and Charles Boni, 1930), 1:79–82; Henry F. May, *The Enlightenment in America* (New York: Oxford University Press, 1976), 274, 303–304, 315–317; Charles F. O'Brien, "The Religious Issue in the Presidential Campaign of 1800," *Essex Institute Historical Collections* 107 (1971): 82–93; Constance B. Schulz, "'Of Bigotry in Politics and Religion': Jefferson's Religion, the Federalist Press, and the Syllabus," *Virginia Magazine of History and Biography* 91 (1983): 73–91.

5. Ludovicus Weld, *A Sermon, Delivered on the Day of the Annual Fast, in Connecticut, March 30, 1804* (Windham, Conn., 1804), 11. Washington's most famous remark on the importance of religion to society is found in the Farewell Address, in which he wrote, "reason and experience both forbid us to expect that National morality can prevail in exclusion of religious principle" (*The Writings of George Washington from the Original Manuscript Sources, 1745–1799,* ed. John C. Fitzpatrick, 39 vols. [Washington, D.C.: U.S. Government Printing Office, 1931–1944], 35:229). For typical illustrations of the standing order's praise of Washington, see Aaron Bancroft, *An Eulogy on the Character of the Late Gen. George Washington. Delivered Before the Inhabitants of the Town of Worcester, Commonwealth of Massachusetts, on Saturday the 22d of February 1800* (Worcester, Mass., 1800); David Osgood, *A Discourse, delivered December 29, 1799, the Lord's-Day Immediately Following the Melancholy Tidings of the Loss Sustained by the Nation in the Death of its most Eminent Citizen, George Washington, who departed this life on the 14th instant, Ætat. 68* (Boston, 1800). For further illustrations, see also Robert P. Hay, "George Washington: American Moses," *American Quarterly* 21 (1969): 780–791; James H. Smylie, "The President as Republican Prophet and King: Clerical Reflections on the Death of Washington," *Journal of Church and State* 18 (1976): 233–252.

6. William Emerson, *An Oration Pronounced July 5, 1802, at the Request of the Inhabitants of the Town of Boston, in Commemoration of the Anniversary of American Independence* (Boston, [1802]), 23. Likewise, prior to the election of 1800, Aaron Bancroft subtly endorsed Adams when he urged his listeners to "transmit inviolate to posterity, our fair national inheritance. Raise characters of worth to elective offices: Then, as an ADAMS has succeeded a WASHINGTON, to him shall succeed an uninterrupted line of illustrious Statesmen and Patriots" (*Eulogy on the Character of the Late Gen. George Washington,* 20).

7. Nathanael Emmons, *A Discourse, Delivered on the Annual Fast in Massachusetts, April 9, 1801* (Wrentham, Mass., 1801), 6–7, 12, 22. David Osgood provided another example of drawing creative, partisan parallels between current events and biblical stories. He contrasted Gideon and Washington to Abimelech and Jefferson in *A Discourse, Delivered before the Lieutenant-Governor, the Council, and the two Houses composing the Legislature of the Commonwealth of Massachusetts, May 31, 1809* (Boston, 1809).

8. Elijah Parish, *A Discourse, Delivered at Byfield, on the Annual Thanksgiving, in the Commonwealth of Massachusetts, Nov. 29, 1804* (Salem, Mass., 1805), 11–15, 18–19, 5. "To hold that it is immaterial what the religious principles of a ruler are, or whether he have any or not, is preposterous," agreed Zebulon Ely, the preacher at Connecticut's general election in 1804. "One might as well deny all connection between cause and effect through the whole moral world. . . . It must surely very materially affect the best interest of a people, whether a ruler be a votary of Jehovah the God of Israel, or of Bacchus, Venus or the Gallic goddess of reason" (*The Wisdom and Duty of Magistrates. A Sermon, Preached at the General Election, May 10th, 1804* [Hartford, Conn., 1804], 25). David Daggett, a former Connecticut assemblyman and future U.S. senator and justice of the state Supreme Court, also scorned Jefferson's approval of

what we would call religious pluralism in *Three Letters to Abraham Bishop, Esquire, containing Some Strictures on his Oration, Pronounced, in the White Meeting-House, on the Evening Preceding the Public Commencement, September 1800, with Some Remarks on his Conduct at the Late Election* (Hartford, Conn., 1800), 29–30. On Daggett's background, see David Hackett Fischer, *The Revolution of American Conservatism: The Federalist Party in the Era of Jeffersonian Democracy* (New York: Harper & Row, 1965), 296.

Almost ten years later, Parish renewed his charge that Jefferson, and now Madison, too, were infidels: "If the late President, the sage of Montecello [*sic*], proud of his infidelity, has employed Printers to *publish* his contempt for the writings of Moses; if he has pronounced the universal deluge *an impossibility*; if his successor has given the whole nation every possible reason, except his public avowal, to believe that his deism is, as fixed as the ice of the poles; if his profanations of the sabbath, if his common, his habitual, his notorious neglect of public worship, are as complete evidence, as the most candid confessions, that he has no part nor lot in *Him*, who was crucified on Calvary, and rose from the tomb of Joseph, is it strange, that a swarm of scoffing infidels should darken the country, where these exalted personages reside?" (*A Discourse, Delivered at Byfield, on the Public Fast, April 7, 1814* [Newburyport, Mass., 1814], 15).

9. Samuel Spring, *Two Sermons Addressed to the Second Congregational Society in Newburyport, Fast Day, April 6, 1809* (Newburyport, Mass., 1809), 5; Samuel Austin, *A Sermon, Preached at Worcester, on the Annual Fast, April 11, 1811* (Worcester, Mass., 1811), 24; Festus Foster, *The Watchman's Warning to the House of Israel. A Sermon, Delivered before the Congregation in Petersham, November 21, 1811, being the Day Appointed for Thanksgiving throughout the Commonwealth* (Worcester, Mass., 1811), 17.

Interestingly, Northern clergymen revived their assault on Jefferson in the 1860s. They blamed him for holding a licentious idea of liberty and for propagating states' rights, both of which they thought were leading causes of the Civil War. James H. Moorhead, *American Apocalypse: Yankee Protestants and the Civil War, 1860–1869* (New Haven: Yale University Press, 1978), 135–140.

10. Samuel Austin, *The Apology of Patriots, or The heresy of the friends of the Washington and peace policy defended. A Sermon, preached in Worcester, Massachusetts, on the day of the National Fast, Thursday, August 20, 1812. Observed in Compliance with the Recommendation of James Madison, President of the United States; and in Consequence of the Declaration of War Against Great-Britain* (Worcester, Mass., 1812), 10–11.

11. Austin, *A Sermon, Preached . . . April 11, 1811*, 24; Henry Cumings, *A Sermon, Preached at Billerica, April 9th, 1801; Being the Day of the Annual Fast* (Amherst, N.H., 1801), 20–26; Parish, *Ruin or Separation*, 17; Foster, *Watchman's Warning*, 18–19.

12. James M. Banner Jr., *To the Hartford Convention: The Federalists and the Origins of Party Politics in Massachusetts, 1789–1815* (New York: Knopf, 1970), 36–46.

13. Weld, *A Sermon, Delivered . . . March 30, 1804*, 21; Asahel Hooker, *The Moral Tendency of Man's Accountableness to God; and its Influence on the Happiness of Society. A Sermon, Preached on the Day of the General Election, at Hartford, in the State of Connecticut, May 9th, 1805* (Hartford, Conn., 1805), 24; Ely, *Wisdom and Duty of Magistrates*, 26.

14. Stephanie A. Munsing, *Made in America: Printmaking 1760–1860. An Exhibition of Original Prints from the Collections of the Library Company of Philadelphia and the Historical Society of Pennsylvania, April–June 1973* (Philadelphia: Library Company of Philadelphia, 1973), 13–14; William Murrell, *A History of American Graphic Humor*, 2 vols. (New York: Whitney Museum of American Art, 1933–1938), 1:49; Allan Nevins and Frank Weitenkampf, *A Century of Political Cartoons: Caricature in the United States from 1800 to 1900* (New York: Charles Scribner's Sons, 1944), 20. Regarding Jefferson's letter to Mazzei, see also John C. Miller, *The Federalist Era, 1789–1801*, The New American Nation Series (New York: Harper & Row, 1960), 202–203.

15. Weld, *A Sermon, Delivered . . . March 30, 1804*, 12; Emmons, *A Discourse, Delivered . . . April 9, 1801*, 26–27; Osgood, *A Discourse, Delivered . . . May 31, 1809*, 7–8; Samuel Austin, *A Sermon, preached in Worcester, Massachusetts, on the occasion of the Special Fast, July 23d, 1812* (Worcester, Mass., 1812), 17–18. See also Foster, *Watchman's Warning*, 9. As James M. Banner Jr. has written, to the Federalists "the Democratic-Republican Party was the repository of the morally diseased" (*To the Hartford Convention*, 82).

16. Osgood, *A Discourse, Delivered . . . May 31, 1809*, 27, 16; Spring, *Two Sermons . . . April 6, 1809*, 7–18, quote on 16; Elijah Parish, *A Sermon, Preached at Boston, Before His Excellency Christopher Gore, Governor, His Honor David Cobb, Lieut. Governor, the Council and Legislature, Upon the Annual Election, May 30, 1810* (Boston, 1810), 18.

17. Austin, *A Sermon, Preached . . . April 11, 1811*, 21.

18. Joseph Lathrop, *The Constancy and Uniformity of the Divine Government, Illustrated and Improved in a Sermon, Preached in Springfield, April 7, 1803, which was a day of Public Fasting and Prayer* (Springfield, Mass., 1803), 13–14; Austin, *A Sermon, preached . . . July 23d, 1812*, iii.

19. Austin, *A Sermon, preached . . . July 23d, 1812*, iii; Joseph W. Phillips, *Jedidiah Morse and New England Congregationalism* (New Brunswick, N.J.: Rutgers University Press, 1983), 85–89; Jedidiah Morse, *A Sermon, Delivered at Charlestown, July 23, 1812. The Day Appointed by the Governor and Council of Massachusetts, to be Observed in Fasting and Prayer Throughout the Commonwealth; in Consequence of a Declaration of War With Great Britain* (Charlestown, Mass., 1812), 5–13; Abiel Holmes, *A Sermon, Preached at Cambridge April 6, 1809, the Day of the Public Fast* (Cambridge, Mass., 1809), 4. Elijah Parish anticipated that his 1808 sermon, discussed at the beginning of this chapter, would be "treated with contempt and scorn"; after all, "the children of Lot ridiculed his story of fire from heaven; doubtless the Antideluvians [*sic*] derided Noah for his ship, his navigation, and his tale of a universal deluge." Nevertheless, Parish—not one ever to tone down his remarks for fear of rebuke—would bravely do his duty: "Had I a voice to be heard from Maine to Georgia, gladly would I meet the torrent of sarcasms, which, like the foam of Niagara, might burst forth, for the privilege of commenting on the text, and most affectionately warning the people" (*Ruin or Separation*, 18).

20. Emmons, *A Discourse, Delivered . . . April 9, 1801*, 29; Holmes, *A Sermon, Preached . . . April 6, 1809*, 4; Weld, *A Sermon, Delivered . . . March 30, 1804*, 3–22, quote on 22. Added Samuel Spring, "The Prophet was not the subject of passive obedience and non-resistance" (*Two Sermons . . . April 6, 1809*, 3). Samuel Austin compared himself not to a prophet of Israel but to the Apostle Paul; he, too, would proclaim the truth in the face of hostility (*Apology of Patriots*, 5–6). For use of the "watchman" theme, see Austin, *A Sermon, preached . . . July 23d, 1812*, iv; Timothy Dwight, *A Discourse, in Two Parts, Delivered July 23, 1812, on the Public Fast, [and August 20, 1812, on the National Fast,] in the Chapel of Yale College*, 2d ed. (Boston, 1813), 31; Foster, *Watchman's Warning*, 3–5; Morse, *A Sermon, Delivered . . . July 23, 1812*, 15–17, 25; Parish, *A Discourse, Delivered . . . Nov. 29, 1804*, 21; Samuel Worcester, *Calamity, Danger, and Hope. A Sermon, Preached at the Tabernacle in Salem, July 23, 1812. The Day of the Public Fast in Massachusetts, on Account of the War with Great-Britain* (Salem, Mass., 1812), 4.

21. Spring, *Two Sermons . . . April 6, 1809*, 27–28, 31; Nathan Perkins, *The National Sins, and National Punishment in the Recently Declared War; Considered, in a Sermon Delivered, July 23, 1812, on the Day of the Public Fast Appointed by the Governor and Council of the State of Connecticut, in Consequence of the Declaration of War Against Great-Britain* (Hartford, Conn., 1812), 28. Samuel Austin also clearly defined what was needed: "The united call of prophets and apostles is to repentance. . . . There is no possible way for us to become purged from the pollutions which dishonor our country and menace our destruction, but by repenting. There is no possible way to escape the plagues which in succession are to desolate our country with the world, but by repenting. We must bring to our offended and much injured

Creator, the sacrifice of a broken heart. We must fast with godly mourning. We must be reformed. We must condemn the wickedness of others by forsaking our own. We must individually, and we must nationally, break off our sins by righteousness, and our iniquities by turning unto God" (*A Sermon, Preached . . . April 11, 1811,* 30). See also William Ellery Channing, *A Sermon, Preached in Boston, July 23, 1812, the Day of the Publick Fast, Appointed by the Executive of the Commonwealth of Massachusetts, in Consequence of the Declaration of War Against Great Britain* (Boston, 1812), 16–17; Cumings, *A Sermon, Preached . . . April 9th, 1801,* 26–27; Dwight, *A Discourse, in Two Parts,* 27; Holmes, *A Sermon, Preached . . . April 6, 1809,* 18; Morse, *A Sermon, Delivered . . . July 23, 1812,* 26–28; Nathan Strong, *A Fast Sermon, Delivered in the North Presbyterian Meeting House, in Hartford, July 23, 1812* (Hartford, Conn., 1812), 18–19; Stephen West, *A Sermon, Delivered on the Public Fast, April 9th, 1801* (Stockbridge, Mass., 1801), 25–26; Worcester, *Calamity, Danger, and Hope,* 18–24.

22. Aaron Bancroft, *A Sermon, Preached before his Excellency Caleb Strong, Esq. Governour, the Honourable the Council, Senate, and House of Representatives of the Commonwealth of Massachusetts, May 27, 1801, the Day of General Election* (Boston, 1801), 13; Joseph Strong, *A Sermon, Preached on the General Election at Hartford in Connecticut, May 13, 1802* (Hartford, Conn., 1802), 7; Chauncey Lee, *The Government of God the True Source and Standard of Human Government. A Sermon, preached on the day of the General Election, at Hartford, in the State of Connecticut, May 13th, 1813* (Hartford, Conn., 1813), 26. The tune sung by Bancroft harmonized with Lee on this point. Speaking in 1801, he said, "Another dark appearance in our political horizon, is a system of philosophy, which, under the spurious pretence of raising man to his perfectibility, destroys the fine feelings and ingenuous sensibilities of the human heart. . . . The apostles of this philosophy disregard the wisest maxims of experience, and endeavour to introduce a national administration in politicks and morality, upon abstract principles" (*A Sermon, Preached . . . May 27, 1801,* 14). See also Reuben Puffer, *A Sermon, delivered before His Excellency Caleb Strong, Esq. Governour, His Honour Edward H. Robbins, Esq. Lt. Gov, the Honourable the Council, Senate, and House of Representatives, of the Commonwealth of Massachusetts, May 25, 1803, Being the Day of General Election* (Boston, 1803), 31.

23. Instead of the hurricane, Aaron Bancroft chose a number of different metaphors to convey this idea. "The axe soon prostrates the tree, which time and nature have reared. . . . The evil pens and contagious examples of some few characters of splendid talents and captivating address, may weaken the moral principles and corrupt the manners of a community, which required ages to establish, and which have formed the characters of successive generations of men. The publick opinion once corrupted, and the religious and moral habits of the people destroyed, the strong band of society is broken, and civil liberty is no more" (*A Sermon, Preached . . . May 27, 1801,* 16).

24. Benjamin Trumbull, *The Dignity of Man, especially as Displayed in Civil Government. A Sermon, Preached on the General Election at Hartford, in Connecticut, May 14, 1801* (Hartford, Conn., 1801); Strong, *A Sermon, Preached . . . May 13, 1802;* Bancroft, *A Sermon, Preached . . . May 27, 1801,* 28. In 1803, Matthias Burnet took his theme from Ps. 11:3, "If the foundations be destroyed what can the righteous do?" (*An Election Sermon, Preached at Hartford, on the Day of the Anniversary Election, May 12, 1803* [Hartford, Conn., 1803]).

25. Bancroft, *A Sermon, Preached . . . May 27, 1801,* 23. Seconded Matthias Burnet, "Without education, and that knowledge which is the effect of it, men are ever liable to be imposed upon and led astray. Ignorant of the true nature of things they are degraded and depressed by the grossest superstition, or blown up by the wildest enthusiasm. They are duped and lead blindfold by every designing demagogue, or tamely crouch down under every lordly despot" (*An Election Sermon,* 9–10).

26. William Ellery Channing, *A Sermon, Preached in Boston, April 5, 1810, the Day of the*

Public Fast (Boston, 1810), 16. Regarding the diffusion of information, Channing said, "Let me entreat all, who are interested in this great object, the improvement and elevation of public sentiment, to adhere to such means only as are worthy that great end; to suppress and condemn all appeals to unworthy passions, all misrepresentation, and all that abuse, which depraves public taste and sentiment, and makes a man of a pure mind ashamed of the cause, which he feels himself bound to support" (ibid., 19). See also Puffer, *A Sermon, delivered . . . May 25, 1803*, 16. Comments Daniel Walker Howe, "Unitarians found the education of the conscience at once liberating and regulating. Such an education offered the ultimate solution to the problems of society: train good men and they would freely make a good society" (*The Unitarian Conscience: Harvard Moral Philosophy, 1805–1861*, rev. ed. [Cambridge: Harvard University Press, 1970; Middletown, Conn.: Wesleyan University Press, 1988], 261).

27. Trumbull, *Dignity of Man*, 23. For Trumbull's background, see Franklin Bowditch Dexter, *Biographical Sketches of the Graduates of Yale College: With Annals of the College History*, 6 vols. (New York, 1885–1912), 2:621–627.

28. Strong, *A Sermon, Preached . . . May 13, 1802*, 12. See also Amos Bassett, *Advantages and Means of Union in Society. A Sermon, Preached at the Anniversary Election, in Hartford, May 14th, 1807* (Hartford, Conn., 1807), 13–16.

29. Jesse Appleton, *A Sermon Preached in Boston, at the Annual Election, May 25, 1814* (Boston, 1814), 16; on Appleton's background, see Nehemiah Cleaveland and Alpheus Spring Packard, *History of Bowdoin College. With Biographical Sketches of its Graduates from 1806 to 1879, inclusive* (Boston, 1882), 114–117. For the importance of women's role in raising the next generation, see Samuel Nott, *Prayer, Eminently the Duty of Rulers, in the Times of Trial; and the Nation Happy, Whose God is the Lord. A Sermon, Preached at Hartford, in Connecticut, on the General Election. May 11th, 1809* (Hartford, Conn., 1809), 10; Burnet, *An Election Sermon*, 24.

30. Joseph Goffe, Diary, 15 Jan., 22 Feb., and 31 Mar. 1800, Joseph Goffe Papers, 1721–1846, AAS. The funeral ceremony at Oxford is described in the *Massachusetts Spy, or Worcester Gazette*, 22 Jan. 1800. Goffe's "electioneering piece" may be the one signed "Numbers" in the 2 April 1800 issue of the *Massachusetts Spy*; it is dated 31 Mar. and concerns the election in Sutton. Regarding the Federalists' use of ceremonies honoring Washington, see David Waldstreicher, *In the Midst of Perpetual Fetes: The Making of American Nationalism, 1776–1820* (Chapel Hill: University of North Carolina Press, 1997).

31. Trumbull, *Dignity of Man*, 16. See also Strong, *A Sermon, Preached . . . May 13, 1802*, 9, 13; Ely, *Wisdom and Duty of Magistrates*, 7; Hooker, *Moral Tendency*, 17–18; Nott, *Prayer, Eminently the Duty of Rulers*, 8, 23–24.

32. Burnet, *An Election Sermon*, 14–15; Ely, *Wisdom and Duty of Magistrates*, 12–16.

33. Parish, *A Sermon, Preached . . . May 30, 1810*, 12. See also Bancroft, *A Sermon, Preached . . . May 27, 1801*, 20; Trumbull, *Dignity of Man*, 25–26; Strong, *A Sermon, Preached . . . May 13, 1802*, 13–14; Puffer, *A Sermon, delivered . . . May 25, 1803*, 19; Ely, *Wisdom and Duty of Magistrates*, 13, 27; Nott, *Prayer, Eminently the Duty of Rulers*, 29.

34. Strong, *A Sermon, Preached . . . May 13, 1802*, 14; Puffer, *A Sermon, delivered . . . May 25, 1803*, 24.

35. Trumbull, *Dignity of Man*, 25; Bassett, *Advantages and Means of Union*, 20; Ely, *Wisdom and Duty of Magistrates*, 26.

36. Ely, *Wisdom and Duty of Magistrates*, 34; Lathrop, *Constancy and Uniformity*, 13. Chauncey Lee built upon Ely and Lathrop's points: "With what reason or propriety, then, is the principle professed, and even by some contended for, that *between religion and government there exists no connection?* — yea, that they are severally contaminated by a mutual touch; and the influence of each is hostile and baneful to the interests of the other? Can a man believe his Bible, and subscribe to a doctrine so absurd? The reverse of it is truth, and the deeper

our researches in this subject, the deeper will be our conviction. It is separating what God hath joined together, and bidding defiance to reason and experience, as well as to scripture" (*Government of God*, 21–22).

37. Bancroft, *A Sermon, Preached . . . May 27, 1801*, 21–23, quote on 21; Ely, *Wisdom and Duty of Magistrates*, 33. See also Bassett, *Advantages and Means of Union*, 25–29; Nott, *Prayer, Eminently the Duty of Rulers*, 18; Parish, *A Sermon, Preached . . . May 30, 1810*, 8–9. In the estimation of Nathan Perkins in 1808, Connecticut had struck the ideal solution to the question of state support of religion: "Perhaps, in our own free and happy state, our government has hit upon the golden mean, of not interposing too much or too little in matters of religion. It is one of the chief glories of our civil constitution, or government that it encourages, countenances, and provides for piety and morality;—looks up with reverence to the christian religion; and interposes for its maintenance. But there is no resemblance of a religious hierarchy in our state, or any improper interference of our government in matters of religion" (*The Benign Influence of Religion on Civil Government and National Happiness—Illustrated in a Sermon, preached before His Excellency Jonathan Trumbull, Esq. Governor; His Honor John Treadwell, Esq. Lieutenant Governor: The Honorable the Council: and House of Representatives of the State of Connecticut, on the Anniversary Election, May 12th, 1808* [Hartford, Conn., 1808], 35).

38. Paul Goodman, *The Democratic-Republicans of Massachusetts: Politics in a Young Republic* (Cambridge: Harvard University Press, 1964), 154.

39. Banner, *To the Hartford Convention*, 132–148, 155–167, 256–257, quotes on 144, 257, 147–148, 155.

40. Bassett, *Advantages and Means of Union*, 21; Dan Huntington, *The Love of Jerusalem, the Prosperity of a People. A Sermon, Preached at the Anniversary Election, Hartford, May 12, 1814* (Hartford, Conn., 1814), 29, 32.

41. Donald M. Scott, *From Office to Profession: The New England Ministry, 1750–1850* (Philadelphia: University of Pennsylvania Press, 1978), 29. Especially revealing is the incident from Connecticut recounted by Scott. In 1811, party leaders declined to back Gov. John Treadwell, whose "bearing so resembled the Republican portrait of the Puritan bigot that the party managers feared he would lead the Federalists to political disaster." This blatant political sacrifice of a candidate of otherwise impeccable integrity and virtue mortified the state's Congregational clergymen (ibid.).

42. Morse to Joseph Lyman, Feb. 9, 1805, quoted in Banner, *To the Hartford Convention*, 164, n. 2.

43. Stephen W. Stebbins, *God's Government of the Church and World, the Source of Great Consolation and Joy: Illustrated in a Sermon Preached at Hartford, May 9, 1811. Before the General Assembly of the State of Connecticut, at the Anniversary Election* (Hartford, Conn., 1811), 30; Lee, *Government of God*, 34.

44. Morse, *A Sermon, Delivered . . . July 23, 1812*, 11–13, 29, 32, quote on 11; Elijah Parish, *A Protest Against the War. A Discourse Delivered at Byfield, Fast Day, July 23, 1812* (Newburyport, Mass., 1812), 13–17, quotes on 15, 17.

45. William Ellery Channing, *A Sermon, Preached in Boston, August 20, 1812, the Day of Humiliation and Prayer, Appointed by the President of the United States, in Consequence of the Declaration of War Against Great Britain* (Boston, 1812), 14–15; Dwight, *A Discourse, in Two Parts*, 49–51, quote on 51. For an interpretation emphasizing the moderation of most of the antiwar Congregationalists, see William Gribbin, *The Churches Militant: The War of 1812 and American Religion* (New Haven: Yale University Press, 1973), 31–39.

46. Austin, *A Sermon, Preached . . . April 11, 1811*, 7.

47. Worcester, *Calamity, Danger, and Hope*, quote on 13; Austin, *A Sermon, Preached . . . April 11, 1811*, 12–18; Perkins, *National Sins, and National Punishment*, 10–13.

48. John Smith, *The People of God Invited to Trust in Him amidst His Judgments upon Sinful Nations. A Sermon Delivered on the Annual Fast at Salem, N.H. March 25, and at the South Parish in Andover, Mass. April 3, 1813* (Haverhill, Mass., 1813), 12–13. Likewise, Samuel Austin was aghast to report, "How many errors, under the names of Arminianism, Socinianism, Arianism, Universalism, and Deism are received! And how do the receivers of these errors treat with neglect, with open opposition, and even with scorn, the truth! What irreverent things are said of the Holy Scripture!" (*A Sermon, Preached . . . April 11, 1811*, 14). See also West, *A Sermon, Delivered . . . April 9th, 1801*, 16.

49. Austin, *A Sermon, preached . . . July 23d, 1812*, 9–10; Perkins, *National Sins, and National Punishment*, 5, 8–9. David Osgood put an interesting, partisan spin on the theme of ingratitude. He argued that Americans were guilty of it, because they had turned the Federalists out of office despite their fine service (*A Discourse, Delivered . . . May 31, 1809*, 22).

50. Weld, *A Sermon, Delivered . . . March 30, 1804*, 23; Spring, *Two Sermons . . . April 6, 1809*, 22.

51. Regarding religious opposition to the war, see the excellent study by Gribbin, *Churches Militant*, 16–60.

52. Nathan O. Hatch, *The Sacred Cause of Liberty: Republican Thought and the Millennium in Revolutionary New England* (New Haven: Yale University Press, 1977), 6–7.

53. Austin, *Apology of Patriots*, 17–18. See also Parish, *A Protest Against the War*, 18; Strong, *A Fast Sermon, Delivered . . . July 23, 1812*, 15.

54. Perkins, *National Sins, and National Punishment*, 25. See also Channing, *A Sermon, Preached . . . July 23, 1812*, 6, 12.

55. Morse, *A Sermon, Delivered . . . July 23, 1812*, 18; Perkins, *National Sins, and National Punishment*, 26; Parish, *A Protest Against the War*, 19–20. Governor Strong's pro-British remarks are found in *By His Excellency Caleb Strong, Governor of the Commonwealth of Massachusetts, A Proclamation, For a Day of Public Fasting, Humiliation and Prayer* (Boston, 1812). See also Gribbin, *Churches Militant*, 20, 41–51. Channing summed up the feelings of Unitarians and evangelicals alike when he said, "When I view my country taking part with the Oppressor [Napoleon's France] against that nation [Britain], which has alone arrested his proud career of victory, which is now spreading her shield over desolated Portugal and Spain—which is the chief hope of the civilized world—I blush—I mourn" (Channing, *A Sermon, Preached . . . July 23, 1812*, 13).

56. Parish, *A Protest Against the War*, 11; Strong, *A Fast Sermon, Delivered . . . July 23, 1812*, 12; Worcester, *Calamity, Danger, and Hope*, 16–17; Parish, *A Sermon, Preached . . . May 30, 1810*, 13; Dwight, *A Discourse, in Two Parts*, 27; Morse, *A Sermon, Delivered . . . July 23, 1812*, 23–24. Similarly, Channing advised, "we deem alliance with France the worst of evils, threatening at once our morals, our liberty and our religion. The character of that nation authorizes us to demand, that we be kept from the pollution of her embrace—her proffered friendship we should spurn—from her arms, stained, drenched with the blood of the injured and betrayed, we should scorn and should fear to receive aid or protection" (Channing, *A Sermon, Preached . . . July 23, 1812*, 14).

57. Austin, *A Sermon, Preached . . . April 11, 1811*, 23; Lee, *Government of God*, 43; Dwight, *A Discourse, in Two Parts*, 24; Morse, *A Sermon, Delivered . . . July 23, 1812*, 30; Perkins, *National Sins, and National Punishment*, 17. The critique of the Constitution as a godless document reemerged during the 1860s. A group calling itself the National Reform Association, endorsed by "several denominations," proposed that the preamble be revised so that it would contain an explicit acknowledgment of the Christian basis of national government (Moorhead, *American Apocalypse*, 141–142).

58. Noah Webster, *An Oration, Pronounced before the Knox and Warren Branches of the Washington Benevolent Society, at Amherst, on the Celebration of the Anniversary of the Dec-*

laration of Independence, July 4, 1814 (Northampton, Mass., 1814); Banner, *To the Hartford Convention*, 338–343, and passim.

59. Cf. Perry Miller, who wrote that in making the transition to revivalistic liberalism, "they [the devout] did not need to renounce the Declaration, nor even to denounce the Constitution, but only henceforth to take those principles for granted, yield government to the secular concept of the social compact, accept the First Amendment, and so to concentrate, in order to resist Deism and to save their souls, upon that other mechanism of cohesion developed out of their colonial experience, the Revival" ("From the Covenant to the Revival," in *Religion in American Life*, ed. James Ward Smith and A. Leland Jamison, vol. 1, *The Shaping of American Religion* [Princeton, N.J.: Princeton University Press, 1961], 350).

60. Perkins, *National Sins, and National Punishment*, 3; Worcester, *Calamity, Danger, and Hope*, 3; Spring, *Two Sermons . . . April 6, 1809*, 20. Added Jedidiah Morse, "Our country, in the Providence of God, and as a just punishment for our national sins, is now involved in a state of calamity and danger, which loudly calls for the exercise of all the wisdom of our wisest men, and for all the best exertions of christians of every class and denomination. A darker day for our country, I believe, was never witnessed by the oldest of the present generation, and probably by none of our ancestors" (*A Sermon, Delivered . . . July 23, 1812*, 3).

61. Worcester, *Calamity, Danger, and Hope*, 7–10; Smith, *People of God Invited*, 11–16; Perkins, *National Sins, and National Punishment*, 17.

62. Austin, *A Sermon, preached . . . July 23d, 1812*, 14; Morse, *A Sermon, Delivered . . . July 23, 1812*, 21; Worcester, *Calamity, Danger, and Hope*, 10.

63. Worcester, *Calamity, Danger, and Hope*, 4–5; Foster, *Watchman's Warning*, 24. John Smith provided another illustration of a foreboding text. He chose Isa. 26:20–21, "Come, my people, enter thou into thy chambers, and shut thy doors about thee: hide thyself as it were for a little moment, until the indignation be overpast. For, behold, the LORD cometh out of his place to punish the inhabitants of the earth for their iniquity: the earth also shall disclose her blood, and shall no more cover her slain" (*People of God Invited*).

64. Smith, *People of God Invited*, 6. Added Samuel Austin, "As the morning of the millennium draws near, things proceed with dispatch. Every individual, family, society and nation, that does not bow to the Saviour and take refuge in his redeeming mercy, shall be destroyed" (*A Sermon, Preached . . . April 11, 1811*, 29).

65. Smith, *People of God Invited*, 9; Dwight, *A Discourse, in Two Parts*, 4; Parish, *A Protest Against the War*, 8–9.

66. Parish, *A Discourse, Delivered . . . April 7, 1814*, 20. As John F. Berens concludes, "The providential thought articulated during the War of 1812 contained a special irony. New England, which had originally contributed its special Puritan themes to the nation's providential legend . . . had now, in a sense, rejected its offspring" (*Providence and Patriotism in Early America 1640–1815* [Charlottesville: University Press of Virginia, 1978], 164).

67. Smith, *Loving Kindness of God*, 13–14, 32. Similarly, Joseph Barker, a rare combination of Congregational minister and Democratic-Republican, reminded a July Fourth audience in 1803 that back in 1776, "the word *democracy*, had no frightful sound; nor were our greatest and best men ashamed to call themselves DEMOCRATS" (*An Address to a Respectable Number of Citizens, from Several Towns in Plymouth County, Convened in Halifax, July 4th, 1803, to Celebrate the Anniversary of American Independence* [Boston, 1803], 6).

68. Goodman, *Democratic-Republicans of Massachusetts*, 204.

69. My discussion of New England's first party competition in this and the next paragraph is based upon these standard works: Banner, *To the Hartford Convention*; Fischer, *Revolution of American Conservatism*; Ronald P. Formisano, *The Transformation of Political Culture: Massachusetts Parties, 1790s–1840s* (New York: Oxford University Press, 1983); Goodman, *Democratic-Republicans of Massachusetts*; Richard J. Purcell, *Connecticut in Transition:*

1775–1818 (Washington, D.C.: American Historical Association, 1918; reprint, Middletown, Conn.: Wesleyan University Press, 1963); Edmund B. Thomas Jr., "Politics in the Land of Steady Habits: Connecticut's First Political Party System, 1789–1820" (Ph.D. diss., Clark University, 1972). The change in political culture is also conveniently summarized in Scott, *From Office to Profession,* 18–22.

70. Dexter, *Biographical Sketches,* 5:99–103; Formisano, *Transformation of Political Culture,* 8; Ezekiel Bacon, *An Oration, Delivered at Williamstown, on the 4th of July, 1799. Being the Anniversary of American Independence* (Bennington, Vt., 1799), quotes on 9–10, 24, 22. For an allegation of a gigantic conspiracy aimed at establishing monarchy on the part of "a powerful aristocratic, monarchic, Britannic faction" of Federalists, see Abraham Bishop, *Connecticut Republicanism. An Oration on the Extent and Power of Political Delusion. Delivered in New-Haven, On the Evening preceding the Public Commencement, September, 1800* ([New Haven?], 1800), 63.

71. In Paul Goodman's interpretation, it was "the acid influence of a diplomatic and commercial crisis which gradually split the country into two hostile camps" (*Democratic-Republicans of Massachusetts,* 47).

72. Banner, *To the Hartford Convention,* 174–176, 271–275, quotes on 271 and 275. For Connecticut, see Purcell, *Connecticut in Transition,* 146–189, 211–235; Thomas, "Politics in the Land of Steady Habits," 132. Rhode Island avoided political polarization to a greater extent than its neighbors until 1805, when Governor Arthur Fenner, who had held the office since 1790 and "appeared to stand above partisan strife," died. After Fenner's death, a two-party contest ensued, with Democratic-Republicans prevailing in gubernatorial races until 1811, when their party's national policies turned the state toward Federalism. The Federalists then controlled the governorship from their victory in 1811 to their defeat in 1817 (Patrick T. Conley, *Democracy in Decline: Rhode Island's Constitutional Development, 1776–1841* [Providence: Rhode Island Historical Society, 1977], 174–183, quote on 175). Nathan O. Hatch describes how Benjamin Austin's *Independent Chronicle,* a Boston newspaper of Jeffersonian bent, politicized two ordinary men, William Manning and Elias Smith; see his "Elias Smith and the Rise of Religious Journalism in the Early Republic," in *Printing and Society in Early America,* ed. William L. Joyce et al. (Worcester, Mass.: American Antiquarian Society, 1983), 262–264.

73. Quoted in Andrew Delbanco, *William Ellery Channing: An Essay on the Liberal Spirit in America* (Cambridge: Harvard University Press, 1981), 18.

74. Joseph McKeen, *A Discourse against Speaking Evil of Rulers: Delivered on the Anniversary Fast in Massachusetts, April 9th, 1801* (Salem, Mass., 1801), 10–16. For biographical information on McKeen, see Cleaveland and Packard, *History of Bowdoin College,* 111–113; Sprague, *Annals,* 2:216–221.

75. West, *A Sermon, Delivered . . . April 9th, 1801,* 4, 19–25, quotes on 4, 24–25. Six years later, Edmund Mills of Sutton, Massachusetts, issued a lament very similar to West's. Taking as his text the Golden Rule of Matt. 7:12, he chastised the political press for mudslinging. "How many Gazettes, (and perhaps none can justly be excepted,) have been circulated, injudiciously fraught with idle surmises, and with low vulgar attempts at detraction? Important characters, emphatically interesting to the United States, have been treated in manner, very dishonorable to an enlightened people." Like West, Mills, too, feared that people would get so caught up in politics that religion would fall by the wayside. He advised his listeners to "seriously consider, what it shall profit a man, to carry into effect all his worldly desires and political purposes, and at last meet with infinite loss" (*A Discourse, Delivered on the Annual Fast, in Massachusetts, April 9th, 1807* [Sutton, Mass., 1807], 15–17).

76. Goodman, *Democratic-Republicans of Massachusetts,* 227, n. 43, lists six Congregational ministers who were Republicans. Banner, *To the Hartford Convention,* 152, n. 2, writes

that "to Goodman's own list of six Republican Congregational clerics, I have been able to add only two more." These two lists provide the identification of Republican Congregationalists for the following paragraphs. William Bentley is identified as a Democratic-Republican in Francis S. Drake, *Dictionary of American Biography* (Boston, 1874), 84.

77. William Bentley, *A Sermon, before the Governor, the Honorable Council, and Both Branches of the Legislature of the Commonwealth of Massachusetts, on the day of General Election, May 27, 1807* (Boston, 1807), 6; William G. McLoughlin, *New England Dissent, 1630–1833: The Baptists and the Separation of Church and State*, 2 vols. (Cambridge: Harvard University Press, 1971), 2:1066–1067, 1073–1074. "True religion is the only foundation of human happiness," noted Thomas Allen in a conventional formulation. "The gospel of Jesus Christ contains a system of religious truth and duty, the best adapted to promote personal, domestic, and national good. . . . The sacred volume gives us the most ample instructions with respect to all social and relative duties; and it points out the design of civil government, and makes known the duty of rulers" (*A Sermon, preached before His Excellency, James Sullivan, Esq. Governor; His Honor, Levi Lincoln, Esq. Lieutenant-Governor; The Honourable Council, and Both Branches of the Legislature of the Commonwealth of Massachusetts, on the day of General Election. May 25th, 1808* [Boston, 1808], 5).

78. John Giles, *Two Discourses, delivered to the Second Presbyterian Society in Newburyport, August 20, 1812: the Day Recommended by the President of the United States, for National Humiliation and Prayer* (Newburyport, Mass., 1812), 17; Joseph Richardson, *The Christian Patriot Encouraged. A Discourse, Delivered before the First Parish in Hingham, on Fast Day, April 8, 1813* (Boston, 1813), 3; idem, *A Discourse Addressed to the First Parish in Hingham, on the Day of Fasting, April 5, 1810* (Boston, 1810), 8. Like a Federalist member of the standing order, Thomas Allen decried extravagance, Sabbath-breaking, and vice (*A Sermon . . . May 25th, 1808*, 15).

79. Richardson, *Christian Patriot Encouraged*, 6.

80. Richardson, *A Discourse . . . April 5, 1810*, 10; Allen, *A Sermon . . . May 25th, 1808*, 16; Giles, *Two Discourses . . . August 20, 1812*, 14–15.

81. "Your Sermons [Spring's *Two Sermons Addressed to the Second Congregational Society in Newburyport, Fast Day, April 6, 1809*] have a tendency to destroy religion and morality. They keep up the old tune of Jefferson and infidelity; which has been sung by federalists, not only in newspapers, but in large public assemblies; not to augment the spirit of devotion in any; but to quench it in thousands. This has been a greater detriment to religion among us, than the Age of Reason, and all other Deistical writings. Publications of the tenor of your Sermons degrade and weaken the influence of the christian ministry. The people feel that such publications are pleading the cause of England in all her aggressions against the rights of this country. And when things so palpably untrue, and inconsistent are handed to them from the pulpit and the press, it genders a distrust of their veracity and honesty as men; and proportionably diminishes their reverence and respect for their persons, and consequently for the religion they preach. When ministers are disposed to come forward and traverse the political field, and condemn those public measures which are approved by a vast majority of the nation, and criminate and slander our rulers, they will be confronted by thousands of the yeomanry, who know as much about public men and measures as they do. This has destroyed the influence of ministers in this Commonwealth more than all their other imprudencies" (*A Letter, addressed by the Rev. Solomon Aiken, A.M. Pastor of the first Church in Dracutt, to the Rev. Samuel Spring, D.D. Pastor of the second Congregational Church in Newburyport, on the subject of his Sermons, delivered April the 6th, 1809* [Haverhill, Mass., 1809], 32).

82. Bentley, *A Sermon . . . May 27, 1807*, 22; Aiken, *A Letter . . . to the Rev. Samuel Spring*, 19. Thomas Allen also lauded Jefferson. "We believe that the administration of our general government has been correct, and that the President of our country has for many years em-

ployed his talents in pursuing the public good, and that he has displayed in his life many virtues honourable to his character. . . . Believing this, and as we know it to be the duty of a people to respect their rulers, we must express disapprobation of all instances, wherein opposition has been shown to what is considered as right, and wherein there has been any violation of a christian duty" (*A Sermon . . . May 25th, 1808*, 16). For similar praise of Madison's "patriotism, wisdom and integrity," see Richardson, *A Discourse . . . April 5, 1810*, 16.

83. Stanley Griswold, *Truth Its Own Test and God Its Only Judge. Or, An Inquiry,—How Far Men May Claim Authority Over Each Other's Religious Opinions? A Discourse, delivered at New-Milford, October 12th, 1800* (Bridgeport, Conn., 1800), 30. Griswold's position united political sentiment with personal biography; just three years earlier, his ministerial association had censured him for unsound doctrine. In 1802, Griswold left the ministry on account of the inhospitality accorded his Republicanism in Connecticut, and he spent the rest of his life in various Republican patronage posts. Dexter, *Biographical Sketches*, 4:476–479.

Although a Yale-educated minister, Griswold does not well fit the description of the Republican Congregationalist given here. His radical separation of religion and government is closer to that of a Baptist (see later). "On the whole, to talk of religion as a servile tool of government, to me appears degrading to the high, dignified character of the former, and as savoring very much of insincerity respecting it in those who thus talk. It looks like placing the things of the eternal world beneath those of this, the things of our everlasting peace beneath the things of a moment! . . . But if religion be a *reality*, then it infinitely transcends all temporal purposes, and ought not to be placed *beneath* any, nor have any so connected and interwoven with it as to endanger its being warped from its native purity and be loaded with corruptions. As we before observed, religion, though free, will always be friendly to lawful government: and this is enough. These remarks, I think, are perfectly agreeable to what we find in the bible. There we find our Saviour expressly disclaiming all temporal views and designs whatever in the religion he taught, declaring that 'his kingdom was not of this world,' but infinitely above this world and all the purposes of it" (*Truth Its Own Test*, 19–20).

84. Allen, *A Sermon . . . May 25th, 1808*, 13–14; Richardson, *Christian Patriot Encouraged*, 5, 9, quote on 5; Aiken, *A Letter . . . to the Rev. Samuel Spring*, 8–10; Richardson, *A Discourse . . . April 5, 1810*, 14. For an extended discussion of the pro-war stance of Republicans from different denominations, see Gribbin, *Churches Militant*, 62–103.

85. Harry S. Stout, *The New England Soul: Preaching and Religious Culture in Colonial New England* (New York: Oxford University Press, 1986), 29–30; Sprague, *Annals*, 2:268; Formisano, *Transformation of Political Culture*, 94–95; Parish, *A Sermon, Preached . . . May 30, 1810*, 2.

86. Noah Webster, *A Rod for the Fool's Back* (New Haven, Conn., 1800), 7; Scott, *From Office to Profession*, 27.

87. Bishop, *Connecticut Republicanism*, iv; Drake, *Dictionary of American Biography*, 723; Gribbin, *Churches Militant*, 23; William Plumer, *Address to the Clergy of New-England, on their Opposition to the Rulers of the United States* (Concord, N.H., 1814), iii. As James M. Banner Jr. notes, "in a state [Massachusetts] where the vast majority of citizens were practicing or professed Congregationalists, the Republican Party could hardly have won a single election without having attracted thousands of Congregational votes" (*To the Hartford Convention*, 197). Like Bishop and Plumer, the "anticlerical" Connecticut Republican politician, Christopher Manwaring, also denied the Federalists' accusations that the Jeffersonians were "*atheists, deists, hereticks [sic], jacobins, infidel philosophers, enemies to God and man, and in league with the devil, Frenchmen, and infernal spirits* to destroy all government, order, and religion, and turn the world upside down" (*Republicanism & Aristocracy Contrasted: or, the Steady Habits of Connecticut, Inconsistent with, and Opposed to the Principles of the American Revolution. Exhibited in an Oration, Delivered at New-London, [Con.] July 4th, 1804. On the Cel-*

ebration of American Independence [Norwich, Conn., 1804], 4). For a brief description of Manwaring's religious liberalism and political radicalism, see McLoughlin, *New England Dissent*, 2:1022.

88. Plumer, *Address to the Clergy*, iii, 23–25, quotes on 25 and iii; Bishop, *Connecticut Republicanism*, 20.

89. Bishop, *Connecticut Republicanism*, 3–23, 38–39, 44, quotes on 38–39 and 44; Plumer, *Address to the Clergy*, 8–19.

90. David Waldstreicher and Stephen R. Grossbart, "Abraham Bishop's Vocation; or, The Mediation of Jeffersonian Politics," *JER* 18 (1998): 617–657.

By using the lump term *dissenters*, I do not mean to suggest that denominational differences had ceased to be important. Denominational identities and particularities remained strong. William G. McLoughlin, for instance, noted bitter competition between Baptists and Universalists, Methodists, and Elias Smith's Christians. *New England Dissent*, 2:709–710, 745–749. Furthermore, intellectually, socially, and politically speaking, the Episcopalians might not seem to fit a general category of "dissenters." Ibid., 2:1026. Boston's John S. J. Gardiner, for example, could "out-Federalize even the Congregational clergy" (Banner, *To the Hartford Convention*, 57). But, as will be seen later, Episcopalians, Baptists, and Christians all lined up to take their shots at the Congregational establishment. These diverse denominations shared a common antipathy toward the standing order. Even the supposedly staid Episcopalians produced the vitriolic John Cosens Ogden.

91. John Cosens Ogden, *An Appeal to the Candid upon the Present State of Religion and Politics in Connecticut* (Stockbridge, Mass., 1799), 14; Nehemiah Dodge, *A Sermon delivered, at West-Springfield, Massachusetts, On the 5th of July,* A.D. *1802, to the inhabitants who met to celebrate the Anniversary of the 4th of July* (Hartford, Conn., 1802), 4. On Ogden's background, see Richard A. Harrison, ed., *Princetonians 1769–1775: A Biographical Dictionary* (Princeton, N.J.: Princeton University Press, 1980), 93–97. For other invocations of John 18:36, see John Leland, "A Blow at the Root: being a Fashionable Fast-Day Sermon, delivered at Cheshire, April 9, 1801," in *The Writings of the Late Elder John Leland, including some Events in his Life, written by himself, with Additional Sketches, &c,* ed. L. F. Greene (1845; reprint, New York: Arno Press and the New York Times, 1969), 242; Asahel Morse, *An Oration, delivered at Winsted, July 5th,* A.D. *1802. In Commemoration of the Declaration of Our National Independence, on the Memorable Fourth of July,* A.D. *1776* (Hartford, Conn., 1802), 13. On Dodge's and Morse's July Fourth sermons, see also McLoughlin, *New England Dissent*, 2:1006–1008.

92. Nehemiah Dodge, *A Discourse, Delivered at Lebanon, in Connecticut, on the Fourth of March, 1805, at the New Meeting-House; before a large concourse of respectable citizens, met in honor of the late Presidential Election of Thomas Jefferson* (Norwich, Conn., 1805), 3–12, 24; McLoughlin, *New England Dissent*, 2:1017–1018. For another example of the Baptists' separation of Old and New Testaments, see John Leland, "The Government of Christ a Christocracy," in *The Writings of the Late Elder John Leland*, 274–275.

93. Dodge, *A Sermon delivered . . . On the 5th of July,* A.D. *1802,* 18–19, quote on 18. "To myself," agreed John Leland, "there remains no doubt, that the religious establishments of Massachusetts, and all state establishments of Christianity in the world, are all of them ANTI-CHRISTOCRACIES" (Leland, "Christocracy," 281).

94. Leland, "Christocracy," 277; Dodge, *A Sermon delivered . . . On the 5th of July,* A.D. *1802,* 6.

95. John Leland, "An Oration, delivered at Cheshire, July 5, 1802, on the Celebration of Independence; containing Seventeen Sketches, and Seventeen Wishes," in *The Writings of the Late Elder John Leland*, 267; idem, "A Blow at the Root," 247; Elias Smith, *[No. I.] The Clergyman's Looking-Glass, or Ancient and Modern Things contrasted. 1—Concerning Ministers. 2—Concerning Baptism. 3—Concerning the Church. Ancient things as they stand in the*

Scriptures. Modern things as they are practised in the present day, 2d corrected and enlarged ed. (Portsmouth, N.H., 1803), iii–iv, 5. For the contention that the established clergy was motivated chiefly by a love of "filthy lucre," see ibid., 11–12; Dodge, *A Discourse . . . on the Fourth of March, 1805,* 27.

96. Dodge, *A Sermon delivered . . . On the 5th of July,* A.D. 1802, 19. See also Smith, *Clergyman's Looking-Glass,* 16–21.

97. Ogden, *Appeal to the Candid,* 11; Smith, *Loving Kindness of God,* 18. Asahel Morse also wished that the constitutions of the New England states contained the same provisions as the first amendment to the U.S. Constitution (*An Oration, delivered at Winsted,* 7–8). John Leland gave this glimpse of the chicanery to which dissenters were subjected, and one wonders how widespread such practices were: "But is there a single article in the state, in which so much deceit, fraud, and cruelty have been used, as in the article of religion? How often have ministerial taxes been mixed with town taxes, that the man taxed might pay the ministerial tax without knowing it? How often have men, who have made use of the law to draw their money back, been flung out of it, under one pretence [*sic*] or another? and if they have gained their cause, being in the town, they have had their proportionate part of the costs to pay. How many times towns have hired ministers to preach, not being ordained over them; and if the dissenters have been exempted from paying the stipulated salary, yet the charge of the committee, and the boarding of the priests, have been put into the town rate. Where meeting-houses are built for one society for town meetings, what specious arguments are made use of to make all pay for building them. Can an honest man look on all this, and much more, and not feel his heart rise with indignation against that religion which gives birth to all this?" ("A Blow at the Root," 252–253).

98. Sidney E. Mead classically stated the theme of the convergence of interests between "rationalists and sectarian-pietists" (*The Lively Experiment: The Shaping of Christianity in America* [New York: Harper & Row, 1963], 38–43, 60–62). The Baptists were not entirely comfortable to be aligned with a reputedly infidel party, wrote William G. McLoughlin, but they reasoned, "better to side with a party which cared little about religion but much for liberty against a party which professed to be thoroughly orthodox in theology but which wanted a favored position for one denomination" (*New England Dissent,* 2:1013).

99. Dodge, *A Sermon delivered . . . On the 5th of July,* A.D. 1802, 4; Ogden, *Appeal to the Candid,* 10. Dodge stated his allegation as a question: "Do [established clergymen] not meet together in caucusses [*sic*], called ministers meetings, and consult what sort of representatives will be most likely to promote rulers, and laws, favorable to their Jewish plan [of an established church combining Moses and Aaron]; then with great pretension to piety, like his holiness, the Pope, from the sacred desk, as it is profanely called, extol, recommend, and exalt to heaven, as near as they can, those characters for rulers, who are most blind, through selfishness, to the gospel plan, and the inalienable rights of man, and most fond of making laws to support hypocrisy?" (Dodge, *A Discourse . . . on the Fourth of March, 1805,* 28).

100. Ogden, *Appeal to the Candid,* 20–21; Leland, "A Blow at the Root," 238; Smith, *Clergyman's Looking-Glass,* 5. A few quotations from Benjamin Trumbull's 1801 Connecticut election sermon will demonstrate the standing order's rejection of the small government ideal. "Their [rulers'] whole authority, powers and influence should be employed to keep and promote the public peace and happiness; to maintain all the natural, civil and religious rights of their subjects, to suppress all immorality, and to countenance and support every thing which is useful, virtuous and praise-worthy. They are represented as the very pillars of the earth, which support it, and prevent its dissolution. In what can the dignity of man be possibly more displayed than in sustaining these high and momentous offices, and in a zealous, wise and faithful discharge of them?" "Civil government is arduous, and requires the knowledge of a great variety of things, with a singular prudence in the management of public affairs." "The af-

fairs of government are high, above the reach of vulgar minds, though they may be good, and have the best designs towards the community" (*Dignity of Man*, 15, 18, 20).

101. Morse, *An Oration, delivered at Winsted*, 4. As noted in chapter 2, no one more vigorously advocated the inalienable rights position than John Leland. See Leland, "A Blow at the Root," 239–242. He also argued for religious toleration in words reminiscent of *Notes on the State of Virginia*, a book ridiculed by Federalists like Elijah Parish. Ibid., 249.

102. Ogden, *Appeal to the Candid*, 2–9, 14, quotes on 9, 2, 14.

103. Smith, *Loving Kindness of God*, 32; Leland, "An Oration, delivered at Cheshire, July 5, 1802," 263. As Michael G. Kenny writes, "Smith and his friends were redefining the meaning of liberty in a manner whereby the traditional Christian concept of liberty—liberty from sin gained through faith in Christ as Savior—began to elide with conceptions of political and personal liberty derived from the Revolution and enshrined in the Declaration of Independence and the federal Constitution" (*Perfect Law of Liberty*, 13–14). For another striking example of ideological fusion, see Leland, "Christocracy," 275, where he wrote, "Liberty and equality, the boast of democracy, is realized in the church. The saints are set at liberty from the prison of sin, and freed from the curse of the law. They are all one in Christ; the poor are exalted, and the rich are brought low."

104. Leland, "A Blow at the Root," 255. As Nehemiah Dodge said, "Was he governor of Connecticut, I am fully convinced that every denomination of christians, would enjoy the liberty of worshipping God when, where, and how bible and conscience should dictate, as an inalienable privilege, and not as a favor granted from any ruling power of man whatever" (*A Discourse . . . on the Fourth of March, 1805*, 29). See also McLoughlin, *New England Dissent*, 2:1004–1005, for the mutually admiring correspondence between Jefferson and Connecticut Baptists, in which Jefferson announced "the doctrine of 'a wall of separation between Church and State.'"

105. Smith, *Clergyman's Looking-Glass*, iv; Dodge, *A Discourse . . . on the Fourth of March, 1805*, 28; idem, *A Sermon delivered . . . On the 5th of July*, A.D. 1802, 19–20; Kenny, *Perfect Law of Liberty*, 24–25, 112, quote on 25. Similarly, said Asahel Morse the same year, "God suffered us, for a little while past, to feel the weight of heavy taxes, and the burden of a standing army, which was imposed upon us in a time of peace; to experience the evil of a sedition law, and an alien bill. But [Ps. 126:3] the Lord who hath done great things for us, hath reserved the scene; the overruling hand of his providence hath regulated and so disposed the great council of our nation, to act upon the calm and peaceable spirit of republican principles, that our country will yet shine as the glory of the world, the ensign of peace, the nursery of arts and sciences, the theatre of freedom and liberty, and a refuge of protection for oppressed humanity. Gentlemen, we have now a bright star in the presidential chair, which arose in the time of British tyrannical darkness in our country, whose brilliant rays of republican light dawned over our land, and illuminated the minds of our citizens, and inspired them with the love of freedom, and with ardor and zeal for our independence and liberty" (*An Oration, delivered at Winsted*, 10). Leland, "An Oration, delivered at Cheshire, July 5, 1802," 259, linked the American Revolution, the French Revolution, and Jefferson's election, an unthinkable combination for the standing order.

106. Morse, *An Oration, delivered at Winsted*, 3. See also Smith, *Loving Kindness of God*, 3–4.

107. The basic pattern, writes Ronald P. Formisano, looked like this: "the dominant Congregational churches were strongly Federal, while dissenting religious groups, especially the Baptists and Methodists, gave the Republicans their surest sources of support" (*Transformation of Political Culture*, 15). However, he also adds that "more precise statements about Congregational political loyalties, or those of other religious groups, are difficult to make" (ibid., 156). Politicians, aware of the sectarian division of the electorate, exploited it to rally their core con-

stituencies. "Federalists usually defended the establishment as received and more often wrapped their candidates and cause in an aura of Christian piety, while trying to stigmatize their opponents with deism, infidelity, irreligion, or immorality. Republicans tended to associate themselves with 'religious liberty' and 'toleration,' and protested vigorously against Federal priestcraft and oppression" (ibid., 155).

108. Stephen Reed Grossbart, "The Revolutionary Transition: Politics, Religion, and Economy in Eastern Connecticut, 1765–1800" (Ph.D. diss., University of Michigan, 1989), 3–4; McLoughlin, *New England Dissent*, 2:919. McLoughlin lists the number of dissenting churches as follows: Baptist 85, Episcopal 74, Methodist 53, Separate 2, and Sandemanian 1. He also lists (pp. 919–920, n. 7) a handful, probably not more than 10, of other religious societies, including Shakers, Quakers, Rogerenes, and Universalists, but notes the unreliability of any precise tabulation. Grossbart's enumeration is somewhat different: "When the new constitution disestablished the Congregational Church in 1818, only 44% of the state's 474 churches were Congregational; 19% were Baptist, 17% Episcopalian, and 15% Methodist" ("Revolutionary Transition," 3–4).

109. Banner, *To the Hartford Convention*, 198.

110. James Thayer Addison, *The Episcopal Church in the United States, 1789–1931* (New York: Charles Scribner's Sons, 1951), 78, 92–93, quote on 78.

111. Jedidiah Morse, *The True Reasons on Which the Election of a Hollis Professor of Divinity in Harvard College, Was Opposed at the Board of Overseers, Feb. 14, 1805* (Charlestown, Mass., 1805). For more on this incident and a fuller account of the orthodox-Unitarian separation, running from the 1790s to the 1810s, see Phillips, *Jedidiah Morse*, 129–151, 157–160.

112. Conrad Wright, *The Beginnings of Unitarianism in America* (Boston: Starr King Press, 1955), 245–251.

113. Howe, *Unitarian Conscience*, 29–56. Banner, *To the Hartford Convention*, 201, writes that, "Behind this schism were the subtle differences of age and experience." He attempts to show (pp. 201–202) that a younger generation of religious liberals opposed an older cohort of conservatives. However, one could just as easily construct a list similar to his showing a group of old liberals (such as Charles Chauncy, Jonathan Mayhew, and Aaron Bancroft) and young conservatives (Lyman Beecher, Heman Humphrey, and Leonard Woods). Indeed, as Conrad Wright notes, "The Unitarian controversy added nothing significant to familiar theological arguments . . . the [Unitarians'] doctrine itself, even in Channing's Baltimore sermon, did not represent a break with the tradition of Chauncy, Mayhew, Gay, Belknap, and Bancroft" ("Institutional Reconstruction in the Unitarian Controversy," in *American Unitarianism, 1805–1865*, ed. Conrad Edick Wright, Massachusetts Historical Society Studies in American History and Culture, no. 1 [Boston: Massachusetts Historical Society and Northeastern University Press, 1989], 4).

114. "When the [orthodox-Unitarian] division [of the Congregational churches] was completed, it was found [around 1830] that the whole number of Congregational churches in Massachusetts was 544 (leaving out of the account such as had become extinct, or were merged in others), of which 135 were Unitarian and 409 Orthodox" (Joseph S. Clark, *A Historical Sketch of the Congregational Churches in Massachusetts, from 1620 to 1858. With an Appendix* [Boston, 1858], 234–235, 272, quote on 272). See also Conrad Wright's fine sketch of the division of Dorchester's Second Parish, which he calls (p. 6) "the Unitarian controversy in miniature" ("Institutional Reconstruction," 6–26).

115. "Jedidiah Morse founded the *Panoplist* in 1805. The Andover Theological Seminary was established in 1808, and the first steps leading to the establishment of the Harvard Divinity School were taken three years later. The Park Street Church was gathered in 1809. The American Board of Commissioners for Foreign Missions was organized in 1810. A General Association of Ministers on an evangelical basis, formed in 1802, finally began to attract wide sup-

port from the orthodox after 1810. The *Christian Disciple*, forerunner of the *Christian Examiner*, dates from 1811. In short, the institutionalization of the split between the two parties was well advanced before the period of liveliest theological debate [after 1815]" (Wright, "Institutional Reconstruction," 5, 14–22, quote on 5).

116. Banner, *To the Hartford Convention*, 208–210.

117. For the exhaustive account of the disestablishment movements in New England, upon which the following relies, see McLoughlin, *New England Dissent*, vol. 2. For a more concise rendering of Massachusetts disestablishment, see John D. Cushing, "Notes on Disestablishment in Massachusetts, 1780–1833," *WMQ* 26 (1969): 169–190.

118. "The Republican Party was born, flourished and died in Massachusetts without ever advocating Jefferson's position on disestablishment" (McLoughlin, *New England Dissent*, 2:1067).

119. Ibid., 2:1084.

120. Ibid., 2:1102. See also Goodman, *Democratic-Republicans of Massachusetts*, 163–166.

121. McLoughlin, *New England Dissent*, 2:1145–1157.

122. Ibid., 2:985–1005, 1024–1028, 1043–1062, quote on 2:1024.

123. Harry Croswell, *A Sermon Preached at the Anniversary Election, Hartford, May 14, 1818* (Hartford, Conn., 1818), 11, 7.

124. Harrison, *Princetonians*, 101, recounts this incident, but erroneously gives the date as 1817. However, in 1817 the election preacher was not an Episcopalian, but Abel McEwen, minister of the First Congregational Church of New London. See Abel McEwen, *A Sermon Preached at the Anniversary Election, Hartford, May 8, 1817* (Hartford, Conn., 1817); Dexter, *Biographical Sketches*, 5:680–683.

Chapter Four

1. Aaron Bancroft, *A Sermon, Preached before his Excellency Caleb Strong, Esq. Governour, the Honourable the Council, Senate, and House of Representatives of the Commonwealth of Massachusetts, May 27, 1801, the Day of General Election* (Boston, 1801), 5–6, 12, 14, 28; Samuel Austin, *A Sermon, Preached at Worcester, on the Annual Fast, April 11, 1811* (Worcester, Mass., 1811), 7, 23, 27; idem, *A Sermon, preached in Worcester, Massachusetts, on the occasion of the Special Fast, July 23d, 1812* (Worcester, Mass., 1812), 14, 17.

2. E[lam] Smalley, *The Worcester Pulpit; With Notices Historical and Biographical* (Boston, 1851), 109–110, 284–285; Isaac Davis, *An Historical Discourse on the Fiftieth Anniversary of the First Baptist Church in Worcester, Mass., Dec. 9th, 1862* (Worcester, Mass., 1863), 9–18. A copy of the petition from those parishioners upset by Austin's Federalist and antiwar preaching can be found in Church Record Book, 1787–1830, Worcester, Mass., Old South Church Records, 1724–1920, folio vol. 1, AAS.

3. [Joseph Goffe], *The Result of an Ecclesiastical Council, published at Princeton, March 7, 1817; and the Protest of the Minority: with Remarks, Notes, and Observations* (Worcester, Mass., 1817), quotes on 13–14; Aaron Bancroft, *A Vindication of the Result of the late Mutual Council convened in Princeton* (Worcester, Mass., 1817), iv; [Joseph Goffe], *The Result of Council at Princeton incapable of vindication: or, a Review of Dr. Bancroft's Vindication of the Result of the late Mutual Council convened in Princeton* (Worcester, Mass., 1817); Joseph Goffe, Diary, 20 Dec. 1796 and 9 April 1797, Joseph Goffe Papers, 1721–1846, AAS.

4. Goffe, Diary, 27 May 1807 and 30 April 1800.

5. Timothy Dwight, *A Sermon Preached at the Opening of the Theological Institution in Andover; and at the Ordination of Rev. Eliphalet Pearson, LL.D. September 28th, 1808* (Boston, 1808), 23–27, quotes on 24–25.

6. Samuel Dunham, *An Historical Discourse delivered at West Brookfield, Mass., on occasion of the One Hundred and Fiftieth Anniversary of the First Church in Brookfield, October 16, 1867* (Springfield, Mass., 1868), 12–13; H[iram]. A. Tracy, *A Brief History of the First Church in Sutton, Mass. Contained in a Sermon Preached Jan. 2d, 1842* (Worcester, Mass., 1842), 10–15; John L. Brooke, *The Heart of the Commonwealth: Society and Political Culture in Worcester County, Massachusetts, 1713–1861* (New York: Cambridge University Press, 1989; Amherst: University of Massachusetts Press, 1992), 66–96, 176–179; Joseph Goffe, Autobiography, Joseph Goffe Papers, 1789–1846, box 3, folder 3, AAS. The two best recent treatments of the Second Great Awakening in Connecticut are David W. Kling, *A Field of Divine Wonders: The New Divinity and Village Revivals in Northwestern Connecticut, 1792–1822* (University Park: Pennsylvania State University Press, 1993), and James R. Rohrer, *Keepers of the Covenant: Frontier Missions and the Decline of Congregationalism, 1774–1818* (New York: Oxford University Press, 1995).

7. Goffe, Autobiography; idem, Diary, 24 April, 14 Aug., and 2 Nov. 1800. "What set New Divinity revivals apart from others," writes David W. Kling, "was their preoccupation with doctrine" (*A Field of Divine Wonders*, 4).

8. Goffe, Diary, 1800, quotes from 28 and 22 Jan., 7 Aug., 23 and 31 Jan., and 30 Sept. Likewise, "the religious conference functioned as the basic organizational unit and transmitter of the revival among Congregationalists in northwestern Connecticut" (Kling, *A Field of Divine Wonders*, 67–72, quote on 68).

9. Goffe, Diary, 1800. For a similar case of ministerial cooperation, see also Kling, *A Field of Divine Wonders*, 65–67.

10. Goffe, Diary, 7 Dec. 1796 and 26 Jan. 1800; idem, Autobiography.

11. Goffe, Diary, 3 and 4 June 1806, 6 Oct. 1807, and 12 Aug. 1802; Brookfield Association, 22 June 1757, Records, 1757–1837, CL.

12. Goffe, Diary, 28 Feb., 30 June (Ballou), 4 Nov., 19 Sept., and 2 June 1800 (in Providence), 1 and 2 Nov. 1803 (in Boston), 17 and 18 Jan. 1804 (in Boston), and 26 Nov. 1805 (Mr. Andrews); idem, *Spirits in Prison: A Discourse, delivered at Upton, Lord's Day, April 10th, 1803* (Worcester, Mass., 1803); Stephen A. Marini, *Radical Sects of Revolutionary New England* (Cambridge: Harvard University Press, 1982), 72–75 (regarding Rich). The entry for 30 June 1800 refers only to "Ballou" without any further identification. I interpret this to be a reference to the Universalist Hosea Ballou, based on his entry in Allen Johnson, ed., *Dictionary of American Biography*, 20 vols. (New York: Charles Scribner's Sons, 1928–1936), 1:558, which notes that "on Sept. 11, 1796, Ballou established a home in Dana, Mass., as the center of extensive circuit preaching (1796–1803)." On the respectability and conservatism of Samuel Stillman and his church, see Michael G. Kenny, *The Perfect Law of Liberty: Elias Smith and the Providential History of America* (Washington, D.C.: Smithsonian Institution Press, 1994), 75–76, 82.

13. Goffe, Diary, 16 Nov. 1800; idem, Autobiography.

14. Goffe, Diary, 31 Jan., 31 May, and 30 Sept. 1801.

15. Tracy, *Brief History of the First Church in Sutton*, 19; Goffe, Autobiography.

16. Goffe, Diary, 30 Sept. 1803, 11 April 1801, and 4 May 1804; idem, "An Inventory of my Library," in Account Book, 1794–1815, Joseph Goffe Papers, 1721–1846, AAS.

17. Nathan O. Hatch has argued that the standing order stumbled before the dissenters' challenge. "In the wake of the Revolution," he contends, "dissenters confounded the establishment with an approach to theological matters that was nothing short of guerilla warfare. The coarse language, earthy humor, biting sarcasm, and commonsense reasoning of their attacks appealed to the uneducated but left the professional clergy without a ready defense" (*The Democratization of American Christianity* [New Haven: Yale University Press, 1989], 34). I try to show rather that the Congregational clergy responded vigorously and creatively.

In the interpretation of Donald M. Scott, the standing order sounded a retreat from the lost world of the eighteenth century. To "the nineteenth-century evangelicals," he writes, "the conquest of worldliness consisted, not in organizing the world along godly lines, but in providing the individual with a set of inner and institutional barriers against it. The fabric of evangelical institutions, associations, and commitments with which churchmen surrounded their communicants thus provided a kind of quarantine against the outer world" (*From Office to Profession: The New England Ministry, 1750–1850* [Philadelphia: University of Pennsylvania Press, 1978], 45). I disagree with his interpretation of these institutions as a strategy of withdrawal and stress, instead, the church as a beachhead for further assault upon the world.

18. William Ellery Channing, *A Sermon, Preached in Boston, April 5, 1810, the Day of the Public Fast* (Boston, 1810), 5; Dan Huntington, *The Love of Jerusalem, the Prosperity of a People. A Sermon, Preached at the Anniversary Election, Hartford, May 12, 1814* (Hartford, Conn., 1814), 7. See also Daniel Chaplin, *The Dispensations of Divine Providence Considered as Generally Corresponding with the Moral Character of a Nation, and the Morals of New England at the Present Day Briefly Compared with the Morals of our Ancestors; with some Observations on the Duty of Electors, to Give their Suffrages to Men of Christian Character. A Sermon Delivered at Groton Jan. 12, 1815, Being the Day of the National Fast* (Cambridge, Mass., 1815), 3–4.

19. Nathan Perkins, *The Benign Influence of Religion on Civil Government and National Happiness—Illustrated in a Sermon, preached before His Excellency Jonathan Trumbull, Esq. Governor; His Honor John Treadwell, Esq. Lieutenant Governor: The Honorable the Council: and House of Representatives of the State of Connecticut, on the Anniversary Election, May 12th, 1808* (Hartford, Conn., 1808), 20. For the same argument, see also Zebulon Ely, *The Wisdom and Duty of Magistrates. A Sermon, Preached at the General Election, May 10th, 1804* (Hartford, Conn., 1804), 28; Huntington, *Love of Jerusalem*, 22–23.

20. Asahel Hooker, *The Moral Tendency of Man's Accountableness to God; and its Influence on the Happiness of Society. A Sermon, Preached on the Day of the General Election, at Hartford, in the State of Connecticut, May 9th, 1805* (Hartford, Conn., 1805), 7. "National calamities," noted Joseph Lathrop, "always originate, in national vice and corruption" (*The Constancy and Uniformity of the Divine Government, Illustrated and Improved in a Sermon, Preached in Springfield, April 7, 1803, which was a day of Public Fasting and Prayer* [Springfield, Mass., 1803], 7). See also Jesse Appleton, *A Sermon Preached in Boston, at the Annual Election, May 25, 1814* (Boston, 1814), 13–14.

21. Perkins, *Benign Influence of Religion*, 24–25. See also Ely, *Wisdom and Duty of Magistrates*, 29; Huntington, *Love of Jerusalem*, 10–14; Joseph Strong, *A Sermon, Preached on the General Election at Hartford in Connecticut, May 13, 1802* (Hartford, Conn., 1802), 5–6.

22. Matthias Burnet, *An Election Sermon, Preached at Hartford, on the Day of the Anniversary Election, May 12, 1803* (Hartford, Conn., 1803), 5–9, quote on 9; Reuben Puffer, *A Sermon, delivered before His Excellency Caleb Strong, Esq. Governour, His Honour Edward H. Robbins, Esq. Lt. Gov, the Honourable the Council, Senate, and House of Representatives, of the Commonwealth of Massachusetts, May 25, 1803, Being the Day of General Election* (Boston, 1803), 25–26; Perkins, *Benign Influence of Religion*, 22–23. Ten years later, Chauncey Lee of Colebrook, Connecticut, said almost the exact same thing as Puffer: "Let it, then, be received, as an axiom in politics; let it be engraven upon our hearts, as with the point of a diamond; that *Religion is the only sure foundation of a free and happy government.* It is the great palladium of all our natural and social rights" (*The Government of God the True Source and Standard of Human Government. A Sermon, preached on the day of the General Election, at Hartford, in the State of Connecticut, May 13th, 1813* [Hartford, Conn., 1813], 42). Benjamin Trumbull, minister of North Haven, Connecticut, concurred with Burnet: "When conscience is lost, and moral motives have no influence, a people can be governed by severe laws and punishments only; by Newgates, swords and cannon. In just such proportion as the influence

of moral principles and motives are annihilated, the restraints of law must be increased, and the natural rights and liberties of the subjects be diminished" (*The Dignity of Man, especially as Displayed in Civil Government. A Sermon, Preached on the General Election at Hartford, in Connecticut, May 14, 1801* [Hartford, Conn., 1801], 22).

23. Ely, *Wisdom and Duty of Magistrates*, 17; Perkins, *Benign Influence of Religion*, 17; William Ellery Channing, *A Sermon, Preached in Boston, July 23, 1812, the Day of the Publick Fast, Appointed by the Executive of the Commonwealth of Massachusetts, in Consequence of the Declaration of War Against Great Britain* (Boston, 1812), 4; Lyman Beecher, *A Reformation of Morals Practicable and Indispensable: A Sermon Delivered at New Haven on the Evening of October 27, 1812*, 2d ed. (1812; Andover, Mass., 1814), reprinted in *Lyman Beecher and the Reform of Society: Four Sermons, 1804–1828*, Religion in America: Series 2, ed. Edwin S. Gaustad (New York: Arno Press and New York Times, 1972), 5. On Perkins's background, see Richard A. Harrison, ed., *Princetonians 1769–1775: A Biographical Dictionary* (Princeton, N.J.: Princeton University Press, 1980), 97–101. Reuben Puffer, too, raised the image of Jesus as patriot in *A Sermon, delivered . . . May 25, 1803*, 17.

24. Stephen West, *A Sermon, Delivered on the Public Fast, April 9th, 1801* (Stockbridge, Mass., 1801), 14; Trumbull, *Dignity of Man*, 37; Samuel Spring, *A Sermon, Delivered before the Massachusetts Missionary Society, at their Annual Meeting May 25, 1802. The Annual Report also of the Trustees, and Several Interesting Things relative to Missions* (Newburyport, Mass., 1802), 29; Dwight, *A Sermon Preached at the Opening*, 25. See also Timothy Dwight, *A Discourse, in Two Parts, Delivered July 23, 1812, on the Public Fast, [and August 20, 1812, on the National Fast,] in the Chapel of Yale College*, 2d ed. (Boston, 1813), 20–23.

25. Spring, *A Sermon, Delivered . . . May 25, 1802*, 30; West, *A Sermon, Delivered . . . April 9th, 1801*, 15; Huntington, *Love of Jerusalem*, 39. "God has graciously shed down the influence of his Spirit on the inhabitants in some parts of the land, by which there is reason to believe, a considerable gathering has been made of souls to Christ, and thousands of Christians have been greatly enlivened and strengthened in the holy faith. The Lord has also put it into the hearts of many Christians in this country as well as in other parts of Christendom, to form societies, and to give their time, their labor and money for the purpose of furnishing the bible and other books of piety to the destitute, and sending a preached gospel amongst them by pious and able ministers. The missionary spirit at the present day is truly wonderful, which the world never witnessed before in so great a degree; we ought to acknowledge the visible hand of God in it, and thankfully hope it to be the forerunner of happier times, of times of refreshing from the presence of the Lord, or of a general reformation, plainly spoken of in the word of God, which Christians expect in the latter day" (Chaplin, *Dispensations of Divine Providence*, 11).

Timothy Dwight, meanwhile, predicted millennial ramifications in the founding of Andover Seminary. "The period, my Brethren, is hastening: the morning star will soon arise, which will usher in that illustrious day, destined to scatter the darkness of this melancholy world, and cover the earth with light and glory; the second birth-day of truth, righteousness, and salvation. Soon shall the Church [Isa. 52:1] *awake, and put on strength*. Soon shall she *be clothed with beautiful garments*. . . . Ministers, [Matt. 13:52] *instructed unto the kingdom of heaven*, faithful, zealous, [Dan. 12:3] *wise*, and thus fitted to *turn many to righteousness*, will be the instruments, by which the SPIRIT of truth will accomplish this divine transformation. To form, and furnish, such ministers, therefore, is to contribute to this glorious work; to convey the blessing down to succeeding ages, and to the remote regions of the earth; to awaken the song of transport in lands yet untraversed, and in millions yet unborn; to become benefactors to the nations of the Millenium [*sic*]; and to increase the multitude, the happiness, and the glory, of heaven" (Dwight, *A Sermon Preached at the Opening*, 26–27). See also Dwight, *A Discourse, in Two Parts*, 44.

26. Connecticut Bible Society, *Report of the Directing Committee of the Connecticut Bible Society; Exhibited to the Society at their Meeting, May 12, 181* [sic] (Hartford, Conn., 1814), 5–6; Stephen W. Stebbins, *God's Government of the Church and World, the Source of Great Consolation and Joy: Illustrated in a Sermon Preached at Hartford, May 9, 1811. Before the General Assembly of the State of Connecticut, at the Anniversary Election* (Hartford, Conn., 1811), 14; Spring, *A Sermon, Delivered . . . May 25, 1802,* 6. Similarly, the Missionary Society of Connecticut commented that "the only consideration which can give consolation to the mind, amidst these changes and revolutions among the nations of the earth, is that the Lord omnipotent reigneth. . . . All events shall be made ultimately to advance his glorious designs respecting his Church; and there is reason to hope that the violent convulsions which agitate so great a part of the earth, are a prelude to that happy state of things, spoken of in the prophetical writings, when nations shall no more rise up against nation, and the inhabitants of the earth shall learn war no more" (*An Address from the Trustees of the Missionary Society of Connecticut, to the Ministers and People of the State: and a Narrative on the Subject of Missions, For the year 1806. To which are Subjoined, a Statement of the Funds of the Society, and a List of Books, Sent to the New Settlements* [Hartford, Conn., 1807], 11–12).

27. West, *A Sermon, Delivered . . . April 9th, 1801,* 15; Dwight, *A Sermon Preached at the Opening,* 24.

28. Franklin Bowditch Dexter, *Biographical Sketches of the Graduates of Yale College: With Annals of the College History,* 6 vols. (New York, 1885–1912), 4:463–467.

29. John Elliott, *The Gracious Presence of God, The Highest Felicity and Security of Any People. A Sermon, Preached before his Excellency the Governor, and the Honorable Legislature of the State of Connecticut, Convened at Hartford, on the Anniversary Election, May 10th, 1810* (Hartford, Conn., 1810), 8–9, 12, 32, 13, 34.

30. Ibid., 18–19, 25–26. "The greatest accessions are made from the militant, to the triumphant Church" (ibid., 30).

31. Ibid., 30, 32, 43.

32. Ibid., 15.

33. Ibid., 44–49. For an overview of benevolent initiatives from the 1790s to 1810s, see Phillips, *Jedidiah Morse,* 109–124. The phrase "evangelical America" comes from Mark A. Noll, *A History of Christianity in the United States and Canada* (Grand Rapids, Mich.: Eerdmans, 1992), 220–232, 242–243. Likewise, Richard Carwardine writes that "evangelical Protestantism [was] the principal subculture in antebellum America" (*Evangelicals and Politics in Antebellum America* [New Haven: Yale University Press, 1993], xv and passim).

34. Williston Walker, *A History of the Congregational Churches in the United States,* The American Church History Series, vol. 3, ed. Philip Schaff et al. (New York, 1894), 309–313; Rohrer, *Keepers of the Covenant;* Spring, *A Sermon, Delivered . . . May 25, 1802,* 45–50; Connecticut Bible Society, *Report of the Directing Committee,* 6; Smalley, *Worcester Pulpit,* 107–108.

35. Randolph A. Roth, *The Democratic Dilemma: Religion, Reform, and the Social Order in the Connecticut River Valley of Vermont, 1791–1850* (New York: Cambridge University Press, 1987), 41–79; Robert H. Abzug, *Cosmos Crumbling: American Reform and the Religious Imagination* (New York: Oxford University Press, 1994), 58–59; Rohrer, *Keepers of the Covenant,* 145–147. Compare the efforts of the Congregational Massachusetts Missionary Society in Spring, *A Sermon, Delivered . . . May 25, 1802,* 35–36, with the Methodists' in Leroy M. Lee, *The Life and Times of the Rev. Jesse Lee* (Richmond, Va., 1848), 265.

36. Walker, *History of the Congregational Churches,* 313, 322–326; Nancy F. Cott, *The Bonds of Womanhood: "Woman's Sphere" in New England, 1780–1835* (New Haven: Yale University Press, 1977), 132–159; Carolyn J. Lawes, *Women and Reform in a New England Community, 1815–1860* (Lexington: University Press of Kentucky, 2000), 45–81; Goffe, Diary, 19,

26, 28, and 29 May 1805; idem, Autobiography. Regarding the subject of publications, Jedidiah Morse made a signal contribution. In 1803 he founded "the Massachusetts Society for Promoting Christian Knowledge, the first tract society in the United States." "In 1805 he began publishing the *Panoplist*, a religious magazine" (Joseph W. Phillips, *Jedidiah Morse and New England Congregationalism* [New Brunswick, N.J.: Rutgers University Press, 1983], 117–120, quotes on 117 and 119). The *Panoplist* further fueled the evangelical movement by attacking Unitarianism wholeheartedly; see Peter S. Field, *The Crisis of the Standing Order: Clerical Intellectuals and Cultural Authority in Massachusetts, 1780–1833* (Amherst: University of Massachusetts Press, 1998), 151–161.

37. Brookfield Association, Records, 5 Jan. 1803, reports on the "Convention of Committees from several Ass.'s in the Western Counties" of Massachusetts held at Northampton on July 7, 1802, at which the plan for a General Association was first floated. Ephraim Ward to Joseph Lyman, 12 Feb. 1805, and Joseph Sumner to David Osgood, undated letter [1805?], Organization Records, 1805, Massachusetts General Association Records, 1805–1891, series A, folder 1, CL. Sumner was then moderator of the Worcester Association, to which Bancroft also belonged; see Joseph Allen, *The Worcester Association and its Antecedents: A History of Four Ministerial Associations: The Marlborough, The Worcester (Old), The Lancaster, and The Worcester (New) Associations. With Biographical Notices of the Members, accompanied by Portraits* (Boston, 1868), 127.

38. The Congregational Library has a volume, the spine of which reads "Minutes of the Gen'l Association of Massachusetts, 1807–1830." It contains clippings of the minutes from the years that they were printed in the *Panoplist*, bound with the separately printed pamphlets. The report of the formation of the Massachusetts Society for the Suppression of Intemperance comes from *Extracts from the Minutes of the General Association of Massachusetts Proper* (Boston, 1813), 2. Brookfield Association, Records, 29 Sept. 1813; *Extracts from the Minutes of the General Association of Congregational Ministers in Massachusetts Proper—1814. Together with Some Interesting Ancient and Modern Ecclesiastical Documents, Relating to the History of these Churches* (Boston, 1814), 3.

39. Walker, *History of the Congregational Churches*, 347–353, quote on 352; Dwight, *A Sermon Preached at the Opening*, 14; Charles I. Foster, *An Errand of Mercy: The Evangelical United Front, 1790–1837* (Chapel Hill: University of North Carolina Press, 1960), 134–135; Natalie A. Naylor, "The Theological Seminary in the Configuration of American Higher Education: the Ante-Bellum Years," *History of Education Quarterly* 17 (1977): 18–19, quote on 25. The recollections of Ephraim Abbot, a student in the first Andover graduating class of 1810, provide ironic confirmation of Dwight's prediction that going through the seminary would have a "powerful influence on the character and conduct" of the scholars. Abbot felt singled out and pressured to conform on account of his tepid Calvinism. "Not being a Hopkinsian," he recalled, "I could not always assent to what others believed; and therefore was sometimes accused of wanting a teachable disposition, and of being too fond of giving my own explanations" (Ephraim Abbot, Autobiography, 1779–1827, p. 10, Ephraim Abbot Papers, 1801–1904, box 2, folder 6, AAS).

40. *Constitution and Address of the Religious Charitable Society in the County of Worcester, Mass.* ([Worcester, Mass.], [1812?]); Benjamin Wood, *Labourers needed in the harvest of Christ. A Sermon, Delivered at Sutton, (S. P.) March 18, 1812, as Preliminary to the Formation of a Society, in the County of Worcester, for the Aid of Pious Young Men, with a View to the Ministry* (Worcester, Mass., 1812); Religious Charitable Society in the County of Worcester Records, 1812–1845, American Education Society Records, 1815–1894, series 06, subseries A, box 10, folder 6, CL. Specifically, the foregoing paragraph is based upon the following entries: 20 May and 16 Sept. 1812 (officers chosen), 15 Sept. 1812 (dispersal of money to students), 18 Sept. 1816 (seventeen branches), 20 April 1814 (Waldos), and 21 Sept. 1814 (Harvard Female So-

ciety). On the Waldo family and its patronage of religious causes, see Lawes, *Women and Reform*, 11–12. For the founding of the Religious Charitable Society, see also *Centennial History of the Town of Millbury, Massachusetts, Including Vital Statistics, 1850–1899* (Millbury, Mass., 1915), 201–202.

41. *Constitution and Address*, 1; Religious Charitable Society Records, 16 Sept. 1818; *Religious Charitable Society in the County of Worcester* ([Worcester, Mass.], [1814?]), 2.

42. See the excellent analysis, on which the following draws significantly, in Scott, *From Office to Profession*, 31–35, quote on 31. See also Foster, *An Errand of Mercy*, 133–136.

43. This same list of social ills is found in all of the following: Nathanael Emmons, *A Discourse, Delivered November 3, 1790, at the particular request of a number of respectable men in Franklin, who were forming a Society, for the Reformation of Morals* (Providence, R.I., 1790), 17–23; Beecher, *A Reformation of Morals*, 9; Heman Humphrey, *The Efficacy and Importance of Combined and Persevering Action. Illustrated, in a Sermon, Delivered at New-Haven, Oct. 19, 1814, Before the Connecticut Society, for the promotion of Good Morals* (New-Haven, Conn., 1815), 17; Ebenezer Porter, *Great effects result from little causes. A Sermon, delivered Sept. 13, 1815, at the Anniversary of the Moral Society in Andover* (Andover, Mass., 1815), 21; Noah Porter, *A Sermon, Delivered at the Meeting of the Connecticut Society for the Promotion of Good Morals, in New-Haven, October 16, 1816* (New Haven, Conn., 1816), 8, 14. Advised Timothy Dwight, "A public, open, determined resistance is also to be made to all the immoralities, which have been recited as deforming, and disgracing our land. Among the best means of discountenancing and subduing these iniquities, would be the establishment of one great and general, and many subordinate societies, for the suppression of idleness, gaming, drunkenness, profaneness, and sabbath-breaking" (*A Discourse, in Two Parts*, 55).

44. Heman Humphrey in 1814 explicitly tied the wicked and disastrous War of 1812 to the moral reform cause: "My brethren and friends, if ever there was a time since the settlement of this country, which demanded the united wisdom, prayers and exertions, of rulers and people for the preservation of every thing dear, it is the present. Weary with long forbearance, God has come out of his place to punish us. Laden with sin enough to sink a world, our little bark has been strangely launched, and sent out, to contend with the Leviathan of the deep. Our commerce is annihilated. . . . A powerful enemy hovers upon our coasts, and menaces our towns. The national treasury is empty. . . . All the skirts of our horizon, are now lighted up with the flames of war. Our Capital has been ingloriously abandoned by its defenders, and taken by a handful of the enemy. A dark and heavy cloud hands over the nation. Every day, we hear its murmuring thunders. . . . Surely, it is high time, for every one, who values the legacy of our fathers, to 'arise, and call upon God.' We may still hope, by repentance and reformation, to turn away his fierce anger from us. In the mean time, let all, rally round our liberties, laws and institutions" (*Efficacy and Importance*, 27–28).

45. Emmons, *A Discourse, Delivered November 3, 1790*, 15–16; Beecher, *A Reformation of Morals*, 23–24, 16, 18; Porter, *A Sermon, Delivered . . . October 16, 1816*, 12.

46. Humphrey, *Efficacy and Importance*, 24. See also Beecher, *A Reformation of Morals*, 8–10; Porter, *A Sermon, Delivered . . . October 16, 1816*, 16.

47. Porter, *A Sermon, Delivered . . . October 16, 1816*, 10–11, 16; Beecher, *A Reformation of Morals*, 6.

48. Emmons, *A Discourse, Delivered November 3, 1790*, 25–26. See also Bancroft, *A Sermon, Preached . . . May 27, 1801*, 20; Beecher, *A Reformation of Morals*, 11–12. Clearly, as these examples indicate, British organizations provided important inspiration and models for the American societies. Mark A. Noll emphasizes how transatlantic the evangelical movement since the First Great Awakening was in "Evaluating North Atlantic Religious History, 1640–1859. A Review Article," *Comparative Studies in Society and History* 33 (1991): 425.

Charles I. Foster, too, points to the British factor, but exaggerates its influence (*An Errand of Mercy*, 10, 62–63, 156).

49. Humphrey, *Efficacy and Importance*, 21. See also Porter, *A Sermon, Delivered . . . October 16, 1816*, 17.

50. Scott, *From Office to Profession*, 31; Beecher, *A Reformation of Morals*, 18, 27, 7.

51. Porter, *Great effects*, 22. Heman Humphrey argued similarly, "A general reformation then, if there is ever to be one, must be brought about, by the blessing of God, upon the exertions of the virtuous and pious. Nor must they expect to do much, in the present state of things, without concert. They must unite" (*Efficacy and Importance*, 12). He made an interesting and unusual pitch for jumping on the reform bandwagon. He cited the story of the Tower of Babel, usually a tale of human folly and sin, and put a positive spin on it, arguing that it showed "the mighty efficiency of united and persevering efforts, for the attainment of whatever great object, they may be employed" (ibid., 4).

52. *An Address to the Branches of "the Society for the Reformation of Morals in the County of Worcester"* ([Worcester, Mass.?], 1815), 1–2; Micah Stone, *Address, Delivered before the Moral Society in Brookfield, April 15, 1817* (Brookfield, Mass., 1817), 8–12; Thomas Snell, *A Sermon, Preached before the Auxiliary Society for the Reformation of Morals, in Brookfield, April 15th, 1816* (Brookfield, Mass., 1816), 13.

53. Porter, *Great effects*, 22.

54. Asahel Morse, *An Oration, delivered at Winsted, July 5th*, A.D. 1802. *In Commemoration of the Declaration of Our National Independence, on the Memorable Fourth of July*, A.D. 1776 (Hartford, Conn., 1802), 9.

Chapter Five

1. In using the term *evangelical*, I follow the usage of the British scholar D. W. Bebbington in his *Evangelicalism in Modern Britain: A History from the 1730s to the 1980s* (London: Unwin Hyman, 1989), 1–17. Bebbington defines (pp. 2–3) "the four qualities that have been the special marks of Evangelical religion" as "*conversionism*, the belief that lives need to be changed; *activism*, the expression of the gospel in effort; *biblicism*, a particular regard for the Bible; and what may be called *crucicentrism*, a stress on the sacrifice of Christ on the cross. Together they form a quadrilateral of priorities that is the basis of Evangelicalism." There is nothing problematic in my adopting the usage of a historian of British evangelicalism, in that the evangelical movement had always been a transatlantic one.

2. Ronald P. Formisano, *The Transformation of Political Culture: Massachusetts Parties, 1790s–1840s* (New York: Oxford University Press, 1983), 63–64, 82, 93–97, 117–127, quotes on 117–118; *Independent Chronicle*, 8 July 1817, quoted in Len Travers, *Celebrating the Fourth: Independence Day and the Rites of Nationalism in the Early Republic* (Amherst: University of Massachusetts Press, 1997), 203; David Waldstreicher, *In the Midst of Perpetual Fetes: The Making of American Nationalism, 1776–1820* (Chapel Hill: University of North Carolina Press, 1997), 300; Edmund B. Thomas Jr., "Politics in the Land of Steady Habits: Connecticut's First Political Party System, 1789–1820" (Ph.D. diss., Clark University, 1972), 263–271; Patrick T. Conley, *Democracy in Decline: Rhode Island's Constitutional Development, 1776–1841* (Providence: Rhode Island Historical Society, 1977), 219.

3. See chapter 3.

4. Peter Eaton, *A Sermon, delivered before His Excellency John Brooks, Esq. Governor; His Honor William Phillips, Esq. Lieutenant Governor; the Honorable Council; and the two houses composing the Legislature of Massachusetts, on the Anniversary Election, May 26, 1819* (Boston, 1819), 3; Abel Flint, *A Discourse, Occasioned by the News of Peace, delivered at the South Meet-*

ing-House in Hartford, February 14, 1815 (Hartford, Conn., 1815), 10–11; Samuel Austin, *An Oration, pronounced at Newport, Rhode Island, July 4, 1822. The Forty Sixth Anniversary of the Independence of the United States of America* (Newport, R.I., 1822), 7; Franklin Bowditch Dexter, *Biographical Sketches of the Graduates of Yale College: With Annals of the College History*, 6 vols. (New York, 1885–1912), 4:250.

5. William Gribbin, *The Churches Militant: The War of 1812 and American Religion* (New Haven: Yale University Press, 1973), 129–135. Writes Gribbin (p. 129), "The ended war was still wicked to those who had always deemed it so, justified to those who had originally cheered it."

6. John Smith, *The People of God Invited to Trust in Him amidst His Judgments upon Sinful Nations. A Sermon Delivered on the Annual Fast at Salem, N.H. March 25, and at the South Parish in Andover, Mass. April 3, 1813* (Haverhill, Mass., 1813), 11–16, quote on 15; idem, *The goodness of God in restoring peace to the United States. A Sermon, Preached April 13, 1815. Being the Day Appointed for Thanksgiving throughout the United States, on Account of Peace with Great Britain* (Haverhill, Mass., 1815), 5–12, quotes on 6 and 12. A number of years would pass before New Englanders could take a more balanced, circumspect view of the War of 1812. In an 1826 July Fourth oration, Henry Colman, a Unitarian minister from Salem, Massachusetts, tried to smooth over any lingering differences between the war's advocates and opponents by recognizing each side's claims. "I am aware of the extreme and bitter diversity of opinion which prevailed among her best citizens in regard to the recent war. But as at this distance of time we can view the subject calmly, and weigh its merits with justice, candid minds, whatever may be their views of its expedience or management, will find it difficult to doubt that the motives in which it originated were patriotic. . . . And unsuccessful as it may be deemed by any in the attainment of its avowed objects, the country came out of it, bringing new trophies of an illustrious heroism, and of a devotion to what many might reasonably deem the cause of liberty and right, worthy of those who hold alliance to the heroes of the revolution" (*An Oration Delivered in Salem, July 4, 1826, at the Request of the Town, on the Completion of a Half Century since the Declaration of American Independence* [Salem, Mass., 1826], 11–12). On Colman's background, see Francis S. Drake, *Dictionary of American Biography* (Boston, 1874), 208.

7. Smith, *The goodness of God*, 12; Elijah Parish, *A Sermon Preached at Ipswich. Sept. 29, 1815. At the Ordination of Rev. Daniel Smith and Cyrus Kingsbury, as Missionaries to the West* (Newburyport, Mass., 1815), 7–8.

8. Samuel Austin, *A Sermon, Preached at Worcester, on the Annual Fast, April 11, 1811* (Worcester, Mass., 1811), 23; idem, *An Oration, pronounced . . . July 4, 1822*, 12–13; Eleazar T. Fitch, *National Prosperity Perpetuated: A Discourse: Delivered in the Chapel of Yale College; on the day of the Annual Thanksgiving: November 29, 1827* (New-Haven, Conn., 1828), 7; Dexter, *Biographical Sketches*, 6:316–317.

9. N. L. Frothingham, *Christian Patriotism: A Sermon, on occasion of the Death of John Adams, preached in Chauncy-Place, Boston, July 9th, 1826* (Boston, 1826), 7–8, 11–12; Nathaniel Bouton, *Christian Patriotism. An Address Delivered at Concord, July the Fourth, 1825* (Concord, N.H., 1825), 8; Drake, *Dictionary of American Biography*, 108. "The Harvard Unitarians," adds Daniel Walker Howe, "relied on the public sentiments to sustain the state" (*The Unitarian Conscience: Harvard Moral Philosophy, 1805–1861*, rev. ed. [Cambridge: Harvard University Press, 1970; Middletown, Conn.: Wesleyan University Press, 1988], 129–130, quote on 129). However, Howe passes over the "anti-patriotism" of the Unitarian clergy during the War of 1812.

10. Charles A. Boardman, *The Agency of God, Illustrated in the Achievement of the Independence of the United States. A Sermon, Delivered at New-Preston, Connecticut, July 4, 1826, being a Religious Celebration of that Day* (New-Haven, Conn., 1826); Joseph Dana, *A Discourse, Delivered in Ipswich, Massachusetts, on the Fourth of July, 1827, Being the Fifty-First Anniversary of the Declaration of American Independence, on July 4th, 1776* (Ipswich, Mass.,

1827), 5. William B. Sprague concurred with the analyses of Boardman and Dana: "I know that a spirit of atheism lurks in the human heart; and though God is speaking to us by a thousand voices every moment, yet, because he holds back the face of his throne, and is seen and heard only in the regular march of his administration, we overlook, in a great measure, his agency, and limit our views to second causes. But the history of our revolution furnishes a rebuke to this spirit. In every part of it, we behold the footsteps of an All wise and Almighty God" (*Religious Celebration of Independence: A Discourse delivered at Northampton, on the Fourth of July, 1827* [Hartford, Conn., 1827], 12–14, quote on 12). Sprague is remembered today as the editor of the nine-volume *Annals of the American Pulpit; or, Commemorative Notices of Distinguished American Clergymen of Various Denominations, from the early settlement of the country to the close of the year eighteen hundred and fifty-five* (New York, 1857–1869), but in 1827 he was the pastor of the First Congregational Church of West Springfield, Massachusetts.

11. Eaton, *A Sermon, delivered . . . May 26, 1819*, 25; Fitch, *National Prosperity Perpetuated*, 5–10; Nathaniel Thayer, *A Discourse, pronounced before His Excellency John Brooks, Esq. Governor, His Honor William Phillips, Esq. Lieutenant Governor, the Honorable Council, and the Two Houses, composing the Legislature of Massachusetts, on the Anniversary Election, May 28, 1823* (Boston, 1823), 5–10. Peter Eaton offered a very similar list: "It has been remarked, that in America, our lofty mountains, majestic rivers, and extended forests, show that nature has wrought upon her largest scale. Our country affords the productions of every clime. Its rapid growth and increasing prosperity encourage the most flattering hopes. Blessed with constitutions of civil government, tested by experience, to be equal to the exigencies, and adapted to the habits and character of the people; favored with statesmen distinguished for talents, patriotism, and love of order; enjoying a religion, mild and benificent [*sic*]; originating numerous institutions whose bounty flows in the channel of Christian charity, forming a swelling stream, which not only enriches and fertilizes our own country, but remote nations; with laws, just and equal, and numerous seats of science for the education of youth, what expectations may we not form of the rising glory of this western world?" (*A Sermon, delivered . . . May 26, 1819*, 25).

12. L. Ives Hoadly, *An Address, delivered at the Union Celebration of Independence, at Sutton, Mass. July 5, 1824* (Worcester, Mass., 1824), 7; Leonard Bacon, *A Plea for Africa; Delivered in New-Haven, July 4th, 1825* (New Haven, Conn., 1825), 8. Henry Colman added his assent to these optimistic predictions in 1826. "The brilliancy of her [America's] achievements will send their cheering light into the dark places of the earth. The full tide of her glory will roll on, until she has taught mankind the most valuable of all political lessons; that justice and honor are the foundations of national as well as individual happiness and glory; that liberty and equality are the natural and inalienable rights of man; that the only ends of civil government are the security, peace, improvement, and happiness of the governed; that all the liberty a good man can desire, is compatible with all the security a good man can need; that the rights of conscience are gifts from GOD, upon which no infringement or restraint is ever to be permitted; and that with knowledge and virtue and religious principle, mankind are always competent to govern themselves" (*An Oration Delivered in Salem*, 23).

13. James H. Moorhead, "Between Progress and Apocalypse: A Reassessment of Millennialism in American Religious Thought, 1800–1880," *JAH* 71 (1984): 524–533; Sprague, *Religious Celebration of Independence*, 18. See also Joseph W. Phillips, *Jedidiah Morse and New England Congregationalism* (New Brunswick, N.J.: Rutgers University Press, 1983), 180–181.

14. Dumas Malone, ed., *Dictionary of American Biography*, 11 vols. (New York: Charles Scribner's Sons, 1958–1964), 10:558–560; Dexter, *Biographical Sketches*, 5:248–249. According to William G. McLoughlin, Wayland was "the greatest Baptist spokesman of the nineteenth century" (*New England Dissent, 1630–1833: The Baptists and the Separation of Church and State*, 2 vols. [Cambridge: Harvard University Press, 1971], 2:1111).

15. Francis Wayland, *The Duties of an American Citizen. Two Discourses, delivered in the First Baptist Meeting House in Boston, on Thursday, April 7, 1825. The Day of Public Fast* (Boston, 1825), 10, 27, 31.

16. Lyman Beecher, *A Sermon, addressed to the Legislature of Connecticut; at New-Haven, on the day of the Anniversary Election, May 2d, 1826* (New Haven, Conn., 1826), 6–13, quotes on 6, 11, and 13.

17. Thayer, *A Discourse, pronounced . . . May 28, 1823*, 4.

18. "At bottom, the real issue between [Unitarians and Calvinists]," writes Daniel W. Howe, "came down to this: had those persons who attained true virtue done so by natural or supernatural means, through their own efforts or through the grace of God?" (*Unitarian Conscience*, 103–104).

19. Howe, *Unitarian Conscience*; Conrad Wright, *The Beginnings of Unitarianism in America* (Boston: Starr King Press, 1955); Sydney E. Ahlstrom, "Introduction," in *An American Reformation: A Documentary History of Unitarian Christianity*, ed. Sydney E. Ahlstrom and Jonathan S. Carey (Middletown, Conn.: Wesleyan University Press, 1985), 3–41.

20. My emphasis on the Unitarians' many conventional positions contrasts with that of James M. Banner Jr., who writes that "the Unitarians, from the 1790's on, increasingly stressed pragmatic values, extolled worldly success, and moved rapidly away from the customary emphasis upon social hierarchy and harmony" (*To the Hartford Convention: The Federalists and the Origins of Party Politics in Massachusetts, 1789–1815* [New York: Knopf, 1970], 157, n. 8). I likewise reject the interpretation of Peter S. Field, who claims, "Almost to a man, Brahmin ministers had begun [by the early nineteenth century] to eschew the kind of active participation in politics entailed in the election-day sermons and fast days of the colonial era" (*The Crisis of the Standing Order: Clerical Intellectuals and Cultural Authority in Massachusetts, 1780–1833* [Amherst: University of Massachusetts Press, 1998], 91–92).

21. William Ellery Channing, "Unitarian Christianity," in *The Unitarian Controversy, 1819–1823*, ed. Bruce Kuklick, 2 vols. (New York: Garland, 1987), 1:9–10, 6, 37–39; Aaron Bancroft, "Sermon on Eph. 4:31," 20 April 1834, p. 3, Aaron Bancroft Papers, 1789–1839, vol. 2, AAS. Daniel W. Howe calls the Baltimore sermon "the [Unitarian] party's platform" (*Unitarian Conscience*, 19). He adds, "Unitarians believed that only what was rationally plausible could be accepted in religious faith" (ibid., 71). For more of Howe's commentary on "Unitarian Christianity," see ibid., 100–102; for a fuller discussion of the dangers Unitarians perceived from the passions, see ibid., 60–62.

Nathaniel Thayer agreed with Channing's criticism of the Calvinist model of conversion. "We disavow our belief in the excitements and disorders which are by some called revivals of religion, and express our apprehension that some who are the subjects of them are given up to strange delusion. . . . We are the advocates of a religion which has warmth and ardour, but it is a religion which is under the direction of a sober mind and a sound judgment" (*Means by which Unitarian Christians may refute misrepresentations of their faith. A Discourse, Delivered at Townsend, Massachusetts, February 10, 1828* [Lancaster, Mass., 1828], 8). For further Unitarian criticism of revivals, see Howe, *Unitarian Conscience*, 163–164.

22. In contrast, Channing said, "it is a great excellence of the doctrine of God's unity, that it offers to us ONE OBJECT of supreme homage, adoration, and love, one Infinite Father, one Being of beings, one original and fountain, to whom we may refer all good, in whom all our powers and affections may be concentrated, and whose lovely and venerable nature may pervade all our thoughts" (Channing, "Unitarian Christianity," 17).

23. Peter Whitney, *A Discourse Delivered in Quincy, at the Interment of John Adams, Late President of the United States. July 7th, 1826* (Boston, 1826), 9.

24. William E. Channing, "Spiritual Freedom. Discourse Preached at the Annual Election, May 26, 1830," in *The Works of William E. Channing, D.D.*, 8th ed., 6 vols. (Boston and

New York, 1848), 4:72, 85; Henry Ware, *A Sermon Delivered Dec. 18, 1821. At the Ordination of the Rev. William Ware, to the Pastoral Charge of the First Congregational Church in New-York* (New York, 1821), 5–8, quote on 8. "Among the Unitarians' most attractive traits," in Daniel W. Howe's estimation, "was their professed commitment to free inquiry" (*Unitarian Conscience*, 207).

Like Ware, Aaron Bancroft contrasted the Calvinists' "metaphysical confessions" to the Unitarians' reliance on the unfiltered Word (*A Vindication of the Result of the late Mutual Council convened in Princeton* [Worcester, Mass., 1817], 30). However, Joseph Goffe countered that Bancroft's comparison "carried to its utmost length, it would sweep all commentaries and books on scriptural subjects from our libraries, and all expositions and sermons from our pulpits, and leave us with nothing but the bare text, without note or comment." Moreover, although Bancroft and Ware denigrated confessions as contrary to the spirit of the Reformation, Goffe pointed out both that all of the Reformers had written creeds and that Bancroft had published a catechism of his own, too. "When all this is taken into view," concluded Goffe, the orthodox minister of Millbury, Massachusetts, "it may be fairly presumed, that Dr. B.'s opposition to creeds and confessions would cease, provided they were consistent with his views of Christian truth; and that the reason why he is now opposed to them, is not so much because they are unscriptural, as because they present such formidable barriers against the dissemination of doctrines which he approves" (*The Result of Council at Princeton incapable of vindication: or, a Review of Dr. Bancroft's Vindication of the Result of the late Mutual Council convened in Princeton* [Worcester, Mass., 1817], 20–22, quotes on 20–21).

25. Aaron Bancroft, *The Nature and Worth of Christian Liberty. Illustrated in a Sermon delivered before The Second Congregational Church and Society in Worcester, On the Twenty-Third Day of June, 1816* (Worcester, Mass., 1816), 3–4, 23. Bancroft was reacting to an abortive attempt, led by Jedidiah Morse, to set up "a presbyterian structure of consociation like that of the Connecticut Congregationalists." Morse and his allies hoped to use such an ecclesiastical structure to enforce orthodoxy throughout the standing order (Field, *Crisis of the Standing Order*, 198). Four years later, Bancroft reiterated these arguments in *A Discourse delivered before the Convention of Congregational Ministers of Massachusetts, at their Annual Meeting in Boston, June 1, 1820* (Boston, 1820), 16–19. Bancroft spoke from personal experience; remember from chapter 1 that he had had to endure a period in his early years in Worcester during which the neighboring clergy shunned him for his "doctrinal belief" and refused to grant him the customary pulpit exchanges (Sprague, *Annals*, 8:134).

26. N. L. Frothingham, *A Plea Against Religious Controversy, delivered on Sunday, Feb. 8, 1829* (Boston, 1829), 16, 6. Abiel Abbot, minister of Beverly, Massachusetts, also professed to be fed up with theological hair-splitting over "matters of judgment and mere opinion." He instructed the convention of Congregational ministers in his state that "the gospel makes *love and peace necessary*, but not agreement in opinions" (*Ecclesiastical Peace Recommended. A Discourse delivered before the Annual Convention of the Congregational Ministers of Massachusetts, in Boston, May 31, 1827* [Boston, 1827], 11–12).

27. Field, *Crisis of the Standing Order*, 89. He adds, "At the urging of the young, energetic Congregational ministers, Boston's elite commenced a wave of philanthropy, the first of its kind in America, which underwrote projects as varied as social libraries, the Harvard Medical School, literary journals, the Massachusetts Historical Society, the Lowell Institute, and the Boston Athenaeum" (ibid., 84). See also Howe, *Unitarian Conscience*, 174.

28. Henry Ware Jr., *The Criminality of Intemperance. An Address delivered at the Eleventh Anniversary of the Massachusetts Society for the Suppression of Intemperance* (Boston, 1823), 11. Similarly, Unitarian work among the Boston poor was based upon the same ideas of personal improvement and the elevation of the mind. "The conditions of slum life were inimical to the cultivation of a Christian character, to the self-development and self-fulfillment that Unitari-

ans prized as the essence of religion and the chief end of man" (Howe, *Unitarian Conscience*, 245–246). Naturally, the Unitarians' extensive involvement in education grew out of this commitment to unlocking people's intellectual potential (ibid., 255–256).

29. "The most capable Trinitarian Congregationalists, like Moses Stuart, pointed out that Unitarians were actually not so much defending free religious expression as trying to hush up an embarassing [*sic*] division in the establishment. The hesitancy of Harvard Liberals to stand up and be counted might be charitably attributed to an ecumenical spirit. But it also manifested their deep-seated social conservatism: their fear lest the weakening of the Standing Order by internal strife pave the way for disestablishment" (Howe, *Unitarian Conscience*, 215–216, quote on 216).

30. Francis Parkman, *The Providence of God Displayed in the Revolutions of the World: A Sermon Preached in the New-North Church, on Lord's Day, Sept. XIX. Occasioned by the Recent Revolutions in the Government of France* (Boston, 1830), 6; Channing, "Unitarian Christianity," 4. Howe quotes this same excerpt from Channing and remarks that "passages depicting God as vengeful or passionate could properly be explained away on these grounds" (*Unitarian Conscience*, 99–100, quote on 100). Regarding Unitarian Arminianism, see Wright, *Beginnings of Unitarianism*, 3, and Howe, *Unitarian Conscience*, 67–68.

31. Joseph Goffe to Eliza Goffe, 4 Feb. 1833, Joseph Goffe Papers, 1826–1842, box 3, folder 4, AAS; Samuel Barrett, *A Sermon, Preached in the Twelfth Congregational Church, Boston, Thursday, August 9, 1832, the Day Appointed for Fasting, Humiliation, and Prayer, on account of the Approach of the Cholera* (Boston, 1832), 17–18; Christopher T. Thayer, *A Discourse, delivered in the First Church, Beverly, at The Fast observed in Massachusetts on Account of the Prevailing Cholera. August 9, 1832* (Salem, Mass., 1832), 3; John G. Palfrey, *A Discourse delivered in the Church in Brattle Square, Boston, August 9, 1832, the Day Appointed for Fasting and Prayer in Massachusetts, on account of the Approach of Cholera*, 2d ed. (Boston, 1832), 10–11, quote on 11.

32. Howe, *Unitarian Conscience*, 207.

33. Henry Ware, *A Sermon, delivered before His Excellency John Brooks, Esq. Governor, His Honor William Phillips, Esq. Lieutenant Governor, the Honorable Council, and the Two Houses composing the Legislature of Massachusetts, on the Anniversary Election, May 30, 1821* (Boston, 1821), 3–5, quote on 5; Eaton, *A Sermon, delivered . . . May 26, 1819*, 19–20. "The habitual attendance on the duties of the sabbath, has a benign influence on the domestic state, social intercourse, ordinary transactions, general manners," agreed Nathaniel Thayer. "It tends to allay the turbulence of passion, liberalize the feelings and sentiments, restrain corrupt propensities, give a regular and moral direction to the whole conduct" (*A Discourse, pronounced . . . May 28, 1823*, 10). On the Unitarians' "moral elitism," see Howe, *Unitarian Conscience*, 131–137.

34. Thayer, *A Discourse, pronounced . . . May 28, 1823*, 9; Eaton, *A Sermon, delivered . . . May 26, 1819*, 10. On the importance of a ruler's religion, see also Aaron Bancroft, *A Sermon Delivered July 9th, 1826, the Sunday following the Death of the Hon. John Adams, a former President of the United States* (Worcester, Mass., 1826), 3–12; James Walker, *A Sermon delivered before His Excellency Levi Lincoln Governor, His Honor Thomas L. Winthrop Lieutenant Governor, the Hon. Council, the Senate, and House of Representatives of the Commonwealth of Massachusetts, on the day of General Election, May 28, 1828* (Boston, 1828), 10–12; Howe, *Unitarian Conscience*, 205–206.

35. Eaton, *A Sermon, delivered . . . May 26, 1819*, 22; Thayer, *A Discourse, pronounced . . . May 28, 1823*, 21; Ware, *A Sermon, delivered . . . May 30, 1821*, 23. See also Howe, *Unitarian Conscience*, 211–215.

36. William Ellery Channing, *Religion a Social Principle. A Sermon, delivered in the Church in Federal Street, Boston, December 10, 1820* (Boston, 1820), 6, 9, 13.

37. Ibid., 6.

38. The ensuing discussion of disestablishment in Massachusetts is based upon McLoughlin, *New England Dissent*, vol. 2, Part XIII, "The Final Downfall of the Massachusetts Establishment, 1820–1833."

39. Twenty-four years after disestablishment, the Congregationalists were still the single largest denomination in the Bay State. However, as this 1857 listing of churches by denomination makes clear, non-Congregational denominations had grown rapidly. "Orthodox Congregationalists, 490; Episcopal Methodists, 277; Baptists, 266; Unitarians, 170; Universalists, 135; Episcopalians, 65; Roman Catholics, 64; Christ-ians, 37; Friends Meetings, 24; Free-will Baptists, 21; Protestant or Independent Methodists, 20; Second Adventists, 15; Wesleyan Methodists, 13; Swedenborgians, 11; Presbyterians, 7; Shakers, 4 communities; nondescript religious assemblies, that cannot be classed with any of the above, nor yet with one another, 12. Total, 1,625" (Joseph S. Clark, *A Historical Sketch of the Congregational Churches in Massachusetts, from 1620 to 1858. With an Appendix* [Boston, 1858], 282).

40. McLoughlin discussed the Dedham case in *New England Dissent*, 2:1189–1197.

41. Ibid., 2:1195. Added McLoughlin, "it was the psychological shock of finding themselves among the dissenters which, as much as anything, turned the Trinitarians against the prevailing system" (ibid., 2:1191, n. 4).

42. Abbot, *Ecclesiastical Peace Recommended*, 18; Bancroft, *A Discourse delivered . . . June 1, 1820*, 26–27.

43. McLoughlin, *New England Dissent*, 2:1205–1206, 1209–1212, 1230–1237, 1245–1262. The vote in favor of ratification was "32,234 to 3,273" (ibid., 2:1259).

44. The biographical data on Beecher, Humphrey, and Porter is found, respectively, in Dexter, *Biographical Sketches*, 5:247 and 761, and Drake, *Dictionary of American Biography*, 730. The second date given is the year in which each man received his bachelor of arts degree.

45. Diodate Brockway, *A Sermon, Preached at Hartford, before the Honorable General Assembly, of the State of Connecticut, on the Anniversary Election, May 11, 1815* (Hartford, Conn., 1815), 6, 20; John Bartlett, *A Sermon, Preached in Wintonbury Meeting-House, Windsor; on the occasion of the Annual Thanksgiving, December 6th.* A.D. 1821 (Hartford, Conn., 1822), 7–13, quote on 11. In another concise statement of the rule of Providence, Abel Flint said, "As the great first cause, he so regulates and controls the operation of second causes, as to produce events according to his holy will" (*A Discourse, Occasioned by the News of Peace*, 9).

46. Bouton, *Christian Patriotism*, 3; Sprague, *Religious Celebration of Independence*, 20. "Prayer for national blessings, is an acknowledgement that his government extends to the concerns of nations," said the president of the Andover Theological Seminary, Ebenezer Porter, in 1831 (*The Christian Citizen; or the Duty of Praying for Rulers. Two Sermons, Preached in the Chapel of the Theological Seminary, Andover, on the State Fast. April 7, 1831*, 2d ed. [Boston, 1831], 5). A dozen years earlier, Andrew Eliot of New Milford, Connecticut, made an argument very similar to Porter's. "To pray acceptably for Rulers," he taught, "we must look up to God as the moral governour of the world; as having dominion over the hearts and consciences of men; and as willing to hear the 'supplications' that are offered up to him through faith in Jesus Christ" (*A Sermon, Preached on the Day of the General Election, at Hartford, in the State of Connecticut, May 5th, 1819* [Hartford, Conn., 1819], 9). See also Hoadly, *An Address, delivered . . . July 5, 1824*, 3; Joseph Dana, *A Sermon, Delivered at Ipswich, (Mass.) on the day of the Annual Thanksgiving, November 23, 1820* (Newburyport, Mass., 1820), 4–8; Thomas Snell, *A Sermon, preached before His Excellency John Brooks, Esq. Governor; His Honor William Phillips, Esq. Lieutenant Governor, The Honorable Council, and the Two Houses Composing the Legislature of the Commonwealth of Massachusetts, May 28, 1817. Being the Anniversary Election* (Boston, 1817), 20–22.

47. Gardiner Spring, *A Tribute to New-England: A Sermon, delivered before the New-*

England Society of the City and State of New-York, on the 22d of December, 1820. Being the Second Centennial Celebration of the Landing of the Pilgrims at Plymouth (New York, 1821), 14, 32; Dexter, *Biographical Sketches*, 5:791–793. Likewise, Eleazar T. Fitch added, "The survey [of American history] presents to us impressive evidence, that the Lord of heaven and earth is our highest benefactor" (*National Prosperity Perpetuated*, 15). The Massachusetts General Association voted that churches throughout the state mark December 22 as a thanksgiving day, since "signal have been the merciful dispensations of Divine Providence, towards our beloved country; and to no part of it more so, than to New England" (*Extracts from the Minutes of the General Association of Massachusetts, assembled at Beverly, June 27, 1820* [Andover, Mass., 1820], 11).

48. Porter, *Christian Citizen*, 36; Francis Wayland, *Encouragements to Religious Effort: A Sermon delivered at the request of the American Sunday School Union, May 25, 1830* (Philadelphia, 1830), 24–25. In another parallel with Wayland, Lyman Beecher also observed that "no punishments of Heaven are so severe as those for mercies abused" (*A Plea for the West*, 2d ed. [1832; Cincinnati, 1835], 46). Asa Cummings, a tutor at Bowdoin College and recently a student at Andover Seminary, reminded his listeners on the annual fast of 1820 that they bore responsibilities "as individuals, and as members of the community." "You have been lamenting your individual sins; you have entered the sanctuary of God, grieving for your personal transgressions. Now, my brethren, add to these our national sins, and let your sorrows flow forth afresh. The blots which cleave to our publick character, call also for your tears. . . . We will remember, that this is a day of *publick* fasting and humiliation; and it is peculiarly appropriate, that, together with our own, we should make the public sins, the burden of our grief" (*A Discourse delivered at Brunswick, (Maine,) April 6, 1820, the Day of the Annual Fast in Maine and Massachusetts* [Brunswick, Maine, 1820], 6). On Cummings's background, see Nehemiah Cleaveland and Alpheus Spring Packard, *History of Bowdoin College. With Biographical Sketches of its Graduates from 1806 to 1879, inclusive* (Boston, 1882), 65–68.

49. Brockway, *A Sermon, Preached . . . May 11, 1815*, 26; Ludovicus Weld, *The kingdom of Grace merits universal patronage. A Sermon, Delivered at Hartford, before the Legislature of the State of Connecticut, at the Anniversary Election, May 2d, 1821* (Hartford, Conn., 1821), 15–16.

50. Samuel Austin, *Religion the Glory of a Community. A Sermon, Preached on the Day of General Election, at Montpelier, October 10, 1816, before the Honorable Legislature of Vermont* (Montpelier, Vt., 1816), 16. The year before, Austin had concluded a twenty-five-year pastorate over Worcester's First Church in order to become president of the University of Vermont. He reasoned that a godly community would be protected, because God would always act in defense of the church. "While the nations who know not God are wasted by their follies and their crimes, as the effect of the wars they wage, and the indignation from above which they provoke, the Church proceeds, lengthening her cords and strengthening her stakes. Let religion, then, pervade throughout a civil community, and it will become at once an integral portion of the Church, united to God by covenant bonds, and enjoying his protection. This protection would be the munition of rocks. It would be a better defence than the greatest number of ships of war, or veteran armies" (ibid., 19). For similar logic, see also Hoadly, *An Address, delivered . . . July 5, 1824*, 18.

51. Eliot, *A Sermon, Preached . . . May 5th, 1819*, 16. As Thomas Snell of North Brookfield, Massachusetts, similarly argued, "One active and insidious enemy in the bosom of a State, who has access to the feelings of his fellow citizens, and knows how to strengthen their prejudices and inflame their passions, can do more to sap the foundations of the government, disturb the tranquility and overturn the liberties of a nation, than a host of avowed enemies without. Aspiring men of talents and subtility, but void of religious principle, are ever dangerous characters. . . . [But] men of christian benevolence, whose object is usefulness, rather than gain, are unshaken friends of the Commonwealth" (*A Sermon, preached . . .*

May 28, 1817, 13–15, quote on 14). See also Austin, *Religion the Glory of a Community,* 12–14.

52. "What security have you that any man, entrusted with office and influence, if he has not the fear of God in his heart, will faithfully seek the public good?" asked Ebenezer Porter (*The Character of Nehemiah, or Jerusalem Built Up. A Sermon, Preached on the Public Fast, April 4, 1816 in the Chapel of the Theological Seminary at Andover* [Andover, Mass., 1816], 19). See also Moses Stuart, *A Sermon delivered before His Excellency Levi Lincoln Esq. Governor, His Honor Thomas L. Winthrop Lieutenant Governor, The Hon. Council, The Senate, and House of Representatives of the Commonwealth of Massachusetts. May 30, 1827, Being the Day of General Election* (Boston, 1827), 31.

53. John Codman, *Home Missions. A Sermon delivered before the Massachusetts Society for Promoting Christian Knowledge, in Park Street Church, Boston, May 31, 1826* (Boston, 1826), 10. "Is it important that social and civil order should be supported," asked Andover Seminary's Leonard Woods, "that sound morality should prevail; and that mankind, delivered from violence and cruelty, should live in peace? Just so important is it, that the servants of Christ should faithfully preach the truths of revelation" (*The usefulness of the sacred office. A Sermon delivered, March 9, 1819, at the Funeral of the Rev. Samuel Spring, D.D. Pastor of the North Congregational Church in Newburyport* [Newburyport, Mass., 1819], 6). See also Samuel Austin, *The Nature, Obligations, and Benefits of the Public Worship of God. A Discourse delivered at the Dedication of the New Meeting-House erected for the use of the Calvinist Church and the Society connected with it, in Worcester, Mass. October 13, 1823* (Worcester, Mass., 1823), 16–17. As discussed previously, Francis Wayland depicted the United States as a model for Catholic and despotic Europe. The United States, therefore, had to be safeguarded, and Wayland's recommendation was much the same as Codman's: "If we would see the foundations laid broadly and deeply, on which the fabrick of this country's liberties shall rest to the remotest generations; if we would see her carry forward the work of political reformation, and rise the bright and morning star of freedom over a benighted world; let us elevate the intellectual and moral character of every class of our citizens, and specially let us imbue them thoroughly with the principles of the gospel of Jesus Christ" (*Duties of an American Citizen,* 45–46).

54. Heman Humphrey, *An Address, delivered at the Collegiate Institution in Amherst, Ms. By Heman Humphrey, D.D. on occasion of his Inauguration to the Presidency of that Institution, Oct. 15, 1823* (Boston, 1823), 28–29; see also Wayland, *Encouragements to Religious Effort,* 26. Fitch, *National Prosperity Perpetuated,* 22; for a very similarly worded argument, see also Stuart, *A Sermon delivered . . . May 30, 1827,* 29–30. Regarding France's bad example, see Humphrey, *An Address, delivered . . . Oct. 15, 1823,* 26–27; Austin, *Religion the Glory of a Community,* 9–11. For a reiteration of all the points in this paragraph, see Nathaniel W. Taylor, *A Sermon, Addressed to the Legistature [sic] of the State of Connecticut, at the Annual Election in Hartford, May 7, 1823* (Hartford, Conn., 1823), 6–17.

55. There are exceptions to most such generalizations. William B. Sprague's endorsement of the establishment in 1825 came surprisingly late from an orthodox Congregationalist; see *The Claims of Past and Future Generations on Civil Rulers. A Sermon, preached at The Annual Election, May 25, 1825* (Boston, 1825), 10–11, 28–29. Perhaps—and this is purely speculative—Sprague's location in the Connecticut River valley of west-central Massachusetts made him more supportive of the establishment. There, in the heart of Congregational orthodoxy, he might have been distanced somewhat from the conflict with the Unitarians and the most bitter fights over parish control. On the valley as the place where "Congregational Orthodoxy reigned more securely—one might say more *purely*—than anywhere else in Massachusetts," see Formisano, *Transformation of Political Culture,* 151.

56. Taylor, *A Sermon . . . May 7, 1823,* 25; Hoadly, *An Address, delivered . . . July 5, 1824,* 11.

Over in Massachusetts, John Codman shared Taylor's assessment. "We confess," Codman said, "we are among those, who do not envy the nations of Europe the advantages of an established church. We believe that its advantages, great as they undoubtedly are, are more than counterbalanced by the evils that grow out of the system. A rich and powerful hierarchy does not appear to us friendly to the propagation of the pure faith of the gospel." However, disestablishment also presented a weighty challenge: "It obliges us to rely upon *our own resources* and the *help of our God.* We have no laws to secure tithes to the priesthood—no presentations of livings to the church—no motives to climb the ladder of ecclesiastical preferment. We cannot expect an act of our National Legislature, like that recently passed by the British Parliament for the erection of a large number of new churches" (*Home Missions,* 12–13). In the 1831 Massachusetts election sermon, Newbury's Leonard Withington also expressed a mixture of acceptance and hesitation over disestablishment. "Do [ministers] wish the legislature to pass a law for their legal support and establish a State church? No, by no means. . . . We wish for your personal esteem but not for your legal protection. We do not even ask for the present feeble support of religious worship which now blots your statue book. If religion cannot support itself, and must sink, we will sink with it" (*A Sermon, preached at the Annual Election, May 25, 1831, before His Excellency Levi Lincoln, Governor, His Honor Thomas L. Winthrop, Lieutenant Governor, the Honorable Council, and the Legislature of Massachusetts* [Boston, 1831], 47–48).

57. Robert H. Abzug, *Cosmos Crumbling: American Reform and the Religious Imagination* (New York: Oxford University Press, 1994), 38; Lyman Beecher, *The Faith Once Delivered to the Saints. A Sermon, delivered at Worcester, Mass. Oct. 15, 1823, at the Ordination of the Rev. Loammi Ives Hoadly, to the Pastoral Office over the Calvinistic Church and Society in that Place* (Boston, 1823), 27. Abzug discusses this sermon in *Cosmos Crumbling,* 51–53. The title, "religious virtuoso," comes from Max Weber (ibid., 4).

58. Beecher, *A Sermon . . . May 2d, 1826,* 11; idem, *Faith Once Delivered to the Saints,* 28.

59. Beecher, *Faith Once Delivered to the Saints,* 28–31.

60. Ibid., 33. In his election sermon, Beecher made the same argument, albeit more concisely: "Multitudes of christians and patriots have long since abandoned party politics, and, not knowing what to do, have abandoned almost the exercise of suffrage. This is wrong. An enlightened and virtuous suffrage may, by system and concentration, become one of the most powerful means of promoting national purity and morality" (*A Sermon . . . May 2d, 1826,* 21). Earlier, while a pastor on Long Island in 1804, Beecher had proposed using the Christian electorate to vote duelists out of office. See John G. West Jr., *The Politics of Revelation and Reason: Religion and Civic Life in the New Nation* (Lawrence: University Press of Kansas, 1996), 92.

61. "The kingdom of Christ is so far from being sustained and strengthened by the secular arm, that hitherto it has invariably languished when constrained to lean upon the civil power. . . . It wants no Jeffries, nor Star Chamber, to enforce its discipline—no compulsory tythes [*sic*] to support its teachers—no military to extend its conquests or guard its sacred towers. . . . The church has always flourished most, when it has been left alone" (Humphrey, *The Kingdom of Christ: A Sermon Preached Before the Annual Convention of the Congregational Ministers of Massachusetts, in Boston, May 29, 1830* [Boston, 1830], 14–15).

62. Ibid., 6–8; Porter, *Christian Citizen,* 31. Interestingly, Beecher's reliance on the Christian electorate caused him some anxiety in the 1830s. The rise in immigration from Roman Catholic countries alarmed him because he feared that Catholics would form their own voting bloc. The Catholic vote, he argued, could be tightly controlled by means of a chain of command stretching from the parish priest to Rome and then back to Vienna and the forces of antiliberal politics. Therefore, Beecher warned, Protestants had to be even more vigilant, lest European monarchy subvert the republic by using this fifth column. *A Plea for the West,* 51–72.

63. Howe, *Unitarian Conscience*, 7–9, 137–148.

64. Stuart, *A Sermon delivered . . . May 30, 1827*, 20–21; Beecher, *A Sermon . . . May 2d, 1826*, 6.

65. Joseph Goffe to Eliza Goffe, 10 Jan. 1832, Goffe Papers; Brookfield Association, 7 Jan. 1829, Records, 1757–1837, CL. For additional descriptions of revival from the 1820s, see, for instance, Bartlett, *A Sermon, Preached in Wintonbury Meeting-House*, 5–6; Noah Porter, *Memorial of a Revival. A Sermon, Delivered in Farmington, at the Anniversary Thanksgiving, December 6, 1821. With an Appendix* (Hartford, Conn., 1822), 6–8. "The powerful revivals of 1799 were prolonged at least till 1805," summarized Williston Walker, "and then, though lessened, did not wholly cease. In 1802 Yale College was greatly stirred. The years 1807–08 were seasons of quickening in Rhode Island and western Massachusetts. From 1815 to 1818 a sixth of all the towns in Connecticut were visited, Massachusetts and New Hampshire were much moved, while in Rutland County, Vt., there was almost a spiritual revolution. Again in 1820–23 extensive revival movements appeared in New England and the West, and once more in 1826–27; but these were surpassed in turn by the religious interest of 1830–31. Yet later, in 1841–42, and in 1857–58, very extensive awakenings took place. Thus, for two generations, the revival became the characteristic feature of Congregational religious life" (*A History of the Congregational Churches in the United States*, American Church History Series, vol. 3, ed. Philip Schaff et al. [New York, 1894], 320).

66. Brookfield Association, Records, 2 Oct. 1827; Porter, *Memorial of a Revival*, 11–12; Daniel Dana, *Conversion the Work of God. A Sermon Delivered Dec. 31, 1831; a Day Devoted by Several Churches in Newburyport and its Vicinity, to United Praise for the Spiritual Blessings of the Year* (Newburyport, Mass., 1832). In ordaining a minister as an evangelist who did not have his own settled parish, the Brookfield Association was following the example of the missionary societies. As early as 1797, the North Hartford Association had ordained an "evangelist at large" to work along the upstate New York frontier. See James R. Rohrer, *Keepers of the Covenant: Frontier Missions and the Decline of Congregationalism, 1774–1818* (New York: Oxford University Press, 1995), 58–60.

67. Ebenezer Porter, *Signs of the Times. A Sermon Preached in the Chapel of the Theological Seminary, Andover, on the Public Fast, April 3, 1823* (Andover, Mass., 1823), 5–6. According to Noah Porter, the present was "a period in which the Holy Spirit is given with peculiar freeness and power, and in which, according to the sure word of prophesy, this shall be more and more the fact, until [Joel 2:28] 'the Spirit shall be poured out upon all flesh,' and [Hab. 2:14] 'the earth be filled with the knowledge of the Lord'" (*Memorial of a Revival*, 10–11).

68. Porter, *Memorial of a Revival*, 9. Lyman Beecher linked the onset of the revivals to the end of the establishment in a sort of providential rescue mission: "At the very time when the civil law had waxed old and was passing away, God began to pour out his Spirit upon the Churches, and voluntary associations of christians arose to apply and extend that influence, which the law could no longer apply." As a result, he continued, the revivals would shake the world. "The revivals of religion which prevail in our land among christians of all denominations, furnish cheering evidence of the presence of evangelical doctrine, and of the power of that Spirit by which the truth is to be made efficacious in the renovation of the world" (*A Sermon . . . May 2d, 1826*, 11–12).

69. Heman Humphrey, *A Glorious Enterprize. A Discourse, Delivered in the College Chapel, Amherst, Mass. June 29, 1834* (Amherst, Mass., 1834), 19. Humphrey had issued his initial call at least fifteen years earlier. He said in 1819, "As the nation of Israel was then [at the time of the conquest of Canaan] *militant*, so is the church now. As the land of Canaan belonged to Israel, in virtue of a divine grant, so does the world belong to the church; and as God's chosen people still had much to do, before they could come into full and quiet possession of the land, so has the church a great work to accomplish, in subduing the world 'to the

obedience of Christ'" (*The promised land. A Sermon, delivered at Goshen, (Conn.) at the Ordination of the Rev. Messrs. Hiram Bingham & Asa Thurston, as Missionaries to the Sandwich Islands, Sept. 29, 1819* [Boston, 1819], 5). Similarly, Noah Porter proclaimed, "on looking over our country how much is to be done for their conversion! how many a dark corner to be illuminated! how many American heathen to be instructed! how many thousands, and tens of thousands untaught in the word! And on looking over heathen lands, O what a scene of guilt and misery! how many millions of immortal souls in the kingdom of darkness and under the power of satan! How can you render a more suitable tribute of gratitude to the Father of the whole family for the great things he hath done for you, than by employing the means which he has put into your hands, for the redemption of the world?" (*Memorial of a Revival*, 15).

70. Bartlett, *A Sermon, Preached in Wintonbury Meeting-House*, 13–14. Elias Cornelius, the orthodox Congregational pastor of the Salem, Massachusetts, Tabernacle Church, argued in 1823 "that the direction of Heaven to Christians at this day in respect to the cause of Missions, is, that they GO FORWARD" (*A Sermon, delivered in the Tabernacle Church, Salem, Mass. Sept. 25, 1823, at the Ordination of the Rev. Edmund Frost, as a Missionary to the Heathen: and the Rev. Messrs. Aaron W. Warner, Ansel D. Eddy, Nathan W. Fiske, Isaac Oakes, and George Sheldon, as Evangelists* [Boston, 1823], 4). "The kingdom of Christ," Humphrey added, "is not, like other kingdoms, liable to be subverted by political revolutions. It may feel the shock, and often does, when human governments are overthrown. But it has already survived hundreds of such convulsions, and will survive many more" (*Kingdom of Christ*, 16). See also Brockway, *A Sermon, Preached . . . May 11, 1815*, 25–26.

71. Daniel Crosby, *Who Troubles Israel? A Discourse Delivered in Conway, Mass. on the day of the Annual Thanksgiving, November 29, 1832* (Amherst, Mass., 1833), 22; Charles Stanley Pease, ed., *History of Conway (Massachusetts), 1767–1917* (Springfield, Mass.: Springfield Printing and Binding, 1917), 131. See also Porter, *Signs of the Times*, 5–6.

72. Wayland, *Encouragements to Religious Effort*, 24; Beecher, *A Plea for the West*, 7–12. One should note that Mark Y. Hanley has argued that Beecher's scenario was both unusual and criticized by contemporaries (*Beyond a Christian Commonwealth: The Protestant Quarrel with the American Republic, 1830–1860* [Chapel Hill: University of North Carolina Press, 1994], 64–66). In 1815, Elijah Parish cautioned, in contrast to the optimism of Beecher and Wayland, that there was much work to do before the millennium. Although current events such as international peace and missionary work did "forebode the reign of the Prince of Peace," the millions of unchristianized people around the globe demonstrated that there was a big job left ahead. "The man of Sin is not *dead*," Parish concluded (*A Sermon Preached at Ipswich*, 14–15).

73. Bouton, *Christian Patriotism*, 11; Cummings, *A Discourse delivered . . . April 6, 1820*, 29–31; Porter, *Character of Nehemiah*, 13, 17.

74. Harry S. Stout, *The New England Soul: Preaching and Religious Culture in Colonial New England* (New York: Oxford University Press, 1986), 293. Like Porter, Francis Wayland also set the goal of restoring America as a metaphorical Jerusalem. "I would plead with you, instead of engaging in political strife, to put forth your hands to the work of making your fellow citizens wiser and better [especially through Bible societies and Sunday schools]. . . . And specially would I charge you to give to this cause not only your active exertions, but your unceasing prayers. Ye who love the Lord, keep not silence, and give him no rest, until he establish this his Jerusalem, and make her a praise in the whole earth" (*Duties of an American Citizen*, 48). For other invocations of Nehemiah's example, see also John Elliott, *The Gracious Presence of God, The Highest Felicity and Security of Any People. A Sermon, Preached before his Excellency the Governor, and the Honorable Legislature of the State of Connecticut, Convened at Hartford, on the Anniversary Election, May 10th, 1810* (Hartford, Conn., 1810), 19; Lyman Beecher, *A Reformation of Morals Practicable and Indispensable: A Sermon Delivered at New*

Haven on the Evening of October 27, 1812, 2d ed. (1812; Andover, Mass., 1814), reprinted in *Lyman Beecher and the Reform of Society: Four Sermons, 1804–1828*, Religion in America: Series 2, ed. Edwin S. Gaustad (New York: Arno Press and New York Times, 1972), 11; Ebenezer Porter, *Great effects result from little causes. A Sermon, delivered Sept. 13, 1815, at the Anniversary of the Moral Society in Andover* (Andover, Mass., 1815), 13.

75. Beecher, *A Sermon . . . May 2d, 1826*, 13, 17–18.

76. Porter, *Signs of the Times*, 26.

77. Walker, *History of the Congregational Churches*, 322–329; Phillips, *Jedidiah Morse*, 172–176; Ebenezer Porter, *A Sermon, Delivered in Boston, on the Anniversary of the American Education Society, October, 4, 1820*, New England Tract Society, no. 135 (Andover, Mass., 1821), 5–6; Charles I. Foster, *An Errand of Mercy: The Evangelical United Front, 1790–1837* (Chapel Hill: University of North Carolina Press, 1960), viii and passim; "Report of the Directors of the Rel. Char. Soc. in the County of Worcester at their 16th anniversary at Upton, Sept. 16, 1828," CL.

78. Joseph Goffe to Joseph and Eliza Goffe, 25 July 1828, Goffe Papers; Harmony Conference of Churches record book, 1828–1833, 17 June 1828, 15 Sept. 1829, and 11 June 1833, Worcester County, Mass., Church Associations Collection, 1805–1935, vol. 1, AAS; Brookfield Association, Records, 7 Jan. 1824 and 10 June 1834. When the Brookfield Association divided up the calendar on 3 Jan. 1837, it supported all of the same organizations as the Harmony Conference except the American Colonization Society, which had fallen into disfavor by that time.

79. H. Richard Niebuhr, *Christ and Culture* (New York: Harper & Brothers, 1951), 195, 43.

80. McLoughlin, *New England Dissent*, 2:698, 1108, 1119–1121, 1264; E[lam] Smalley, *The Worcester Pulpit; With Notices Historical and Biographical* (Boston, 1851), 290–295, quote on 294; Wayland, *Encouragements to Religious Effort*, 20, 37f., quote on 20. International missionary work was a project common to the Congregationalists and Baptists; see Wayland, *The Moral Dignity of the Missionary Enterprise. A Sermon delivered before the Boston Baptist Foreign Mission Society on the Evening of October 26, and before the Salem Bible Translation Society on the Evening of Nov. 4, 1823* (Boston, 1824). As McLoughlin added, "Like Lyman Beecher, the editor of the *Christian Watchman* [a Baptist periodical] talked of 'the Church' with a kind of proprietorial ownership which assumed that all evangelicals were at one in desiring to convert the world and bring on the millennium" (*New England Dissent*, 2:1265). The rise of interdenominational evangelicalism is also a theme in Phillips, *Jedidiah Morse*, 5–7, 168, 176.

81. McLoughlin, *New England Dissent*, 2:1134, 1267.

82. Beecher, *Faith Once Delivered to the Saints*, 5; Porter, *Signs of the Times*, 5; idem, *A Sermon, Delivered . . . October, 4, 1820*, 6. In 1826, Beecher added that "jealousies and ambitious collisions between religious denominations should give place to christian courtesy and the magnanimity of an hearty co-operation for the glory of God, and the salvation of the world" (*A Sermon . . . May 2d, 1826*, 18). "One feature of the evangelical movement suggestive of an established church was its Protestant ecumenicism," observes Daniel W. Howe. This ecumenicism "reflected a decline of interest in the theological distinctions that had often formed the basis for denominational differentiation accompanied by a rising sense of American nationality and national moral responsibility" ("The Evangelical Movement and Political Culture in the North during the Second Party System," *JAH* 77 [1991]: 1224).

In the 1830s, one of Beecher's problems with Roman Catholics was that they did not play by the new rules of denominational friendship. He charged that they were an exclusive group, bent on grabbing power: "Did the Catholics regard themselves only as one of many denominations of Christians, entitled only to equal rights and privileges, there would be no such cause for apprehension while they peaceably sustained themselves by their own arguments and well doing. But if Catholics are taught to believe that their church is the only church of Christ, out of whose inclosure [*sic*] none can be saved, . . . that heresy is a capital offence . . . that the pope and the councils of the church are infallible, and her rights of ecclesiastical jurisdiction universal and as far as possible and expedient may be of right, and ought to be as a matter of duty, enforced by the civil power, — that to the pope belongs the right of interference with the political concerns of nations, . . . if these things are so, is it invidious and is it superfluous to call the attention of the nation to the bearing of such a denomination upon our civil and religious institutions and equal rights? It is the *right of* SELF-PRESERVATION, and the denial of it is TREASON or the INFATUATION OF FOLLY" (*A Plea for the West*, 69–72).

83. Brookfield Association, Records, 14 Oct. 1829; Harmony Conference record book, 15 Sept. 1830; Joseph Allen, *The Worcester Association and its Antecedents: A History of Four Ministerial Associations: The Marlborough, The Worcester (Old), The Lancaster, and The Worcester (New) Associations. With Biographical Notices of the Members, accompanied by Portraits* (Boston, 1868), 276; Smalley, *Worcester Pulpit*, 237; David Damon, *A Sermon, preached at Charlton, Massachusetts, Sept. 14, 1826, at the Annual Meeting of the Auxiliary Bible Society in the County of Worcester* (Worcester, Mass., 1826), 18; Membership book, 1816–1859, Worcester County, Mass., Bible Society Records, 1816–1866, vol. 1, AAS; Sam'l Crocker to A. D. Foster, 21 Oct. 1833, Worcester County, Mass., Bible Society Records, box 1, folder 2 [contribution from Fitchburg Baptists].

84. Channing, "Spiritual Freedom," 4:88.

85. Nathaniel S. Wheaton, *The Providence of God displayed in the rise and fall of Nations. A Sermon, delivered at the Annual Election, in Trinity Church, New-Haven, On Wednesday the 7th of May, 1828* (New-Haven, Conn., 1828), 11. Compare Wheaton's sermon with Harry Croswell's 1818 election sermon, analyzed at the end of chapter 3, which took a decidedly more separatist tone. Croswell was another Episcopalian, the rector of Trinity Church, New Haven. See Croswell, *A Sermon Preached at the Anniversary Election, Hartford, May 14, 1818* (Hartford, Conn., 1818).

86. Wheaton, *Providence of God*, 17. The Methodists' stance on the issue of a public religious commitment was less clear. Willbur Fisk was one of the few Methodists to deliver an election sermon in southern New England during the half-century following the American Revolution. He was a minister and served in 1829 as the principal of "the Wesleyan academy" in Wilbraham, Massachusetts. His sermon epitomized the picture of evangelicals bidding a retreat from a corrupting world and adopting a holy lifestyle, because the end of the world was fast approaching. See Fisk, *A Sermon delivered before His Excellency Levi Lincoln, Governor, His Honor Thomas L. Winthrop, Lieutenant Governor, The Hon. Council, The Senate, and House of Representatives of the Commonwealth of Massachusetts, on the Day of General Election, May 27, 1829* (Boston, 1829). Early Methodist leaders such as John Wesley and Francis Asbury had also been apolitical, but later Methodist clergymen preached about the need for societal godliness, aided the Democratic-Republican party, and by the 1830s warned, like Lyman Beecher, about Catholicism's threat. See George Claude Baker Jr., *An Introduction to the History of Early New England Methodism, 1789–1839* (Durham, N.C.: Duke University Press, 1941), 45–48. Apparently, the Methodists followed a trajectory toward "respectability" similar to the Baptists, but as a newer denomination, they moved more slowly into the evangelical consensus regarding public Christianity. Regarding the Methodists' upward social mobility by the second quarter of the nineteenth century, see also John H. Wigger, *Taking Heaven by Storm: Methodism and the Rise of Popular Christianity in America* (New York: Oxford University Press, 1998), chapter 8.

87. Anne C. Loveland, *Southern Evangelicals and the Social Order, 1800–1860* (Baton Rouge: Louisiana State University Press, 1980), 109; Daniel L. Dreisbach, "Introduction: A Debate on Religion and Politics in the Early Republic," in *Religion and Politics in the Early*

Republic: Jasper Adams and the Church-State Debate, ed. Daniel L. Dreisbach (Lexington: University Press of Kentucky, 1996), 7–10.

88. As McLoughlin wrote, "the old springs of disdain and distrust still flowed too deeply" for the Baptists and orthodox to come together too closely before the late 1820s (*New England Dissent*, 2:1129). See especially ibid., 2:1136–1138, where he recounts a flap arising within the American Education Society in 1820. The Baptists accused the predominantly Congregational leadership of discriminating against Baptist students in its awarding of scholarships.

89. Joseph Goffe, Diary, 1 Nov. 1803, Joseph Goffe Papers, 1721–1846, AAS; Joseph Goffe to Eliza Goffe, 4 Feb. 1833, Goffe Papers; Porter, *Signs of the Times*, 17.

90. Stuart, *A Sermon delivered . . . May 30, 1827*, 15. Nathaniel S. Wheaton, an Episcopal priest, made the same link between judgment and morality as Stuart had, saying, "The ascendency of law can be maintained in such a world as ours, only by the hope of reward or the fear of punishment" (*Providence of God*, 11). Asa Cummings displayed the typical orthodox detestation for the Universalists when he asked, "Now what is this,—call it infidelity, or universalism, or by any other specious name,—what is it, but to charge falsehood upon God? to allege, that his anger is not to be dreaded,—his grace not to be desired,—the overtures of his mercy not to be regarded? While they thus trample under foot the blood of the Son of God, and do despite to the spirit of grace, let them remember, that he, whose sentence will decide the destinies of men, hath declared, that [Mark 6:16] '*he that believeth not shall be damned*'" (*A Discourse delivered . . . April 6, 1820*, 17–18). Regarding the Baptists' and Methodists' equally intense antipathy toward the Universalists, see, respectively, McLoughlin, *New England Dissent*, 2:717–722, and Baker, *Early New England Methodism*, 39–40.

91. Hosea Ballou, *Orthodoxy Unmasked. A Sermon, delivered in the Second Universalist Meeting in Boston, on Sabbath Morning, June 24, 1827, in which some notice is taken of Professor Stuart's Election Sermon* (Boston, 1827), 13–15, quote on 15.

92. McLoughlin, *New England Dissent*, 2:1133–1134, quote on 2:1133. For the idea of the Unitarians as a negative reference group that served to unify the orthodox Congregationalists, see Lawrence B. Goodheart and Richard O. Curry, eds., "The Trinitarian Indictment of Unitarianism: The Letters of Elizur Wright Jr., 1826–1827," *JER* 3 (1983): 281–296. Elizur Wright Jr. was then a recent graduate of Yale and teacher in Groton, Massachusetts. His letters depict the Unitarians in Groton as a morally decadent and religiously apostate elite. As Goodheart and Curry point out (pp. 282–283) in their discussion of "the wider cultural ramifications of the Trinitarian indictment of Unitarianism," "Trinitarians . . . perceived Unitarianism as a serious threat to traditional social values—in fact, a threat to the stability of the republic itself."

93. Abraham Bishop, *Connecticut Republicanism. An Oration on the Extent and Power of Political Delusion. Delivered in New-Haven, On the Evening preceding the Public Commencement, September, 1800* ([New Haven, Conn.?], 1800); Edward D. Griffin, *An Address delivered on the 13th, May 1824, at the Anniversary of the Presbyterian Education Society in the City of New-York* (New-York, 1824), 3; Dexter, *Biographical Sketches*, 4:17–24; Abraham Bishop, *Remarks on Dr. Griffin's Requisition for 700,000 Ministers* (New Haven, Conn., 1824), 4–5.

94. Bishop, *Remarks on Dr. Griffin's Requisition*, 22–23.

95. Ibid., 38–39.

96. The biographical information comes from Sprague, *Annals*, 2:221–228, quote on 226, and Caleb J. Tenney, *Mysterious Events to be Explained. A Sermon, Preached at Glastenbury, December 8th, 1830, at the Funeral of the Rev. Samuel Austin, D.D.* (Hartford, Conn., 1831), 13–24.

97. Samuel Austin, *An Address, Pronounced in Worcester, (Mass.) on The Fourth of July, 1825, being the Forty-Ninth Anniversary of the Independence of the United States, before an As-*

sembly Convened for the Purpose of Celebrating this Event Religiously (Worcester, Mass., 1825), 6, 10–11, 16, 18, 20, 22; Austin, A Sermon, Preached . . . April 11, 1811, 23.

Chapter Six

1. Francis Wayland, Encouragements to Religious Effort: A Sermon delivered at the request of the American Sunday School Union, May 25, 1830 (Philadelphia, 1830), 35–36.

2. Mark A. Noll, A History of Christianity in the United States and Canada (Grand Rapids, Mich.: Eerdmans, 1992), 287.

3. Robert H. Abzug, Cosmos Crumbling: American Reform and the Religious Imagination (New York: Oxford University Press, 1994), 33.

4. Len Travers, Celebrating the Fourth: Independence Day and the Rites of Nationalism in the Early Republic (Amherst: University of Massachusetts Press, 1997), 4. For examples of star-spangled July Fourth oratory, see Horace Mann, An Oration, Delivered at Dedham, July 4th, 1823, on the Forty-Seventh Anniversary of American Independence (Dedham, Mass., 1823), 3–4; George Washington Adams, An Oration Delivered at Quincy, on the Fifth of July, 1824 (Boston, 1824); Francis Bassett, An Oration, delivered on Monday, the Fifth of July, 1824, in Commemoration of American Independence, before the Supreme Executive of the Commonwealth, and the City Council and Inhabitants of the City of Boston (Boston, 1824); George Bancroft, An Oration Delivered on the Fourth of July, 1826, at Northampton, Mass. (Northampton, Mass., 1826); Josiah Quincy, An Oration, delivered on Tuesday, the Fourth of July, 1826, it being the Fiftieth Anniversary of American Independence, before the Supreme Executive of the Commonwealth, and the City Council and Inhabitants, of the City of Boston (Boston, 1826).

5. Asa Cummings, A Discourse delivered at Brunswick, (Maine,) April 6, 1820, the Day of the Annual Fast in Maine and Massachusetts (Brunswick, Maine, 1820), 10–11; Leonard Bacon, A Plea for Africa; Delivered in New-Haven, July 4th, 1825 (New Haven, Conn., 1825), 6. Similarly, Heman Humphrey, president of Amherst College, was sick and tired of the Fourth's high-flying patriotism. "The birth-day of our nation is the brightest era in the political history of the world; and may the fourth of July never dawn, without exciting in every American bosom the warmest gratitude to Heaven, for the blessings of civil and religious liberty. . . . But the popular and stereotyped topics of the anniversary, I do not intend to introduce on the present occasion. Enough will be said by others to satisfy, if not to surfeit, the very genius of patriotism—about liberty in its cradle and in its armour; in its perils and in its triumphs. Enough there will be of boasting—of our ancestors, or ourselves, and especially of our posterity: enough of Mars, and the Bird of Jove, and our star-spangled banner. Indeed, so many bows of promise and halos of glory have already been painted on every cloud, that there is no room left upon the face of the heavens for another" (Parallel Between Intemperance and the Slave Trade. An Address delivered at Amherst College, July 4, 1828 [Amherst, Mass., 1828], 3).

6. Cummings, A Discourse delivered . . . April 6, 1820, 11–12, quotes on 11; William B. Sprague, Religious Celebration of Independence: A Discourse delivered at Northampton, on the Fourth of July, 1827 (Hartford, Conn., 1827), 5; Travers, Celebrating the Fourth, 129. I do not know how widespread the practice was, but I have come across at least three July Fourth addresses that were delivered before Christian audiences with the expressed purpose of marking Independence Day in a godly manner. In addition to Sprague's Religious Celebration of Independence, see also Samuel Austin, An Address, Pronounced in Worcester, (Mass.) on The Fourth of July, 1825, being the Forty-Ninth Anniversary of the Independence of the United States, before an Assembly Convened for the Purpose of Celebrating this Event Religiously (Worcester, Mass., 1825), and Charles A. Boardman, The Agency of God, Illustrated in the

Achievement of the Independence of the United States. A Sermon, Delivered at New-Preston, Connecticut, July 4, 1826, being a Religious Celebration of that Day (New-Haven, Conn., 1826).

Boston's 1811 Fourth of July festivities likewise struck Edward A. Pearson as "heathenish rather than christian." In a letter to his future brother-in-law, Ephraim Abbot, a recent Andover Seminary graduate then on a missionary tour of Maine as agent for the Massachusetts Bible Society, Pearson charged that "very many" people "made [Independence Day] a day of excess" that "serves to disunite rather than unite the people." However, he also wrote that he was "pleased to learn by a Southern paper the manner in which the day was kept by a Society of Methodists in Philadelphia, they met at their place of worship & gave thanks to the Almighty for the blessings which the day comm[em]orated" (E. A. P. to Ephraim Abbot, 13 July 1811, Ephraim Abbot Papers, 1801–1904, box 1, folder 1, AAS).

.7. William Lloyd Garrison, "Garrison's First Anti-slavery Address in Boston. Address at Park Street Church, Boston, July 4, 1829," in *Old South Leaflets*, vol. 8, no. 180 (Boston: Directors of the Old South Work, Old South Meeting House, 1907), 78, 81. For background on Garrison, see Abzug, *Cosmos Crumbling*, 136–142.

8. Heman Humphrey, *Indian Rights & Our Duties. An Address delivered at Amherst, Hartford, Etc. December, 1829* (Amherst, Mass., 1830), 13, 10, 24.

9. Ibid., 24.

10. See, for instance, *To the Public. An Address from the Ministers of the Association in and about Cambridge, at their stated Meeting on the second Tuesday in October, 1796* (Boston, 1796). For the colonial background and a concise overview of the Sabbatarian movement, see Abzug, *Cosmos Crumbling*, 111–116.

11. Richard R. John, "Taking Sabbatarianism Seriously: The Postal System, the Sabbath, and the Transformation of American Political Culture," *JER* 10 (1990), 522, 535, 527–528; Ebenezer Porter, *The Character of Nehemiah, or Jerusalem Built Up. A Sermon, Preached on the Public Fast, April 4, 1816 in the Chapel of the Theological Seminary at Andover* (Andover, Mass., 1816), 20. Likewise, Lyman Beecher warned, "So let the stream of pleasure and of worldly cares bear away the population of the land from the house of God, and from the duties of devotion on the Sabbath; and ignorance of God, and of His laws will with equal certainty ensue; irreligion will prevail, and immorality and dissoluteness, to an extent utterly inconsistent with the permanence of republican institutions" (*A Sermon, addressed to the Legislature of Connecticut; at New-Haven, on the day of the Anniversary Election, May 2d, 1826* [New Haven, Conn., 1826], 16). "Were we to go to the prison of this state [of Massachusetts]," predicted the president of Williams College, Zephaniah Swift Moore, in 1818, "we should probably not be able to select one, who after an honest and correct analysis of his character, and of the influences, which led him to the commission of crimes, of whom it would not be true, that he began his downward course by a neglect and contempt of the duties of the sabbath" (*The Sabbath a Permanent and Benevolent Institution. A Sermon, preached at the Annual Election, May 27, 1818, before His Excellency John Brooks, Esq. Governor; His Honor William Phillips, Esq. Lieutenant Governor; The Honorable Council; and the Legislature of Massachusetts* [Boston, 1818], 20).

12. Moore, *The Sabbath a Permanent and Benevolent Institution*, 27; Thomas Snell, *A Sermon, preached before His Excellency John Brooks, Esq. Governor; His Honor William Phillips, Esq. Lieutenant Governor, The Honorable Council, and the Two Houses Composing the Legislature of the Commonwealth of Massachusetts, May 28, 1817. Being the Anniversary Election* (Boston, 1817), 23. Charles A. Boardman, then of New Haven's Third Congregational Church, most clearly analyzed the way in which "the gospel and its institutions [may] be properly upheld by the rulers of the people." He rejected the establishment, but said that civil rulers could, among other things, pass Sabbatarian legislation. According to Boardman, Chris-

tianity could be "upheld by the rulers of the people; — so upheld as never to encroach upon the rights of conscience; never to invade denominational privilege; never to compel men to assume the badge of discipleship, as a test of official qualification; but so upheld by the example of those in high places, and by their adoption of appropriate measures, as to protect the sabbath from profanation, give unrestrained efficacy to the gospel in the hands of an enlightened and efficient ministry, — room and privilege to charitable and benevolent associations to do their work, and for the church of God to accomplish her high and holy enterprise, under the blessing of the Holy Ghost sent down from heaven; [so that] from the mightiness and all pervading nature of this cause, we may expect the perpetuity of our free institutions, the steady advance of national prosperity, and individual elevation and blessedness, and God will look down upon the land with favor, and lay it over with the manifestations of his presence and glory" (*The Duties and Embarrassments of Rulers. A Sermon, addressed to the Legislature of the State of Connecticut, at the Annual Election in New-Haven, May 5, 1830* [New-Haven, Conn., 1830], 8).

13. John, "Taking Sabbatarianism Seriously," 523–526, 535–544, quote on 540; *Extracts from the Minutes of the General Association of Massachusetts Proper, Holden at Royalston, on the Fourth Tuesday, viz. the 27th day of June,* A.D. *1815, and continued by adjournment to the 29th of the same month* (Boston, 1815), 21; *Extracts from the Minutes of the General Association of Massachusetts Proper* (Boston, 1816), 3. For a thorough exposition of the arguments for and against halting the Sunday mails, see also John G. West Jr., *The Politics of Revelation and Reason: Religion and Civic Life in the New Nation* (Lawrence: University Press of Kansas, 1996), 137–170.

14. Joseph Goffe to Eliza, Eben[eze]r, and Joseph Goffe, 30 May 1828, Joseph Goffe Papers, 1826–1842, box 3, folder 4, AAS. West, *Politics of Revelation and Reason,* 107, notes that "more than 400 temperance societies had been established" nationwide by 1828.

15. Abzug, *Cosmos Crumbling,* 93–104. For a lengthier discussion of the temperance movement, see also Ian R. Tyrrell, *Sobering Up: From Temperance to Prohibition in Antebellum America, 1800–1860,* Contributions in American History, 82 (Westport, Conn.: Greenwood Press, 1979). However, Tyrrell consistently downplays or overlooks the religious aspects of the issue. To take one example from his introduction, Tyrrell notes the predominance of New England and the upper Midwest in temperance, but attributes this to economics, not religious culture. "Explaining this uneven geographic dispersal of the temperance and prohibitionist agitations is not difficult," he tells us (p. 13). "The Northeast first felt the disruptive changes of industrialization, urbanization, and the increasing commercialization of agriculture, which called forth the organized temperance movement." This is typical of Tyrrell's antireligious bias.

16. As Heman Humphrey declared, "If there is any evil which hardens the heart faster, or fills the mouth with 'cursing and bitterness' sooner, or quickens hatred to God and man into a more rapid and frightful maturity, I know not what it is" (*Parallel Between Intemperance and the Slave Trade,* 25).

17. William B. Sprague, *Intemperance, a just cause for alarm and exertion. A Sermon, Preached at West Springfield, April 5th, 1827, the Day of the Annual Fast* (New York, 1827), 8. See also Henry Ware Jr., *The Criminality of Intemperance. An Address delivered at the Eleventh Anniversary of the Massachusetts Society for the Suppression of Intemperance* (Boston, 1823), 12–15; Luther Fraseur Dimmick, *Intemperance: A Sermon, delivered at the North Church in Newburyport, on the occasion of the Publick Fast, April 1, 1824* (Newburyport, Mass., 1824), 13–16.

18. Heman Humphrey, Roswell R. Swan, and William Bonney, *Intemperance: An Address, to the Churches and Congregations of the Western District of Fairfield County, (Connecticut)* (1813; Schenectady, N.Y., 1814), 16; Humphrey, *Parallel Between Intemperance and*

the Slave Trade, 28. "As you love your country, then, and desire her prosperity," William B. Sprague said in the same vein, "as you wish that her noble institutions may be perpetuated, and that it may be seen by the world, that though the floods should come and the winds beat, the fabric of her government cannot fall, being founded upon a rock; I exhort you to endeavor to arrest the progress of this deadly evil" (*Intemperance*, 24).

19. Ware, *Criminality of Intemperance*, 5–6; Sprague, *Intemperance*, 12–22, quotes on 22.

20. Humphrey, *Parallel Between Intemperance and the Slave Trade*, 39; Sprague, *Intemperance*, 26; Tyrrell, *Sobering Up*, 33–86. Like Humphrey, Luther Fraseur Dimmick of Newburyport, Massachusetts, also counted on the same triumvirate of "the Patriots, and Philanthropists, and Christians, in the different parts of our land" to petition for "the suppression of this evil" (*Intemperance*, 19–20).

21. John, "Taking Sabbatarianism Seriously," 527, 535; Abzug, *Cosmos Crumbling*, 106–107, 114; Daniel Walker Howe, "The Evangelical Movement and Political Culture in the North during the Second Party System," *JAH* 77 (1991): 1216–1239; Harry L. Watson, *Liberty and Power: The Politics of Jacksonian America* (New York: Hill and Wang, 1990), 177–179; Tyrrell, *Sobering Up*, especially 125–134.

22. Boardman, *Duties and Embarrassments of Rulers*, 13; William E. Channing, "Spiritual Freedom. Discourse Preached at the Annual Election, May 26, 1830," in *The Works of William E. Channing, D.D.*, 8th ed., 6 vols. (Boston and New York, 1848), 4:84.

23. Wayland, *Encouragements to Religious Effort*, 7–18.

24. Eleazar T. Fitch, *National Prosperity Perpetuated: A Discourse: Delivered in the Chapel of Yale College; on the day of the Annual Thanksgiving: November 29, 1827* (New-Haven, Conn., 1828), 6–7, 21. For the same tension between celebrating material prosperity and worrying over its effects among the Unitarian clergy, see Daniel Walker Howe, *The Unitarian Conscience: Harvard Moral Philosophy, 1805–1861*, rev. ed. (Cambridge: Harvard University Press, 1970; Middletown, Conn.: Wesleyan University Press, 1988), 227–235.

25. Howe, "Evangelical Movement and Political Culture," 1222, n. 14; L. Ives Hoadly, *An Address, delivered at the Union Celebration of Independence, at Sutton, Mass. July 5, 1824* (Worcester, Mass., 1824), 12.

26. Sprague, *Religious Celebration of Independence*, 26. Likewise, noted Asa Cummings in disgust, "A nation of freemen, who glory in their liberties; who are sensible to every insult offered to their sovereignty; who would hazard their lives and their treasures sooner than surrender the most inconsiderable right; whose very watchword has been, *liberty or death*; this nation holds myriads of human beings in bondage" (*A Discourse delivered . . . April 6, 1820*, 23)!

27. Cummings, *A Discourse delivered . . . April 6, 1820*, 24. Eleazar T. Fitch's antislavery remarks of 1827 were prophetic in two senses of the word; they were a message about God's justice and a prediction (accurate, as things turned out in the 1860s) of future calamity. "If the South and the North now unite as the brethren of one common country, and as friends of the enslaved Africans, and commit their undertaking to him who has hitherto conducted the destinies of this nation in kindness; there is hope that we may yet blot this stain from our annals, and avert this impending scourge from our country. But if the North will reproach and refuse her aids and sympathies, and if the South will be jealous and refuse her assent and co-operation; if they will not unitedly come before God and commit to him the issues of the cause, waiting on him in their appropriate duties; our hope is gone, and we or posterity shall smart for our injustice towards man and ingratitude towards God" (*National Prosperity Perpetuated*, 31).

28. Hoadly, *An Address, delivered . . . July 5, 1824*, 14; Nathaniel Bouton, *Christian Patriotism. An Address Delivered at Concord, July the Fourth, 1825* (Concord, N.H., 1825), 15, 18. See also Joseph W. Phillips, *Jedidiah Morse and New England Congregationalism* (New Brunswick, N.J.: Rutgers University Press, 1983), 182–194; Abzug, *Cosmos Crumbling*, 133–134.

29. Bacon, *A Plea for Africa*, 18. For a similar argument, see also *Report of the Managers of the Worcester County Auxiliary Colonization Society, at the Annual Meeting Held in Worcester, December 14, 1831* (Worcester, Mass., 1832), 6. Bacon's moderate antislavery position is carefully illuminated in Hugh Davis, *Leonard Bacon: New England Reformer and Antislavery Moderate* (Baton Rouge: Louisiana State University Press, 1998). Davis discusses Bacon's *A Plea for Africa* on p. 60.

30. Garrison, "First Anti-slavery Address in Boston," 83–86. Robert Abzug has pinpointed Garrison's significance similarly to the way I have. He argues for Garrison's critical role because the abolitionist "reached beyond prior campaigns of equal moral urgency by emphasizing the imperative of racial equality along with the sin of slavery, and by casting his appeal in the language of militant New England evangelical reform" (*Cosmos Crumbling*, 130). Abzug discusses Garrison's biography at ibid., 129, 136–138, and analyzes the Park Street Address at ibid., 142–145.

Epilogue

1. Daniel Walker Howe, *The Unitarian Conscience: Harvard Moral Philosophy, 1805–1861*, rev. ed. (Cambridge: Harvard University Press, 1970; Middletown, Conn.: Wesleyan University Press, 1988), 222–224, 255, 294–295.

2. Edward D. Griffin, *An Address delivered on the 13th, May 1824, at the Anniversary of the Presbyterian Education Society in the City of New-York* (New-York, 1824), 4. John Codman, the orthodox Congregational minister of Dorchester, Massachusetts, issued similar words of warning in 1826: "The growth of our country, my hearers, is unparalleled in the history of the world; and we might indulge our patriotick feelings by dwelling on her prosperity and anticipating her future glory.—But our subject calls us to a different object of contemplation—to meditate upon her *moral* condition. Her unequalled growth, while it calls forth the effusions of patriotick sensibility, awakens in the bosom of the Christian emotions of a different kind. He well knows, that, in the rapidity of her growth, she has outstripped her moral and religious cultivation" (*Home Missions. A Sermon delivered before the Massachusetts Society for Promoting Christian Knowledge, in Park Street Church, Boston, May 31, 1826* [Boston, 1826], 9).

3. Lyman Beecher, *A Plea for the West*, 2d ed. (1832; Cincinnati, 1835), 15–18; John Scholte Nollen, *Grinnell College* (Iowa City: State Historical Society of Iowa, 1953), 29–50. On the spread of Congregationalism into the Western states, see Williston Walker, *A History of the Congregational Churches in the United States*, American Church History Series, vol. 3, ed. Philip Schaff et al. (New York, 1894), 371. For a visual representation of Congregationalism's expansion into the old Northwest, refer to the map entitled "Congregational Churches: 1850," in Edwin Scott Gaustad, *Historical Atlas of Religion in America*, rev. ed. (New York: Harper & Row, 1976), 60. Gaustad's map clearly shows the denomination's concentration in its original, New England hearth and its spread across upstate New York and the Great Lakes belt of Ohio, Michigan, Illinois, and Wisconsin, and on into Iowa.

4. Heman Humphrey, Roswell R. Swan, and William Bonney, *Intemperance: An Address, to the Churches and Congregations of the Western District of Fairfield County, (Connecticut)* (1813; Schenectady, N.Y., 1814), 16. John Codman similarly conglomerated moral and economic themes in a Whiggish manner. In 1826, he called for the linkage of evangelism to the market, transportation, and communications improvements then underway. "The spirit of enterprise and internal improvement, which has recently manifested itself in our country, calls loudly for concomitant exertions on the part of all the friends of Zion. Let but the same energy and zeal, which is displaying itself in the various schemes of internal improvement, be manifested by the friends of God in efforts to diffuse among our growing population the knowledge

of the gospel, and, as we shall one day be the greatest and most powerful, so we shall also be the happiest and most holy nation upon the face of the earth.

"Wherever new sources of communication are opened by the persevering enterprise of our fellow citizens, let the Bible and the tract be transported with the bale of merchandize [*sic*], and the produce of the soil. Wherever a clearance is made in the mighty forests for the habitations of men, there let the church and the school house be the centre of the thriving settlement" (*Home Missions*, 19).

5. Daniel Walker Howe, "The Evangelical Movement and Political Culture in the North during the Second Party System," *JAH* 77 (1991): 1223; Richard Carwardine, *Evangelicals and Politics in Antebellum America* (New Haven: Yale University Press, 1993); Daniel Walker Howe, *The Political Culture of the American Whigs* (Chicago: University of Chicago Press, 1979).

6. Howe, "Evangelical Movement and Political Culture," 1224, 1226–1228, quote on 1226.

7. Harmony Conference of Churches record book, 1828–1833, 11 June 1832, Worcester County, Mass., Church Associations Collection, 1805–1935, vol. 1, AAS; Brookfield Association, 20 April 1831, Records, 1757–1837, CL; Joseph Goffe to Eliza Goffe, 12 Oct. 1831, 4 Feb. 1833, and 13 Aug. 1833, Joseph Goffe Papers, 1826–1842, box 3, folder 4, AAS; Sydney E. Ahlstrom, *A Religious History of the American People* (New Haven: Yale University Press, 1972), 419–422, 458–461; Joseph Goffe, "Sermon on Titus 3:8 at a meeting of the General Association of Massachusetts at Andover," no. 1736, 24 June 1829, pp. 16–17, Joseph Goffe Collection, 1787–1832, box 1, folder 2, WHM.

8. Robert H. Abzug, *Cosmos Crumbling: American Reform and the Religious Imagination* (New York: Oxford University Press, 1994), 106. James H. Moorhead provides another sketch of the tensions and ambiguities within the clergy's public Christianity from the 1830s to 1850s in *American Apocalypse: Yankee Protestants and the Civil War, 1860–1869* (New Haven: Yale University Press, 1978), 6–22, 83–96. Issues such as reform movements, politics, and slavery divided Protestant ministers. As Moorhead concludes (p. 22), "Everyone sensed the imminence of crisis, perhaps of catastrophe, but there were no commonly accepted marching orders as struggle loomed in view. The situation represented a failure for the churches. They had launched evangelical crusades to make the United States a fit millennial instrument and had hoped to turn aside the divine judgments that harried other peoples; but after seven decades under the federal Union, their efforts had not prevented moral confusion and political disorder."

9. Walker, *History of the Congregational Churches*, 362–363; James H. Moorhead, "Social Reform and the Divided Conscience of Antebellum Protestantism," *CH* 48 (1979): 416–430. Moorhead shows that Finney's theology led him into the reformist camp. Indeed, Finney uttered this classic expression of the clergy's public Christianity in 1846: "'Now the great business of the church is to reform the world—to put away every kind of sin. . . —to reform individuals, communities, and governments, and never rest until the kingdom [triumphs around the globe]'" (ibid., 422–423, where Moorhead is quoting from p. 11 of the *Oberlin Evangelist* of 21 Jan. 1846). However, Moorhead also argues (p. 422), that Finney was "notoriously unwilling to proceed as far or as fast as many reformers wished."

10. Abzug, *Cosmos Crumbling*, 145–161; Howe, *Unitarian Conscience*, 270–297. Howe notices an interesting parallel between Unitarian clergymen's revulsion toward revivalists and abolitionists; they viewed both types as passionate demagogues (ibid., 288–289).

11. *Proceedings of the Convention of Ministers of Worcester County, on the Subject of Slavery; Held at Worcester, December 5 & 6, 1837, and January 16, 1838* (Worcester, Mass., 1838), quotes on 19, 21, and 5.

12. Abzug, *Cosmos Crumbling*, 209–228, quote on 228.

13. Harriet Beecher Stowe, *Uncle Tom's Cabin; or, Life among the Lowly* (1852; New York: Penguin, 1981), 629.

14. Moorhead, *American Apocalypse*, chapter 2, "The Armageddon of the Republic."

15. "Burial Hill Declaration" (1865) quoted in J. William T. Youngs, *The Congregationalists*, Denominations in America, 4 (Westport, Conn.: Greenwood Press, 1990), 144.

16. Josiah Strong, *Our Country*, ed. Jurgen Herbst, John Harvard Library (1886; Cambridge: Harvard University Press, Belknap Press, 1963), quotes on 201–202, 213, 215, and 218. Herbst's introduction provides the sales data for *Our Country* (p. ix) and the information regarding Strong's Cincinnati post (p. xvi).

17. Walker, *History of the Congregational Churches*, 423–424. Daniel W. Howe draws a similar link between the Unitarians' corporate ethic and Progressivism in *Unitarian Conscience*, 304–305.

Index